The Arch... Coursebook
Third Edition

Fully updated and restructured, this third edition of the best-selling title *The Archaeology Coursebook* is a comprehensive guide for students studying archaeology for the first time. Including new methods and case studies, it provides pre-university students and teachers, as well as undergraduates and enthusiasts, with the skills and technical concepts necessary to grasp the subject.

This fully revised edition now includes:

- introductions to the most commonly examined archaeological methods, concepts and themes, and provides the necessary skills to understand them
- explanations on how to interpret the material students may meet in examinations and how to succeed with different types of assignments and exam questions
- supporting case studies, key sites, key terms, tasks and skills development
- illustrated concepts, interpretations and commentary with over 400 photographs and drawings of excavation sites, methodology and processes, tools and equipment
- an improved companion website with new interactive study skill activities and links to other key websites in archaeology at a similar level: www.routledge.com/textbooks/9780415462860
- new material on 'Issues in Modern Archaeology', 'Sites and People in the Landscape' and 'People and Society in the Past'; new case studies chosen to illustrate key debates and the development of vocabulary; new methods, examples, boxes, photographs and diagrams.

Jim Grant is a Chief Examiner in A Level Archaeology and Assistant Principal at Cirencester College. He has experience in field archaeology. **Sam Gorin** is Chief Moderator for A Level Archaeology and was formerly a Curriculum Director at Newark and Sherwood College. He has been widely involved in field archaeology in the East Midlands. **Neil Fleming** is a Chief Examiner in A Level Archaeology and Upper-Sixth House Master at Christ's Hospital, Horsham. He is a highly experienced teacher of archaeology who also has field archaeology experience.

The Archaeology Coursebook

Third Edition

An **introduction** to themes, sites, methods and skills

Jim Grant, Sam Gorin and **Neil Fleming**

Routledge
Taylor & Francis Group

LONDON AND NEW YORK

First edition published 2001
Second edition published 2005
This third edition first published 2008
by Routledge
2 Park Square, Milton Park, Abingdon, Oxon OX14 4RN

Simultaneously published in the USA and Canada
by Routledge
711 Third Avenue, new York, NY 10017

Routledge is an imprint of the Taylor & Francis Group, an informa business

© 2001, 2005, 2008 Jim Grant, Sam Gorin and Neil Fleming

Typeset in Palatino and Bell Gothic by
Florence Production Ltd, Stoodleigh, Devon
Printed and bound in Great Britain by CPI Group (UK) Ltd, Croydon, CR0 4YY

British Library Cataloguing in Publication Data
A catalogue record for this book is available from the British Library

Library of Congress Cataloging in Publication Data
Grant, Jim, 1958–
   The archaeology coursebook: an introduction to themes, sites, methods,
   and skils/Jim Grant, Sam Gorin, and Neil Flemming. –3rd ed.
      p. cm
   1. Archaeology – Study and teaching (Higher) 2. Archaeology – Methodology.
   3. Archaeology – Examinations – Study guides. I. Gorin, Sam, 1946–
   II. Flemming, Neil, 1955– III. Title
   CC83.G7 2008
   930.1076 – dc22
                               2008017818

ISBN 10: 0–415–46286–X
ISBN 13: 978–0415–46286–0

Brief Contents

Contents

Figures

Acknowledgements

Once again we would like to thank those who contributed to previous editions of this book, much of which is retained here. In particular Julie Gardner at Wessex Archaeology, Amanda Hart, Dave Jones, Mick Jones, Brona Langton, James Megoran, Royston Clark, Sarah Cole, Don Henson, Richard Reece, Nick Trustram-Eve, and Robin Wichard. Once more thanks are due to Moira Taylor for guidance and patience and to Matthew Gibbons for backing the project.

Our students at Cirencester College and Christ's Hospital School have continued to be guinea pigs for much of the material and in some cases provided material for the book. We've also had lots of useful feedback from students and teachers of archaeology about what you would like to see more or less of. Hopefully you will find this new edition even more useful.

In addition to new sections of several chapters Sam has researched and updated technical information and I have tried to increase the size and usefulness of the case studies. Several people made valuable contributions to this including John Dewar, Mike Morris (Chester City Council) and Craig Spence (Lindum Heritage). Other material was provided by Matt Reynolds, Marnie Grant and Ben Maggs. Three A Level students also kindly allowed extracts from their excellent personal studies to be included as examples. They are Paul Allison, Keith Scholes and Rebecca Suddick.

Many case studies are difficult for readers coming to archaeology for the first time to visualise, but I hope that the quality of the new drawings will help. In particular I'd like to thank Sarah Scott for her many stunning illustrations, such as those of Head Smashed In and Mask, which really bring them to life.

Finally, a huge thank-you to my family, Dawn, Zack and Marnie for putting up with me writing it up.

Jim Grant
Jan 2008

Illustration
Acknowledgements

We are very grateful to those below for supplying illustrations and permission to use them. All other illustrations are the Authors'.

Paul Allison (13.10, 13.11, 13.12)
Ginny Baddiley, Nottinghamshire SMR (1.4)
Paul Brooker (1.10)
Chris Butler (1.18 and 5.9)
Royston Clarke (3.18, 7.9, 7.10)
Christina Cliff (7.15)
Sarah Cole (5.10)
Controller of Her Majesty's Stationery Office (1.22)
John Dewar (6.50)
Empingham Archive (2.23, 6.14, 10.16)
Julie Gardner – Wessex Archaeology (2.4, 2.21, 2.29, 3.23, 4.2, 9.37)
Jamie Gibson (11.7)
Martin Green (2.6)
Amanda Hart and Jude Barratt, Corinium Museum (6.53, 7.13, 9.10)
Gwilym Hughes (2.18)
Institute of Archaeology (11.1)
Colin Jarvis (13.13)
Dave Jones (1.12, 2.10, 2.11, 2.12, 2.13, 2.34, 3.14, 6.47)
Mick Jones, Lincoln Unit (2.17)
William Killbride (ADS) (13.9)
David Knight (2.35 and 2.36)
Brona Langton (2.1, 5.15)
Ben Maggs (5.16)
Marine Sonics (1.19)
Marnie Moo (2.28, 3.8, 8.11, 9.27, 9.32, 11.2)
Mike Morris (English Heritage and Chester City Council) (2.2, 2.3)
Harold Mytum (10.18 and 10.19)
Norfolk Archaeology and Environment Division (2.20)
Andy Payne (English Heritage) (1.17)

Francesca Radcliffe (1.20 and 7.21)

Matt Reynolds (1.11, 1.13)

Clive Ruggles (11.10)

Jim Russell (11.9)

Dan Schofield (3.11 and 3.27)

Keith Scholes (13.2)

Aidan Scott (8.6 and 9.11)

Sarah Scott (3.5, 3.13, 3.22, 3.34, 4.2, 5.14 (after Reynolds and Klausmeyer),
  7.2, 7.4, 7.7, 7.24 (after Stone & Zimansky), 7.25 (after Binford), 7.26
(after Binford),
  7.27 a/b (after Drewett), 7.32, 8.5, 8.13, 8.20, 8.26, 8.38, 8.40, 8.43, 8.50
(after Svendsen),
  8.51 (after Burov), 9.9, 9.15, 9.24, 9.30, 9.38, 9.40 (after Wenke), 9.42,
9.43, 10.6, 11.8)

Rebecca Suddick (13.6, 13.7)

Jane Timby (2.22)

Nick Trustram-Eve (1.5, 1.9, 13.4, 13.14, 13.15, 13.16)

Jonathan Tubb (2.24, 8.8 and 8.8)

University of Cambridge Air Photos (1.24)

Tracy Wellman MoLAS (2.33)

Robin Wichard (2.7, 5.2, 6.49, 8.37)

Brian Williams (3.15)

Kate Walton (3.29, 3.32, 6.3, 6.17, 13.8 (after Lake))

Several illustrations are drawings based on other examples. Those not credited
in the captions are 2.26 (after Milner), 7.3 (after Fischer), 7.8 (after Garrney),
7.14 (after a Hedges & b Renfrew), 8.18 (after Waddell), 9.26 (after Whitelaw),
9.27 (after Whitelaw), 9.31 (Ammerman & Cavalli-Sforza), 9.33 (after Whittle),
9.39 (after Isaacs), 9.41 (after Gamble).

A number of photographs are of interpretive displays at the following
museums: Andover Museum of the Iron Age (5.11), Burren Centre, Kilfenora
(9.4), Devizes (8.60), Isibister Tomb of the Eagles (6.11, Moesgård (3.10,
Museum of Antiquities, Newcastle (6.46), National Museum, Copenhagen
(6.28), Smithsonian Museum of Natural History, Washington DC (6.21, 8.10),
Sutton Hoo (9.11)

Introduction

The Archaeology Coursebook is about archaeological literacy. Whether you are a student or someone who wants to know more about archaeology, you probably have not studied it previously. This means that you have a whole new technical language and set of concepts to grasp. This text will enable you to get to grips with them. It does not pretend to cover the whole of a degree programme nor is it a specialist guide to archaeological methods. There is a fantastic array of books and websites already available which fulfils these functions. The aim of this book is to get you started with understanding archaeology, to help you succeed in your academic study and to point you in the direction of additional resources for topics you want to investigate in greater depth.

As authors our collective experience includes professional and amateur archaeology and teaching in both state and private schools and in colleges. As teachers and examiners of archaeology we have considerable experience of successfully preparing students of all ages on A Level, IB, Access and HE programmes. In writing this new edition we have responded to feedback from students, teachers and general readers of the *Archaeology Coursebook* about what they liked and what was less useful. Amongst these changes are:

■ Increasing the range and length of case studies. This includes several new topics related to the transition to farming.

■ Improving and adding to the range of diagrams and illustrations used to explain ideas.
■ Moving most of the weblinks and text recommendations to the new companion website so that they can be kept up to date and added to more readily.
■ Moving material to assist you in studying archaeology to a separate section so that it is easier to access.

We have updated several chapters to reflect continuing changes in archaeology including excavation and managing the past. We have also tried to highlight the way new scientific methods are leading us to review our view of the past and expand the limits of what can be known about it. An increasing amount of archaeological knowledge is emerging from the lab particularly with recent advances in biochemistry.

The structure of the book follows the AS and A2 Level Archaeology courses studied by students in England and Wales. These are changing from 2008 and 2009 so we have addressed these by:

■ Improving the introductions to religion and ritual to include Rome and Egypt and adding more detailed case studies on some of the prescribed topics.
■ Moving detail on scientific analysis to the topics where it is having a major impact so that it can be understood in context.

■ Adding a section to social archaeology on human origins.

For those of you studying archaeology we hope this book will be of use to you at every stage of your course, from understanding new terminology to producing your major study. It is intended to be relevant and useful for all students studying the subject up to first-year undergraduate level. If it equips you to produce pass-level essays and to understand what is being discussed in lectures and seminars it will have done its job. You will, of course, need other sources too including other case studies and to look at examples of fieldwork reports. The companion website will provide suggestions for these. From year 2 of university you will need greater depth of material. However, by then you will know everything that is in this book!

Throughout the book we have introduced the most commonly examined archaeological methods, concepts and themes. Whole books have been written on the meanings of particular terms and there may not be consensus on their use. We have concentrated on providing you with working definitions and examples rather than debating meaning. We have organised the book into four broad sections:

■ *Part I Understanding archaeological resources* is an introduction to how archaeologists work. How they find sites, excavate them and analyse and interpret the material they recover and how we get archaeological knowledge.

■ *Part II Studying themes in archaeology* covers the broad topics of religion and ritual, settlement, economics and material culture and society. These will be relevant to you whether your course follows a period-based or thematic approach. We have concentrated on providing examples defining key terms and highlighting the sources and methods used to explore these themes.

■ *Part III Issues in world archaeology* covers the protection and management of our archaeological heritage. It addresses the social and political role of archaeology and introduces a number of current debates. It also looks at how archaeological knowledge is presented.

■ *Part IV Examination success and beyond* guides you through how to produce a successful

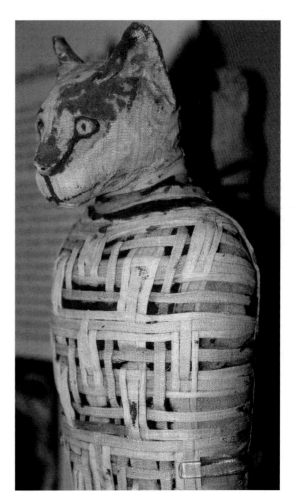

Figure 0.1 *Ecofact or Artefact?*

These are two of the first terms you will encounter in archaeology. Inside this Egyptian cat-mummy are the remains of an animal (natural material). However, it has been transformed by human activity including mummification, wrapping and painting into a ritual object.

archaeological project and helps you develop study skills and prepares you for passing your exams. It shows you how to approach different kinds of questions and material and how to use the case studies in the book to address them. The final chapter is a guide to some additional sources of information and further study opportunities. These are developed in more detail on the companion website.

A key feature of this book is that it is designed to be used alongside your PC. The companion website follows the same structure as the book and provides access to a huge range of websites to look for examples and illustrations. Archaeology is such a visual subject and so well served by many excellent sources on the Net that it is foolish not to use it.

HOW TO USE THIS TEXT

There are so many different ways in which lecturers can structure courses that it is unlikely you will follow the exact order of our contents sequence in your own study. We have taken this into account by providing a full index and contents list which includes all the main sub-headings. We have also used a system of cross-referencing throughout the book from one topic to related topics. Content, skills and resources are all linked. Look out for the following signposts which all provide links from the text immediately preceding them.

▶ (arrowhead) guides you to related material on another page

✎ (trowel) indicates a key text or website

Examples are given for most of the points we make and a range of case studies is provided to deepen your understanding of the ideas and methods discussed. Where they are relevant to your course [they are about the right length and detail for essays up to year 2 at university] you can use them as content to support your written work. We have introduced and defined key terms as they have arisen in the text. The glossary on p. 430 contains a working definition of all the words printed in **bold** in the text.

Key sites and key studies can be used to address a range of different questions. To help you with this we have used icons to indicate where a case study in one section would also be useful in another. You will find them in the top left of each site box.

 Social archaeology

 Economics and material culture

 Settlement

 Religion

Figure 0.2 *And this one?*

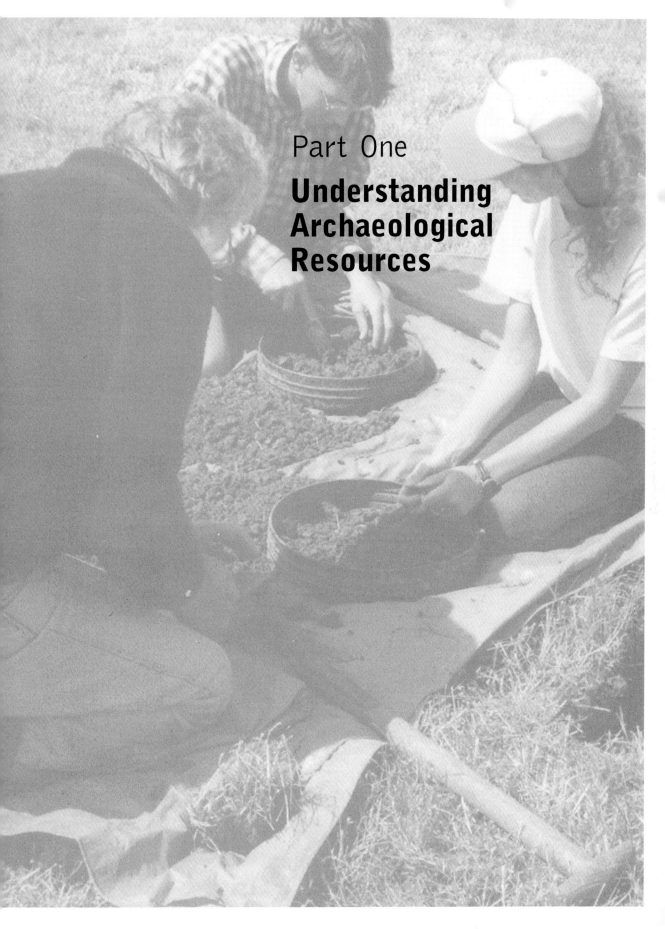

Part One
Understanding Archaeological Resources

Chapter 1

Archaeological Reconnaissance

YOUR GOALS

You need to be able to

■ understand the key methods used by archaeologists to locate and define sites

■ identify some strengths and limitations of the most important techniques

■ suggest appropriate methods for locating and exploring sites in particular circumstances.

Archaeologists use a wide range of reconnaissance techniques to locate archaeological sites and to investigate sites without excavating them. Some archaeologists predict that future advances in non-invasive, and non-destructive, methods will see them emerge as an alternative to excavation. Reconnaissance techniques are also used to map evidence of human activity in the

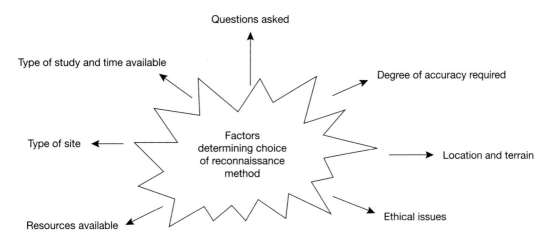

Figure 1.1 Factors influencing the choice of reconnaissance methods

landscape. The appropriate methods in each case will relate to the time and resources available as well as to the particular case being investigated.

Every year hundreds of new sites are located. Some are spotted from the air or even from satellites in space, others through the discovery of artefacts by metal detectorists. Quarrying, dredging and peat cutting all regularly produce unexpected finds while some of the most important have come about completely by chance.

The discoveries of the body of Ötzi the Ice Man by skiers and of the Altamira cave art by children are classic examples. So too was the discovery of the Neolithic tomb at Crantit in Orkney, which was found when a digger fell through the roof!

Equally, some sites were never 'lost' to begin with. Stonehenge and the Pyramids were well known before the development of archaeology and many of the buildings of the last 200 years are still in use. Other named sites were documented by historians and located by using written sources. Schliemann's discovery of Troy is the classic example but many historic battlefields also fall into this category. In addition, a considerable number of new discoveries are made during the exploration of known sites.

To locate or explore sites through research or ahead of development there are four broad and complementary categories of methods that are commonly used:

- desktop study
- surface survey
- geophysical or geochemical survey
- aerial survey

In addition there is a range of newer techniques, most of which can be labelled **remote sensing**.

Reconnaissance should not be seen simply as the precursor to the real business of digging. In some cases it can provide all or most of the evidence needed to answer questions. The pioneering Shapwick project which investigated the development of an estate owned by Glastonbury Abbey used a battery of reconnaissance methods alongside limited sampling of deposits through shovel pit testing, geochemical survey and excavation. The results when combined with evidence from maps, historical sources, and environmental data enabled the production of regression maps showing the development of settlement in the area.

DESKTOP STUDY

As its name suggests, this is an office-based investigation using existing records. Some archaeologists, usually concerned with shipwrecks, aircraft or the investigation of historical individuals, continue to use written sources to track down or identify particular sites. More generally, most excavations and all research in Britain today begins with a search of information that has already been recorded. The majority of these investigations are part of the planning process. Their purpose is to determine whether there are likely to be archaeological remains which might be threatened by development (▶ p. 341).

Desktop study involves researching maps and historical or archaeological documents including aerial photographs about the area under investigation. If they are not in private hands, these are most likely to be held in planning departments, county records offices, historic environment record, local **Sites and Monuments Record (SMRs)** or the **National Monuments Record (NMR)** offices.

Historical documents

A diverse assortment of documents may be of value to the archaeologist. These will vary by county, area and period. In much of the country known documents are archived or recorded in the County Records Office. In many areas, useful sources have also been catalogued in a volume

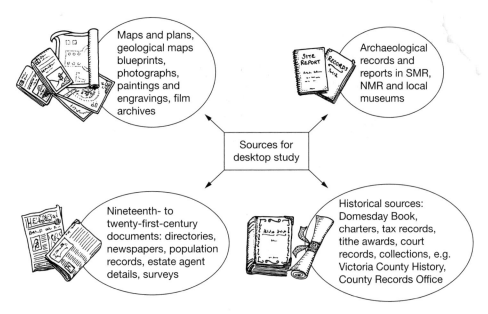

Figure 1.2 *Sources commonly used for desktop study*

of the Victoria County History (VCR). This is often the first resource researchers turn to. Only a fraction of early records have survived and those that have need translation and interpretation. Amongst the potential range available, the following categories are important.

Legal documents. Records of ownership such as Anglo-Saxon charters or court records of disputes often included physical description of boundaries and occasionally land use. Wills and inventories which can be linked to particular buildings may provide lists of contents. These can provide clues to that building's use.

Tax records. These are particularly valuable in helping to identify landowning units and their economic uses. The Domesday Book is the best known but later tax surveys and tithe awards are often of more direct use.

Economic records. Order and sales books are invaluable to industrial archaeologists while nineteenth-century directories are useful in

exploring functions of buildings. Estate agents' bills are increasingly being preserved to record changes in important buildings.

Pictorial records. Paintings, engravings and photographs can be of value both in identification and in tracing changes. They are particularly valuable when studying standing buildings. Archives of aerial photographs (APs) such as the RAF 'or Luftwaffe' surveys of Britain in the 1940s are key documents in tracing landscape change in the last sixty years. They are often the only record of many sites.

Written accounts. Descriptions of places in books, diaries and travelogues are of use in identifying the function, construction methods and identity of many sites. The work of early antiquarians such as Stukeley is particularly valuable for descriptions of monuments as they were before the modern period.

Archaeological records. There are three main sources here. If there are early excavation or

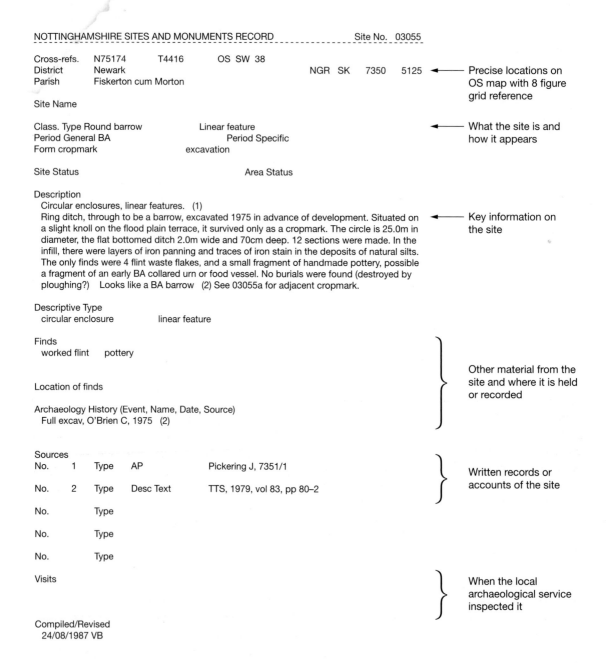

NOTTINGHAMSHIRE SITES AND MONUMENTS RECORD ------------------------ Site No. 03055

Cross-refs.   N75174   T4416   OS SW 38
District   Newark   NGR SK   7350   5125 ◄─────── Precise locations on
Parish   Fiskerton cum Morton   OS map with 8 figure
Site Name   grid reference

Class. Type Round barrow   Linear feature   ◄─────── What the site is and
Period General BA   Period Specific   how it appears
Form cropmark   excavation

Site Status   Area Status

Description
    Circular enclosures, linear features.   (1)
    Ring ditch, through to be a barrow, excavated 1975 in advance of development. Situated on   ◄───── Key information on
    a slight knoll on the flood plain terrace, it survived only as a cropmark. The circle is 25.0m in   the site
    diameter, the flat bottomed ditch 2.0m wide and 70cm deep. 12 sections were made. In the
    infill, there were layers of iron panning and traces of iron stain in the deposits of natural silts.
    The only finds were 4 flint waste flakes, and a small fragment of handmade pottery, possible
    a fragment of an early BA collared urn or food vessel. No burials were found (destroyed by
    ploughing?)   Looks like a BA barrow   (2) See 03055a for adjacent cropmark.

Descriptive Type
    circular enclosure   linear feature

Finds
    worked flint   pottery
                                                                                          } Other material from the
Location of finds   site and where it is held
                                                                                             or recorded
Archaeology History (Event, Name, Date, Source)
    Full excav, O'Brien C, 1975   (2)

Sources
No.   1   Type   AP   Pickering J, 7351/1
                                                                                          } Written records or
No.   2   Type   Desc Text   TTS, 1979, vol 83, pp 80–2   accounts of the site

No.   Type

No.   Type

No.   Type

Visits   } When the local
                                                                                             archaeological service
                                                                                             inspected it

Compiled/Revised
    24/08/1987 VB

Figure 1.3 *How to read an SMR printout*

survey results they can often be accessed through libraries or local museums. Local collections of finds and reports will also be held in local museums. Details of previous archaeological work and stray finds for much of Britain are held in local SMRs. These records are increasingly computerised and a national version is being built up at the various NMR offices. Printouts which include lists of earlier research can be made by inputting grid references.

Oral accounts. While living people may provide clues to the use and location of recent buildings, farmers and others who work on the land or the built environment may have valuable knowledge for archaeologists. Farmers, for example, may be able to identify areas where building rubble has been ploughed up or where dressed stones have been removed. Sometimes estate management records may hold this information for earlier periods.

Maps

Maps are amongst the most basic tools and sources used by archaeologists. They are used to locate and explore sites and to answer questions about previous use of the landscape. They are of particular value in tracking changes through time (settlement shape and location, boundaries, land units, fields and hedges). They can also be used to relate sites to geology and topography. Medieval archaeologists are often able to produce their own maps for periods before mapping began. They do this by working back from the oldest available map and cross-referencing historical sources and fieldnames. This technique is known as **regression**.

A wide variety of maps are used by archaeologists, including the following.

Early maps
Maps from the sixteenth century tend to show the properties of the rich. They are not always to scale but may provide visual information such as illustrations of specific buildings. From the seventeenth century there are also route maps such as Ogilvy's Road Book, which is a series of linear strips. Maps were produced to show the proposed routes of turnpikes, canals and railways in order to gain permission from parliament for building to take place.

Changes in rural landownership from the eighteenth century onwards were recorded on enclosure award maps, while taxes owed to the church by landowners were sometimes written on tithe award maps. Occasionally these can be cross-referenced and both can provide information about fieldnames, routes and boundaries, which are vital for landscape archaeology. Other maps show landscaped gardens, battlefields or provide plans of factories and mines.

These early maps are often held in county record offices. Some may be in private hands or belong to churches.

Ordnance Survey (OS) maps
During the early nineteenth century the OS mapped each county at 1 inch to 1 mile. From the 1880s OS 6 inch to 1 mile maps provided more detail of individual buildings and even hedge species. OS maps established a new standard in accuracy and a comprehensive system of coding and keys for features. A grid system was used which covered the whole country and enabled precise references to be given. By examining a succession of maps for any area, changes in land use and the built environment can be easily seen.

• www.ordsvy.gov.uk

Maps used in archaeological
The OS 1:25000 Pathfinder or Leisure series show the location of some archaeological sites but planning maps that use the OS grid system are needed for investigations. 1:10000 (old 6 inch) maps are sometimes the most detailed available for mountainous, remote and some rural areas but 1:2500 (old 25 inch 1 mile) rural or 1:1250

urban planning maps are normally used. For field walking 1:10000 or 1:2500 is used and for excavation the 1:2500 or 1:1250 provides a base. A 1:2500 map allows you to identify individual metre squares with a 10-figure grid reference. These maps are held in county or district planning offices.

Other maps sometimes used include the Geological Survey series, street maps, factory plans, vegetation and climatic maps, land use and classification, soil surveys and specialist archaeological maps. Increasingly archaeologists are using computerised mapping systems based around Geographical Information Systems (**GIS**).

As an archaeology student you need some basic map skills including the ability to:

- identify and interpret common archaeological features from maps
- 'read' contours and hachures
- use scales and at least 6-figure grid references
- produce basic cross-sectional sketches from maps
- interpret simple archaeological plans and diagrams
- use other evidence such as photographs and written accounts to interpret maps and plans.

SURFACE SURVEYS

This term can be used to encompass **fieldwalking**, **surveying** and even planned aerial photography. We will use it to describe non-destructive visual surveys at ground level. These can range from slow, painstaking searches on foot to quite rapid examinations of a landscape by Landrover, looking for upstanding earthworks. Since most sites lack visible features, the former is more common. Fieldwalking is largely concerned with finding traces of unrecorded sites. Scatters of building rubble or artefacts or slight undulations in the surface can reveal where there are buried walls or house platforms. Differences in soil or vegetation may also be indicative of past human activity. For studies of the **Mesolithic** and **Neolithic** in Britain, scatters of flint and

KEY TERM

Geographic Information Systems (GIS)

This refers to powerful databases which can store many layers of data against individual map grid references. This can include details of topography, geology and vegetation as well as archaeological data. GIS can integrate data from satellites with field recordings. It can produce topographic maps and site plans in three dimensions and perform complex statistical analysis. It is revolutionising the presentation and interrogation of archaeological data. It can even be used to predict site locations based on known patterns.

- http://www.esri.com/industries/
  archaeology/index.html

KEY TASK

Sourcing information

Take each of the following examples and list the types of source you might find useful in investigating it.

Next take a real example of one of them and find out what actual sources exist. You may be surprised.

A round barrow or cairn

A Roman villa or Saxon church

A deserted medieval village or abbey

An eighteenth-century farm or canal

A nineteenth-century railway line or factory

A twentieth-century pillbox or airfield

animal bone are often the only traces of human activity visible in the landscape. To study the activities of these mobile populations, careful identification and plotting of these scatters is essential. A variation on this is the study of hedges and woodlands for traces of past economic activities and to help locate settlement areas (▶ p. 202). Surface surveys can cover large areas such as Webster and Sanders' work in the Copan Valley of Mexico or woods such as the Thetford Forest project in East Anglia.

Surface investigations of known sites include **micro-contour surveys** of the topography. These involve detailed and precise use of surveying tools to build up a picture of variations in height and levels. Data is increasingly being entered on databases to enable computer enhancement of

the landscape. These surveys can often reveal hidden features that could not be detected with the naked eye.

In most studies, the areas to be surveyed are measured using surveying equipment or Global Positioning Systems (GPS) and set out with rows or squares of pegs, cane or marker poles. This is to enable accurate sampling and recording.

Recording standing buildings

One specialised area of archaeological surveying focuses on the built environment and links archaeology to architectural science. Detailed studies of the material and construction techniques of structures are made both to enhance knowledge of the development of buildings and

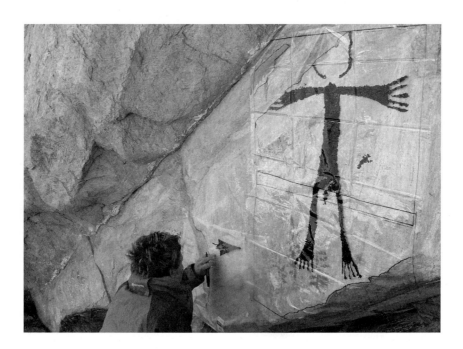

Figure 1.4 *Rock art survey using GPS and GIS*

The survey of rock carvings or petroglyphs illustrates many aspects of reconnaissance and recording techniques. In addition to a detailed record being made by tracing and photograph, the position of each petroglyph is identified by GPS. Its height above sea level and orientation are also measured and the information entered into a GIS database. This enables 3D presentations to permit study of relationships between petroglyphs and topography or each other.

KEY TERM

Sampling

Whatever is deposited is a fragment of past material culture. Dependent upon the material, a variable portion of these deposits will survive. Archaeologists will recover a sample of these. Not every site can be fieldwalked, let alone excavated. Choices have to be made. If these choices are arbitrary (non-probabilistic) they could lead to bias in the **archaeological record** with certain types of evidence being neglected and others over-represented. For example, if archaeologists chose only to study hill forts from the Iron Age or, as often happens, if development only permitted excavation in one part of a town, it might create an unrepresentative picture of life in the past.

When archaeologists design research strategies they use some form of probabilistic sampling to reduce bias in recovery. This means that the chance of anything being recovered is known. Rigorous sampling is used in most aspects of archaeological reconnaissance and excavation.

Firstly the plan of the total area or site to be surveyed is divided up either into a grid pattern of numbered squares or a series of equidistant parallel lines or transects (▶ p. 12). Both are usually aligned north–south to link into the national survey grid although sometimes grids in fields are aligned on a particular boundary. With large areas it is common to select a sample

Figure 1.5 *Models of different approaches to sampling*

of grids and then use transects within them. The scale varies according to the task. An initial surface survey of a whole landscape might start with 100 metre or kilometre squares and then have transects between 10 and 50 metres apart depending on terrain and resources. For test pitting on a known site the initial grid might be 1 metre square. You need to understand four basic approaches to sampling. Our illustration is for grids but the principles are the same for transects.

A simple *random sample* works like a lottery. The numbered units are selected by computer or number table. This is fair as each unit has an equal chance of being selected, but it can also lead to clustering and thus miss features.

Stratified sampling overcomes clustering bias by first dividing the sample universe into sections. For example, if the site has natural zones such as hills, valley and plain then numbers are selected randomly for each zone in proportion to its area.

KEY TERM *cont.*

Sampling

Systematic sampling overcomes clustering by selecting at evenly spaced intervals, for example every third grid or every 10 metres. This ensures a more even selection although it could miss things that are regularly distributed. It usually requires a higher number of samples.

   Stratified systematic sampling combines the last two methods and could be used to take more samples in particular zones than others.

• http://archnet.asu.edu/archives/theory/sampling/sampling.html

to provide a record against future destruction or decay. For example laser scanning is used in some buildings which are covered with lichen to see how they are constructed. Records will range from written description to CAD (computer-aided design) based recording of every brick or stone. Most recording of buildings occurs as part of the planning process (▶ p. 347) or during conservation work. A recent example is the Defence of Britain project, which collected records on surviving defensive monuments of the Second World War.

• www.britarch.ac.uk/projects/dob/index.html

Fieldwalking

Fieldwalking, or **surface collection**, involves systematic collection of artefacts from the ploughsoil which might be indicative of human settlement. This is based on the reasoning that material on the surface reflects buried remains. Sometimes high density scatters of particular materials such as building rubble or broken pottery enable specific sites such as buildings or kilns to be identified. More typically, the method helps identify areas of settlement or activities such as hunting. Ceramics and worked stone are the most commonly gathered but metal, bone and burnt stone are often also collected. The method is destructive in that archaeological material is

removed, but as it has been disturbed by ploughing, it is not in its original context anyway.

Decisions about sampling have to be made when planning fieldwalking. Not everything will be collected, particularly when building rubble is involved. For instance, will all ceramics be collected or just diagnostic pieces? Decisions also have to be taken about the width of transects or size of grids.

Timing is important. Ideally ploughed soil should have been broken down by weathering and recent rain will have cleared dust from the surface. Walkers either proceed along a transect in a series of stints or search a grid. These have been carefully set out with marker flags or poles. Grids tend to be used when total coverage of a field is required. The material collected is bagged and tagged with the number of the grid or stint for processing and analysis.

Once washed and identified, finds are counted for each grid or stint. This can then be plotted on a distribution map to show patterns and concentrations. There are many ways of displaying this information. Phase maps or a series of clear plastic overlays for each period or type of find are commonly used. Computer displays using GIS have an edge here since several types of data can be linked to any point and comparisons easily made.

Fieldwalking is a well established method because it has many strengths. It is a relatively

Figure 1.6 *A Level students fieldwalking*

The experience and training of fieldwalkers and the conditions on the day are factors affecting what is recovered (▶ p. 117).

KEY TERMS

Transects, traverses and stints.

A transect is a sampling line which could be across a single site or an entire landscape. It is usually aligned north–south and tied into the national grid. In fieldwalking transects are usually divided up into manageable chunks or stints of 10 to 50 metres where one walker will use one collecting bag. 'Traverse' is a term used largely in geophysics and sometimes aerial photography to describe the straight, parallel paths passed over by the surveyor. So a magnetometer survey might use traverses set at 0.5 metres apart.

cheap way of surveying large areas since volunteer labour can be used to collect and wash finds. It can help establish the function and period of a site without excavation and provide insights into location and exchange.

Fieldwalking can indicate the spread and foci of evidence. It does, however, have important limitations too. It is only really useful on arable land where access has been granted and then only at certain times in the agricultural cycle. In addition, its results cannot be taken at face value. For example, medieval manuring practices transferred much domestic refuse to the plough-soil, creating a doughnut shape pattern of pottery distribution. Chris Gerrard's work on the Shapwick Project has explored two other major limitations.

Different materials behave differently in the same soil. In Shapwick, rewalking the same fields

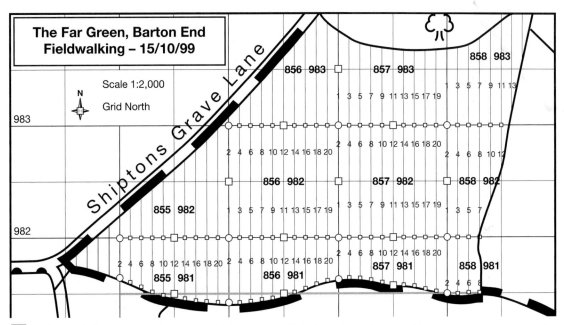

Figure 1.7 *A planned fieldwalk which has been linked to the national grid system. Transects are 10m apart with 50m stints*

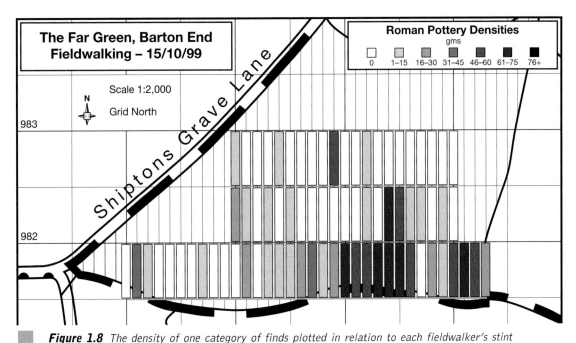

Figure 1.8 *The density of one category of finds plotted in relation to each fieldwalker's stint*

Amounts of selected materials can also be shown with shapes or dots where the size and colour or shading represent the numbers of finds.

Figure 1.9 *An excellent example of a flint arrowhead recovered during fieldwalking at Thetford*

Figure 1.10 *A total station*

The total station combines the functions of theodolite, EDM and data logger. It is highly accurate in calculating heights, angles and distances and can be used to rapidly set out grids or to record the position of hundreds of points. These can later be downloaded and with the right software, used to produce 3D maps of the survey area.

and monitoring ceramics in them showed that some material migrates further than others. Patterns for pottery from different periods were also very different. It was not always a good indication of settlement. A second variable was the differential collection by different field-walkers. Analysis of their finds showed that some were good at recognising and collecting one type of material but poor with another. This applied to experienced walkers as well as novices. Their performance varied according to weather and slope. Taken together it means that what is recovered is a sample of what was in the topsoil and the topsoil holds a sample of what lies below. In both cases the sample varies for each type of find. Fieldwalking results therefore need to be cross-checked with other data before conclusions can be drawn.

There are a number of other prospection methods which provide alternatives to field-walking although all are more destructive. **Shovel pit testing** can take place in woods, pasture and gardens where fieldwalking is impossible.

Coring and **augering** are also used to sample the subsoil. This can provide a snapshot of the

stratigraphy and the sample can be examined for artefactual or environmental evidence. **Probing**, which involves driving a rod into the ground, is more useful for tracing shallow buried features such as walls on known sites ▶ p. 253.

GEOCHEMICAL PROSPECTION

These relatively new methods and expensive techniques attempt to locate areas of past human activity by detecting differences in the chemical properties of the soil. All living things produce organic phosphate as waste or through decay. Unlike phosphate in fertiliser, this remains in the soil where it was deposited. Samples of soil

Figure 1.12 *Auger sampling*

An auger is driven or screwed into the ground. It extracts a sample of the subsoil in much the same way as an apple corer.

Figure 1.11 *Shovel pit testing*

This approach to sampling is very common in the USA. Only the top few centimetres are sampled. In each sample a standard volume of soil is sieved through a fine mesh for ecofacts and artefacts.

are taken and levels of phosphate measured in a laboratory. Once plotted, concentrations of organic phosphate may indicate settlements or animal enclosures. Similar principles apply to heavy minerals such as lead and cadmium and to lipids (fats). These may become increasingly important in the future. One possibility is that different chemical combinations could identify 'signatures' (▶ p. 125) for different activities.

GEOPHYSICAL SURVEYS

This term covers techniques that detect features through their physical differences with the surrounding soil. The most common techniques detect magnetic and electrical anomalies and require considerable skill to interpret. With the increasing involvement of archaeology in planning development and a shift in emphasis

amongst archaeologists in favour of preservation rather than excavation, these techniques are now commonplace. The manufacture of increasingly reliable instruments for archaeology has seen magnetometry become a standard technique.

- http://www.geoscan-research.co.uk
- www.brad.ac.uk/acad/archsci/sbject/ archpros.htm

Resistivity survey

There are differences in the ability of different soils to conduct electricity. This can be detected by passing an electric current through the ground and comparing readings. Electricity is conducted through the soil by mineral salts contained in water. The more moisture there is the better the conductivity of the soil. A buried ditch or grave will generally retain water better than the surrounding soil. A buried wall or road will conduct poorly and therefore resist the current more than the surrounding soil. Electrical current flows close to the surface so it can be measured using shallow probes. The method works better with some soils than others. Clay retains moisture

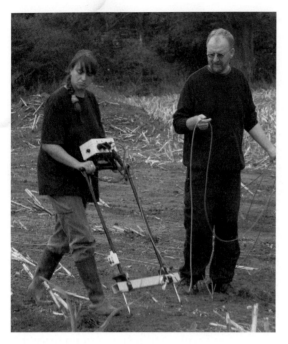

well, so differences in resistance between the soil and buried ditches or pits may be impossible to detect. This also applies to many soils if they become waterlogged in wintertime. Plants, rocks and variations in the depths of soils can also create misleading readings.

Resistivity can also be used to create pseudo-sections of buried features. This involves taking a series of readings from a line of probes placed across a buried feature such as a ditch. Wider spacing produces data on deeper parts of the feature than narrowly spaced probes. The depth to which this technology penetrates the soil is limited and readings require considerable inter-pretation, as the sensitivity of the meters is not great. At Hindwell in Wales, a 4-metre wide ditch identified by resistivity turned out after excavation to be a series of massive postholes with construction ramps.

Figure 1.13 *Resistivity surveying*

Meters are usually mounted on a 'zimmer-like' frame and have a data logger on board to record results. While relatively easy to use they are not fast and are best suited to detailed exploration of a site rather than initial prospecting.

Magnetometer surveying

The earth's magnetic field is generally uniform in any one place. However, local magnetic distortions can be caused by past human activity. Topsoil contains haematite (Fe_2O_3), an iron

RESISTIVITY

The resistivity meter works by detecting anomalies (differences) in the ability of subsurface remains to conduct electricity compared with the surrounding soil.

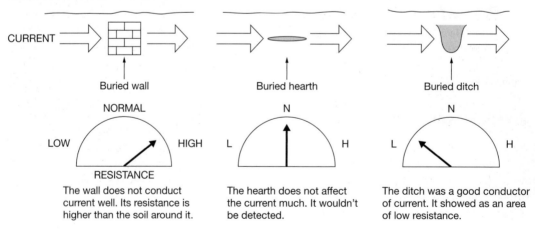

CURRENT

Buried wall

Buried hearth

Buried ditch

NORMAL

LOW / HIGH

RESISTANCE

The wall does not conduct current well. Its resistance is higher than the soil around it.

The hearth does not affect the current much. It wouldn't be detected.

The ditch was a good conductor of current. It showed as an area of low resistance.

Figure 1.14 *A simplified diagram illustrating the principles of resistivity*

oxide. In some forms its crystals are magnetic. A ditch which has filled up with topsoil will contain more haematite than the surrounding area. Its fill will therefore be slightly different magnetically and may be detected by sensitive, modern magnetometers.

A second type of distortion is caused where topsoil has been subject to considerable heat. This erases the magnetic properties of the iron oxides. For Haematite 675 °C is required. When the soil cools the iron oxides become permanently magnetised according to the polarity of the earth's magnetic field at that time. Since this field changes over time the sites of kilns and hearths appear as magnetic anomalies.

The earliest magnetometers were cumbersome and slow to use. The development of hand-held fluxgate gradiometers has enabled the technique to be used to rapidly scan quite large areas to highlight anomalies. Magnetometers are also used in detailed site investigations where they can detect small features up to 1 metre down and provide images of some buried features. For very detailed work traverses are set 0.5 metres apart with samples every 0.5 metres. 1 metre gaps and sample intervals are more common.

Figure 1.15 *Magnetometer survey*

Magnetometers are either hand-held or as in this example, mounted on a frame. The twin fluxgate gradiometer shown here has two vertically mounted sensors a metre apart to maximise speed and sensitivity on large searches.

MAGNETOMETER SURVEY

RESISTIVITY SURVEY

Figure 1.16 *Resistance and Magnetometer plots compared*

The essential complementary nature of these techniques can be seen in these plots from English Heritage's survey of White Barrow.

• http://www.archaeotechnics.co.uk/

To be able to detect anomalies, the magnetic background of the soil has to be measured and magnetometers calibrated against it. The measuring of this **magnetic susceptibility** of the topsoil can also be used as a crude but rapid survey technique in its own right. Magnetic hotspots suggest areas of past settlement or industrial activity, which could be surveyed using other methods.

Sensitive magnetic instruments are easily disturbed by iron, including nails, pipes and wire fences as well as the zips and piercings of the archaeologist. A further limitation can be background interference from magnetic bedrock or where a long period of occupation has left a magnetic layer over a wide area. Sandy and clay soils often do not provide sufficient contrast. Fluctuations in the earth's magnetic field also have to be taken into account. It requires considerable skill and experience to interpret the results.

Caesium vapour (CV) magnetometers

These are many times more sensitive than conventional magnetometers and are more commonly used in Germany and Austria. Typically several machines are used close together on a large wooden handcart. They work by pumping caesium vapour and taking rapid measurements at around 25cm intervals. This alkali is so sensitive to minute variations in magnetism that it can detect and define the edges of buried features formed by traces of magnetite. This iron oxide (Fe_3O_4) is concentrated in the remains of the bacteria which consumed the wooden structures such as posts which once stood there. It is being used at a number of well-documented sites to reveal more of their secrets. Recent work at Stanton Drew stone circle revealed the 'ghosts' of hundreds of postholes in concentric circles. Caesium magnetometers suffer less from the background 'noise' which occurs with hand-held devices but at £40,000 per machine and

KEY TASK

Test your understanding of geophysics

Which of the two main geophysical methods would normally be effective in detecting these buried features? Answers on p. 429.

1 Hearths	6 Large pits
2 Cobbled floors	7 Stakeholes
3 Stone walls	8 Building platforms
4 Graves	9 Small pits
5 Kilns	10 Ditches

perhaps four machines on a cart, this technique is expensive.

Other methods

Metal detectors are useful for metal objects down to about 15 cm. Some archaeologists use them on site to provide information in advance of digging such as the position of burial deposits. Skill is required to avoid time being wasted exploring buried slag or modern metal debris. Similarly they can sweep areas in advance of detailed geophysics to identify concentrations of metal that might distort readings.

Ground penetrating radar (GPR) which was developed for defence and engineering is starting to be used in archaeology. Aerial versions can highlight buried landscapes and rivers. GPR works by transmitting pulses of energy into the ground and recording the time taken and strength of the return signal. This can indicate the density and depth of buried deposits. Data based on different energy wavelengths can be plotted as a series of 'time slices' to build up a 3D picture of buried remains.

Sonar, which was developed to detect submarines is a form of acoustic sensing. Side scan sonar measures sound waves as they 'bounce back' and can map the sea bed and reveal the

Figure 1.17 *Handcart mounted GPR*

Ground versions of GPR are useful for detecting buried floors, voids and walls. It has been particularly effective in revealing the internal structures of buildings and exploring burials. It is the only effective geophysics technique in city centres where it can even penetrate tarmac. Due to its cost and the availability of quicker methods it has not been used widely outside urban areas in the UK although this is starting to change. It also works poorly on clay soils.

depth and form of sunken structures. *Bosing* is a crude form of acoustic sensing used on land. It involves hitting the ground with a mallet and listening for variations in resonant sounds. These may indicate buried ditches or walls.

Finally there is *dowsing*. This is a traditional method by which skilled dowsers use wooden rods to detect water or archaeology underground.

All of these geophysical techniques are limited in the type of work they can do and they should therefore be seen as complementary. None of them are particularly useful on waterlogged sites. Their value is often in pinpointing or exploring features rather than finding new sites.

AERIAL PHOTOGRAPHY

The first aerial photographs (APs) were taken from balloons. Today, most photographs are taken from light aircraft although even kites or balloons are used on occasions. APs are used for mapping, finding new sites rapidly over large areas and illustrating and exploring known sites. Substantial archives of aerial photographs are available publicly and commercially so new pictures may not always be needed.

- http://aarg.univie.ac.at/
- http://www.nmia.com/~jaybird/AANewsletter/

Figure 1.18 *Side scan sonar image of a submerged aircraft*

This scan of a US Navy PB4Y-2 Bomber was recorded by sonar mounted in a towfish device. The aircraft is at the bottom of Lake Washington in the USA under 164 feet of water. http://www.marinesonic.com/

Other information on marine surveys is at http://www.uri.edu/artsci/his/mua/MUA.htm

Verticals and obliques

Aerial photographs used for mapping are taken with the camera pointing straight down at the ground (*verticals*) with the aircraft flying along grid lines. Often these are taken from high altitude. This is the case with the RAF archives dating from the 1940s which are now housed at the NMR. These also provide an excellent desktop source for initial study of landscape developments. Overlapping vertical photographs can be viewed through a stereoscope to see the landscape in 3D. Their main value is in planning and illustrating sites. Where some dimensions in the photograph are known, reasonably accurate plans can be drawn of sites, including their contours. This is known as photogrammetric mapping.

Oblique photographs are the most widely used in archaeology to locate sites and illustrate features. These are taken from low-flying aircraft with the picture taken at an angle to the ground. Aerial reconaissance usually precedes field survey. While this is fast and gives good coverage, it can be expensive and can miss features if their **signatures** are not visible from the air. Equally, there may be features which are invisible at ground level and this provides the only means of recording them. There are three main ways in which archaeological sites show up from the air.

Shadow sites

In low light, either at the start or end of the day, shadows are at their longest and even quite minor variations in ground level cast shadows, for instance ploughed out barrows or the remains of early field systems.

APs taken from a low-flying aircraft and recorded with a camera pointed into the sun have a distorted perspective which emphasises shadows. The technique is best used for illustrating existing sites and locating details within them, for example features inside a hill fort. However, shadows are also created where crops are at different heights (▶ p. 23) and occasionally new sites can be detected. Winter is the best season for photography as the sun is low and vegetation which might mask sites has often died down. Snowfall and flooding can accentuate the appearance of hollows and earthworks and create some of the most dramatic images of **shadow sites**.

Cropmarks

The ripening and growth rate of crops is related to the amount of moisture their root systems can access. Plants with better access to moisture will often grow taller and turn a different tone or

Figure 1.19 *An excellent view of the deserted medieval village (DMV) of Bingham's Melcombe, which shows up because of shadows cast by low sunlight. Traces of houses, enclosures and trackways are all visible*

Note how features at right angles to the sun show up best.

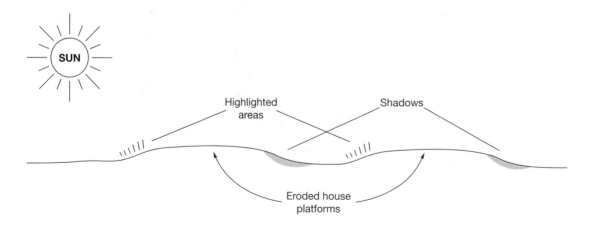

Figure 1.20 *Why earthworks are visible as 'shadow sites'*

colour than those plants around them. If there are buried archaeological features under a field this can result in patterns showing in the crop. A buried ditch with its infill of humus and topsoil will often hold moisture, creating a dark green line in the crop above. This 'positive' **cropmark** is visible from the air. The opposite occurs in plants over a buried wall. They are likely to be stunted and produce a yellowish, 'negative' cropmark. 'Parch marks' show on grass for the same reason.

Cropmarks sometimes only show for a few days a year. Repeatedly flying over areas over time can pick up new and different features. Some only show up in drought conditions when crops with access to moisture have the greatest advantage and colour contrast is exaggerated. The technique works best on quickly draining soils such as river gravels but is less good on clay or areas of deeper topsoil, where the soil retains moisture well. Cropmarks show up best in cereal crops such as wheat and particularly barley. They do not show up in many crops, for example peas and beans, and the effect of differential moisture can be overcome or masked by irrigation or fertiliser. Care has to be taken with interpretation, as geological features such as periglacial cracks and modern field drainage and underground pipelines also create crop-marks. Trial excavation is often the only way to firmly identify many sites. Cropmarks are the most prolific source of new sites, particularly for the late Neolithic to early medieval periods, and are also used to investigate existing sites such as the extent of the harbour at Fishbourne Palace.

Figure 1.21 *An Iron Age 'banjo' enclosure on Cranborne Chase showing as a dark cropmark*

The crops growing over the ditches of the feature are darker because their roots have better access to moisture than the surrounding crops. Crown Copyright 1955 & 1959/MOD.

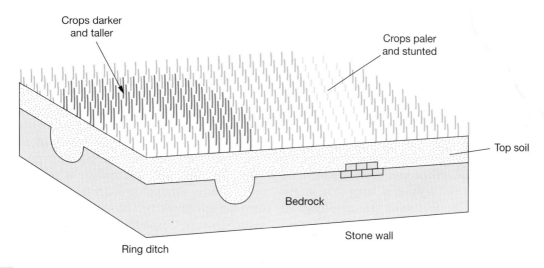

Crops darker and taller

Crops paler and stunted

Top soil

Bedrock

Stone wall

Ring ditch

Figure 1.22 *Three-dimensional cross section of cropmarks*

Soil marks

On soils where there is a marked contrast between the colour of the topsoil and subsoil, evidence of ploughed-out monuments can occur as **soil marks**. On chalk, the dark brown of ditch infill will contrast with the chalk rubble of a bank and the lighter brown of the plough soil. At Flag Fen a Roman road appeared as an orangey stripe against the black peat soil. Soil

Figure 1.23 *Winterbourne Stoke round barrow cemetery showing as soil marks*

The difference in tone between the top soil and the material used for the barrow provides a clear contrast. The monuments would not be easily detected on the ground.

marks are sharpest in winter when vegetation is low.

Remote sensing

This can be a rather confusing term. Usually it is used to distinguish between the imaging techniques used from planes and satellites and those of ground based prospection. Sometimes it is used to describe all techniques that don't remove material. When you come across it, be sure to check which sense it is being used in. We are using it in the first sense. The results of all these techniques need to be checked at ground level.

• http://www.arcl.ed.ac.uk/arch/remotesense/

A variety of airborne and satellite techniques, including thermal imaging and infrared photography, are able to record temperature, dew and frost dispersal variations invisible to light-sensitive film. They all work on the principle that anomalies such as disturbed earth or buried walls will absorb and retain heat or moisture at different rates to the surrounding ground. Commercial equipment is really only suitable for large features although military developments to increase sensitivity will no doubt filter through to archaeology. Currently such equipment is too expensive for most archaeological surveys.

Figure 1.24 *Loughcrew*

The area around Loughcrew in Ireland is packed with neolithic monuments, however, little is known about other use of the landscape. Current research is using a technique called airborne Lidar (Light Detection and Ranging) to map all the earthworks within 3km of the site. The Lidar device is mounted in a light aircraft and transmits a scanning laser beam which is reflected back from the ground surface and recorded on sensors. The time taken determines the precise distance from the aircraft. This method is more sensitive than conventional photographs of shadows and is revealing early field systems within the modern landscape which survive as slight earthworks.

Excavation

To many people, archaeology simply means excavation. Often their interest in archaeology stems from witnessing an excavation or viewing one on television. Excavation is often the public face of archaeology. It is only when people 'dig' deeper into the subject that they are able to recognise the role that excavation plays in the wider nature of the discipline. It has its own methodology, which constantly changes to reflect current thinking and improving technologies. There can never be one set of rules for excavation although there is general agreement on key elements of the process. This chapter will try to reflect that current consensus.

WHY EXCAVATE?

Any removal of the accumulated evidence of the past is a finite act. Once disturbed, trowelled, shovelled and bucketed away that material cannot be replaced as it was before the excavator removed it. Hence it has been frequently said that 'all excavation is destruction'. Today no one condones excavation as it took place in the nineteenth century: for the pleasure of the excavators and to establish collections of artefacts. In all but those extreme circumstances, where chance discovery of remains demands a prompt response, there should be controlled planning. This should establish the rationale for excavation and formulate a series of questions, which it is hoped, the excavation might answer.

Often the record of a site can be remarkably full if a wide range of reconnaissance methods has been applied and there are sufficient clues about hidden features or structures. In many cases, once the record of such survey activities is carefully housed in an appropriate archive, for example the local SMR, archaeologists leave the physical remains untouched. If, however, a decision is made to excavate, it should be viewed as a very serious step. While most scientific experiments can be repeated over and over again in the laboratory, archaeological excavation, although scientific in its approach, does not, by its very nature, allow a second chance. Some excavation procedures, somewhat confusingly referred to as sampling strategies, have been developed to try and ensure that not all the evidence is removed in the primary investigation of a feature or deposit. Nevertheless, in essence, excavation means destruction. However, that 'destruction' is minimised if the archaeologist pays appropriate care and attention to the way the excavation is conducted and particularly to the quality of the records kept. This is sometimes referred to as 'preservation by record'

There are other considerations. A balance must be struck between the desire to protect archaeological remains for future generations and the need to develop the discipline and advance our knowledge through excavation. It is also important that archaeology is kept sufficiently in the public eye to receive the support it needs in the wider political forum. All these issues are explored further in Chapter 10.

Today, excavators are expected to:

■ provide justifications for digging a site
■ use survey techniques to plan excavation strategies

Figure 2.1 *No it isn't a row of onions*

The reuse of ceramic containers for drainage purposes in the town walls at Cremona in Italy presents an archaeological dilemma. Should all the vessels be recorded in situ and excavated by hand or treated as fill and a sample of complete and diagnostic pieces kept and the rest discarded?

KEY STUDY

Chester Amphitheatre project

A major partnership between English Heritage and Chester City Council was launched in 2004 to sponsor a major research programme focused on, but not wholly devoted to, a re-examination of the archaeological evidence for the Roman amphitheatre. The first main phase of the project ran for three years from 2004–2006. Central to the aims and principles established for the project was that it should have a strong basis of community links and involvement and this can be seen exemplified by the contents of a dedicated website: www.chester.gov.uk/amphitheatre

The main aims of the programme were:

■ Non-destructive research involving, amongst a range of techniques, ground penetrating radar and photography including photogrammetry and aerial photography
■ Large scale excavations
■ Reinterpretation of the site
■ Focus on the amphitheatre but also its contemporary Roman context (in particular the adjacent legionary fortress) and possible post-Roman early Christian development

These first four objectives embodied the archaeological mission to validate and enhance the data recovered from previous excavations, to reappraise the evidence and the quality of its survival,

Figure 2.2 *Location of Chester amphitheatre*

Plan of Chester in Roman times showing (1) the relationship of the amphitheatre to the fortress and (2) the location of Area A in the north-west quadrant of the amphitheatre. (English Heritage and Chester City Council)

KEY STUDY *cont.*

Chester Amphitheatre project

to establish the occupation/building phases of the site pre-amphitheatre, during the amphitheatre's development and in the subsequent use of the site post-amphitheatre.

- To establish a new Research Centre with a community focus that would engage and interest the people of Chester
- To encourage visitor interest – an important economic factor
- To have an educational emphasis through display, development of teaching and learning materials and, during the excavations, to enable local people to be trained in basic archaeological field techniques
- To plan for the future of the site

These latter four objectives ensured that this was not another 'unit' excavation undertaken behind fences and inaccessible through Health and Safety legislation. The whole process was conducted in full view of the public (special viewing platforms were erected and guided tours arranged) and the media played their part in recording and broadcasting updates.

Figure 2.3 *Excavation of Chester amphitheatre*

Area A from the east. The two lines of the curving external amphitheatre walls are visible with the earlier one on the left and the one from the enlarged site on the right. Note the very public display of excavation in this community project. (English Heritage and Chester City Council)

KEY STUDY *cont.*

Chester Amphitheatre project

Following the three seasons of excavation and related research the following phases had been identified on the main site:

1. Pre-Roman soil levels produced pollen samples which suggested the area may have been the site of an Iron Age farm.
2. The first amphitheatre, probably built AD 80–100, had a stone outer wall and a stone arena wall with clay dumped in between the two and timber seating erected on this. Upper seats were reached by external stairways. Outside the amphitheatre post-holes cut into a cobbled surface provide unique evidence for the presence of booths and stalls – in today's context the souvenir/programme stand and burger van. A possible small shrine was found near the north entrance and may have been dedicated to the goddess Nemesis (Fate).
3. At a date not yet determined the first amphitheatre was partly demolished and replaced by a much grander construction, the biggest amphitheatre in Roman Britain, with new foundations 2m outside the original line and 2.7m deep. These supported a large stone outer wall with added buttresses, stone entrances and the upper rows of the tiered seating would have been carried on vaulting reminiscent of similar sites elsewhere in the Roman world e.g. Nimes in Provence.
4. At some time possibly in the tenth or eleventh centuries and certainly before the twelfth and thirteenth centuries the main walls of the amphitheatre were robbed out, first the inner wall and secondly the massive outer wall of the later rebuild.
5. From the twelfth century onwards over much of the site medieval cess pits were dug through the Roman levels. These have provided a wealth of finds and particularly environmental evidence such as seeds, fish bones and parasite remains.

- adjust to subsequent changes on site
- put a complete recording system is in place
- select and maintain appropriate samples for analysis
- have facilities for all aspects of post-excavation work
- interpret a site from a limited excavation or sample
- 'publish' the results of the work so that they are available to other interested parties
- maintain professional standards while working under time and economic constraints.

If this is done then excavation can move beyond the possible results of survey and get to the real core of archaeology – the hard evidence left by previous people of their existence.

TYPES OF EXCAVATION

Excavations today usually fall into one of two broad categories depending on the main reason for them: research or rescue.

Research excavations

These are usually excavations on sites where there is no immediate threat of destruction. The site is selected by archaeologists for its suitability to answer the questions they wish to answer. It can be excavated according to archaeological needs rather than prompted by the threat of development. Research excavation is only undertaken when the perceived benefits to archaeological understanding outweigh the loss of the original site, or part of it, to future generations.

Occasionally there may be re-excavation to recover samples which were never collected at the time or to extend the area of a site. Current work at Star Carr is a good example.

There is some public or commercial funding of research excavation for example exploration of the North Sea bed (▶ p. 351) which is funded by a levy on aggregate companies. However, in most cases archaeologists have to finance investigative work by alternative means. For instance, universities that run 'training excavations' for their undergraduates may also accept paying 'volunteers' (▶ p. 358). Applied research agencies, for example the British Academy, provide some support for research projects. An example is the Stonehenge riverside project which involves several universities, English Heritage and organisations such as the Society of Antiquaries and the Prehistoric Society. Much research is also multidisciplinary involving specialists from fields as diverse as chemistry, computing and ecology working in conjunction with archaeologists.

Rescue excavations

'Rescue excavation' was a term coined in the 1960s when much of our archaeological heritage was destroyed by development and road building. It involved trying to excavate and record as much as possible in the time before the builders began work. Occasionally sites were not discovered until land clearance began. Rapid recording and rushed excavation in these circumstances was often the best that could be done. This was often called 'salvage archaeology'. Some excavations in inter-tidal areas (▶ p. 56) still fall into this category. The term is used in the USA interchangeably with 'rescue archaeology'.

Today most digs are rescue excavation. These take place within the framework of the planning process. (▶ See Chapter 10.) Exploratory excavations are often used alongside remote sensing to establish the nature and extent of archaeological deposits. These 'impact assessments' inform discussions between archaeologists, planners and contractors. To avoid the heavy costs and delays in construction caused by full excavation, a series of 'mitigation strategies' (▶ p. 348) are often adopted. These involve building whilst trying to minimize damage to archaeology. This is known as 'preservation in situ' (▶ p. 348). However, where excavation does go ahead, archaeologists will often set their priorities against research questions as well as time and cost considerations. Unless they miscalculate or uncover unexpected remains they have time to carry out their work according to proper archaeological principles. Once the contractors move in, archaeologists keep a 'watching brief' (▶ p. 348). This means that they can stop building work to record archaeology which turns up unexpectedly.

Amongst the key differences between the two approaches is the ability of research archaeologists to select sites and also to fully excavate all sites. Rescue archaeology has sometimes resulted in many tiny 'keyhole' excavations into parts of sites rather than always revealing large parts of them. However, sometimes the differences can be overstated. The Channel Tunnel rail link from London to Dover resulted in the largest archaeological project to date in the UK. Engineers and archaeologists from eight different groups worked together to ensure that archaeological issues were fully considered. All forms of survey work were carried out; over 2,000 trial trenches and test pits were dug. Fieldwork informed the setting of priorities about where to excavate. Some 55 hectares of the route were identified as requiring detailed archaeological investigation. Planning of the work gave archaeologists time to 'painstakingly' record the archaeological deposits on the sites selected for detailed work. Other areas were subject to watching briefs. In this particular scheme the archaeologists were empowered to stop construction work if 'features of significance' were identified. Over forty sites were excavated with dates ranging from the Palaeolithic to the Second World War. The impact of the new evidence will alter many current perceptions of Kent's archaeology.

• See *Current Archaeology 168*.

Figure 2.4 *Excavations on the site of Heathrow Terminal 5*

Only the largest archaeological units are capable of bidding for infrastructure projects such as this and often only in collaboration with others. In this instance several units came together to form Framework Archaeology. This proved to be the largest single site excavation in the UK with over 100 hectares being dug and 80,000 artefacts recovered. Unusually, finds were recorded and analysed on-site rather than after excavation. Environmental data has enabled reconstruction of the sequence of land use from the Upper Palaeolithic onwards. The earliest signs of settlement were forager cooking pits from 6500. During the Neolithic, the linear feature in the photograph was constructed. This was not an earlier runway but the Stanwell Cursus, a 4km long ritual monument. Perhaps the most important discovery was that from around 2000 BC the landscape was divided by field boundaries. This is about 500 years earlier than previously thought and pollen evidence suggests that hedges were used as boundaries. The earliest boundaries respected the line of the Cursus but from around 1500 they cut across the Cursus and suggest that sedentary farming was associated with religious change. Boundaries also restricted access to the rivers so waterholes were dug. Deliberate deposits of artefacts in these suggest that water may have been significant in ritual at the time. Some of the boundaries established in the Bronze Age were used up to the twentieth century.

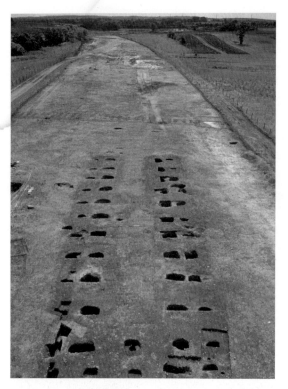

Figure 2.5 *Rescue excavation of a Roman barn*

The M6 Toll motorway created a huge transect across the West Midlands. Many sites were located and recorded along the route including the post settings of this Roman barn.

EXCAVATION STRATEGIES AND THE PROCESS OF EXCAVATION

The decision to dig will originate either in a research project or because remains are due to be destroyed. In either case the excavation director will make plans based on what is known from desktop surveys and reconnaissance. These plans will aim to answer a series of questions at different levels. An example of a question linked to wider debates might be 'Did towns decay early in the 4th century AD?' A more specific question might be 'Why was this site abandoned?' Below that might be a whole series of questions such as establishing the date of deposits and

understanding site formation processes (▶ p. 112). These questions along with constraints of time and money will lead to decisions about where and how to dig.

Defining the site in question is the first issue (▶ p. 198). In excavation terms some 'sites' are in fact a series of smaller 'sites' in themselves. For example, cropmarks may indicate a series of **features** (enclosures, pits, tracks) which can be separated out for investigation while a Roman town has a street plan and a variety of public and private buildings each capable of individual excavation. Sites are set within a landscape context and a successful excavation needs to take note of that factor too. So the director needs to decide whether it is the entirety of the site that is the focus of their attention or whether concentration on certain parts offers the best chance to answer their questions.

If there are many similar features it is likely that a number will be sampled rather than excavating every one. This can mean that some deposits are not recorded to the same extent as others. For example Georgian housing might be more speedily excavated and recorded because the main interest is in an underlying Roman forum.

• http://museums.ncl.ac.uk/raunds/

There is no set manual for archaeological field practices either in relation to where to put the holes in the ground or in how to proceed once the excavation trench is underway. This is not because archaeologists have a laissez-faire attitude to standards and procedures but because of variety in the nature of sites, evidence and questions asked. Most texts on excavation express their ideas about appropriate 'good practice' and as new methods evolve so they too appear in print. The archaeological world constantly shares its experiences and a general consensus of current good practice is evident when one looks at images of modern excavations. Practitioners learn from one another and try to keep

KEY TERMS

Features and cuts

Features are traces in the soil of past human activity. A distinction can be made between

* Constructed features which were deliberately built such as a wall, fish trap or pond
* Cumulative features which develop from repeated actions. Middens, hollow-ways and the shallow gullies known as drip rings which encircled round houses are good examples.

While some features are obvious, many are not. Only the faintest traces of a stakehole may survive as slight variations in the colour or texture of soil only detectable by an experienced excavator. Many small features such as ditches or postholes may in fact be elements in one larger feature which is only revealed when excavation recording is complete. The term 'cut' is increasingly used to describe dug features such as pits, ditches and postholes.

The site below is seen topstripped before Green's (2000) research dig. The major features or cuts are revealed as discolorations in the chalk but excavation was required to identify them. They proved to be a ring of pits with a central pit 10m wide and 1.5m deep. Hidden in this pit was a burial of a woman and three children and a 7m deep shaft down to a seam of flint.

Figure 2.6 Features at Neolithic ritual site at Monkton Up Wimborne

their methods in line with current thinking and therefore ensure that their results, when published, stand up to scrutiny and are accepted by their peers. For example, many archaeological units use the Museum of London excavation manual.

The nature of the archaeological record in the ground is often complex. Human nature and life circumstances ensure that most sites have a developmental history, which the archaeologist needs to unravel. The people who left the evidence went about their daily business without a thought for how their activities might leave traces for future investigators. They were not simply creating 'features' much of the time, nor did they often build a structure and leave it unaltered. However, their constructional or daily activities will have created a sequence of deposits, layers or **contexts** (the words are often used interchangeably) which build up to create the archaeological record. Contained within these deposits, which are linked to features and structures, are the **artefacts** of pottery, metalwork, etc. and **ecofacts**, which provide sources for understanding the chronological, cultural and environmental nature of the site.

One further issue which excavators have to be aware of is the health and safety of their diggers. Precautions range from hardhats and reflective clothing on developer sites to ensuring that deep trenches are properly shored up or have stepped sides. Safety issues are most evident on underwater sites where air supply, currents, cold and sharks are amongst the potential hazards not faced on land.

How to dig?

The excavation methodology debate centres on the fact that all sites have two key elements. A vertical sequence of layers containing structures and finds, and the horizontal layout of an occupation area or individual structure. It is difficult for a method to explore both equally well but to record both elements is vital. Unless the archaeologist can establish the correct succession of levels an excavation will have limited, if any, value. Similarly the inability to produce the plan (layout) of a building or a cemetery leaves the researcher well short of the required results. Archaeologists have therefore developed a series of methods appropriate to different types of site.

Trenches and test pits

The term 'trench' has been applied to any linear excavation and sometimes to any hole cut into the ground by archaeologists, whatever its surface shape. A stricter definition is a rectangular shaped excavation of variable width and length. Test pits or 'sondages' are essentially square trenches, usually 1 metre square. Trenches and test pits are used either to evaluate the stratigraphy of a site before a decision is made on whether or not to excavate or as part of an excavation sampling strategy. By digging down either to bedrock or the top of the archaeological deposits the vertical profile of part of the site can be examined. This provides information about depth of deposits and complexity of contexts. It can also provide an opportunity for sampling environmental remains. Sometimes mechanical diggers are used to dig part or all of the trench in which case the trench width is determined by the dimensions of the digger's bucket.

Those of you who have watched the TV programme 'Time Team' will be familiar with the use of trial trenches to investigate possible features identified by reconnaissance methods. This is also done on many sites after 'top-stripping' of topsoil (◀ p. 32). In very large sites trenches are used to investigate linear archaeological features such as defensive **earthworks** by being placed at 90° to the alignment of the feature. The trenches cut by Alcock through the defences of South Cadbury hill fort in Somerset provide a classic example. By strategically placing a series of 2-metre wide trenches around the hill he was able to study and report on the developmental

KEY CONCEPTS

Stratigraphy, contexts and phases

In any text about archaeological sites you will come across terms such as level, layer, deposit, stratum. They describe the make-up of the excavated ground in terms of layers. These were created either by people or nature. Archaeologists attempt to carefully record these strata – the **stratification**. By studying their relationship they can build up a sequence of events on the site. The study of the strata is known as stratigraphy.

If no intrusive features are present (for example a pit dug from an upper/recent layer down through lower/older layers) it would be safe to assume that layers at the bottom of any sequence are older than those at the top. Each successive layer was deposited after the one directly below it. The 'higher' the layer, the later it is. This is sometimes referred to as 'the law of **superposition**'. But life and archaeological sites are not usually that simple. Archaeologists need to establish which layers overlie others and which cut into earlier layers or are cut by later ones.

It is within the layers that the artefactual, environmental and dating evidence is located. Layers are a time capsule. Materials in any layer are likely to be broadly contemporary and can be dated by association with dateable evidence from that layer. The layer holds the clues to the immediate context of finds and structures.

Figure 2.7 *A picture that demonstrates how the law of superposition can tell a story*

The female skeleton is lying above the mosaic at Kingscote and covered by building debris. The interpretation is that she was one of a number of 'squatters' who occupied the derelict villa building but was killed, apparently trying to escape, when it collapsed.

Plotting the position of each layer within the site helps determine chronological patterns. Other archaeologists will use published data about the stratification to assure themselves of the authenticity of the conclusions reached about phasing on a site.

Increasingly **context** is used for both layers and features. Each individual element in the stratigraphy is a context. A context might result from a single event such as a fire or roof collapse or a build up of soil against a wall over several years. The task of the digger is to identify each context and to trace the boundaries or 'interfaces' between contexts. This may only be detectable by minute changes in the colour, texture or composition of the soil. Typically contexts will be identified in the side of a trench by nails and labels. (▶ p. 39). A description is also noted on a **context sheet** (▶ p. 44). Once recorded, the stratigraphic relationship between contexts can be determined and a vertical, chronological sequence based on successive 'events' established. Stratigraphy is usually

KEY CONCEPTS *cont.*

Stratigraphy, contexts and phases

recorded in section drawings (▶ p. 44). However, since 1973 the Harris Matrix has revolutionized the presentation of the sequences in schematic diagrams. This interpretative system can be applied to standing buildings and rock art as well as to excavated remains.

KEY

☐	Fills and layers	
○	Cuts	
[ ]	Built features	

③	Pit fill
②	Rubbish pit
①	Topsoil
⑤	Dark fill
④	Tree throw
⑥	Ashy layer
⑨	Backfilled pit
⑧	Robber cut
⑦	Sandy layer
⑩ ⑪ ⑬	Dark layers
⑫	Humic layer
[⑭] [⑰]	Stone walls
⑮ ⑱	Foundation cuts
⑯	Clay layer

Figure 2.8 *A Harris matrix*

Down to layer 7 in this example the law of superposition can be applied. Layers 10, 11 and 13 are similar but may not be exactly the same because of the building floor 12. These are shown in parallel. Similarly, the 2 walls are likely to be contemporary.

Context is also used in a general sense when talking about finds and their relationship to layers. This is based on the principle that objects found together in the same layer are roughly from the same period and can be dated by association with dateable evidence from that deposit (▶ p. 97). Associated finds may also have a relationship. They may help to explain each other because they were used in the same activity or process. If the context of an artefact is not known, it is usually of little use to archaeologists.

Once sequences and associations of finds are established, different phases of the site can be determined. This relies on recognizing significant changes in the assemblages of artefacts or ecofacts or type of structures. For example, the first phase with pottery on a site might be preceded by a final aceramic phase.

http://www.harrismatrix.com

sequence of the site's fortifications. This had the added bonus of disturbing a small proportion of the site in return for a large volume of evidence. Most of the site was left undamaged for future archaeologists. Other linear features such as roads and boundaries can be cross-sectioned in this way. Offa's Dyke, an early medieval feature running from north to south Wales, has been the focus of a long-term study by Manchester University and over 100 trenches have been put across it to check and confirm details of its construction.

Sometimes test pitting is the main method used. The site is gridded with 1 metre squares and sampling used to select a number of locations to dig. This produces a series of vertical profiles across the site which gives some idea of the horizontal plan. On very shallow sites with little stratigraphy, shovel pit testing (◀ p. 15) is sometimes used for this. Cutting lots of test pits or trial trenches into a site is quick, cheap and provides valuable information about stratigraphy. For this reason they are the most common type of excavation in the UK. However, they are relatively poor as a means to understand how a site fitted together.

Area excavation

This is the most common form of excavation of whole sites as can be seen in most reports or archaeological magazines. 'Area' or 'open-stripping' occurs where the extent of the features to be uncovered determines the size of the excavation. This does not mean that whole sites are always laid bare. This can be an outcome but more frequently other factors limit the total recovery of evidence or perhaps development only threatens part of the site and the rest is left 'in situ'. On some research digs such as those run by universities digging may take place over several seasons. Different parts of the site are dug and recorded each year. Danebury hill fort is a well known example of this strategy (▶ p. 120). Finally there may be research considerations. Only a sample of the site may be needed to

Figure 2.9 *A 'cut' feature quartered in order to give four internal section profiles*

This will enable excavators to determine the depth, shape and fill of the pit as well as any internal stratigraphy.

answer the director's questions. Financial constraints may limit the amount of digging.

Although destructive, area excavation has become the key approved method for several reasons.

- Complete structures can be studied.
- Complex relationships between features can be clarified.
- It provides excellent recording possibilities.
- A total understanding of horizontal relationships is possible.

When area excavation became fashionable there was criticism from those traditionalists who had used trenches. The sides of trenches have the advantage of revealing the vertical sequence of deposits (stratigraphy) and there was concern that this essential record might be lost. The depth of deposits can vary and the issue is of great significance where the stratification is deeper and more complicated. This problem can be addressed by leaving baulks (undug strips of ground) at strategic points or, increasingly, by carefully recording the horizontal picture of a site

Figure 2.10 *Area excavation at Goldfields Farm*

The training dig (▶ p. 358) on this Romano-British site has adopted an area approach. Once topstripped the individual features such as the ditch in the foreground are sectioned or excavated. Barrow runways ensure spoil is quickly and safely removed and protect the surface.

layer by layer and feeding the data into a computer. This process is referred to as 'single context recording'. The data can be interrogated to produce sections along any chosen line. The problem is that without baulks no check is left in place if the director wishes to refer back, so the recording systems must be of the highest quality. To provide a check, the contexts and their relationships are sometimes photographed.

Box-grid or quadrant systems

These sit in an intermediate position between trenches and area excavation. They offer archaeologists the better aspects of each by giving access to both the horizontal view and the vertical cut simultaneously.

The box-grid system owes its origins to the work of Sir Mortimer Wheeler in the first half of the twentieth century. He would set out a grid of square 'boxes' to be excavated with baulks left in between them. This resulted in a dig resembling a patchwork quilt. An advantage was the chance to record four sections for every 'box'. Removal of spoil was also easier as baulks provided barrow runs. However, the whole layout of a site was not revealed until the baulks were finally removed. Important relationships between features or structures would not be understood while digging, which might depend on such an understanding, was progressing. The system was complex, costly of time and manpower and of little use on sites with very

Figure 2.11 *Recording a section across an excavated ditch*

This approach to features is typical of area excavations. The planning frame against the vertical section helps the recorder to produce an accurate profile on gridded paper. The context labels on the face of the section ensure that slight changes in the fill which might be very difficult to see or photograph are recorded.

deep stratigraphy. It is little used in the UK today although it is still popular in other countries, particularly India.

The 'quadrant system' is a similar approach that is still sometimes employed. It is particularly relevant in the case of sites that are approximately circular in nature, such as round barrows, (▶ p. 47) although a smaller scale version of this method can be used on hearths, pits or even postholes. The feature is cut into four quarters by lines intersecting at the middle. Opposing quadrants are excavated first. It is possible after only removing half the remains to see patterns of features in plan (which if they show common elements suggest that they continue under the undug areas) and to totally record the vertical profile of the site in two directions.

Planum excavation

On most sites features can be identified once a surface has been cleared and trowelled. However, if a site lacks clear stratification and generally comprises soil rather than stones or building materials, the identification of contexts can present problems. In this case an alternative approach is to 'plane' off a predetermined thickness of deposit across the whole site, plan and photograph the revealed surface and then repeat the process. In effect slices are removed across the site to reveal and record a series of images much the same as an MRI (Magnetic Resonance Imaging) body scan provides cut-through views of the human body for doctors.

One application of this method is the excavation of grave fills where ground conditions have adversely affected the survival of the burial and/or any associated objects. The painstaking excavation of cave deposits at Creswell Crags took the planum method one step further by also dividing the deposits vertically so as to create small cubes of cave earth for precision in recording ecofacts and artefacts.

KEY SITE

Boxgrove

The chance discovery in 1993 of a human shin bone in a quarry by Mark Roberts led him to initiate the most famous recent example of box-grid excavation. The ongoing excavations have revealed much about the lifestyle and environment of Homo Heidelbergensis, one of the earliest of our ancestors to reach Britain. The bone enabled scientists to suggest that these hominids were large and heavily built like a modern sprinter. Cut marks on two human teeth found nearby showed that they used their teeth to hold meat while they cut it. The geology revealed that the site had been a beach backed by chalk cliffs. A spring at the foot of the cliffs fed a small fresh water pool that attracted animals. In and around the pool were scatters of animal bones and flint tools including 450 well made hand axes and hammer stones (for removing marrow from bone). Many of the bones had cut marks from the tools and even fragments of flint in a knife cut.

Figure 2.12 Box sections

Box sections enabled precise cross referencing of the freshwater sediments laid down by the stream. Chalk ensured excellent preservation and enabled scatters of flint and bones to be studied where they had fallen. Some of the silts were so fine grained that individual episodes could be recorded and in one case it was possible to tell from waste flakes how the flint knapper was sitting.

KEY SITE *cont.*

Boxgrove

SEM examination of a rhinoceros bone revealed human butchery marks under the tooth marks of a scavenging carnivore. In other words, the human had got there first. Hunting evidence came in the form of a horse scapula with a very neat circular perforation on the outside and a splintered 'exit wound'. This suggested a high velocity projectile, perhaps a fire-hardened wooden spear such as the ones discovered at Lehringen. Experimental archaeology (▶ p. 125) involving a javelin thrower and a deer carcass produced very similar damage to excavated bones. This suggests that these hominids were hunters rather than scavengers. They used speed and throwing weapons to kill and strip the meat from the horses, deer and possibly rhinoceros visiting the pool. The hominids repeatedly exploited their understanding of animal behaviour at the waterhole while evading other predators. Their presence is evident from wolf teeth marks on the shin bone.

The base of each section was marked with the site grid to ensure precise planning. Each find was given a coloured flag depending on the material and both compass direction and angle of dip recorded in order to determine whether water movement had moved them (▶ p. 114). Figure 2.13 illustrates spit level sections.

Faunal dating (▶ p. 99) showed that the site was in use during a warm interglacial period 500,000 years ago. Lions, elephants and tuna bones suggest a warmer climate than today. As well as bones of large grazing animals, wet sieving enabled the recovery of bird and fish bone and the remains of extinct water voles. These tiny rodents evolve rapidly. For example their teeth lost their roots over time. Minute differences and the extinction of many species have enabled researchers to construct a detailed picture of vole evolution in Europe for a million years. Voles can be used to date the stratigraphic layer they are found in. Since different species have different habitats, they also help us understand local ecology at the time. The level of development of vole teeth enabled Boxgrove to be compared to examples from other sites dated using absolute methods (▶ p. 101). The 'vole clock' showed that Boxgrove was older than 478,000 BC.

The find of an 'antler hammer' potentially provides a new perspective on human mental capacity and behaviour for this period. It suggests a degree of planning, fore-thought and 'curation' that was believed to be beyond the capacity of hominids at this stage in evolution. The hammer also provided corroborative faunal dating evidence. The antler came from a giant elk which became extinct around 500,000 years ago.

Figure 2.13 *Living floor*

THE PROCESS OF EXCAVATION

Archaeologists have developed a variety of methods for removing archaeological deposits from the ground in which they have lain to suit the varying circumstances of archaeological sites. The topsoil is removed by mechanically topstripping with a digger or by using picks, mattocks and shovels. This is either mechanically lifted or wheelbarrowed away to start a spoil heap. This has to be far enough away to avoid it spilling over and contaminating deeper layers or burying the diggers. Although mechanical diggers can be used for trial trenches, most excavation is by hand. According to the time available and the nature of the deposits, tools could range from shovels to dentistry instruments for recovering tiny fragments of material. The most familiar toolkit includes a mattock, a short pointed trowel, a dustbrush, a coalshovel and a bucket. In the USA long handled shovels are used which are better for a digger's back than spades, while in some countries hand hoes are an alternative to trowels. Eventually, and very neatly, what was an archaeological resource is converted into a hole in the ground. The extracted evidence must be subjected to a rigorous recording process or the excavation will have destroyed the site and its potential. Recording requirements will vary for sites with less obvious collectable material or with particular distributions of evidence.

Layers of deposits in the ground are recognised, labelled and removed in sequence. On many sites such as Roman or medieval where pottery sherds and animal bones are common, their collection is linked to the contexts in which the material is found. They are collected in labelled 'finds trays' so that all the finds from each layer can be put together. They will subsequently be washed, dried and coded to their particular layer for recording.

On the same sites less common objects like metal, worked bone or stone will usually be classified as special or key 'finds'. A distinct and

KEY TASK

Testing the law of superposition

When you have been working at your desk for a while or after, say, half an hour of a lesson look at the way your books, papers, pencil case, sweet wrappers (or those of your fellow students) have combined in an overlapping manner. If you pick your way backwards through the evidence it should be possible to establish in reverse order the sequence of events that led to the accumulated material being in position. This will not tell you when the build up of items took place but should establish the order. The floor of your room provides an alternative site to examine.

more comprehensive recording system will ensure that the precise location of each find is recorded in three dimensions by triangulation and depth measurements. They are collected in finds trays or plastic bags and given unique reference numbers. On a working floor associated with a prehistoric flint-knapper careful plotting of each flake is necessary to recreate the sequence of the earlier activity. Sometimes their position in a layer is marked by a small flag so that distribution patterns can be recorded. These finds will be kept separately and the nature and fragility of each object will determine their post-excavation scientific treatment.

Recovery of environmental material

Not all the material to be retrieved can be recovered by trowelling. The ground contains much smaller and less obvious evidence, in particular faunal (animal) and floral (plant) evidence such as snail shells, small fish or bird bones, insect remains, seeds and pollen grains. Not all of these are visible to the naked eye. Tiny fragments of metal or worked material such as flint or glass present the same problem. This material can be recovered on-site by using sieving or flotation or by taking strategically selected soil samples for later analysis.

Dry sieving small amounts of soil is carried out in the same way as shovel pit testing (◀ p. 14). On larger sites buckets of soil samples are tipped into a large sieve usually suspended from a frame and riddled over a barrow to ensure that finds not detected in the digging process are retrieved. A series of sieves with increasingly finer mesh improve collection chances and also collect different sized material in each sieve. The introduction of water to create 'wet-sieving', whether by spray or dipping into a tank, helps to remove the soil particles. Wet material is often easier to identify and locate by colour contrast.

Flotation

This involves putting soil samples into water. Lighter materials such as plant remains float to the surface while the soil drops to the bottom of the container. Improvements to this basic methodology include adding oil to hold tiny particles on the surface and bubbling air from below the water to create a froth, which holds and separates lighter organic material. Water is drained from the top through a sequence of increasingly finely meshed sieves.

Soil sampling

Some recovery of environmental remains occurs off-site. Bags of soil samples are taken from selected locations such as pits, ditches or other similar diagnostic features or layers. On peat sites, long sampling tins are hammered vertically into the sides of freshly dug sections, removed and quickly sealed in plastic to avoid contamination. They are then placed in cold storage before detailed analysis in the laboratory. The pollens and plant remains in them will be used to provide vegetation sequences and help date the site. Soil may also be sampled for chemical analysis, particularly for phosphates (◀ p. 14). One aspect of soil sampling which has often

Figure 2.14 *Flotation bins*

Soil samples — Film of oil to trap pollen — Outflow

Bubbles carry small particles up

Coarse mesh

Fine mesh

Water flow

Settling tank — Drain

Sludge

Water pumped in

Froth flotation can separate pollens and small ecofacts and artefacts from soil samples.

Sieving, using a series of different meshes is more appropriate for larger finds.

Figure 2.15 *How a flotation bin works*

been neglected is attempting to recover dietary evidence when excavating human remains. Studies have suggested that around 70% of burials have evidence surviving in abdominal soils.

Metal detection

On some excavations, and directly under the control of the director, it is appropriate to use metal detectors. They can be employed as part of the initial survey as a piece of geophysical equipment but they can also be used to check the spoil heap for finds. This would be applicable if the site had been stripped by machine rather than by hand or if soil removal had been by pick and shovel without subsequent sieving. Any such finds would be classed as unstratified. Metal detectors can also be used to alert diggers to

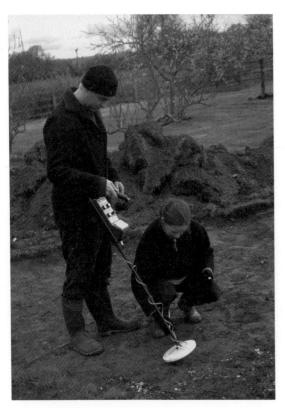

Figure 2.16 *A metal detector on site*

potentially fragile metal objects in areas they are trowelling.

In whatever way the finds are identified and collected it is vital that the methods used allow their full potential to be exploited in post-excavation analysis and dating procedures. Individual directors of excavations have to make valid decisions about the processes they adopt in order to balance the needs of the dig to make sufficient progress with the demands of post-excavation studies.

WHAT RECORDS DO ARCHAEOLOGISTS CREATE?

Different directors will approach the task of recording, as they will the excavation itself, from slightly different standpoints. But certain common themes will feature: context sheets, plans, sections, photographs, artefact collection systems and, increasingly, the use of on-site computer technology. They also make use of a range of surveying equipment to plot the exact positions of finds and features. Each excavation has a complex reference system. A grid allows each point surveyed and key find to be linked to the national grid. Finds are numbered and linked to contexts. Each context has its own distinct number. Alidades, plane tables and theodolites are still in use alongside Electronic Distance Measures (EDMs) but increasingly **total stations** (◀ p. 14) are superseding them.

Context sheets

The 'single context recording system' has, with some slight variations to suit local circumstances, become the established norm for recording purposes. A separate proforma context sheet is used for each identified context which also has its own unique reference number. The context sheet is designed to ensure that the person making the record addresses all possible questions and compiles a clear description including the maximum level of information in order to

CONTEXT RECORDING SHEET

SITE CODE: BGB95 ← Unique reference numbers

Where found. Enables horizontal reconstruction →

CITY OF LINCOLN ARCHAEOLOGICAL UNIT

| AREA TRENCH: 5/6 | GRID SQUARE: 100/0105 | INTERPRETATION L/S FOUNDATIONS | CONTEXT No: 266 |

DESCRIPTION : (COMPACTION : COLOUR : COMPOSITION : INCLUSIONS : THICKNESS & EXTENT & ANY OTHER OBSERVATIONS

SINGLE COURSE OF ROUGHLY SQUARED AND FACED L/S BLOCKS RANGING IN
SIZE FROM 260mm x 230mm x 80mm TO 680mm x 360mm x 80mm
WITH A CENTRAL CORE OF SMALLER IRREG-SHAPED L/S PCS AVE SIZE 170mm x ← Record of distinguising features
170mm x 60mm ALIGNED N–S. NO OBVIOUS BONDING
DIMENSIONS   N–S   4.8m REMAINING
E–W   1.00m
DEPTH 80mm

GRID CO-ORDINATE:

STRATIGRAPHICALLY: SAME AS   105
EARLIER THAN   ← This identifies its place in the sequence of dsposits

LATER THAN
3/5

COMMENTS / INTERPRETATION

PLAN No's:	PHOTOGRAPH B/W No's:	SAMPLE:	FINDS: OTHER
SECTION No's	PHOTOGRAPH COLOUR No's: 35/3/1–3,	NONE ☐ POT ☑	GLASS ☐ OTHER METAL ☑
SKETCH PLAN:	MATRIX LOCATION:	BRICK/TILE ☐	B.M. ☐
HIGHEST LEVEL O.D: 63.12m	LOWEST LEVEL O.D: 62.98m	BONE ☐ IRON ☐	WOOD ☐ LEATHER ☐
PROVISIONAL PERIOD:	PHASE:	CHECKED BY:	RECORDED BY DATE: Y.R. 25/07/95

Links elsewhere in the site archive →

Identifies it on site plan →

Enables vertical reconstruction

Figure 2.17 How to interpret a context sheet

facilitate reliable comparison between one context and another. On larger excavations where all the staff are experienced each site assistant will be autonomous and expected to take responsibility for particular contexts and their recording. Thus the context sheets provide detailed records of layers and other elements of the stratigraphy of the site. They also allow associations between finds to be explored post-excavation. They will be used in post-excavation analysis to reconstruct the phases of use of the site and its features. Other non-standard proformas have been devised for more complex sites to cater for the recording of, for example, masonry structures and skeletons.

Plans

Detailed plans are used to show the location and spread of features, artefacts and structures. On a site employing the single context recording system every context, except fills of small pits and post-holes, will be drawn separately. A complete set of height measurements will be taken and recorded as an essential element in ensuring the context's unique profile is fully monitored. Large-scale plans are used to illustrate individual features. For example, an excavation of an Anglo-Saxon cemetery requires an overall plan to show the relationships between graves and associated features. A detailed plan drawing will be required of each individual grave to show the position of skeletal remains and the location of grave goods. The position of some of the artefacts may be better explained by a close-up drawing featuring, perhaps, the chest area of the burial.

All these drawings relate to the fixed recording grid on the site. Their position is plotted using surveying equipment and their dimensions carefully scaled onto paper. This usually involves placing a planning frame over the feature to assist the production of accurately measured drawings (▶ p. 49). Considerable effort after the excavation often goes into producing cleaned up versions of these plans for publication. Often finds and features will be plotted on a series of overlays related to soil and topography. Increasingly, plans are plotted onto computers because of the flexibility in presenting data they allow. GIS is revolutionising this process. Its 3D database enables the production of any section or plan and the testing of complex models.

Section drawings

The sides of excavation trenches, strategically placed baulks or cuts through the fill of features such as ditches, pits or postholes offer vertical slices through the constituent layers of an archaeological site.

Although methods of recording the horizontal spread and depth of each deposit have improved over recent decades it still remains true that an accurate scaled depiction of the vertical relationship of layers is commonly used to demonstrate the development of a site or feature. For example, the relationship of a 'post pipe' – the evidence for the location of the post itself – within a posthole and to any packing material is best related in drawn form. As with plans, a key advantage of section drawings is that they can highlight subtle differences in the colour, texture or composition of layers. These are difficult to pick up with photographs. Before drawing it is essential that the face of the section is cleaned up and in some instances sprayed with water to improve contrast. Soil structure and Munsell colour charts are some-times used to enable specific and standardised descriptions.

Where a section results from a continuous period of excavation it may be some time before it is ready for recording. Archaeologists note the presence of layers as the dig proceeds by pinning labels to the side of the excavation with context numbers to ensure that when the section is drawn it is still possible to recognise the finer points of the stratification. Such labels are frequently seen on site photographs.

Figure 2.18 *Plan of an excavated barrow at Lockington using the quadrant method of mound removal*

Circular features such as the surrounding ring ditch and palisade gully are revealed in each quadrant. Eight narrow baulks are left for extra sections. A pit containing gold armlets was located on the edge of the barrow. Although clearly important, no relationship could be established by the processes of excavation to link this pit and its contents to the barrow and the cremation burial below it.

■ **Figure 2.19** *A quartered barrow seen in profile. The picture also shows the familiar wheelbarrow runs used to remove spoil from the excavation itself*

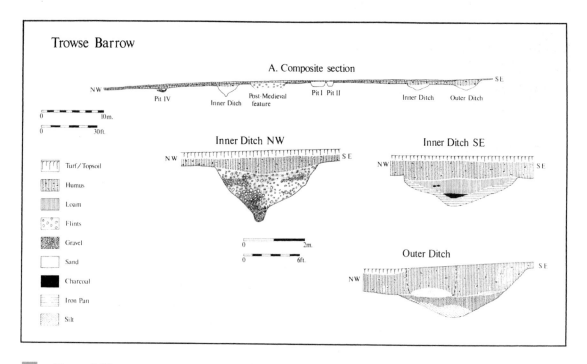

■ **Figure 2.20** *A section drawing of Trowse Round Barrow*

This barrow has two incomplete ditches surrounding it. The main composite cross-section shows the inner ditch twice, the outer ditch once and several other features. The inner and outer ditch sections are enlarged to give greater detail. A key is provided to demonstrate the soil types present. Reproduced with the permission of the copyright holder, Norfolk Archaeology & Environment Division.

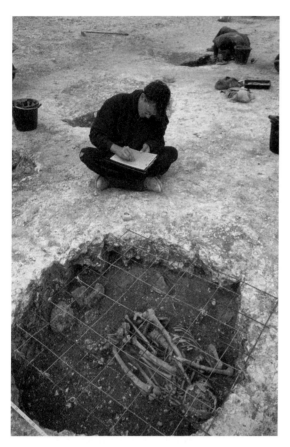

Figure 2.21 *Using gridlines to plan a skeleton*

In this example the soil covering the skeleton has been carefully excavated prior to recording. The gridlines make it easier for the recorder to keep to scale. Measurements are frequently taken during drawing to ensure the finished record is as accurate as possible. Following recording the skeleton will be excavated.

Once completed, drawings are usually accompanied by an interpretation offered in textual or schematic form such as the Harris Matrix. It must be stressed that drawings are always interpretations and the quality of on-site drawings does vary according to the skill of the recorder and the conditions they are working under. Back-up photographs can provide an additional record.

Photographs

The camera is a key aid to recording although archaeologists believe that it is less comprehensive in the detail it can show than the drawn record. Although rulers or ranging rods are usually seen in photographs to give an idea of scale, distances are distorted and film cannot be used to provide precise measurements. The camera clearly offers the chance of accurate views of features and sections whereas the draughtsperson can accentuate elements that the camera might obscure, for example similar coloured soils which have different textures. The camera also provides back up in case the drawings are poor. The two methods complement each other and both are normally used. Many archaeologists continue to use conventional black and white film for recording. Slides were often used to record the dig in progress and for lectures afterwards. However digital photography and film are having a major impact, particularly as a support to the site diary. Digital recording also enables the excavation to be viewed online.

The essence of site photography lies in ensuring that the parts to be captured on film are clean, edges of individual structures or bones are well established and careful spraying is used to accentuate coloration changes and contrasts. The use of photographic towers or other means to get a camera above the excavation is common. Vertical photographs with scales can be used as an aid in the creation of plans.

SPECIAL CASES

Most of the points in this chapter apply to all sites but there are some issues that apply to particular types of sites.

Figure 2.23 *Skeleton from another grave from Empingham*

Note the different information provided by the plan and this photograph.

Figure 2.22 *Burial 74 at Empingham*

A plan of a skeleton in the grave to show positions of bones and grave goods. The skeleton of a male aged about 25–30 years old was accompanied by a shield boss; two board studs, a spearhead, an iron knife, a copper alloy-bound wooden bucket and an iron buckle. Preserved wood remains in the spear socket were identified as willow and poplar and in the bucket as yew.

1 Shield
2–3 Board studs
6 Spear
7 Knife
8 Bucket
9 Buckle

100 mm

Archaeology of standing buildings

In 'traditional' archaeology, interpretation of excavated evidence relies on the basic principle that the deeper the deposit, the earlier it is – the basis of relative dating by stratigraphy. Although standing buildings require a different approach to their study, the basic principles remain the same. One of the objectives of recording is to enable the developmental sequence of the building to be traced. Where a feature has been inserted into an existing one (for example a window or door inserted into a standing wall) it follows that the inserted feature is later than that into which it was inserted. Similarly, later walls may be of different construction to the original or may be butt-jointed (simply butted up against earlier walls rather than properly bonded). All of these clues help archaeologists to build up a sequence of development in the same way as on an excavation. Recording standing buildings may involve reconnaissance techniques (◀ p. 9), dismantling, excavation or a combination of these approaches. The amount of information which may be recovered from a building will depend on many factors. Cosmetic renovation of a structure may give only a few clues (for example

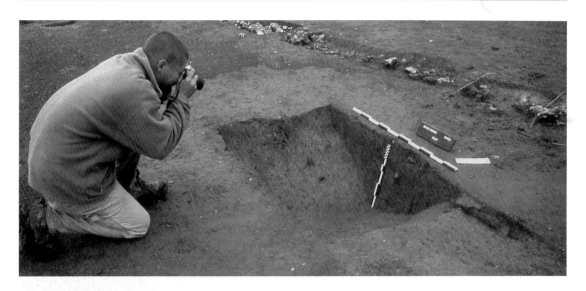

Figure 2.24 *Recording using photography*

This section at Barcombe Roman villa is being carefully photographed to complement the drawn record. To counteract the effects of perspective a horizontal and vertical scale have been placed on the section. Also in view are a north pointer and a board with the feature or context number to enable identification and location afterwards.

glimpses beneath floor boards or behind small areas of plaster) whereas a building undergoing substantial alterations or even demolition will be far more exposed to study. The aim should be to identify the earliest structural remains on the site and then, having plotted them, begin to add in later stages of development. Additions or changes to a building are never random: they will always serve a clear purpose which archaeologists try to detect, for example the extending of a room or rebuilding of a façade.

The recording of standing buildings should be every bit as rigorous as the recording of an excavation. Alongside drawings and written descriptions a full photographic record should be maintained, indicating scale and the exact point on a master plan from which the view was taken, along with any other relevant information. Sampling should include examples of different mortars and plasters. Substantial timbers may be sampled for **dendrochronology**. (▶ p. 101) Details of the fabric and construction of the

building, alterations and dating evidence are gathered through drawing and photography. Elevations of buildings are often drawn stone by stone using grids as the completed drawing can often reveal patterns not obvious to the naked eye. Very precise photographic recording to within 10mm can be achieved using photogrammetry. In this technique, also used for aerial photography, two precision cameras are used together to create a 'stereo' recording. When combined with readings from an EDM, specialists can use CAD to produce a 3D record of the building, including very fine decorative or architectural detail. It is considerably faster than traditional recording and is both cost effective and accurate. It is particularly used where historic buildings are being restored.

Wetland archaeology

Waterlogged sites are where the natural water table has maintained a wet or damp environment since the deposition of the evidence. They have been a major factor in adding to our knowledge of past cultures. **Anaerobic** conditions, which prevent or impede normal bacterial and chemical decay processes, can result in widespread survival of organic material such as wood, leather and textiles which would normally perish. Strategies for excavation, conservation and post-excavation analysis on wetland sites need to take into account the time and cost of dealing with additional evidence as well as the particular problems associated with waterlogged sites. In particular there are often large quantities of environmental material, especially plant remains. While the complete removal of all material for close examination is not usually a viable proposition much emphasis is put on the selection of large numbers of samples of site deposits for laboratory analysis. This has been the case with excavations of London's waterfront. Huge

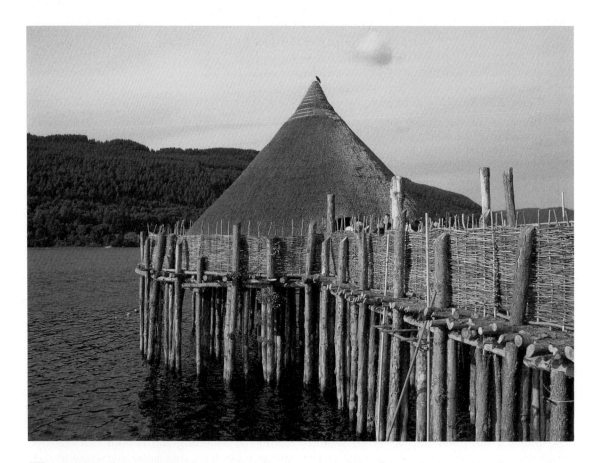

Figure 2.25 Reconstruction of Oakbank Iron Age Crannog

Crannogs are artificial islands with a wooden platform supported by piles driven into lakebeds or boulders dumped on the lakebed. They were used for some 5000 years until the seventeenth century in Scotland and Ireland as farmsteads, halls and defensive refuges. At Oakbank underwater archaeologists were able to recover organic remains including food, artefacts and structural timbers. Exceptional finds included a butter dish containing butter and a canoe paddle. Like many wet sites, Oakbank has shed light on the extent to which large timbers were felled, shaped and moved in the past.

KEY STUDY

Star Carr revisited

Star Carr is Britain's most well known mesolithic site. The excavation by Clark in 1949–51 was one of the first to combine environmental data with material culture in order to understand past economic activity. The site at the western end of what was Lake Pickering had exceptional preservation under a layer of peat. The occupation area was in an area of open birch-wood and featured a brushwood 'living platform', scatters of thousands of pieces of flint debitage and butchery and antler working debris. Lithic tools included arrowheads for hunting and adzes for wood working alongside a range of organic artefacts. These included a canoe paddle, rolls of birch bark, antler 'mattocks' and most famously, 21 'antler headdresses'. The original radio-carbon date for the site was 7600 BC.

Clark interpreted Star Carr as a winter or early spring base camp from where a small band of 4–5 families exploited red deer and made hide and antler artefacts. Over the years many other interpretations were offered including summer occupation, a butchery site (many meat-bearing bones were missing from the assemblage) and a hide processing area (many scrapers were found). Clark himself revised his view to see it as a site used all year round. Much of the debate focussed on whether or not antlers at the site were from fresh kills or had been collected elsewhere as raw material and therefore could not identify the season the site was used. Star Carr was unusual in other ways, being the only local site where axes or large numbers of barbed antler points were found. Despite being well known, its main function remains unclear.

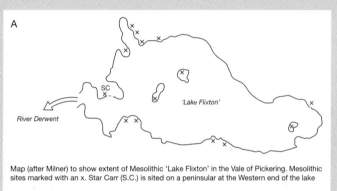

Map (after Milner) to show extent of Mesolithic 'Lake Flixton' in the Vale of Pickering. Mesolithic sites marked with an x. Star Carr (S.C.) is sited on a peninsular at the Western end of the lake

Figure 2.26 *Map of Lake Flixton in the Vale of Pickering showing positions of Mesolithic sites*

KEY STUDY *cont.*

Star Carr revisited

More recently pollen and sediment studies have revealed that the reed swamp around the site had been repeatedly burnt. This may have been to provide a hunting area or perhaps improve access to the lake. Either way it may be the earliest landscape management found in Britain. Charcoal samples provided dates which pushed back the occupation of the site around 1000 years to 8700–8350 BC. Occupation of the site appears to have spanned several hundred years rather than the two decades initially thought. It may therefore be a **palimpsest** where use varied over time. Test excavations near the site revealed that the site extended beyond the area studied by Clark. They also revealed that the site was rapidly degrading and becoming more acidic, possibly in relation to land drainage. Bones were found to have lost their mineral element leaving only a collagen jelly. Currently a major research project is underway to understand more about the local context of Star Carr and to recover more information about the site itself before too much organic material is lost.

Excavations close to Clark's dig have shown that the site was far more extensive than previously thought. The extent of lithic scatters and antler working areas suggest that Clark only excavated the most waterlogged part of the site and that there are more discoveries to be made. One new feature is a 6m platform running out through the reed beds to the edge of the open water. This may have been to provide access for canoes. Wood had been split using antler tines as wedges and along with many wood chippings provides the first European evidence for

Figure 2.28 *Pie charts showing numbers of individual animals processed at Star Carr and their contribution as food in terms of meat poundage*

Figure 2.27 *One of several sets of Antler 'head-dresses' found at Star Carr*

KEY STUDY *cont.*

Star Carr revisited

carpentry. The quantity of wood being processed may also suggest coppicing was going on. As well as axe and adze marks, beaver teeth-marks have been found on some of the wood archive material. Re-examination of Clark's excavation has been hampered by a limited archive and few notebooks. Some of the gaps have been revealed through interviews with Clark's colleagues. In order to manage the huge quantity of finds, Clark imposed a 'fingernail rule' for recovery. This meant that micro-debitage and tiny bones were not collected and almost certainly biased overall findings. Bones of fish-eating birds were recovered but not fish bones. Archaeologists have argued since about whether the inhabitants were exploiting fish.

Research teams have contour-mapped the ancient lake area and are using augers to gain environmental details and test pits every 15m to see if there were other sites close-by. However none has been found so far. Star Carr itself is now known to cover most of a small peninsular at the point where the lake is drained by a stream. Whether this was chosen for economic or social/ritual reasons is unclear. Distributions of finds suggest different activities were taking place in different areas with wood often found on the lake-margin, bone and antler at the swamp edge and flint on drier ground. Painstaking excavation is recovering evidence of single tool-making events. Meanwhile other surveys are looking at other mesolithic activity – mostly flint scatters – across the Vale of Pickering. A possibility is that Star Carr was an **aggregation** site for particular activities for groups widely dispersed across the landscape for much of the year.

amounts of large timbers could not all be preserved. Those selected for recovery enabled the development of carpentry and construction techniques over a long period to be studied. This revealed the way older timber buildings were recycled by builders. Once out of water, organic material will be stored in tanks of water prior to conservation.

The consequence is that while the information from 'wet' sites is considered a real bonus in archaeological study, the costs of obtaining it considerably outstrip those of excavating 'dry' sites.

Unlike 'dry' sites where you can walk carefully across the site, pressure on wetland deposits can cause considerable damage. Excavators at Flag Fen erected a series of platforms on scaffolding to allow diggers to lie above the features

they were excavating. Such restriction to movement makes digging, cleaning, planning and photography all the more difficult.

• http://www.crannog.co.uk/

Underwater archaeology

Although underwater sites follow the same basic rules as dry sites – the need for survey, careful excavation and recording – being below water presents additional challenges. The excavators usually require watertight diving suits, air tanks and weights. In extreme depths remotely controlled vehicles may be used. In addition to underwater hazards, cold temperatures may make it difficult to remain stationary for long periods while poor visibility may require excavation using touch rather than sight!

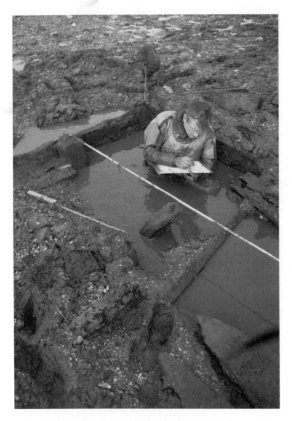

Figure 2.29 *Inter-tidal archaeology presents another specific range of challenges*

Organic material exposed between tides such as shipwrecks or structures has often been well preserved but will rapidly decay. It needs to be excavated and recorded quickly but twice a day it is submerged, covering the site with sand or mud. This makes work difficult or dangerous. A salvage approach is usually adopted with material where possible being removed from immediate danger for study in a laboratory. Unfortunately this action can also destroy the context of the site.

To inform excavation strategy a form of sampling is often employed to gain a feel for the site. One example of this is the Tudor warship the *Mary Rose* whose position and condition was examined and investigated for several years before a full enough understanding enabled full excavation. Where little or no wooden remains

are present and finds are in a dispersed state, plans are drawn and trial trenches excavated to determine the extent of the deposits.

• http://www.abc.se/~m10354/uwa/
• http://www.maryrose.org/

Removal of spoil can employ a combination of hand movement and water dispersal but special tools are usually required. A water lance can shred sediment while a range of water vacuum cleaners can help excavate spoil and keep a site clear of sediment for recording. Objects may have suffered corrosion and created concretions that need to be broken apart. Decisions have to be made as to whether to use hammer and chisel below water or to bring the whole mass to the surface. Ordinary finds are placed in open containers, fragile finds in sealed ones and larger objects lifted by the use of inflated air bags. As with waterlogged sites, organic material is susceptible to damage if it is allowed, even briefly, to dry out during excavation. Once such material is removed from the water it must be quickly put into appropriate storage.

Plastic 2 × 2 or 4 × 4 metre recording grids are set out and the usual land-based methods of planning, context sheets and photography employed where possible. Synthetic paper enables ordinary pens to be used underwater. Photography is likely to be limited to close-up shots or carefully rigged photogrammetry rather than general views. One advantage of underwater excavation is that the archaeologist can cross the site without treading on a trowelled surface!

Urban archaeology

While it is clear that there is a great variety in the nature of archaeological sites in rural areas, archaeologists working on urban sites face very different challenges.

In urban areas open ground is at a premium and so it is usually the clearance of a site for development that provides archaeological

Key

1 Pipe sucking sediment and spoil away
2 Laminated recording sheets
3 Suspended polythene tube grids
4 Finds box
5 Ranging pole
6 Water lance and tube
7 Section (close-up below)
8 Organic materials

Figure 2.30 *Diagram illustrating some of the equipment used in underwater archaeology (after Thomasen in Andersen 1985)*

opportunities. The area involved is often tightly constrained by other buildings and therefore only parts of buried sites are available for study. These do not necessarily correspond to areas which archaeologists would choose if they were making the site selection on academic grounds, a good example of rescue archaeology being dictated by developer activity. Such excavations are like keyholes into the past because a full view cannot be obtained. Nevertheless there has been an increase in the number of urban excavations with much focus on sampling via evaluations and test pits. The depth of stratification is usually much greater than on rural sites because of frequent reuse of the same site over time. Planning permission (▶ p. 347) places an emphasis

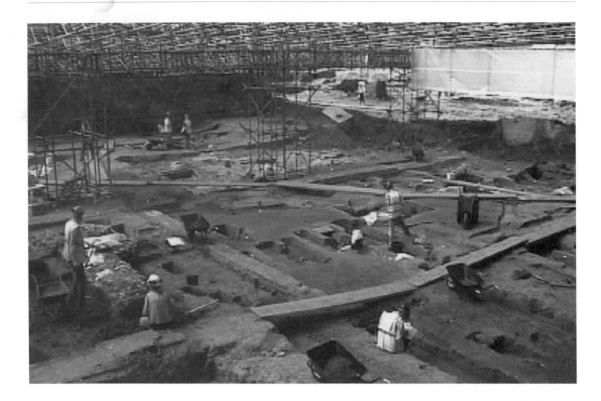

Figure 2.31 *An area excavation of the medieval burial grounds at Spitalfields Market in London*

Note the cover over the site, both for protection of the remains and out of respect for the burials. The relatively confined space is typical of most urban excavations.

on avoiding damage to the stratigraphy and checking the depth of deposits. It is particularly difficult to forecast the range of features, that will be encountered and the time it will take to excavate them all properly. Deep excavation also presents additional safety hazards.

Survey methods applicable to rural sites such as aerial photography and many of the geophysical procedures are ineffectual or inappropriate in preparatory work. Indeed, at a large excavation in London at Number 1, Poultry in the 1990s the evaluation consisted of a desktop survey and four shafts between 3 m and 5 m deep to reach the top of the natural geology. These gave indications of the sequences and structures which might be encountered. The excavation also produced

Figure 2.32 *Using a total station to rapidly plot the position of finds*

At Spitalfields, so many skeletons were discovered that digital means of recording their position were used including barcodes.

Figure 2.33 *Removing a skeleton*

The excavator has dressed to minimise DNA contamination of the remains. Each bone is carefully recovered, sometimes using dental tools. In this instance the body had actually been placed in the grave in pieces.

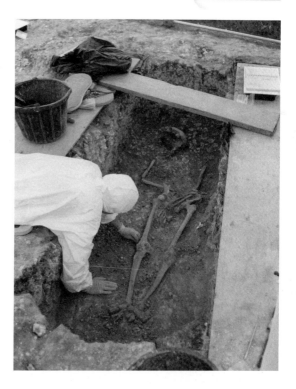

'wet' archaeology including about 1,500 datable (by dendrochronology) Roman timbers. This extensive urban excavation (the on-site budget exceeded £2m) continued for twelve months below the construction of the new building. Normally archaeologists have to complete their work before the building contractors arrive on site.

• *Current Archaeology* 143 and 158

Forensic archaeology

It is quite surprising that forensic ('used in or connected with a court of law') archaeology should only have been seen as a significant contribution of the discipline in the last 20 years. Scientific archaeological excavation has a long history and throughout that time law enforcement agencies have needed high quality of evidence in their enquiries. The material in this chapter and the ones preceding and following it apply equally to archaeologists and forensic investigators. Such agents use search capabilities including geophysics and aerial photography, recovery methodologies largely focused on excavation but also linked to surface depositional activities, identification of evidence and its recording and conservation. Following retrieval of the evidence, their laboratory techniques involve detailed analysis of artefacts and ecofacts just as in a traditional post-excavation context.

One only has to review the detailed examination of bog bodies or Ötzi the 'Ice-man' (▶ p. 93) to recognise that similar processes are also needed for more recent discoveries, often linked to crime. The careful and considerate approach adopted by archaeologists can contribute to a fuller understanding of individual burials or mass graves such as were revealed and investigated in Bosnia recently.

AFTER EXCAVATION

Once the digging is completed attention switches to the laboratories and the processing of finds and site records. This is dealt with in Chapters 3 and 4. The eventual outcome of the excavation used to be a full excavation report with text on the features and structures, catalogues and drawings of finds and specialists' reports. Today the emphasis is on producing a quality 'archive' which can then be adapted as appropriate into reports, more popular publications or to provide research opportunities. Increasingly records are stored digitally which offers tremendous potential for disseminating data to different audiences in different ways.

Figure 2.34 *Skeleton recording sheet*

For dealing with human remains, excavators increasingly use a specialised recording system as this example from the Museum of London demonstrates. Note the Stratigraphic (Harris) matrix which records the burial (context 1439) overlying the grave cut (1441) but underneath the grave fill (1438).

Figure 2.35 *Gamston drawing 1. Gamston was an Iron Age settlement and field system in the Trent Valley*

The result of painstaking excavation and recording can be seen in these plans from an Iron Age settlement and field system at Gamston in the Trent Valley. Figure 2.35 shows a plot of the crop marks which identified the site as being of archaeological interest and a summary of the dug features revealed by excavation. Figure 2.36 shows the sequence of occupation at the site. The evidence for this relied on rigorous attention to stratigraphy.

Figure 2.36 *Gamston drawing 2*

Chapter 3

Post-excavation Analysis

YOUR GOALS

You need to understand

- ▥ the range of specialisms involved in post-excavation work and what they can contribute to site archives

- ▥ the types of analysis carried out on the most commonly analysed materials

- ▥ the basic principles of the main analytical techniques

- ▥ how to integrate a grasp of analytical techniques with specific examples

---

Analytical techniques are often the parts of archaeology courses which most students find difficult. The bulleted points above are sufficient for AS/A Level and some first year undergraduate courses which do not require detailed scientific knowledge. Most degree-level courses will at some point require a greater depth of understanding of scientific techniques and many will involve practical work. The first half of this chapter explains general approaches and some widely used methods applied to a range of materials. The second half considers issues related to particular types of material and illustrates what analysis can achieve. Further examples can be found in Part II of this book.

Reconnaissance and excavation might be the most visible part of archaeology but the longest part of the work takes place after digging has finished. Post-excavation or 'post-ex' encom-

passes all of the processes and interpretation that go on using the materials recovered and the records made by the excavators. The focus now moves indoors to the specialists' rooms at the excavation team's base where the material is stored in a temporary archive. Wessex Archaeology's headquarters in a converted RAF command centre near Salisbury is one such location. At one end of the building corridors are lined with archive boxes, labelled with site and context codes while in the main work area pots are being reassembled and flints sorted and labelled. Another suite of small rooms equipped with sieves and microscopes houses the 'snail people'. They patiently sieve through samples to extract the molluscan remains which will help to reconstruct past environments (▶ p. 200). Other specialists deal with beetles or animal bones. One room is given over to careful technical

Figure 3.1 Post-excavation processes normally take longer, cost more and involve more people than excavation. It is the hidden face of archaeology. This desk is set up for the identification and recording of samples

drawings of finds and of crucial site documents such as plans, sections and elevations, complemented where appropriate with photographs. Close by are housed the site archives from previous excavations and projects – that is the collections of context sheets and registers normally stored in a series of ring-binders until needed for publication. Finally there is the suite of computers in the publishing room which produces the finished site reports. Other teams may have more or less than this. In all cases there will always be some processes they have to outsource. Palynologists (pollen), pathologists and geologists are just some of the specialists who are contracted to analyse material. Radiocarbon dating is also undertaken in more specialist facilities.

• www.wessexarch.co.uk/

INITIAL PROCESSING AND CONSERVATION

On arrival materials are treated differently according to their properties. Robust artefacts such as flint tools or pottery are cleaned in water unless analysis of residues or wear is to be undertaken. Fragile bones, metals artefacts and wood are handled with delicacy and may require conservation work before analysis can begin. For example, bone may require treatment with

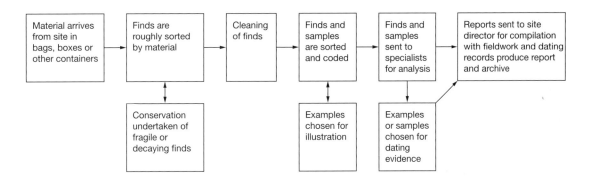

Figure 3.2 Simplified diagram of the post-excavation process

polyvinyl acetate (PVA) to stop it crumbling while organic samples may require mild fungicides to halt decay. The conditions they are kept in will also vary depending on their original context. For example, wood from waterlogged sediments may be kept in water until it can be conserved or analysed. Soil cores for pollen analysis may be kept in a fridge to prevent bacterial decay. In many cases a find code which links the object to its context is written on it in indelible ink.

VISUAL EXAMINATION AND RECORDING

The first analytical stage for most materials involves categorization. Artefacts will be sorted according to physical characteristics or attributes into categories by material and typology. The physical feel of artefacts is often used as well as appearance. Characteristics such as grittiness or greasiness are best determined by touch. Specialists use their knowledge to categorise finds but they will also have a set of 'diagnostics' (e.g. a type-series of pottery sherds) or illustrations to aid identification. These are sometimes called parallels. Some materials, particularly metals, will require further tests. Regular microscopes are frequently used and in particularly well-equipped facilities Scanning Electron

Figure 3.3 *A painstakingly reconstructed beaker from Boscombe Down*

The convention is for plain clay to be infilled in the gaps to recreate the solid shape while making clear which parts are original. Beakers are associated with the cross-over between Neolithic and early Bronze Age. In Europe this is often called the Copper Age or Chalcolithic.

Figure 3.4 *Sorting pottery according to attributes*

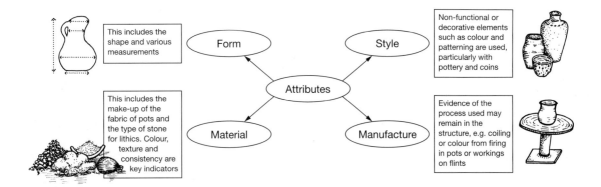

Figure 3.5 *Examples of attributes which could be used to sort material*

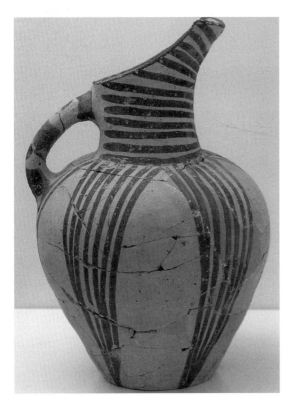

Figure 3.6 *Early Minoan 'Myrtos style' jug*

Some pottery is easily identified by material and decoration and does not require further typological analysis. In this case the fabric and the red lines on light background would be enough. Note how artefact styles are normally named after the site where they were first recognised.

Microscopes (SEM) may also be employed. Microscope examination of marks on some materials can also provide clues to their use. Environmental samples, once removed from soil, are identified by species and then analysed in similar ways, using microscopes for plant and invertebrate remains. Once identified and categorized material is quantified and recorded through drawing or photography. A descriptive report is then produced by the specialist undertaking the work.

CERAMICS

Pottery is very important to archaeology from the Neolithic onwards because it survives well in almost any environment. It provides dating evidence and can be used to make inferences about exchange, economy and society. To categorise sherds, colour is described by reference to the Munsell Soil Colour Charts. There are similar charts for hardness and the grain size of inclusions in the temper. Such analysis may require the use of polarising microscopes. Manufacturing by hand, coil or wheel methods can usually be determined visually, as can form. The key indicators here are sherds from the rim, neck and base of vessels. Where possible pots are reassembled by specialists for recording.

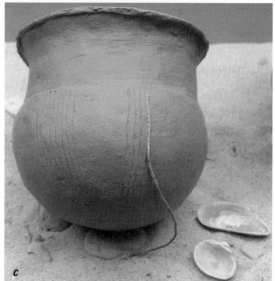

Figure 3.7 *Prehistoric pottery making*

These pictures illustrate the process of local pottery manufacture in much of prehistory. Local clay would be mixed with a variety of tempers (a) which might include grit, chaff, shell or the remains of previous vessels. Mineral inclusions will be the key for archaeologists to sourcing the pot. After kneading the pot shape is formed by coiling (b). This can be detected by examining sherds in cross-section. Decoration is applied – in this instance using cord or shell impressions but twigs, feathers and fingernails were also used (c). These marks are clearly seen through a microscope. Finally the pot would be fired in a bonfire.

1st century black burnished-ware

cm

Figure 3.8 *The standard way to record and illustrate ceramics is to draw the whole vessel in outline but with one quarter cut away. This enables one half to provide a cross-section to show internal and external shape and dimensions. The other half shows external appearance. Sometimes the area of decoration is limited to the area of the actual sherd recovered.*

KEY TERM

Use wear analysis

For some artefacts, including stone tools, tiny scratches and traces are left from past activity. For example, half an hour cutting cereals will leave a polish on a flint blade. Expert analysis backed by examples from experimental archaeology (▶ p. 125) can sometimes identify the signatures of different activities. However, this may only reveal the *last* activity the tool was used for. The detection and description of wear marks can be greatly assisted by the use of a scanning electron microscope (SEM). This sweeps a band of electrons over the surface of the tool being studied and gives much improved depth of focus and higher magnification. This enhanced image can then be displayed on a screen. Recent work has involved the study of starch grains on stone blades In Polynesia and the analysis of blood residues on some of the equipment carried by Ötzi the Ice Man.

Clay is almost entirely formed from eroded sedimentary rocks, but a tiny percentage of the material is made up of trace elements. Petrology and other characterisation techniques can be applied to pottery and bricks although 'fingerprinting' clay sources is much more difficult and well developed than is the case with rocks. In many cases, experts on regional pottery will be able to suggest the origin of artefacts from the temper and inclusions in the pottery, which they identify from visual or microscopic examination.

Their analysis is helped by data from refiring experiments and ethnography (▶ p. 125) which can provide insights into manufacturing techniques. The fabric colour and hardness provide clues to firing temperatures. Clay often contains iron, which forms a red oxide if it is heated in an oxygen rich environment or a black/grey oxide if it is oxygen poor. The colour of the molecules of clay indicates which was the case. If the clay is vitrified (where minerals have melted and fused together) it indicates that firing occurred in a kiln at temperatures in excess of 1100°C. Slips and glazes provide additional clues to origins and period.

In quantifying pottery finds there is debate amongst archaeologists over whether the number or weight of sherds is more useful. On most sites it is rare to recover entire pots either intact or in pieces. A large urn may break into several large but heavy pieces while a small pot may shatter into many small light fragments. Depending on which measure is chosen the results can be widely different. Increasingly archaeologists measure both, but weight used in conjunction with average sherd weight can be used to reduce variability caused by different sizes of vessels. Various attempts have also been made to work out 'estimated vessel equivalents' (EVE) or 'minimum number of vessels' (MNV). Techniques vary from counting elements which only occur once such as the base to dividing the total angles of rim sherds by 360 degrees. The Ashmolean Museum website has an excellent guide to the value of pottery to archaeologists.

• http://potweb.ashmolean.org/

ANALYSIS OF PARTICULAR INORGANIC MATERIALS

Lithics

Lithics or stone tools are virtually indestructible. They have been used for all but the earliest stages of human development and for many sites and periods are the only definite sign of human activity. Examination of their surface can determine whether they were manufactured by fracturing, pecking or polishing the original stone. Reference to experimental or ethnographic examples (▶ p. 125) (including microwear analysis) can help identify signs of techniques such as indirect percussion and pressure flaking and help interpret what they were used for.

Figure 3.9 *Lithics*

This hoard of early Neolithic 'fish-tail' daggers from a Danish bog illustrates a peak in knapping skill. Possibly weapons and certainly prestige items, the design seems unnecessarily difficult for a flint weapon and is probably based on early copper weapons. It is a good example of a form suited to one technology crossing over into another. The drawn record of these daggers would aim to show size, shape, depth and the method of manufacture including direction of flaking.

Figure 3.10 *Pressure flaking*

This is the process of using bone or antler to prise thin flakes away from a part finished artefact to gain greater definition of sharpness. Recording of markings on the artefact would enable informed viewers to understand which technique had been used.

Artefacts can be sorted by type of stone, colour and **typology**. Specialists will use reference material for relative dating and suggestion of function. Manufacturing debris (debitage) is of particular value. It provides evidence of raw materials, the production process and the tools used. Sometimes debitage can be refitted to show the sequence of manufacturing and even whether the knapper was sitting or standing, left- or right-handed. Petrology has been the most widely used means of characterisation for lithics although the other techniques are increasingly used.

Petrology

This is a geological technique for locating the source of minerals. A **thin section** of a stone or ceramic (◀ p. 65) artefact is cut, ground and polished till it is about 0.02 mm thick. It is then examined by microscope. The crystals of each mineral have a distinctive colour and structure. The particular combinations of key minerals enable the original source to be established with reference to geological maps. Thin sections of pottery can also be studied to provide information about manufacturing techniques.

Petrology has contributed greatly to our understanding of exchange. For instance the sources for the early medieval period trade in lava quernstones throughout north-west Europe have been traced back to quarries in the Eiffel Mountains of Germany. The technique can be used for building materials including stone and, in some cases, brick. It has been used extensively in Egypt to identify the quarries ▶ p. 276 used to build the temples at Karnak and the pyramid complex at Giza. Distribution patterns based on extensive studies such as these have helped us understand the complexity of ancient trade routes, transport systems and economic organisation.

Petrology does not work in all cases. Thin sections of **obsidian** and flint look remarkably similar regardless of where they originated. Similarly, ceramics, which lack distinctive mineral tempers, require other techniques in order to source them.

Metallurgical analysis

Some metal artefacts, particularly those which are badly corroded, may be x-rayed. This can enable the object to be identified, to clarify markings on the surface and to identify cracks or seams where several pieces of metal were joined to form complex artefacts. Conservation would include careful treatment to remove corrosion. Used in stereo, x-rays can give a 3D

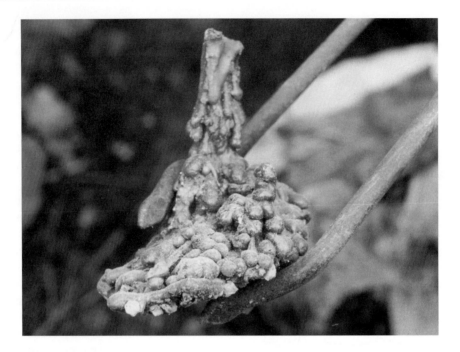

Figure 3.11 *Bloom*

Finds of material from various stages in the production of metals are crucial to understanding manufacturing technology. In this experiment the cooling metal or bloom is being lifted out of the furnace leaving slag behind.

view of an object and reveal elements of the construction techniques and process such as pattern welding in swords: the manufacture of iron sword blades often involved hammering folded layers of metal. This process can also be detected by examining a cross-section of the blade with a powerful microscope. **Metallography** includes examination of the size and shape of the grains of minerals in the material for traces of heating, working and alloying. Where they are available, SEMs are preferred. Their magnification at 1000x may be similar to the best optical microscopes but the depth of field they provide enables fine detail to be identified. This is particularly important when exploring the manufacturing techniques used in jewellery making.

The first recorded use of metal is in the form of jewellery and ritual items. These were made from 'soft' metals (gold and copper) which would be worked by hammering. Early metal artefacts were relatively simple and tended to imitate stone ones. It was not till smiths learnt how to use bellows to reach the high temperatures needed to smelt ores in crucibles that the potential of metals could be realized. This also enabled the production of alloys which were blends of two or more minerals. The most significant was bronze made from copper and tin. One and two piece moulds enabled new shapes including socketed weapons to be produced. A key development was the 'lost wax process' where a model of the desired tool was made in wax and then fired inside a casing of clay. The wax melted when the clay was fired leaving a void in the shape of the tool into which molten metal could be poured. Evidence for this technology comes from stone and clay moulds, crucibles, slag and waste metal as well as the finished products. Artefacts themselves provide evidence

0   50   100   150   200 mm

Figure 3.12 *Anglo-Saxon grave goods from Empingham*

This illustrates many of the conventions for drawing inorganic artefacts. The shield boss is shown partly reconstructed as with pottery. The button and spear are shown in several views so that shape is communicated. Compare this with the photographs and grave plans (◄ p. 50). Aside from the bucket this might look like a warrior grave. However, there is some evidence that such grave goods were a mark of ethnic identity in the early medieval period rather than a direct link with what a person did (► p. 317).

of casting errors, mould seams, cold working after casting and decorative techniques.

Metal objects were frequently ornamented by means of a range of engraving tools or punches whose shapes may be identified when magnified. The Gundestrup Cauldron (▶ p. 290), a magnificent, silver Iron Age feasting bowl found in a bog in Denmark was examined in this way. Analysis of punch-marks with a SEM suggested that several toolkits had been used. Taylor was able to compare manufacturing techniques and imagery to identify Transylvania as the likely location for the workshop and to suggest the ethnic origins of the craftsmen.

• Taylor 1997

Coins are a particularly specialised area of study. For example Roman coins can be used as an approximate form of dating and have been used to explore topics as diverse as trade, territories and particular events. All excavations will have a contact who is a coin expert to interpret the images and inscriptions on their surfaces.

ANALYSIS OF ORGANIC REMAINS

Site reports usually feature chapters produced by individual experts in plants, various types of animal remains and soils and are largely concerned with detailed visual examination and comparison with reference material. With major research projects there has been an increasing trend to use a battery of lab-based analytical methods. These are often delivered by multi-disciplinary teams – for instance in bioarchaeology – based at a few well-equipped universities or commercial companies.

Soil

Geoarchaeology is the study of preserved soils and the natural and human processes which created them. The chemistry of soil can provide clues to the type of vegetation and by extension, fauna and agriculture it could support. The early farmers in central Europe, for example, seemed to favour particular soil types (Loess – a fine glacial soil deposited by the wind) for their farming settlements. Soil change can also record the impact of humans on the land. Sediments in valleys in Cyprus were used to explain the abandonment of Bronze Age sites. Deforestation or overgrazing had led to erosion of topsoil on the hillsides which had then been deposited in the valleys. Understanding sedimentary profiles is essential to interpretation of phasing, dating and the way archaeological sites changed over time. At a microscopic level, soil is also analysed for what it holds. Pollen, invertebrates and even microbes can be recovered to provide clues about environment and economy.

Soils differ in their ability to preserve materials. Pollen survives well in acidic contexts whereas alkaline environments are better for snail shells.

Faunal remains

Zooarchaeology is the study of the remains of animals from archaeological contexts. Humans interact with animals in several ways including using them for food or other resources and indirectly as the occupants of ecological niches alongside them. Faunal (which includes fish and

Figure 3.13 *Animal bones after washing*

birds as well as mammals) remains are vital to archaeologists in two ways: to reconstruct past environments (▶ p. 200) and to identify the contribution which animals made to the human economy (▶ p. 236).

The mineral element in bones can survive well in alkaline soils such as sand or gravel. Acid soils usually dissolve all but burnt bone although in certain conditions bone collagen can sometimes be recovered. Waterlogged, arid and frozen sites provide the best preservation. This means that some sites may have vast amounts of bone whilst others have very little. This bias applies to different types of bone. Larger bones and teeth enamel survive far longer than small bones. Similarly tiny fish and bird bones don't survive as well as cattle bones. Even where they survive, they are rarely recovered unless sieving or flotation is used.

The first task for bone specialists is to identify the type of bone and then the species of animal from which they came. Mammals have similar numbers and types of bones so reference collections supplement the expert's knowledge. This also applies to fish and birds. To understand the significance of particular species in an **assemblage** the number of animals represented has to be determined. However, it is rare for complete skeletons to be recovered so several different ways of counting the bones of each species are used.

- NISP. The number of identified specimens (bones) present. However, only parts of some animals may have been taken to a site.
- Weight. This is biased to animals with heavier bones.
- MNI. Minimum number of individuals. Working out the smallest number of animals which could produce the assemblage. This is done by counting bones which only occur once such as skulls or pelvis.

The raw data only shows the relative abundance of a particular species not how important it was to people and their economy. There is more meat on a cow than on a sheep, so while the MNI for sheep may be greater than for cows, they may contribute much less to the overall diet. (◀ p. 54) Several additional measures have been developed to assess dietary contribution such as meat weight versus bone weight. A further complication arises when we consider the body elements that are present. Some animals may not have been slaughtered on-site and bones that are low in meat, such as the spine and feet, may have been discarded off-site. Careful examination of butchery marks can reveal the process by which animal bone reached the site of deposition.

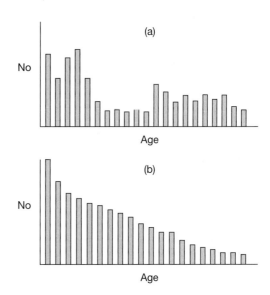

Profiles which plot the age of animals from surviving bones against the number found in each age group.

(a) An attritional profile caused by selective butchery or hunting. A disproportionate number of animals are killed as they reach maturity (probably male) and when they are beyond breeding age. Animals in their prime, particularly females, would be spared.

(b) A catastrophic profile. The whole herd has died. Possibly caused by stampeding over a cliff.

Figure 3.14 *Simplified diagrams to illustrate catastrophic and attritional profiles in animal bone assemblages*

Figure 3.15 *Neolithic animal bone with evidence of human butchery. The cattle bone on the left has cut marks while the sheep skull on the right has been split open with a sharp tool*

Establishing the age and sex of the animals represented in a bone assemblage can help reconstruct the system of hunting or agriculture practised (▶ p. 236). For example, the sex ratio and age structure in herds of cattle kept for dairy products are different from those kept for meat. Assemblages can also indicate particular activities. Large amounts of bones which have not been fully processed are usually interpreted as evidence of feasting. The sex of bones can be identified from anatomical features such as antlers (deer), large canines (pig) and penis bone (dog) in males and pelvic shape and structure in females. The dimensions of bones can also be used as males are larger in many species. The ratio between two or more measurements from one bone is used rather than a single measure (for example length) as size may be dependent on the age of the animal. Identification of changes in the skeleton is useful for establishing age especially patterns of teeth eruption, growth and wear and bone fusion. The ends of long bones are called epiphyses. In a young animal these are joined to the bone by cartilage. As the animal ages this calcifies until by a process known as epiphysial fusion the ends and bones are joined. This allows adults and juveniles to be differentiated. Tooth eruption and antler shedding may also establish the season of death of the animals. However, such analysis is not always reliable, as bones may not have been deposited at the time the animals were killed. Note that Star Carr was thought to be a winter site from antler evidence, but recent discoveries

Figure 3.16 *Processed deer shoulder blade*

This bone has had a circular section cut away with a flint tool to make a ring for personal decoration. Evidence of large scale production of the rings at the Mesolithic site of Ringkloster provides an insight into the range of uses to which animals were put as well as being a source of food. It also indicates a degree of specialisation and probably exchange.

of stork and crane bones suggest it was used in summer. Antlers may have been accumulated over a long period and can therefore be unreliable as a guide to season of occupation.

Biostratigraphy, the principle of using fossil animals to date layers, has been used by archaeologists to help date palaeolithic sites. For example, reindeer bones might indicate a period during the last Ice Age. Smaller mammals such as voles, which evolve quickly, are often the most useful for this (◀ p. 40). It is also possible to analyse bone collagen for dating and for environmental information from the minerals and amino acids it contains. Animals provide clues to the environment although we cannot always be certain that they occupied similar habitats to today's animals. Bones can also provide insights into human behaviour. The spread of species may be related to trade or human migration. DNA research is also shedding light on the origins of modern animal species (▶ p. 246). Analysis of damage to bones provides data on hunting, butchery and craft technology.

Human remains

Human remains can be divided into two major categories: hard and soft tissue. The evidence that these two types provide and the conditions in which they are preserved vary considerably.

Soft tissue

Like other organic remains, soft tissue is only usually recovered on sites with unusually good preservation. They are not likely to be a representative sample of the wider population but are useful none the less.

Desiccated bodies such as Egyptian mummies often preserve facial features well, if a little distorted from the drying process, together with internal organs, nails and hair. Accurate sexing of the body can usually be done from the external sexual organs, or from facial hair. There are always exceptions. 'Mummy 1770', which had probably spent some time in the Nile as a result of an unfortunate encounter with a crocodile, could not be sexed at the time of mummification by the priests. He/she was therefore prepared for either eventuality in the afterlife by being given both a false penis made of a roll of bandage, and gold nipples. In addition to providing details of clothing and **mortuary practices**, tissue samples can be rehydrated to give useful evidence about disease, for example the sand pneumoconiosis suffered by one of 'The Brothers' in Manchester Museum. Dry sites sometimes also provide coprolites. Analysis of these can recover hair, bone, seed and parasites to reveal information about diet and health. Analysis of deposits from the latrines at Bearsden Roman Fort revealed little trace of cholesterol but lots of wheat bran, suggesting that the legionaries ate little meat. The Dungfile website provides all the links you might want.

- http://www.scirpus.ca/dung/dung.shtml

Frozen corpses like Ötzi the Ice Man (▶ p. 93) and the Pazyryk 'Ice Maiden' provide similar evidence to dry bodies except that stomach

Figure 3.17 *A latrine at Housesteads fort. Analysis of soil at similar sites has provided valuable evidence about the diets of legionaries*

Figure 3.18 *'Ginger'*

Nicknamed from his colour, this naturally mummified Egyptian from around 3400 BC is testimony to the preserving power of arid conditions. The hot sand desiccated the body by absorbing its water content. As a dried out piece of leather there was no moisture for the flesh eating bacteria which cause decay. Ginger is surrounded by pre-Dynastic grave goods.

contents are often preserved as well. The general level of distortion and decay is often so low that these bodies can almost seem asleep, not dead. The Peruvian Inca children are especially extraordinary in this respect. In one case the trauma that caused death – a blow to the head – could still be identified in a CAT scan. In another example the red-stained vomit from the symbolic 'achiote' dye that the child had been forced to ingest still marked his face and the front of his clothing. Without Ötzi's preserved skin we would not have known about his tattoos, which may be the earliest evidence of medicinal acupuncture.

Bodies from anaerobic conditions such as the famous 'bog bodies' of northern Europe, including Lindow and Tollund Man, have been used to study diet, internal parasites and trauma. The acid nature of bogs can lead to the almost complete demineralisation of bone while tanning the skin to perfection.

- http://www.pbs.org/wgbh/nova/peru/
- http://www.bbc.co.uk/science/horizon/2001/iceman.shtml
- http://www.archaeology.org/online/features/bog/

In some soil conditions, in East Anglia for example, where the soil is damp and acid, neither hard nor soft tissue survives well. The only surviving trace of a body may be a stain in the bottom of the grave that provides a silhouette of the original corpse. The 'sand man' in Mound 1 at Sutton Hoo may have been such a burial.

• http://www.suttonhoo.org/

Hard tissue

Bone is much more frequently recovered by archaeologists than soft tissue. Similar analysis to that used on faunal remains is carried out to determine the composition of assemblages of human remains. Many techniques for ageing and sexing humans are also similar. However, due to widespread variation amongst males and females no physical method is totally reliable and it is almost impossible to sex children. DNA testing is accurate, but is very expensive. Using wear on bones to estimate age for older individuals is also notoriously unreliable. Theya Molleson made a comparative study on the collection from Spitalfields Crypt where the actual ages were known from the coffin plates. In the case of Louisa Courtauld, the archaeological estimate of her age using bone was wrong by over twenty years. However, a newer technique of thin-sectioning teeth, which relies on measuring the amount of translucence in the root, provided a much closer estimate.

Health. Where a large sample of human bones is recovered one can *start* to gain some tentative insights into age structure and health of the population. Some diseases leave marks on bones. These include polio, tuberculosis and genetic disorders such as cleft palate, along with syphilis and various types of cancer. Early medical treatments such as trepanation (cutting or drilling a hole in the skull) can sometimes be identified. Teeth also provide clues. Harris Lines – horizontal lines in teeth enamel where growth was reduced during a period of stress – can be an indication of disease or of malnutrition. Amongst farmers this is most likely immediately before the harvest period whereas foragers are often at risk in the late spring when plant foods are in short supply. The study of skeletal remains to find out about lifestyle is called Bioarchaeology.

Evidence of trauma and wear on the bones can provide insights into lifestyle and illness. For example a shiny ulna or elbow joint is caused by bone rubbing on bone because the cartilage has been worn out by repetitive action. Possible activities which might cause this include rowing if both ulnae are affected or throwing spears if only one is affected. In the latter case the arm bone in question may be thicker than the other one as a result of greater activity.

Damage to the skeleton through accidents, activities undertaken during life, murder and warfare injuries and even childbirth can all be evidenced by physical traces left on bone. Female skeletons at Tell Abu Hureyra (▶ p. 242) were shown to have traces of arthritis from using grindstones, while the murder of prisoners at the Battle of Towton (▶ p. 328) has recently been investigated through meticulous examination of skeletons from a pit near the battle site. Wear and damage to teeth can also be indicative of particular diets or activities. DNA can be extracted from both soft and hard tissue, including hair but for archaeology bones and teeth are the main sources. DNA analysis (see chapter 9) can be used to reveal information about health, origins, sex and relationships between individuals.

Diet. The main approach to diet relies upon studies of isotopic traces in bone. Particular diets such as one dependent on marine foods or one heavy in maize consumption will leave a signature in the bone collagen (▶ p. 314). Tooth wear is also used to demonstrate gritty diets while earth from the abdominal area of buried skeletons can be analysed for pollen and seeds which may have been in the stomach.

• http://www.brad.ac.uk/acad/archsci/depart/ resgrp/palaeodiet/

Figure 3.19 *Drawings of human skeleton*

The key parts of the skeleton used by archaeologists to sex and age the body are labelled. The close-up of the pelvis indicates the difference between the narrow arch of males and the wider arch in females to allow for the passage of the baby's head during birth. In the blade of the pelvis, below the socket for the hipbone (femur), is the sciatic notch. The rough 'rule of thumb' of the forensic anthropologist Rebecca Storey is, 'You stick your thumb in and if it wiggles it's female and if it doesn't it's male!' The skulls illustrate potential variation between male and female skulls although there is more of a continuum here. Generally male brow ridges are heavier with larger mandibles (jaws) and skulls. The best guide to age is tooth eruption stages and epiphysial fusion. Bones fuse at different rates during an individual's life until full maturity in a person's twenties. There are also changes in bone structure as we age although microscopic analysis would be required to assess it.

KEY SITE

The 'Amesbury Archer'

During housing development in the Stonehenge area, Wessex Archaeology made one of the most significant discoveries of recent years. A burial which was dated to 2300 BC contained the richest assemblage of grave goods found from the period including the earliest gold found in Britain. Most beaker burials have one or two vessels and one archery kit. This man was buried in a wood lined cist with over 100 artefacts including five beakers, two archery sets and an array of rare metal objects. These included copper knives and two gold hair tresses. Shortly after this discovery a second grave was found. This man did not have so many goods but he too had a pair of gold tresses, discovered during micro-excavation of his jaw! These were spectacular finds but analysis of their skeletal remains was to reveal much more.

Figure 3.20 *The grave of the Amesbury Archer*

- Oesteoarchaeological examination suggested the archer was 35–40. He was a robust individual about 5′8″ in height with a badly damaged left knee. His leg would have been withered and oozed with pus. It would have been awkward and may have smelled bad. The second man was in his 20s when he died.

KEY SITE *cont.*

The 'Amesbury Archer'

- The men shared a number of distinctive anatomical traits including similar shaped heads and a rare deformity of their heels. They were related, possibly father and son.
- Carbon isotope analysis suggested that they had eaten diets based around cereals.
- When growing, teeth enamel locks in oxygen from local drinking water. Analysis (▶ p. 214) of the Amesbury Archer's teeth suggested that he originated from somewhere along a line between Sweden and the Alps. This was because his Oxygen isotope profile matched that from water sources in that region. Further study involving analysis of strontium isotopes may narrow the search further. In contrast, the younger man had grown up in southern England.

Analysis of the gold suggested it came from at least 100 miles away – possibly from Europe – as were the two knives. His shale bracelet was from the Dorset coast and other artefacts had also come from some distance. So who was this man with such exotic possessions? The press quickly dubbed him 'the king of Stonehenge' and suggested that he built it. Since Stonehenge is far older that is impossible although he may have been involved in one of its later phases.

The beaker assemblages are one clue. Beakers from the grave have been compared to others from both Europe and Scotland. The origins of the beaker assemblage lie in the central European corded ware tradition (Sherratt, 1997) of individual burials with battle axes, beakers and flint dagger. In the bell-beaker development which reached Britain, archery equipment replaced the battleaxe. This male warrior drinking assemblage might reflect life roles or it might simply be the 'right way' to be buried. Either way, the archer was one of the earliest of such burials so he may have been involved in importing such ideas. He also had equipment for metal working – some of it similar to the Upton Lovell burial (▶ p. 287). Perhaps his status (and wealth) was derived from his craft which initially must have seemed close to sorcery.

Organic artefacts

Organic artefacts are far rarer in archaeology than those made of stone and clay. Inevitably this has distorted our view of the past because so much material culture is invisible to us. Sites where organic finds survive in large amounts are unusual and in some cases may not be 'typical' sites. However, they do provide tantalising glimpses of the skills, culture and economics of the periods in the past from which they came.

Plants

For the archaeologist samples of plant remains divide into the microscopic and the macroscopic.

Both types usually require specialised methods of conservation and analysis. Plants can tell the archaeologist about past climate, economic practices, the nature of past environments and environmental change. We can explore the exploitation of plants for food, medicinal and narcotic purposes while the study of wood leads us into construction, carpentry and woodland management.

Plant macrofossils

Plant macrofossils are specimens that are visible to the naked eye. They include seeds, leaves and twigs. They are usually preserved in the following unusual conditions:

Figure 3.21 *Viking shoes from Aros*

Like other textiles, leather survives only in anaerobic conditions. Survival of examples such as this and others from medieval towns such as Dublin and York enable an understanding of the leather trade, clothing and the exploitation of animals.

Figure 3.22 *Textiles*

Plant and wool based textiles rarely survive outside anaerobic conditions. The earliest woven textiles used thread from plants such as nettle (▶ p. 280) and flax. Grasses (▶ p. 93) and lime bast were also used for some items before wool became widely used in the Bronze Age. This Bronze Age burial from a waterlogged Danish site included a full set of clothes made from plant and animal fibres.

■ Waterlogged, where wet anaerobic conditions inhibit the growth of the bacteria that cause decomposition. For example, bran in Lindow Man's stomach or moss used as 'toilet paper' in Viking York.

■ Carbonised, where charring has converted material to inorganic carbon which is less susceptible to the forces of decay, for example grain in the pits at Danebury. Some plants are more likely than others to have become carbonized during processing which can distort samples (▶ p. 116).

■ Mineralised, where the organic content of the specimen is replaced by minerals such as iron and manganese from groundwater in the soil.

■ Frozen, usually in conditions of permafrost when the ground is always frozen and organic remains within it can be perfectly preserved. For example coriander seeds in the 'Ice Maiden's' grave or the stomach contents of Siberian mammoths.

■ As impressions in mudbrick, pottery or daub, for example corn cobs at Ceren and olives at Pompeii.

Wood

Dealing with wood from archaeological contexts presents huge problems, but may also offer sources of evidence unavailable elsewhere. Wood survives on wet or desiccated sites and in carbonized form. The cellular structure of trees varies so it is possible to identify different species using a microscope. Leaving aside its use for dating through dendrochronology, wood is valuable as physical evidence for structure and artefacts. Living trees are discussed in chapter 7. Archaeologists cannot study carpentry practices from the past, which involved complex joinery, without part of a ship or building to show how the joint was made. The discovery of wooden structures is also important in revealing the huge range of uses to which wood was put in the past.

Shipwrecks (▶ p. 272) such as the Wasa or Mary Rose are time capsules: a moment frozen in time. Inside these two warships were a bewildering array of wooden artefacts from mundane spoons and bowls to sophisticated navigational aids.

• http://dover.gov.uk/museum/boat/home.asp

All of this material is derived from wet contexts. The wood, though flimsy and insubstantial, retains much of its form and details such as axe marks. Wood from dry contexts also sometimes survives but is frequently warped and distorted. Once wood is removed from a wet environment, decay sets in rapidly unless proactive measures are taken. Observations at Oakbank (◀ p. 52) showed that excavated wood when freshly broken retained the colour of fresh timber, but once exposed to the air the wood turned black in about twenty seconds. In the short term wood is kept wet with biocides added to the water to prevent fungal growth. Longer term conservation may involve freeze-drying but this is only a viable option for artefacts and small timbers. Larger specimens require different techniques. Replacing the water in the cells of the wood with a soluble wax such as PEG (polyethylene glycol) treats shipwreck timbers, which have the consistency of wet cardboard and consist of 80–90 per cent water. This treatment can be very time-consuming. The Mary Rose, which has been treated with PEG, is still not ready for display more than ten years after she was raised.

Indirect evidence for the use of wood can also be detected. At Sutton Hoo the imprint of an Anglo-Saxon ship's timbers remained in the sand while at Garton Slack there was a stain from the vanished spokes of a chariot's wheels. Charcoal is a common find on many archaeological sites. In addition to providing samples for radiocarbon dating (▶ p. 102) it can reveal much about local environments. Microscopic analysis can reveal not only species but even whether firewood came from coppiced trees.

Figure 3.23 *Wood from the Corlea Trackway*

Wooden structures not only tell us about carpentry and construction techniques but also about woodland management. In most cases research reveals that specific tree species were selected for specific tasks. At Corlea in 148 BC a 2 km long track way was built across a bog. The timber for the road came from 370 oak trees. This was laid on alder and elm runners above a platform of brushwood. The planks were split skilfully with wooden wedges and were anchored down with pegs through mortises. Causeways are common in the area and are mentioned in Celtic stories such as the Wooing of Etain. However, the scale of Corlea is exceptional and would have required a high degree of social organization to construct. Possibly at tribal level (▶ p. 293). There are no ruts from carts or wear on the surface and unlike the Sweet Track (▶ p. 277) the Corlea sank within a decade. Its purpose can only be guessed at but may relate to ostentatious display.

Other plant macrofossils

The quantity of plant material in natural sediments is usually low but on archaeological sites can be abnormally high, especially where activities such as deposition of food waste and human faeces (**coprolites**) or food processing and storage has have taken place. Archaeologists must also take care in presenting data if the sheer quantity of small seeds produced by some species is not to artificially dominate an assemblage at the expense of other species which produce fewer and larger seeds. A comparison between the size of poppy seeds and almonds makes this point.

On most sites archaeologists will want to know about the local environment and the use of plant foods including crops (▶ Chapter 8). However, biases can occur in samples for a number of reasons. Differential survival may distort the range of plants known from a particular period because some plants do not preserve well or because they grow in locations lacking suitable conditions for preservation. People may also have introduced plants into the site either deliberately through plant collecting or cultivation or by accident as in the case of Ötzi the Ice Man, in the form of cereal grains adhering to his grass cape. This means that the archaeologist must study very carefully the formation processes (▶ Chapter 5) that led to the creation of the deposit that contains the plant remains under consideration.

Plant microfossils

Plant microfossils are remains that can usually be studied only using microscopes. Three types that are important to archaeologists are pollens, diatoms and phytoliths.

Figure 3.24 *Stages in grain processing and the resulting assemblages*

Through ethnographic study (▶ p. 124) of contemporary societies that rely on simple technology, archaeologists can understand the main stages of grain processing. Each stage produces a signature assemblage of plant macrofossils from the waste or what is left. After reaping (1) ears, bits of stalk and various weeds are taken to the farm. Threshing (2) breaks up the ear and separates the grain from the chaff. Winnowing (3) removes straw and husks – often to be fed to animals. Pounding (4) starts to break up the grains. Singeing to remove waste and sieving to remove smaller weed seeds may occur before storage and finally grinding.

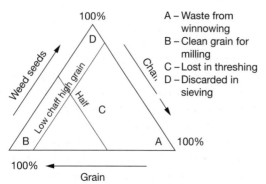

Pollen

The study of pollen is known as **palynology**. The species of individual grains of pollen are readily identifiable by palynologists through their characteristic shapes. They survive well, especially in wet, acid conditions, because they possess a tough outer case. Pollen can be retrieved from most soil samples but is most useful when taken by coring or from a column of samples from a ditch or pit to show vegetation changes. Species frequency in samples can be counted and the numerical data plotted to show relative quantities. Some species produce more pollen then others, so depending on wind, animal and human action a particular assemblage of pollen may represent a very local or a more regional sample.

The relative quantities of pollens provide a record of environmental change. In well-researched areas it has been possible to define pollen zones which characterise particular periods according to the relative amounts of each species. These pollen assemblages can be used to assign relative dates to samples from

Depth of sample in centimetres
or number of sample level

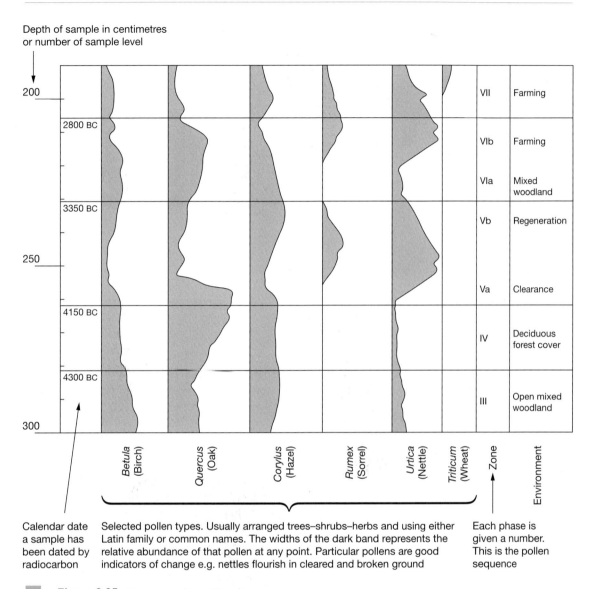

Figure 3.25 *How to read a pollen diagram*

other sites according to where they match the established environmental sequence. This is known as **pollen dating**. The samples can also be dated using radiocarbon dating.

Diatoms

Diatoms are microscopic single-celled plants usually found in open water or in wet conditions such as bogs and waterlogged soils. They are very sensitive to changes in their local water. Their hard outer shell survives well in alkaline or anaerobic conditions. Changes caused by human action such as deforestation or pollution can be inferred from changes in the species of diatom. They have been invaluable in studies around London in determining where the

Figure 3.26 *Drawings of examples of magnified pollen grains of oak, lime and willow illustrating the different shapes for each species*

braided channels of the Thames were in prehistory and whether they were tidal.

Phytoliths

Phytoliths are silica from the cells of plants. They survive well enough in alkaline soils to be identified to particular groups of plants. It has been suggested that sickle gloss on flint blades from the early Neolithic in the Near East is indirect evidence of abrasive cereal phytoliths, while in Mesoamerica maize phytoliths have been used to demonstrate the spread of agriculture. At Amud Cave in Israel phytoliths from both wood and grasses were even recovered from Middle Palaeolithic sediments dating back to before 50000 BP. These have been interpreted as Neanderthal fuel and bedding with seeds being collected as food.

Invertebrates

The shells of many tiny living creatures are surprisingly resilient. They provide evidence of the local environment and in some cases human diet and activity, as with the layers of seashells in coastal middens. Two important categories are beetles and snails.

Beetles

Beetles (or Coleoptera) are one of the most diverse types of invertebrate and they can be found in virtually every environment. The hard shell casing or 'exoskeleton' of a beetle is very resistant and varies sufficiently between species to enable identification under a microscope. In evolutionary terms, beetles have changed very little for tens of thousands of years, so comparison of samples with modern reference collections is relatively straightforward. The large number of types of beetle can make species lists rather unhelpful as there may be up to fifty species present in a collection of 100 specimens with only one or two in each category. A more profitable approach has been to group species together by their food or habitat preferences into classes such as 'phytophages' (plant eater) or 'obligate aquatics' (living in water). Archaeologists can then discover their local habitat and what

KEY STUDY

The decline of the Maya

Rue (1989) collected samples by coring a peat bog to produce a long thin column of sediment which encapsulated the environmental history of the Copan valley. Once processed the data revealed a surprise. The general view was that Maya society declined rapidly after AD 800 so Rue expected this would be reflected in the pollen evidence with maize being less prominent and tree pollen becoming dominant as the forest cover regenerated. In fact maize continued to be planted until at least AD 1100 and only after that did hardwoods like the mahogany, suggestive of fully established rainforest, became apparent on a large scale. Either the standard textbooks about the Maya were wrong or Rue's data were. His results were supported by Freter, who was working on obsidian hydration dating of blades found on Maya sites of this period. Her dates also suggested a long drawn out decline over several hundred years rather than a cataclysmic demise for the Maya. This provided a new 'model' to explain the end of Maya civilisation. It also highlights the view of modern archaeology as a discipline made up of many subdisciplines which often provide complementary evidence and new ways of looking at established ideas.

Ecological disaster at Copan caused by extension of farming onto hillsides and removal of tree cover

Figure 3.27 *Ecological disaster at Copan*

The extension of farming onto thin hillside soils and removal of tree cover led to environmental damage. Rain washed nutrients from the hill soils. The sediments covering valley settlements were caused by topsoil sliding down from the hills.

taphonomic processes (▶ p. 115) led to their decomposition in a particular deposit. The kind of archaeological information provided by the beetles can be summarised as follows:

- Reconstruction of ground surface conditions. Buckland (1976) used beetles to analyse the floors of houses at Reykholb in order to infer the use of different rooms.
- Reconstruction of vegetation and climate. The discovery of Oodes gracilis in southern Britain during the Palaeolithic has been used to infer the existence of much cooler conditions during glacial periods since this species now has a largely Arctic distribution.
- Information about stored products and the utilisation of plant resources. In Roman granaries at York grain beetles have been discovered which prove the exploitation of cereals even though there is no physical evidence of the plants themselves.

Molluscs

Land snail shells are preserved in calcareous, chalky soils because their shells are made of calcium carbonate (chalk). Most snails are so small (around 2 mm) that you can't normally see them. Those larger snails you may have seen, or even eaten, are much bigger and represent only three or four varieties of the hundreds of species of snail. Snails are especially useful to archaeologists as different species have particular vegetation habitats.

Microscopic shells are carefully sieved out of the soil (rather like seeds), identified and counted by the specialist. All snails need shade as they must not dry out, but some species are more tolerant to areas with less shade. This enables classification into three broad groups. Open country species can survive in grassland areas with little shade, unlike the woodland group. A catholic group is frequently found in both habitats, but some have quite specific preferences. Snails do not move far so although you

Figure 3.28 *Laboratory examination of snails. A microscope is used to identify the different species to provide insights into local habitats*

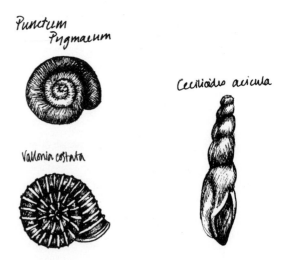

Figure 3.29 *Drawing of magnified snails to illustrate the varied shapes which enable each species to be identified*

cannot tell what any past habitat was like from just one or two shells, you can from a whole assemblage.

ARCHAEOMETRY

Scientific advances have a major impact on archaeology with those in dating, DNA and reconnaissance being the best known. However, just as inventions such as sonar and GPS were developed for military rather than archaeological purposes, archaeologists have adopted an impressive range of techniques from other disciplines. The growth of **archaeometry**, the scientific analysis of archaeological materials, has led to the creation of a whole range of new archaeological specialisms as well as archaeological science degree courses. It has also seen the development of institutions which link archaeological research to wider social issues. For example the Ancient Biomolecules Centre at Oxford University specialises in researching ancient DNA and is funded by Wellcome because the findings will help understand the development of disease and the impact of past climate changes.

Laboratory analysis of finds can determine their composition, structure, date, and in the case of artefacts, their manufacturing history. The type of analysis selected in any particular case will depend on factors including cost, the importance of the individual sample and the questions the archaeologists are asking. For example, **petrology** is relatively cheap, but it is also destructive. **X-ray fluorescence** provides a dearer alternative, which doesn't cause damage, but it can only analyse the surface of objects.

Only selected materials are sent to laboratories and only with clear questions in mind which will help address overall research questions. An excellent range of links for scientific methods is at

• http://www.brad.ac.uk/acad/archsci/

Characterisation studies

Scientific analysis of artefacts and building material can reveal their chemical make-up. This is valuable because while stone or metal of the same type is largely composed of the same elements, their exact chemical composition varies. Each stone or metal ore was extracted from a specific location under particular geological conditions. These unique circumstances mean that they contain slightly different combinations and quantities of 'impurities'. Copper, for example, may contain minute amounts of arsenic, silver and lead. These '**trace elements**' occur as a few parts per million and may have negligible effects on the material, but they provide it with a distinctive 'chemical fingerprint'. Where the geological sources of metal, clay or stone have been mapped, archaeologists may be able to identify the location from which the materials were quarried.

Spectrometry

Spectrometry covers a range of methods that derive from physics and involve using radiation (for example X-rays) to force a small sample of material to produce light (another form of radiation) which can be measured through spectrographic analysis. In the way that sunlight can be split into a rainbow, the light emitted by different elements shows different characteristic patterns when split by a prism into a spectrum. This is projected onto a viewing screen or photographic plate, so that information can be recorded. In a compound of elements, the balance of those elements is shown by the intensity of the lines in the spectrum. This is compared with control spectrums of known composition produced under the same conditions. Trace elements of a few parts per million can be recorded in this way. Spectrometry is a very accurate method for quantitative analysis and only requires small samples (less than 10 milligrams) to be taken. This makes it suitable for valuable archaeological material. It is widely employed for metal analysis but is also used for glass, faience, pottery, obsidian and occasionally flint.

X-ray fluorescence

This technique is one of the cheapest and quickest methods of analysing the surface composition of materials, particularly metals and pottery glazes. It is also non-destructive. A beam of X-rays forces the material to re-emit X-rays. The intensity of energy given off can be measured to indicate the chemicals present and their relative abundance. Since the method does not penetrate deeply it is of little use where materials have a coating of another mineral. A more advanced method uses protons to penetrate more deeply but it is also more expensive.

Neutron activation analysis (NAA)

This is the most accurate and reliable **characterisation** technique. Tiny samples are ground down to a powder and heated to remove moisture and carbonate. They are then bombarded with neutrons in a reactor. This creates unstable isotopes in the sample which give off distinctive patterns of radiation that can be measured. The technique is so sensitive that elements present in a few parts per billion can be detected. This means that clays can be sourced from minute variations in trace elements. The technique has been used at Manching in Germany to explore the distribution of similar types of ceramics across Iron Age Central Europe. It established that technology and designs were exchanged over wide areas rather than pottery. Visual examination alone could have led to the opposite

Figure 3.30 Gold Lunulae from Irish bogs

These incredible gold collar ornaments or Lunulae are rarely found outside Ireland and testify to the great skills of early goldsmiths there. The chemical signature could be accurately determined by NAA but that would mean destroying a sample. XRF would probably be sufficient particularly since the objects are quite thin.

Figure 3.31 *Copper 'oxhide ingots' from Minoan Crete*

Copper was exchanged across the eastern Mediterranean in the early Bronze Age. These distinctive ingots are found at palace sites and also shipwrecks (▶ p. 272). Shape, moulding marks and inscriptions have been studied to identify patterns but lead isotope studies were able to locate the mines to Cyprus.

conclusion. It is useful for a wide range of materials and is particularly appropriate for coins. Unfortunately it is expensive. The analysis of a single sample costs over £100.

Atomic absorption spectrometry (AAS)

Measuring the specific gravity of artefacts and comparing with known examples can identify alloys of gold. A more precise technique is AAS. A minute sample is dissolved in acid and then vaporised. When light of known wavelengths is passed through the gas, the amount that is absorbed indicates the minerals present. This technique has been used to trace the seventh-century debasement of coins in the Merovingian Empire. AAS is also widely used for bronze and copper. A limitation of this technique is that where metal artefacts were made from several sources the 'fingerprint' is obscured. In the ancient world, valuable commodities such as bronze were often recycled with new artefacts made from scrap from a variety of sources.

Isotopic analysis

Atoms of the same element which have the same number of protons and electrons but different numbers of neutrons, are called isotopes. (▶ p. 92) By determining what isotopes are present, and in what proportions, materials can be linked to known sources with the same ratios. This technique was used to analyse metal artefacts from early Bronze Age Crete. These had distinctive Cretan styles but there are no metal ores found on Crete. Ratios for lead isotopes in bronze and silver artefacts enabled the material to be traced to sources on the mainland. This showed that raw materials rather than finished objects were being traded. Trade in copper and marble around the Mediterranean has also been traced using isotopic analysis. In the case of marble, petrology had been unable to do so.

Organic residue analysis

This exciting new technique uses chemical solvents and reagents to dissolve and extract traces of organic materials left in the fabric of pottery sherds. The resulting solution can be tested for sugars, and particularly lipids or fatty acids. Lipids are ubiquitous in nature and are present in nearly all foodstuffs, for example milk, honey, vegetable oil or meat. Each fat has a slightly different molecular structure or 'biomarker'. Research aims to identify the biomarker and compare it with 'fingerprints' known from particular sources. This method can identify the resins of different trees, the fats of different animals and different waxes and oils. Successful matching will indicate what the vessel

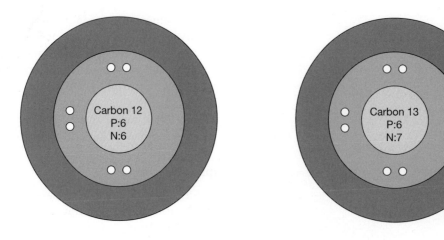

Figure 3.32 *Isotopes*

In this example, carbon-13 has a extra neutron which makes it fractionally heavier than the more common carbon-12.

had been used to store or process. Most prehistoric pottery is unglazed so lipids penetrate deep into the fabric itself. This means that even if there is no visible residue lipids can be recovered. This involves a sample of the wall of the vessel being ground down and then solvents are used to extract the lipids. These are subjected to lab-based processes such as gas chromatography to identify the compounds.

A problem with the method has been the degradation of lipids over time which can make it harder to distinguish between different fats. To some extent this can be overcome by further analysis of the stable carbon isotopes present in different compounds. Lipids are also present in human faeces and in skeletal material. Although expensive the technique is being applied to many different questions. A team from Bradford University has used this technique to study the bulk import of liquids into Bronze Age Egypt through analysis of amphorae sherds while research in Greece has identified some of the glues and waterproof tars being used in the Neolithic. One of the most exciting projects is examining the spread of dairying across Europe (▶ p. 256).

Is archaeology a science?

The adoption of scientific techniques and the overlap between archaeology and biology in the study of human origins led some archaeologists to claim that archaeology was now a science. This would have advantages for university departments since science enjoys higher status and better funding than the humanities. However, the use of scientific techniques in itself doesn't make a subject a science. To be accepted as a science archaeology would have to demonstrate that it is following the principles of empirical methods with a view to establishing 'laws', or 'middle range theory' as it is often called. Although many research archaeologists have adopted the scientific model of generating a hypothesis and then testing, it is difficult for archaeologists to form law-like generalisations from their findings. While the relationships explored by scientists in laboratory experiments can be repeatedly tested under controlled conditions, archaeologists investigate unique events from the past and deal with material which, once removed from its context, can never be re-excavated. However, many people working in archaeology are

KEY STUDY

Ötzi the Iceman

The amazing discovery of an ice mummy of a copper age man from the Alps continues to provide new surprises. The latest news is that not only was Ötzi shot with an arrow, he may have been finished off with blows to the head. The latest forensic techniques have suggested that he may have lost consciousness from blood loss and either hit his head on a rock or someone else hit him with one. Someone also appears to have pulled the arrow shaft from his shoulder.

Ötzi has arguably been the greatest single archaeological discovery of all time. While his individual story is fascinating, scientists have learned a great deal about life and technology in copper age Europe.

His body has provided an insight into life at the time. His various injuries and ailments and the treatments he received – including acupuncture – suggest a difficult existence. However, sourcing the materials he carried including both plant remains and lithics reveals a society where people did move beyond their village and may have had links over a great distance. Isotope analysis of his teeth and of plant remains on his clothes suggests he came from northern Italy but he was a long way from home when he died. Pollen from the hop-hornbeam tree which he had ingested while eating suggested that he died in early summer. Ötzi himself had dangerous levels of arsenic in his hair from working copper. For the first time we have a definite example of one of the mysterious metal smiths who were transforming material culture.

Figure 3.33 *Ötzi the Ice Man*

KEY STUDY *cont.*

Ötzi the Iceman

It is his technology which is staggering. Aside from a few tools and weapons his possessions were largely organic. They include items we may have glimpsed at Mesolithic sites (▶ p. 240) but nowhere has this technology been as fully revealed. His clothes were designed to trap air as those of a modern mountaineer would but he had a grass cape rather than Gore-tex™. His hat was bearskin and bear also was used for the lower part of his boots, deerskin providing the uppers. The boots were stuffed with grass for insulation. He wore a kind of vest, leggings and other clothes made of leather and topped it off with a woven grass cape.

In a pouch on his belt were several fungi including one which may have been medicinal and another which was part of the kind of fire-lighting kit which was in use till modern times. He had a rucksack on his back made from a U-shape birch frame and plant fibre netting and carried two birch-bark containers. Besides a copper axe he had a bow, arrows from a variety of trees and a quiver with a flap to keep the arrows dry.

scientists and in their lab-work are applying scientific methods so the lines are blurred.

AFTER ANALYSIS

Finally all the reports are united with the dating evidence and the fieldwork record as a complete site archive. At this point the archaeological record becomes a collection of written, graphical and electronic data. It still needs to be interpreted. (▶ p. 111) In the tradition of scientific reporting, published archaeological reports tend to be descriptive and analytical with a fairly minimal amount of assessment and interpretation. The archive is there for others to draw their conclusions from. For members of the public and many students, reports are often frustrating. What they want are the works of synthesis and interpretation that are largely produced by academic rather than field archaeologists. The examples and discussions in Part II of this book are largely drawn from these interpretative accounts.

The vast majority of finds from excavations remain in museum or other archives and are only seen by specialist researchers. In some cases material is re-analysed many years later. For example new scientific techniques can be deployed on material excavated many decades earlier as with the studies of lipids using archive collections of ceramics.

Figure 3.34 *After excavation, finds are stored in archive boxes. This enables future researchers to access them*

Chapter 4

Understanding Dating in Archaeology

YOUR GOALS

You need to understand

■ the underlying principles of dating

■ the essence of how the more common techniques work

■ reasons why particular techniques are appropriate for specific situations

■ how to 'read' some of the more common types of charts and diagrams used to present dating data.

Archaeologists have used many different techniques to work out the age of artefacts and sites for which they have no historical dates and the order in which they were used. These dating techniques can be broadly subdivided into two groups:

■ **Relative dating** techniques which identify the order in which sites or artefacts were used in a sequence from earliest to latest.

■ **Absolute** (or chronometric) **dating** techniques that try to establish an exact or approximate calendar date for a site or artefact.

The techniques selected depend on the specific task and evidence as well as practical considerations such as cost. Many of the scientific techniques are expensive and require high levels of technical skill to use and to interpret. The span of human history studied by archaeologists is so vast and environments so varied that techniques suitable for one place and period may be unsuitable for another.

Periods in archaeology

In the historic period, archaeologists make use of period names which are broader and often different from those used by historians. The fifth to seventh centuries AD are a case in point. In history books the period following Roman Britain is usually referred to as the Saxon Period or the Dark Ages. The latter term has been used to relate to both the decline in Christianity and urban life and the paucity of written documents from the period. To archaeologists it is certainly not 'Dark' since there is a wealth of artefactual evidence. In those further reaches of north-western Europe where the Iron Age was not interrupted by Roman occupation it is often referred to as the later Iron Age because of continuity in technology and society or the 'migration period' because of population evidence. In England 'Early Medieval Period' is sometimes used to indicate discontinuity with the Roman period and greater similarity with later centuries. In general, history will refer to peoples or individual royal families while archaeologists use labels that reflect more gradual changes in material culture and social and economic arrangements.

Archaeologists of European prehistory have, since the adoption of the three age system of stone, bronze and iron in the nineteenth century, used material culture and technology to label periods. A key indicator of the Mesolithic, for example, is the development of microlith technology which can be broadly distinguished from the blade based technology of the Upper Palaeolithic. Within these broad periods of several thousand years, subdivisions are often named after sites where variations in artefactual evidence were first noted. These subdivisions differ across wide regions. For example in France and parts of central Europe the term 'Sauveterrian' is used for part of the early Mesolithic. This is named after the type-site of Sauveterre le Lémance where assemblages containing numbers of geometric microliths were first identified. In Northern Europe a broadly similar period is termed 'Maglemosian' after the type-site of Maglemose in Denmark where flint microliths were used alongside a range of wood and bone tools. For the Palaeolithic some archaeologists, particularly those using environmental data, will refer to climatic periods such as Holocene or particular glaciations such as Devensian. It is worth noting that periods often start and finish at different dates in different areas. For example the Neolithic in south-east Europe occurred earlier than that in the north-west and reflects the gradual spread of agriculture out from the Balkan region. By the time Britain was 'in' the Neolithic the Balkans were 'in' the copper age or Chalcolithic.

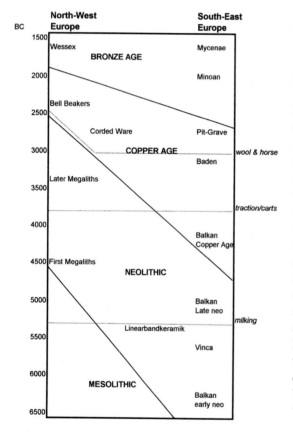

Figure 4.1 *Confusing periods in the past*

This simplified diagram (after Sherratt) illustrates broad patterns between South East and North West Europe during a period where the first metal-using civilisations were developing in the Near East but northern Scandinavians were continuing with the same foraging lifestyle that had been developing since the last Ice Age. So was it the Mesolithic, Neolithic or Bronze Age?

Historical dating

For sites less than 5,000 years old there may be written or artistic evidence which can provide precise dates as long as the original language can be decoded. For example, coins, seals, inscriptions and clay tablets were used by the civilisations of the Mediterranean and Middle

Figure 4.2 *Roman coin from the reign of Nero*

Coins have often been used to establish TPQ dates. In this case, the layer with the coin could not have been earlier than AD 54–68 (the reign of Nero). To help remember the difference between TPQ and TAQ think 'you have to *p*ost a letter before it can *a*rrive'.

East. Sometimes historical records such as dates, calendars or lists of rulers are available. These have allowed sites such as Egyptian tombs or Mayan temples to be precisely dated. When artefacts from these civilisations appear in non-literate areas they can be used to provide approximate dates in those areas. For more recent periods the exact dates for the introduction of many artefacts from clay pipes to beer bottles are known and can be used to date sites. Where artefacts are used for dating it is critical that their precise position within the stratigraphy is accurately recorded. Such 'indirect dating' of sites provides two types of date:

- *Terminus post quem* (**TPQ**): the earliest possible date for an archaeological deposit
- *Terminus ante quem* (**TAQ**):the latest possible date for the deposit

RELATIVE DATING

Typology

In its simplest form, this involves putting a number of finds into chronological order. On

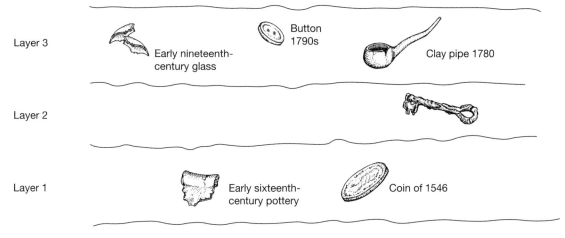

Layer 3 — Early nineteenth-century glass — Button 1790s — Clay pipe 1780

Layer 2 — (key)

Layer 1 — Early sixteenth-century pottery — Coin of 1546

Finds and features in layer 2 could not have deposited before 1546 (TPQ) and must have been deposited by 1780 (TAQ)

Figure 4.3 *The use of finds to provide earliest and latest dates for a layer. The key can be dated by association (◄ p. 36) to the layer*

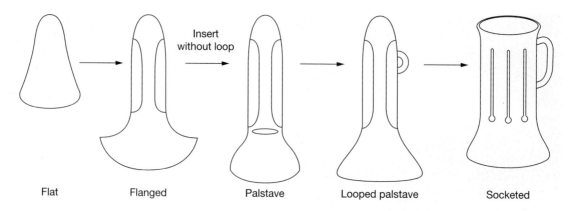

Insert without loop

Flat   Flanged   Palstave   Looped palstave   Socketed

Figure 4.4 *An example of a typological sequence: the development of copper and bronze axes*

a site with a clear and undisturbed stratigraphy, items from lower levels are older than those in higher levels. In the nineteenth century, observations about the types of artefact from different layers led to the creation of a time frame for prehistory known as the '3 age system', based on the introduction of tools made from stone then bronze then iron. Today many flaws are apparent in this scheme but the terms are still used to distinguish different 'periods' in the past. A more sophisticated technique was popularised by Flinders Petrie in the 1900s. He noted that the design and decoration of pottery from the Egyptian tombs he excavated changed gradually over time. He was able to place the different types into a chronological sequence. Once a good typological sequence for an area is established it can be referred to when new finds and sites are discovered and used to 'cross-date' them. In addition to design, the fabric or material used to make the artefact is also analysed. If you take a piece of pottery into your local museum, typology will be used to assign your sherd to a particular period.

Successive groups (or assemblages) of contemporary artefacts, which are commonly found together, have been used to form culture sequences over wide periods. Before the advent of absolute dating techniques this technique enabled a timetable of the spread of 'cultures' across Europe in later prehistory to be constructed, based on changing combinations of grave goods.

Seriation

Most artefact styles appear rarely at first in the archaeological record, then become more common and eventually dwindle in numbers again. This pattern has enabled a sophisticated statistical technique known as seriation (ordering) to be used. Information from a variety of dated sites across a long period is brought together. The frequency with which each form of artefact appears can be plotted as bars on a timeline. Ideally this will produce a shape known as a 'battleship curve' because it looks like an aerial view of a battleship. The changing popularity of each form will appear as a sequence of battleship curves. Other sites can be dated relative to the first site by comparing their seriation.

Problems with these techniques
- Although they can put sites and artefacts into order, they can only be used to provide calendar dates where elements of the sequences are tied to historical data.
- The advent of radiocarbon dating showed that archaeologists had underestimated timespans in prehistory. They had mistakenly

Figure 4.5 *A TRB ceramic assemblage*

This distinctive type of fourth millennium pottery with funnel-neck beakers and a range of stylised containers for liquids is the calling card of the first Neolithic farmers along the Baltic. Debate continues over whether they were incomers or converted foragers (▶ p. 251) but finds of this type provide a relative date for the contexts they are recovered from.

constructed sequences to fit their assumptions that all developments happened around the Mediterranean and then spread north and west to 'less civilised' areas.

■ One type of artefact doesn't always succeed another. For many years it was thought that pointed hand axes were earlier than oval ones after they were found in lower levels on some sites. However, at Boxgrove both were found together suggesting that other influences on choice were important. Seriation assumes that new artefacts are phased in gradually as others are phased out. This does not always happen.

■ **Curation**, the preservation of valued artefacts, can lead to items being deposited a long time after their manufacture. Basing dates on a few isolated artefacts could lead to errors.

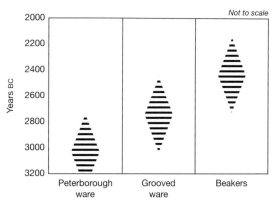

– Length of lines represent proportion of a given type at that point in time

Figure 4.6 *A simplified diagram to show how a model of seriation can be constructed*

The relative proportions of pottery types at a new site would be compared with the seriation chart to give it an approximate date. On our diagram, a site with lots of Grooved ware but only one beaker might be relatively dated to soon after 2800 BC.

Geoarchaeological dating

For early periods of prehistory archaeologists have borrowed techniques from the earth sciences to reconstruct the environments of early people and also to establish relative chronologies based on environmental changes. As the climate alters, so too do the types and relative numbers of different plants and animals. Where organic preservation is good, changes can be traced by analysing pollen (◀ p. 85) contained in sediments and animal bones. (◀ p. 72) To provide a pollen sequence a core through a deposit such as peat is taken and for each layer the proportions of different types of pollen are identified. Sites within these deposits can then be cross-dated to particular phases of climate history in local sequences. Analysis has to take account of many factors including the different amounts of pollen produced by each plant and the different distances the pollen travels. Similarly, sites can be relatively dated from the type of animal bones

Figure 4.7 *Obsidian blade*

This example is too precious to subject to hydration dating. It illustrates one of the other properties of obsidian – its razor-sharp cutting edge. This Aztec ritual blade was used to remove hearts from sacrificial victims.

present (◄ p. 41). This is particularly useful where the sequence of the appearance or extinction of species (for example mammoths) is known. Absolute techniques are needed to date these sequences. For the relative dating of major climatic sequences, deep sea cores and varves (lake deposits) are used.

Obsidian hydration

Obsidian is a volcanic glass that can be worked to provide razor-sharp cutting edges. In the Middle East and Mesoamerica it performed a similar function to flint in northern Europe. As soon as a piece of obsidian is broken it begins to absorb water from the atmosphere at a known rate (in much the same way as a stick of rock which goes soft on the outside). By measuring how far water has penetrated (hydration) into the obsidian on one site a relative date can be estimated compared to other sites. In some cases, results can be calibrated to provide absolute dates but that requires considerable additional data since the speed of hydration varies with local temperatures and the chemical make-up of the obsidian. This is one of the cheaper laboratory dating techniques.

• http://www.peak.org/~obsidian/

Hydration also occurs in other rocks and the potential of quartz for dating is currently being explored. Experiments on artefacts with known dates including Olmec pendants in Mexico has led to claims that quartz hydration may be able to date artefacts between 100 and 100,000 years old. However not all archaeologists currently accept this method.

Figure 4.8 *How obsidian hydration works*

Chemical dating of bones

Buried bones absorb fluorine and uranium from water in the ground whilst their nitrogen content declines as collagen in the bones decays. These processes occur at uniform rates so it is possible to establish the relative age of different bones by measuring the proportions of these chemicals.

ABSOLUTE OR CHRONOMETRIC DATING

Since the middle of the twentieth century new methods have been used to provide calendar dates. With the exception of dendrochronology, they all have margins of error and are expensive to use.

Dendrochronology (tree ring dating)

This is the most accurate chronometric dating method. Early in the annual growing season trees produce thin-walled 'earlywood' cells. Towards the end of the year thick-walled 'latewood' cells are produced. This cycle produces a visible 'ring' in the wood each year under the bark. The rings are wider in good weather conditions than in poor ones and can provide a record of local climatic variation. Trees in the same area will have similar ring patterns which means wood from different periods can be matched in overlapping sequences. These are tied to historical dates by modern trees. Californian Bristlecone Pines, which live for 4,000 years, were used to construct sequences over 7,000 years in the USA while oaks preserved in bogs have been used in Europe to create master sequences going back 11,000 years. The precision of the method is such that the felling date of the central stump of Seahenge (▶ p. 119) which had its bark attached has been pinpointed to between April and June 2050 BC.

Dendrochronology does have some limitations. Sometimes carpenters discard the softer sapwood just under the bark. This is important as in England there may be 15–55 or so 'sapwood' rings on an oak. In such cases researchers can only estimate an 'earliest possible felling date'. Not all areas have sufficiently varied seasons or enough surviving timber to be able to construct sequences. To effectively date wood around fifty years of tree rings are needed. Since this represents quite a thick piece of wood, the technique is better for dating building timbers than artefacts. Its direct use is from the Neolithic onwards when buildings were used and it has

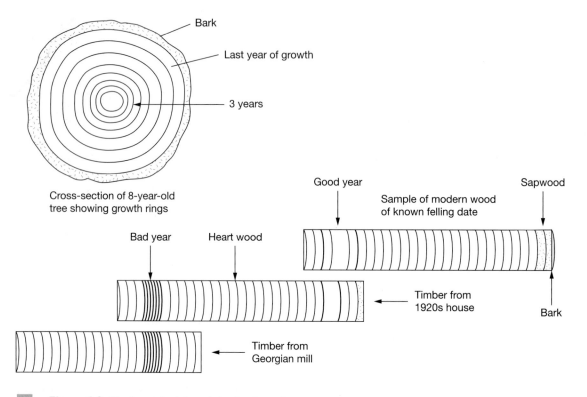

Bark
Last year of growth
3 years

Cross-section of 8-year-old
tree showing growth rings

Good year
Sample of modern wood
of known felling date
Sapwood

Bad year　Heart wood

Timber from
1920s house

Bark

Timber from
Georgian mill

Figure 4.9 *The key principles of dendrochronology*

Principle of tree ring dating: overlaps are matched to take the sequence back from a known date to date old timbers. Samples are taken at 90 degrees to the grain and numbers of rings and their thickness measured by eye or computer.

been widely used on medieval ships and buildings. Dendrochronology actually dates when the tree died or was felled. Where wood has been reused, as often happened with structural timbers in the past, this method can overestimate the age of a structure.

• http://www.ltrr.arizona.edu/

Radiocarbon dating

All living things absorb several types of carbon isotope from the atmosphere in similar ratios. About 1 per cent of this carbon is an unstable isotope known as carbon 14 (C-14) which decays at a known rate. The half-life of radiocarbon is 5730 years which is the length of time it takes

for half the C-14 to decay. By comparing the amount of C-14 remaining with amounts of other carbon isotopes (which do not decay) in organic samples it is possible to work out how much C-14 has decayed. This indicates how long it has been since decay began (and the creature or plant was alive). For many years it was thought that the dates produced by radiocarbon dating were precise. However the original half-life estimate of 5568 has been shown to be too little and the amount of carbon in the atmosphere has varied over time. As a result many dates for the last 8000 years were underestimated. For 5000 BC this was by around 1000 years! To get round this problem, radiocarbon dates are calibrated. More recently scientists have also identified a 'marine reservoir' effect. Carbon in the food chain in the sea is up to 400 years older than that on land with the result that dates based on bones of populations which ate a lot of marine food may be inaccurate.

The usual method of calibrating radiocarbon dates is dependent upon dendrochronology. Even after calibration there is a margin of error that is calculated statistically. This usually means that there is a 68 per cent chance or 'level of confidence' (LOC) that the real date is within the range indicated and a 95 per cent LOC that it is within twice the range. C-14 is mainly used to date organic materials including bone, shell and plant remains. It does not work on cremated bone although it will work for charred bone. It is more precise with wood samples from twigs and nuts than from trees that may have lived for hundreds of years. Radiocarbon's practical use is for periods from 200 to about 10,000 years with less reliability to around 40,000 years. Until recently at least 10 grams of charcoal or 200 grams of bone were needed for results. The development of accelerator mass spectrometry (AMS) has enabled samples as tiny as one grain

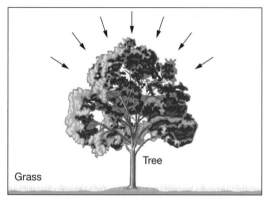

C-14 is formed by cosmic radiation in the atmosphere and absorbed by plants through photosynthesis.

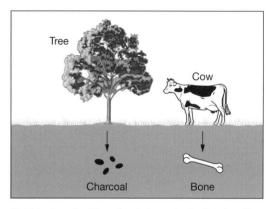

C-14 is absorbed by animals from plants. It enters the archaeological record in burnt wood (charcoal) or bones.

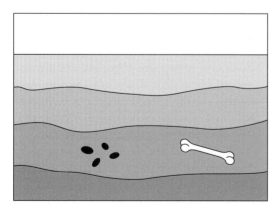

Archaeologists recover charcoal and bone samples to date a layer. Great care is taken to avoid contamination.

Laboratory analysis gives time since animal or plant died and C-14 decay began.

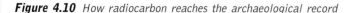

Figure 4.10 *How radiocarbon reaches the archaeological record*

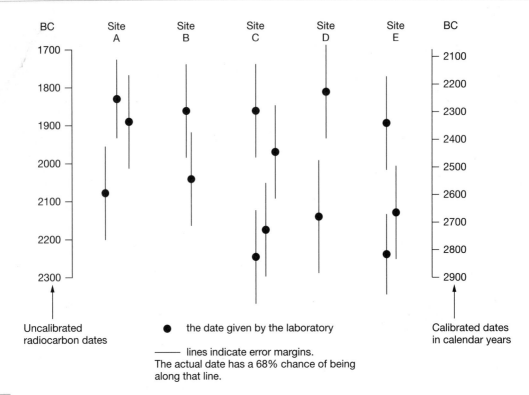

Figure 4.11 *Reading a radiocarbon table*

5820 ± 95BP

Raw result plotted against calibration curve

Calendar dates BC

The 'cloud diagram': another way of plotting R.C. dates

Figure 4.12 *A 'cloud' diagram*

An alternative mode of plotting RC dates shows the date range graphically. Lines underneath indicate 1 and 2 LOC.

of cereal to be dated. This expensive technique uses energy to accelerate the carbon molecules in such a way that they can be separated by weight and then counted.

• http://www.radiocarbon.org/
• http://www.radiocarbon.org/Info/#labs

C-14 dates are expressed in the following ways:

- Lower case letters are often, but not always, used to show that dates are uncalibrated, whereas capitals should mean they have been calibrated. Increasingly 'Cal' is added to a calibrated date to avoid any confusion.
- Calendar dates are expressed as ad or bc (uncalibrated) and BC, AD, Cal BC, Cal AD (calibrated)
- Radiocarbon dates are expressed as BP or Cal BP (calibrated). BP means 'before present' (1950) and is often preferred for early prehistoric periods for which BC and AD are relatively meaningless.

KEY TERM

Calibration

Calibration involves turning measures of time into calendar dates by comparing results from one method with dates from a more precise method. Dendrochronology is the most widely used method for calibration. Essentially, wood of a known age is tested for its C-14 date and the two dates compared. Once a large range of comparisons has been made a chart can be produced which enables scientists to read off a calendar year against a sample date. Calibration curves are modified as new data on ancient wood is published.

RC date (BP)

RC date = 3000 BP
95.4% probability that it is either
1375–1340 BC (82%)
1320–1129 BC (87.2%)

Calibration curve

Calibrated date (cal BC)

- - - - - - - Lines matching up limits of possible dates between RC and cal BC

Figure 4.13 *How calibration works*

This diagram is intended simply to illustrate principles. In the example plotted you can see that where the calibration curve is steeper, raw dates are converted to a relatively short range of calibrated dates while where the curve is shallow the range would be much longer.

A SECOND DATING REVOLUTION? THE APPLICATION OF BAYESIAN STATISTICAL ANALYSIS

Radiocarbon results often contain very broad ranges of possible dates. E.g. 3500 ± 125 years means that the data has a 68 per cent chance of being somewhere within a 250 year period and a 95 per cent chance of lying within a 500 year period. These broad date ranges have meant that archaeologists have been unable to discuss particular events and discussions of sequences and changes have often been at a very general level. The application of a new statistical technique to radiocarbon dates offers the possibility of much greater precision. It is also challenging current beliefs about many periods in the past.

The Rev. Thomas Bayes was an eighteenth century amateur mathematician. He developed a statistical model based on accumulating evidence in order to assess the probability of a given hypothesis being correct. This involves other observations and common-sense knowledge being used to modify probability statements. To take an extreme and simplified example: there might be a 5 per cent chance in any given year of snow falling on 25th December. However if we know that it snowed on 23rd and 24th, the probability of snow falling on the 25th would increase significantly.

If we take our 250-year date range, there are 250 potential outcomes which have equal probability of being the right date. Bayesian inference might lead us to update this hypothesis using other information available to us. For example other dating evidence derived from stratigraphy might lead us to reject one part of the date range. As a result of combining different types of evidence we might update the hypothesis by stating that it was probable that another part of the range contained the probable actual date. In this case we might then believe that the possible date range spanned 30 years rather than 250.

This advance is possible because of recent developments in computer-based simulations and complex mathematical methods of translating archaeological data into formats where it can be analysed statistically. There is some criticism of the approach because it contains elements of subjectivity but it has generally been embraced by dating specialists. Although first applied to radiocarbon dates, Bayesian statistics are being used in a range of other dating methods including thermoluminescence to improve the resolution of dates and in other areas of archaeometry where results are expressed in terms of probability.

English Heritage have illustrated the potential of this technique by using it to carry out a re-dating of skeletal remains from a number of neolithic long barrows in southern England. Previous data from Wayland's Smithy had given a span of dates over a thousand years. This suggested a long period of little change with episodic reuse of the monument. The new data on 14 skeletons narrowed the range to a few decades from 3590 to 3560 BC. This opens up the possibility that the monument was related to one event or series of events. Evidence of injuries on the skeletal remains could suggest that it relates to conflict. Re-processing of radiocarbon dates from four other long barrows including West Kennet and Hazleton revealed that the final burials in each of them date to around 3625 BC. Alex Bayliss who leads the English Heritage team has suggested that instead of seeing the Neolithic as a relatively timeless period, we may now start to be able to identify specific events and change within it.

Figure 4.14 *The façade of Wayland's Smithy*

Fourteen skeletons were excavated in the 1960s from this chambered long barrow in Oxfordshire. Recent forensic examination suggests that three of them may have been killed by arrows. Two of the skeletons may have been scavenged by dogs or wolves as they lay in the open before being recovered and buried. This may suggest that the people were killed at the same time in a raid or feud. Combined with the new dates it may mean that the middle of the fourth millennium BC was a time of social tensions.

Thermoluminescence (TL)

Radioactive decay in the quartz crystals found in clay leads to a build up of electric charge at a known rate. The electrical charge is released as light (luminescence) when the crystals are heated. Each reheating resets the clock. When pottery is discarded it also acquires (gamma) radiation from the surrounding soil. Essentially this means that the flash of light energy released by a given weight of ceramic sample (palaeodose) can be measured in a laboratory to calculate the number of years since the pottery was fired. The more light the longer the time since the 'clock setting event'.

$$\frac{\text{Palaeodose (acquired since last heating)}}{\text{Annual dose}} = \text{Age}$$

The technique can be used for materials such as glass and burnt flint or stone for periods from the present to around 400,000 years ago. It is significantly less accurate than C-14 dating and can give false readings due to radiation from the soil or if the initial firing was at low temperature. However, it is useful for older periods and instances where there are no organic remains such as dating Upper Palaeolithic figurines from Dolni Vestonice. A similar principle underlies **Optically Stimulated Luminescence (OSL)**. Electrons from decaying radioactive elements are trapped in crystals of quartz or feldspar which form part of many sediments. When stimulated with light, the electrons free themselves, giving off luminescence (light energy) in the process. The amount released can be used to date the last 'clock setting event'. Dates from 50 to a million years can be calculated with more accuracy than TL. OSL measures the time since sediments were last exposed to sunlight or in the case of ceramics when they were last heated to over 400°C.

• http://www.uic.edu/labs/ldrl/

Potassium–argon dating

As potassium in rock crystals decays it produces argon gas at a known rate. Measuring the amounts and ratios in a laboratory provides a date at which the crystal was formed. It has been used in volcanic regions to date layers of rock which sandwich human remains. For instance, at Koobi Fora in East Africa early hominid remains were dated to 1.89 million years BP ±0.01 million years. The technique can be used for periods from around 200,000 to several million years ago but it is limited to sites with the right geology.

Other absolute dating techniques

Figure 4.17 covers less commonly used methods, some of which are still at an experimental stage. You do not need to know them in detail although you should be aware of the situations where they might be used. Like radiocarbon dating, most of them rely on data showing known rates of chemical change or decay that can be measured in laboratories. Several of them measure the age of layers rather than the archaeological deposits themselves and are thus limited to particular types of geology. Most methods are used in combination to cross-check dates.

Date in radiocarbon years BP / Laboratory identification code / Margin of error at 1 LOC (68% chance) / Sample identification number

3960 ± 80 BP (Har–6268)

Calibrated / 68% chance that date is within this range / Calendar years

2560 – 2490 Cal BC

Figure 4.15 *Understanding a radiocarbon date*

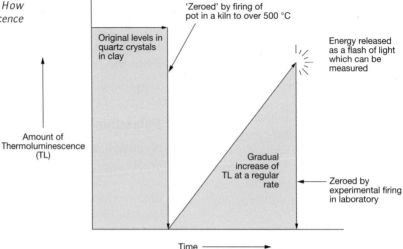

Figure 4.16 *How thermoluminescence works*

'Zeroed' by firing of pot in a kiln to over 500 °C

Original levels in quartz crystals in clay

Energy released as a flash of light which can be measured

Amount of Thermoluminescence (TL)

Gradual increase of TL at a regular rate

Zeroed by experimental firing in laboratory

Time

The amount of energy released is relative to the amount of time since last heated to over 500 °C the 'clock setting event'.

 KEY TASK

Test your grasp of dating methods

1   Which methods might you use to date the following? Check your answers on p. 429.

   ■ A wooden spear tip from 20,000 years ago
   ■ Shells from a Mesolithic midden
   ■ Seeds from a Roman well
   ■ Burnt flint from a palaeolithic hearth
   ■ Walls made from baked mud bricks from an ancient house
   ■ Human bones from a Saxon cemetery
   ■ An Aztec kiln site from Mexico
   ■ Bison bones found in cave deposits
   ■ A terracotta figurine from a Roman temple
   ■ Timbers from a Bronze Age boat

2   Construct a bar chart to show which methods are useful for which period in the past.

   ■ List each method on the vertical axis at regularly spaced intervals.
   ■ List the following dates (in years BP) on the horizontal axis at regularly spaced intervals:
      0, 100, 500, 1,000, 5,000, 10,000, 50,000, 100,000, 500,000, 1,000,000, 5,000,000.
   ■ Shade the period for which each method is useful in the relevant row.

	How it works	What it can be used for	What periods it is used for	Comments/limitations	Examples
Amino acid racemization	The chemical structures of the amino acids found in all living things change slowly over time at a known rate	Bones, teeth and shell	1000 to 1 million years	Must not be cooked Needs calibrating Varies with climate	Ostrich eggs on Palaeolithic sites in Africa
Archeomagnetism	The earth's magnetic field changes over time. When iron oxide is heated to around 600 °C and cools, it records the magnetic field at that time. Variations in the earth's field have been calculated which enables the date of initial heating to be established	Ceramics, lava, hearths and kilns that contain iron oxide	Up to 5,000 years	Local variations in magnetism Sites must be undisturbed when measured. Needs to be calibrated, e.g. by varves Can provide inaccurate dates where the same polarity occurred more than once	Clay ovens in south-west USA
Electron spin resonance (ESR)	Electrical charges build up at a known rate in some crystal structures. The time since the process began can be calculated by measuring the charge	Teeth enamel, shells calcite deposits in caves	50,000 to 1 million years	Works best in dry environments Wide error margins	Palaeolithic sites in Israel and Africa
Fission track dating	Uranium decays regularly through fission (splitting) which releases energy and damages crystalline structures, leaving a 'track'. Tracks or holes are counted to estimate the time the process of decay has taken	Glass, burned obsidian, heated stones containing uranium Sites sandwiched between volcanic layers	Mainly 100,000 to several million years although some recent glass has been dated	Difficulty in differentiating tracks from crystal defects Over 10% error margins	Homo habilis bones at Olduvai Gorge from around 2 million years ago
Uranium series	Uranium isotopes U235 and U238 are soluble in water and decay to produce deposits of thorium and protactinium at known rates. By measuring the ratios of the elements the date at which the deposits were laid down can be established	Analysing calcium carbonate deposits where water containing uranium has seeped into caves and been deposited (e.g. as stalactites) Teeth enamel, shells	Early human sites in Europe 50,000 to 500,000 years	Prone to ambiguous results Needs a high uranium content	Dentine on Neanderthal/ early human teeth in Israel
Varves	Melt-water from glaciers lays down different sediment at different times of year. This creates annual layers like tree rings. Changing climate will lead to changing deposits which can then be cross-referenced over large areas	Analysing cores taken from ancient lake beds. Where they contain pollen they can be tied to geoarchaeological sequences	Up to 20,000 years	Key dating role is by calibrating other techniques such as radiocarbon and archaeomagnetism	A sequence of 17,000 years has been established in Scandinavia and 20,000 in the USA

Figure 4.17 Comparison of other major scientific dating methods

Chapter 5

Archaeological Interpretation

YOUR GOALS

You need to understand

- why the way in which the archaeological record is formed is so important
- the basis of some ideas which archaeologists use to interpret archaeological remains
- the strengths and weaknesses of some of these ideas.

As humans, we use ideas and models to interpret the world around us. It is impossible to describe something or another person without likening them to something or somebody else. The same is true for archaeology. The goal of archaeology is to explain (not really reconstruct) past behaviour, but archaeologists do not dig up behaviour. They excavate material remains from the past and assume that behaviour and the ideas that motivated behaviour will be reflected in these remains. They then use theories from the present to make sense of the archaeological record. For example, you need theory to interpret a dark circular mark as a posthole or a particular burial as that of a chieftain. This way of thinking, which links material remains to their interpretation as evidence, is known as middle-range theory.

Debates between archaeologists often stem from differences in their assumptions about how the archaeological record was created and

KEY TERM

The archaeological record

This is the raw data for archaeology. The physical remains of past activities include features, artefacts and ecofacts (including human remains). The archaeological record comprises these remains in the contexts in which they come down to us. It is not static and constantly changes.

how one should interpret it. On degree-level programmes you will encounter a variety of theories of archaeological knowledge. Before then you don't need to know about specific theories. However a basic grasp of aspects of middle-range theory can help you assess the strengths and weaknesses of different interpretations.

Figure 5.1 *Excavation of this dark circle of earth can define shape, dimension and content. Establishing what it once was will always require interpretation. This example was a lime kiln*

In order to interpret data, and determine its significance, archaeologists have to know which materials go together and can be used to provide evidence of past behaviour. For example, a clustering of broken pottery, burnt stones and processed animal bones could represent a cooking area or it could be the result of people spreading their domestic rubbish on a field as fertiliser. This is where archaeology becomes detective work. To determine which explanation is most likely to be correct we need to understand the processes by which data reached us. Not all the materials used in human activity enter the archaeological record. Once there, some materials survive, others do not. Finally, some archaeologists are better at recovering some materials than others.

Figure 5.2 *Sites contain, and are made up of, features. This stone-built feature from Kingscote Roman Villa was identified as a kiln or corn dryer through reference to other sites, ethnographic example and experiment*

KEY CONCEPT

Relativist theories of knowledge

There are a wealth of texts on this subject and on the debates between rival schools of thought. In recent years, as in most academic disciplines, relativist ideas have become very influential. They share a belief that there are no absolute facts since all knowledge is subjective. For example, the values and assumptions we hold determine the way we think. The way we think structures what we see in such a way that it makes sense to us. So when we think we are discovering patterns in archaeological data, what we are really doing is organising data so that it reflects the structures already in our minds. For example, a female skeleton in a prehistoric burial with a flint arrowhead by her neck might be automatically interpreted as a victim if you have already assumed that only men fired arrows. Archaeologists with other assumptions might *see* her as a hunter or warrior.

TRANSFORMATION PROCESSES

These processes include all the stages by which human behaviour from the past is translated into the data recorded in archaeological reports and all the human and natural forces that shaped that data.

Formation processes

Archaeological data can be used to explain past human behaviour because people helped create that data. This applies to artefacts, ecofacts and much environmental data. The formation of archaeological materials is a complex process involving four broad stages. These need to be understood since evidence can enter the archaeological record at any point.

Figure 5.3 *Spindles*

These composite artefacts for twisting wool into thread are made of both organic and inorganic materials. Only the clay or stone 'whorl' is likely to survive. Interpretation is needed to reconstruct it.

Depositional processes are the ways in which remains actually find their way into the ground. If humans are responsible, we need to try and understand their logic. Why was an artefact discarded rather than being reused, recycled,

KEY TASK

Understanding formation processes

Produce your own table (like Figure 5.4) or illustration to show your understanding of **formation processes**. Use one of the following examples:

1   Remains of a hunted animal
2   A Roman amphora

 KEY TERM

Curation

Deliberately keeping and preserving something. It accounts for why old artefacts sometimes turn up amid much more recent material. Artefacts might be curated for sentimental reasons, rarity, beauty or because they were particularly useful. What has been curated in your home? Curation can distort the record, for example in early medieval Europe fine classical pottery often continued in use while metal vessels were recycled.

repaired or curated? These questions also apply to structures and ecofacts.

Some historical sources were created specifically to deceive. While there have been odd instances of faking such as 'Piltdown Man', it is highly unlikely that archaeological material has been buried to fool later generations. However, there are still codes to be broken. Archaeologists carefully map buried finds to see if there are patterns. Where these exist they may indicate 'structured' rather than random deposition. Natural forces may also have caused particular deposits. These might include erosion, flooding or volcanic activity. By understanding formation and transformation processes, archaeologists learn to differentiate between what was due to humans and what was due to nature.

How does archaeology get buried?

Leaving aside deliberate burial and sites buried by cataclysmic events such as floods, landslides

Stage of formation process	Example	We need to know	May enter the archaeological record as
Acquisition	Collecting flint, feathers and resin, cutting wood	Where and how the materials were gathered Why were they chosen	Flint mine
Manufacture	Shaping the flint, feathers and wood to make an arrow Heating the resin to make glue	What techniques and tools were used	Waste flakes Antler tools
Use/purpose	Used to hunt animals	How it was used, which creatures it was used on	Lost or broken points
Discard	Buried with its owner or in the remains of an animal	Was it thrown away, lost or deliberately abandoned	Arrowhead in burial or bone debris

Figure 5.4 *Example of the way in which a flint-tipped arrow might enter the archaeological record*

Figure 5.5 *Loomweights from Vorbasse*

This line of charred weights was discovered in the burnt out remains of an early medieval farmhouse in Jutland and were some of the few artefacts to survive. The rest of the loom was made of organic material and was burnt. The position of the weights indicates that they fell and were buried in situ rather than being deposited. Finds like this are relatively common and provide evidence of widespread domestic manufacture of textiles (◀ p. 81).

or volcanic eruptions, a key player is the humble earthworm. Worms process waste vegetation and throw up 'worm casts'. Over many years these raise the soil level to cover discarded material and abandoned structures. Time-lapse photography would show the archaeology literally sinking into the ground. In rural areas other burrowing animals such as moles also move topsoil while animal droppings contribute to new soils. Dying vegetation, particularly leaf mould on dry land and peat on wetland, can rapidly cover quite large structures. The wind also deposits dust, sand and eroded soils from elsewhere. In urban areas buildings are often raised on the levelled ruins of earlier structures. This is at its most spectacular on tell sites. Until recently rubbish was often burnt or buried in towns and this increased the depth of soil. In churchyards the addition of human remains and coffins would similarly raise soil levels. As a result archaeological deposits in towns are usually more deeply buried than contemporary remains in the countryside.

Post-depositional factors

Once buried, further modifications take place. The archaeological record is not a safe place for artefacts or ecofacts. The causes of these changes are usually grouped as:

- natural forces or 'N transforms,' including bacteria, acid, water, erosion, ice, worms, sunlight, roots, freezing and thawing, drying out (desiccation), silting, gnawing and oxidisation
- human or cultural 'C Transforms,' including grave robbing, looting, shelling, mining, reuse, ploughing, collecting, trampling, building and draining.

KEY TERM

Structured deposition

Most human societies, including our own, dispose of materials in ways determined by their beliefs and knowledge. By trying to uncover the patterns in which material was deliberately deposited in the past, archaeologists hope to reveal elements of past beliefs. Structured deposition has been particularly influential in recent studies of ritual practices in European pre-history, for example at Flag Fen. Here, the sacrificed bones of dogs were found on the seaward side of an artificial causeway.

 Figure 5.6 *Finds from the Hjortspring hoard.*

This assemblage of weapons, personal ornaments and a sea-going ship from AD 300 represents the sacrifice of booty from a successful battle. Careful plotting of the position of artefacts and tracing links between different piles of equipment enabled archaeologists to establish that this was one big sacrifice rather than deposits over a long period. The objects had been 'ritually killed' prior to being placed in a bog. No human remains were found there.

These factors can result in changes including movement, destruction, partial decay, colour loss, texture and shape changes, and alteration of chemical composition. The extent of change varies between different materials. Inorganic materials are preserved best. Stone, pottery and bronze, for example, are particularly durable. Consequently, there is a systematic bias in the archaeological record towards artefacts made from these materials. By contrast, organic materials such as wool, wood and bodies are far less likely to survive. Where they do it may reflect

particular environmental conditions as much as what happened in the past. **Taphonomy** (the law of burial) is the name commonly given to the study of the effects of such processes on animal and plant remains. The size of buried objects, their depth of burial, climate and the nature of the soil further complicate these basic distinctions. Bones, for example, will decay more slowly than normal in dry soil such as sand and in soils with little oxygen such as clay.

We can get some idea of the wealth of material that is usually lost by studying finds from

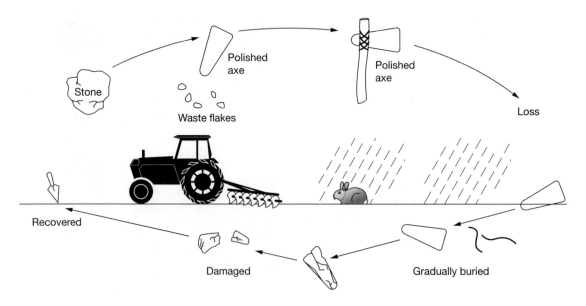

▮ **Figure 5.7** *Examples of transformation processes affecting a polished stone axe*

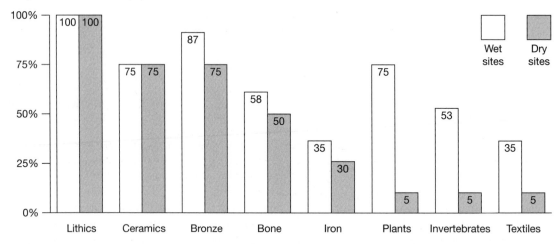

▮ **Figure 5.8** *Examples of differential survival of materials on wet and dry sites*

sites with exceptionally good organic preservation. In these cases remains are protected from the bacteria which normally consume organic material by climatic conditions or low oxygen levels (anaerobic conditions). While these sites remind us that absence of evidence is not evidence of absence, we cannot assume that they are typical sites from their period.

■ Arid sites, often in desert regions, can lead to remains drying out (desiccation) before they have a chance to decay. In the case of

Figure 5.9 *Neolithic spoon*

Finds of wooden artefacts from prehistory are rare except on waterlogged sites. Survivals such as this Neolithic spoon provide an insight into technology and domestic craft skills at a time when most tools would have been made from wood rather than stone.

bodies, this process creates natural mummies. Classic examples include Mesa Verde in the south-west USA where wooden and leather items were preserved.

- Waterlogged sites including lakes and peat bogs have been particularly important in European archaeology. Examples include Flag Fen, Tybrind Vig (▶ p. 240) and the wreck of the *Mary Rose*.
- Frozen sites have produced some incredible finds in recent years. Perhaps the most well known are the bodies of Ötzi the Ice Man from the Alps and the Pazyryk 'Ice Maiden'

from Siberia. Their skin has been so well preserved that tattoos and acupuncture marks can be studied.

- Rapidly buried sites can also reveal much that is normally lost. Examples include Pompeii volcanic ash, Copan (▶ p. 284) earthquake and Ozette in the USA where mudslides also preserved organic material.

Recovery factors

As if these processes were not enough, there is one final hurdle for archaeological remains to cross before they can be used to explain the past. Archaeologists themselves structure the archaeological record in the way they recover data. This results in some materials or sites being better represented than others. Sometimes this may simply be due to chance factors such as discovery or whether archaeologists can get access to particular sites. Decisions about how much of a site to excavate, which samples to take and what period to prioritise (◀ p. 25) all 'structure' what is recorded. Similarly, while pottery and metals finds are usually recorded, animal bone is sometimes not. The techniques

 KEY TASK

Group activity on transformation processes

Brainstorm ideas about what might be left for future generations of archaeologists if a disaster struck your class today. Consider what the effect of post-depositional forces would be. Present your findings in a visual format.

Figure 5.10 *Dry sieving at Barcombe Roman Villa*

Depending on the mesh size, sieving can dramatically increase the recovery of earth coloured pottery, coins, lithics and organic remains. However, even a large riddle like this is relatively slow to process soil and they are not used as widely in Britain as in the USA.

available for recovery are also important. Not all excavations will use flotation techniques to recover pollen, metal debris and small bone fragments or have the laboratory support to analyse them. Finally there is the quality of the diggers and those recording the finds. Inevitably there are some variations. Once away from the site, the care taken in analysis and storage may continue to transform the record.

The net result of all these processes is that archaeologists do not simply piece together recorded data to produce a picture of the past. Archaeological evidence cannot speak for itself and needs interpretation. Whatever was deposited was a fraction of the material used by people in the past. Only some elements of this will survive and only a sample of them will be recovered. By understanding transformation processes, archaeologists gain insights into what shaped the various samples. This enables them to identify which of the patterns in their data are

really the result of human behaviour and to begin interpreting them. For example, human skeletons are often found with the head turned to one side. At face value this might seem significant. However, forensic science has revealed that the slumping of corpses' heads is due to natural processes of decay rather than burial rites.

Partly because of these factors and the limitations of our analytical techniques, archaeological reports often contain minimal amounts of interpretation. Their writers follow a scientific tradition of reporting their findings and analysis of data but leaving interpretation to others.

Analysing spatial patterns

Having identified archaeological material and taken account of various transformation processes, archaeologists try to identify what human behaviour lies behind any patterns that they can detect. Initially this involves plotting vertical and

KEY STUDY

Seahenge

The Bronze Age timber ritual site dated by dendrochronology to 2050 BC illustrates both differential survival and recovery. Until erosion by the sea the timbers and land surface had been preserved, perhaps with associated deposits. By the time it was discovered in 1999 much damage had been done and English Heritage felt it was not worth rescuing. Under pressure from archaeologists they relented and began a fairly basic salvaging of the main timbers amid mud, tides and some angry pagans who saw excavation as sacrilege. Each of the 55 timbers was at least 30cms across which meant that the circle was almost closed and focused on a massive upturned oak stump. Little else was recovered and it provides a good contrast with recovery at Boxgrove (◀ p. 41). In 2007 the conserved timbers were partially reconstructed in a new museum.

• http://www. channel4.com/ history/timeteam/ archive/2000 seahenge.html

Figure 5.11
Seahenge

 KEY TERM

Assemblage

Sub-assemblage: a repeated pattern of arte-facts associated with one activity. Think of it as a toolkit.

Assemblage: the range of toolkits used by a particular community. The term is also used more widely for a cluster of finds in one place as in 'bone assemblage'.

horizontal relationships between finds, structures and sites. Patterning is taken to be evidence for behaviour. For example, a scatter of flint tools amidst the bones of an animal might indicate a butchery or kill site involving humans in scavenging or hunting. The toolkit used is termed a sub-assemblage.

MAKING SENSE OF THE DATA

The next stage of archaeological interpretation tends to vary according to the ideas about knowledge held by the archaeologist. In most cases they will use **analogies** or models to

KEY SITES

Danebury and Butser

The hillfort of Danebury had a huge storage capacity. This took two forms. Amongst 18,000 postholes were hundreds of four and six post structures and 5000 pits. Both forms are common on Iron Age sites but rarely in such amounts. Carbonised grain was recovered from the pits while seeds and snails were recovered from soil samples by flotation and wet sieving. Analysis and interpretation of these finds revealed much about the farming economy.

Microscopic examination of plant assemblages identified the main crops as einkorn and emmer wheat, but also found over 40 types of weed. This suggested that wheat was brought to Danebury unprocessed since weeds had come too. It also showed that wheat came from a wide area since many weeds are particular to certain soil types and locations. Assemblages also contained much chaff which is a by-product of processing (◀ p. 84).

Ethnographic analogy (▶ p. 125) suggested that the four-posters might have been raised granaries. To test this idea several full scale models were built at Butser Ancient Farm. This innovative open air laboratory had already been one of the first places to experiment with 'constructs' based on excavation floor-plans. Apart from the post holes another clue was provided by traces of wattle and daub panels which might have been the walls of these structures. The Butser model made sense as it kept grain out of reach of rats and allowed air to circulate to prevent damp. The walls, beams and roof itself are the product of experimentation based on knowledge of Iron Age carpentry and engineering. Building roundhouses has enabled the exploration of ideas about roof slope, light, efficiency of fires and whether a smoke hole is needed. It has also answered questions about how long a roundhouse might last and the amount of woodland needed to build and maintain it. The site also experiments with Iron Age crop growing and animal husbandry.

Figure 5.12 *Four-poster granaries*

KEY SITES *cont.*

Danebury and Butser

Many of the pits cut into the solid chalk were bell-shaped. They were a metre wide and up to 2 metres deep with a capacity of over 2 tonnes each. Initially it was thought that the pits had been sealed and covered with a basketwork lid so that their contents would last over the winter. How they did this without rotting was unclear. To investigate, the archaeobotanist Hillson conducted a micro-excavation in his lab of a sample of carbonized grain from a pit. As he removed and counted the seeds layer by layer he discovered that there were more germinated seeds at the bottom, next to the chalk.

Reynolds (1979) tested Hillson's findings by digging a 1.5m pit and filling it with grain. Instruments were inserted to measure humidity, temperature and gas exchange. The pit was sealed with an airtight layer of clay. The results were impressive. The grain around the edges, especially when it was in contact with the chalk, began to germinate and produced shoots. This gradually used up the available oxygen and produced carbon dioxide creating an anaerobic environment and germination ceased. While the seal remained intact the grain lay dormant and survived the winter in good condition. When the pit was opened most of the grain could be used except for that around the edges, which was full of mould and fungi. If the pit was to be used again this waste had to be disposed of. Reynolds suggested that it was burnt in the pit, which accounted for the carbonised grain at the bottom. It is likely that the grain was taken out in one go, perhaps for sowing or trading, rather than used as a larder for food.

The zones where grain would germinate and spoil are shown in Figure 5.14. Ladders and baskets or buckets would be needed to empty a pit of this depth. Excavation on contemporary sites suggested that pits were usually backfilled to preserve their narrow entrances from collapse and not present a hazard. It was easier to re-dig them than start a new pit. Curiously this seems to

Figure 5.13 View of Butser Ancient Farm

KEY SITES *cont.*

Danebury and Butser

have been rare at Danebury where many pits contained strange ritual deposits (▶ p. 172).

Compared with the huge number of pits at Danebury a magnetometer survey of the nearby hill fort of Woolbury contained very few. Cunliffe, the excavator, used this finding to support his idea that Danebury was a high status site with a redistributive (▶ p. 268) function.

- Cunliffe 1995
- http://www.butser.org.uk/

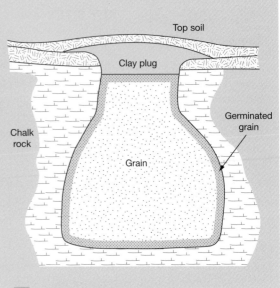

Figure 5.14 *Section of 'Beehive' grain storage pit*

 KEY TERM

Analogy

This involves using something with which we are familiar to interpret a new thing or phenomena. It is based on the idea that if two things are similar in one way then they may be similar in others. When we describe an artefact as a hand-axe or an enclosure as a hill fort, we are using analogies. Analogies range from interpretations of how something was made or worn to what the social systems or patterns of religious belief in the past might have been. Analogies cannot prove anything about the past but they can tell us much about what was possible. They can widen our horizons, generate new lines of enquiry and provide theories to be tested against further evidence to see how robust they are.

formulate theories about what the data can provide evidence of.

Our society does not include all the rich variety of human activity and culture that has existed. To rely on it as the sole source of analogies would be limiting and lead to Eurocentric and anachronistic interpretations. Increasingly, archaeologists have drawn on three major sources of analogies.

Historical accounts or documents of past societies

- Classical accounts of the world such as the descriptions of Ancient Egypt by Herodotus
- Literary and artistic sources such as the poetry of early medieval Europe
- Travelogues written by the first western people to visit areas largely unaffected by European culture. For example, reports by Catholic missionaries on the peoples of Mesoamerica in the sixteenth century. These accounts are often called ethno-histories

KEY STUDY

San Jose Mogote

Flannery and Marcus used several key interpretive methods in their exploration of beliefs from the Zapotec civilisation that flourished in the Oaxaca Valley of southern Mexico between 200 BC and AD 700. There was evidence of great continuity in local populations from Zapotec times until the Spanish conquest in the sixteenth century. The archaeologists were able to use what they termed a direct historical approach (DHA). Spanish priests had documented local 'pagan' customs that were used to form a hypothesis for testing by excavation. The archaeologists predicted that anything with breath (pee) would be sacred and that ancestors would be worshipped. The burning of copal incense and sacrifices of blood, jade, living things and exotic goods would be made to petition elemental forces such as earthquake and lightning. They expected to find evidence of priests who lived in two-roomed houses with sacrifices made in the inner room and who used drugs to reach ecstatic states.

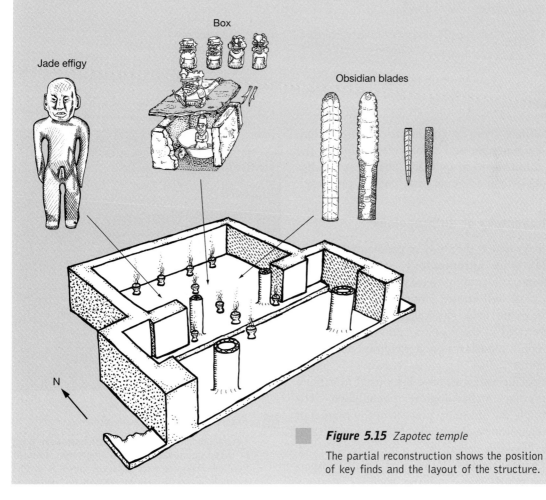

Figure 5.15 *Zapotec temple*

The partial reconstruction shows the position of key finds and the layout of the structure.

KEY STUDY *cont.*

San Jose Mogote

Excavations at San Jose Mogote revealed symbolism in the architecture and repeated patterns of structured deposition. There were a series of two-roomed buildings with the same east–west axis superimposed upon them. The inner rooms had been kept scrupulously clean although there were traces of repeated burning in them. Tiny pieces of debris in the corners were frequently from obsidian blades or stingray stings, used for bloodletting until historic times. Buried in the floor were tiny statues, jade beads and the bones of quail, a bird believed to be pure. The Spanish hadn't recorded this aspect of religion. Underfloor offerings also included effigies of the lightning clouds, hail and wind. Research amongst local people revealed that they called the statuettes 'little people of the clouds'. Ancestors were also known as cloud people. Through a mixture of historical records, analyses of excavated architecture and artefacts, and ethnography, Flannery and Marcus were able to reach conclusions about Zapotec reverence for ancestors and natural forces and the types of ritual practice involved in worship.

- http://www.angelfire.com/ca/humanorigins/religion.html#zapotec
- Marcus and Flannery 1994

■ Where there is continuity in population, environment and some cultural forms, the direct historical approach (**DHA**) uses studies of, or oral accounts from, current peoples.

Ethnography or anthropology

Ethnography is the study of people in the world today while **anthropology** compares human cultures to identify general principles. Amongst the most well known ethnographic studies are those of the Hadza and Kalahari bushmen which were used in the 1960s to provide social and economic models for pre-agricultural humans as 'man the hunter'.

Specific analogies have been used to explore particular archaeological phenomena. For example the mortuary practice of the Merina of Madagascar has been used to provide insights into Neolithic beliefs (▶ p. 158).

General models drawing on broad comparisons across many cultures such as Service's

Figure 5.16 *Romanian six-poster*

Similar ideas to those at Butser have been used in other countries although their own cultural heritage produces very different looks as in this example of an historic building in Romania.

KEY TERM

Signature

To help identify features and their functions, archaeologists use mental templates for common activities in the period they are studying. There will be certain recurring patterns at sites, which have already been studied, which are associated with particular activities. For example, fires or hearths usually colour the earth reddish-orange while smelting or metalworking leaves slag and other waste products.

Archaeologists will 'read' these signatures when they come across similar finds or features on new sites.

band-tribe-chiefdom model of social evolution (▶ p. 293) have been used to categorise and interpret past societies.

However, most ethnographic studies come from the twentieth century when most of the world was already influenced in some way by European civilisations. There is often also a huge gulf in time and place between ancient peoples and the modern groups who are the source of analogies. While taking us beyond western models, ethnography can also limit our imagination. It is highly likely that ideas, social organisations and ways of doing things existed in the past that are not present in any current societies. The greater share of variation in human societies has already been lost. Archaeologists also have to resist the temptation to select the single examples that make most sense to them.

Actualistic studies

These studies involve the use of materials similar to those from the past in order to tie observed behaviour to physical remains.

Ethnoarchaeology

This involves studying how contemporary communities use material culture from an archaeological perspective. By correlating modern activities with physical remains we may start to understand what behaviour is reflected in which data. Studying people who manufacture stone tools and the debris they leave can help us identify the signatures left by different processes. Examining the distribution of remains within modern hunting camps may help identify the functions of particular areas (▶ p. 218). **Ethnoarchaeology** may also help reveal 'invisible' influences such as gender or ethnicity.

Experimental Archaeology

This involves forming a hypothesis about a process, artefact or ecofact and testing it using similar materials to those found on archaeological sites.

- Replica artefacts can be used to test the potential functions of real examples. For example, testing flint axes to see how effectively they can chop down trees and then comparing the wear patterns with Neolithic examples. Experimental studies of lithics have demonstrated that the wear and damage on the surface of tools varies depending on the material being processed (e.g. bone or meat) and the type of action being carried out (e.g. cutting or scraping). Identifying each 'microwear' signature enables the functions of tools from the past to be identified with greater accuracy than traditional typologies and ethnographic analogies. A second approach is to use replication to understand the technology itself. Knapping experiments are the best example of this. The distribution of debitage (waste material) can be compared with archaeological examples to understand the knapping sequence and whether the knapper was standing, seated and left- or right-handed.

Figure 5.17 *Experimentation with flint blades*

Replicating lithics and using them to test their efficacy on a variety of tasks has a long tradition in archaeology. Here flint blades are being used to process a deer. This can help us understand how effective the tools are. The blades can also be examined afterwards for distinctive polishes caused by cutting meat and bone. These can provide signatures to help interpret archaeological examples.

- Reconstructions use data as the basis for models that can be tested. The best known in Britain is probably the constructs of Iron Age roundhouses at Butser Ancient Farm. Where the remains of such an experimental village are examined there might be an overlap with ethnoarchaeology. However, the people in the experiment would clearly be very different from those in archaeological examples. While some recreations are primarily for presenting ideas (▶ p. 374) others are used to test assumptions. The Kon Tiki raft which sailed across the Atlantic to test the possibility that the Ancient Egyptians could have reached Mexico falls into this category. Recreated boats have frequently broadened our understanding of seafaring in the past. The most recent example is the half size replica of the Sutton Hoo ship.

- The final category is taphonomic studies. This involves transformation processes to understand patterns on real sites and their impact on archaeological material. Experiments in Africa have explored the effect of scavengers on the distribution of bones from a carcass or the effects of streams on artefact movement. The bones or artefacts can then be subjected to microwear analysis to identify signatures for particular kinds of processes such as flash flooding or trampling. One example was a square metre which was created to simulate a portion of the palaeolithic site of Klithi in northern Greece. The simulated site was positioned along the path

Figure 5.18 *Replica Viking ships from Roskilde*

Well preserved Viking vessels have enabled the construction of replicas. The Viking museum at Roskilde has built replicas of several different types which are enormously valuable in helping us understand the skills and potential of past seafarers. The building process provided insights into the skills required of specialised shipwrights and the materials they would have needed. The ships themselves help us understand seamanship, speed, range, loads, handling and function. Taken together they help address the question of why the Vikings were so successful as a traders and raiders in the early medieval period.

leading to the site so that it was regularly walked upon by diggers going to and from the site. It was also 'trampled' by the regular passing of goat herds along the valley. After a period of time the simulated site was excavated and the position of the artefacts recorded. Comparisons can then be made between the original position of the artefacts and where they may have moved to giving information about taphonomic changes that may take place on a site. With all experiments replication is a key element in determining their validity. Where several researchers get similar results from similar experiments those results are more widely accepted. The production of lithics falls into this category.

• Schick and Toth 1993

Figure 5.19 *Drilled artefacts*

During the Neolithic stone artefacts were polished and drilled in order to take a haft. Replication can tell us something of the effort that went into this and perhaps by extension, the value. Such artefacts were often made from exotic rocks, which suggests they may have been prestige items. We can also learn of the processes required to manufacture them.

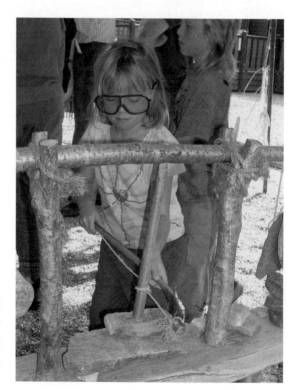

Figure 5.20 *Replication as education*

Reconstructions of tools such as bow drills enable researchers to test their effectiveness on a range of materials and to identify signatures for their use. Replica tools are also widely used at archaeological attractions to enable the public to connect with the past by appreciating the skills of past people.

WHY DO ARCHAEOLOGISTS OFFER DIFFERENT INTERPRETATIONS OF THE PAST?

Since archaeologists disagree about how or whether past behaviour can be reconstructed and because the archaeological record is so flawed, it is hardly surprising that their accounts differ. Data is constantly being reinterpreted as archaeologists ask new questions, use new techniques or find new sources of analogs. They also borrow models and methods from other disciplines. In the 1970s geography provided settlement archaeology with site catchment analysis and central place theory. Since the 1990s developments in biochemistry have provided powerful new tools for interpreting past health, diets and population movements. The continued debate amongst archaeologists is a sign of the subject's vitality.

Figure 5.21 *Accidental experimentation*

When one of the houses at West Stow (▶ p. 319) was burnt by arsonists the archaeologists were naturally disappointed. However, it did provide them with evidence about what would survive from burnt buildings from the past and the signature they would leave in the ground.

Part Two
Studying Themes in Archaeology

The content of archaeology courses can be arranged in many ways. All include methods to some extent. Beyond this they are selective in their areas of archaeological knowledge. Some focus on particular parts of the world, following continuity and change over time, e.g. 'British prehistory'. Others may focus on change but take a whole world perspective, with topics such as 'human origins' or 'the spread of farming'. Some concentrate on particular cultures in more limited periods such as 'the classical world' while others, including A Level, are organised around themes. Whichever course you take you will need to use case studies. In fact the same case studies might be relevant to all these courses (▶ p. 381). For example, the Iron Age settlement at Hengistbury Head could be used to study:

- the emergence of elites and trade in Iron Age Britain
- the development of towns and commercial trade
- the influence of the Roman Empire
- settlement function, exchange and manufacturing themes.

We have chosen to organise this section thematically partly because it mirrors the A Level syllabus and partly because an understanding of the themes is more transferable. A study of Roman temples may not be immediately useful to a student studying Neolithic Britain and vice versa, but an introduction to concepts of religion and ritual will be useful to both. We have included content, but its function is to illustrate. It may well be in just the right size chunks to put into essays but it is there to provide examples of archaeological ideas and debates.

Religion and Ritual

YOUR GOALS

You need to understand

- ◼ the key concepts drawn from sociology and anthropology that archaeologists use to help define and explain past beliefs and rituals
- ◼ the techniques and sources used to interpret evidence of religious belief and practices
- ◼ case studies from your chosen period or area of study, which illustrate religion and ritual

For periods where there are written sources such as Ancient Greece or medieval Europe, archaeologists have tended to use texts as the means to interpret and understand past belief systems. For cultures where there are no written sources, many archaeologists have held the view that uncovering the nature of past religious belief from material remains is beyond their ability. In the 1950s Hawkes argued that there was a hierarchy of inferences which archaeologists could make from their sources. Using material remains they could say a great deal about technology and economics, much less about society and very little about belief. How can you understand thoughts from bones, sherds and postholes? His argument has become known as Hawkes' Ladder of Inference.

Since the 1960s there has been an explosion of interest amongst the general public in prehistoric religions. The reluctance of many archaeologists to discuss religion left a gap that was filled by a range of other explanations, which fed on public interest in ancient monuments. Often these involved projecting current concerns onto evidence from the past. The most famous was Von Däniken's depiction of God as an astronaut. This view attributed great monuments from the past to aliens. For example, the Nazca lines in Peru became alien landing strips. More recently a New Age version of prehistory has linked together sites from various periods as evidence of a universal cult of an earth goddess. Partly in response, archaeologists have borrowed a battery of analytical techniques and concepts from other disciplines including ethnography, sociology and critical theory to explore religion and ritual. It is now a core element of study for many periods. A particularly influential idea has been the fact that for many cultures religion cannot neatly be separated from social

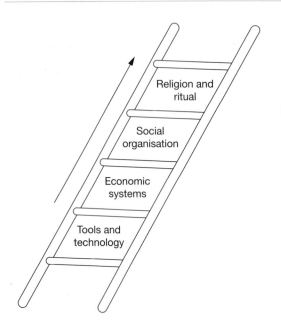

Figure 6.1 Hawkes' Ladder of Inference (after Hawkes 1954). The higher one goes up the ladder the harder it is to make inferences on the basis of archaeological evidence

Figure 6.2 Minoan snake goddess or Potnia Theron (Mistress of the Beasts)

This idol found in a hidden cist at Knossos with other cult objects may represent a female deity. Some have claimed she is evidence of a mother goddess religion. (c. 1600 BC).

organisation or even economics. It influences the way people behave and therefore leaves traces in their material culture.

The analytical power of computers is increasingly enlisted in searching for patterns, particularly in the disposal of artefacts and the siting of monuments. Use of these techniques has in turn led to criticism of written sources for what they omit and because they are often ambivalent. Archaeology may have much to offer the study of religion in the classical period after all.

In this chapter we have tried to explain some of the more unfamiliar concepts which archaeologists have adopted. We have also provided examples of the methods and insights used by archaeologists to tease out clues about belief and ritual from material remains. To illustrate the contribution of archaeology in the past we have included overviews of religion and ritual in later European prehistory, Ancient Egypt and the Roman Empire.

WHAT IS RELIGION?

You are most likely to be familiar with modern world religions. These are atypical. Christianity, Judaism and Islam, for example, are all **monotheistic** (one god) religions which provide codes of conduct for life, have permanent religious institutions and offer life after death to believers. There have been religions that have differed on each of these points. At the other end of the scale from the **states** (▶ p. 295), which have promoted world religions, are hunter-gatherer societies. They tend to see themselves as part of, rather than in control of, nature and their religion may be simply one part of their daily life rather than something done on special occasions. There is far more variety in those small-scale societies which survive today than in world religions. They may provide better insights into the wealth of lost belief systems. After all humans have spent most of history hunting and foraging for food rather than growing it.

Giddens (1989) provides a useful, broad definition of religion as: 'a set of symbols, invoking feelings of reverence or awe . . . linked to rituals or ceremonials practised by a community of believers'. These symbols may be of gods and goddesses, ancestral or nature spirits, or impersonal powers. Rituals can consist of prayers, songs, dances, feasting, drug taking, offerings and sacrifices. People often use them to try to influence supernatural powers and beings to their advantage and to deal with problems that cannot be solved through the application of technology. However, there are some religions without objects of worship. In Confucianism and Taoism, for example, the individual attempts to attain a higher level through correctly following specified principles.

WHAT IS THE FUNCTION OF RELIGION?

Archaeologists are more interested in how religion affected the people practising it rather than whether a particular religion accomplished what its believers hoped. All religions cater to basic human social and psychological needs. Some of these, such as the need to explain what happens when people die, may be universal if we are correct in our interpretation of the archaeological evidence for burial and associated activities from the last 40,000 years. Common functions include:

- Explaining the unknown in order to provide meaning and reduce anxiety. A belief in a

divine force can provide hope and comfort in difficult times. The death of a family member may be easier to cope with if they are believed to exist beyond death. Ritual at a time of crisis may give people the confidence to cope with problems, for example, praying before a battle.

Figure 6.3 *Drawing of the Wakah Kan or 'Raised up sky' from Palenque*

The Mayan 'world tree' linked the underworld, the realm of the living and the sky. The king would dress in the image of the Wakah Kan to emphasise the special relationship between the ruler and the spirit world. He provided a conduit for supernatural powers. Religious belief serves to sustain the authority of the king. Here King Pacal is shown falling into the jaws of the earth monster. Underneath is an altar with a bowl of blood sacrifices burning and thus opening up a portal into another world. The smoking axe in Pacal's forehead is a mark of his divinity and he wears a jade net skirt which reveals that at his moment of death he had become the 'Maize God'. Above him the cross branch of the tree represents the double-headed 'vision serpent' of life and death. This sceptre of power is depicted on altars being handed on from one ruler to the next rather like a relay baton. Von Däniken considered the Wakah Kan was evidence of space travel with the top as the front of the alien craft. www.legendarytimnes.com/

KEY STUDY

The Temple of the Inscriptions at Palenque

The stone temple-pyramids at Palenque, in north central Mexico advertised the special magical authority of the reigning king. The Temple of the Inscriptions has stucco figures on the outside showing the child king Chan-Bahlum (Snake-Jaguar) as a child inheriting power from his ancestors, including Pacal whose body lies in the tomb below. The child king has a prominent umbilical cord that links him to his

Figure 6.4 *The temple-pyramids at Palenque*

famous ancestors and echoes another feature of the temple known as the 'psychoduct'. Other carvings show captives who were sacrificed when the new heir was presented to the people or later when the building itself was dedicated. The costumes worn by Pacal and his relatives are full of symbolic elements such as the net skirt that shows that Pacal personifies the 'First Father'.

Inside, a passage covered with inscriptions and a staircase lead down to the burial chamber of Pacal. The floor of the passage contains the remains of five sacrificial victims. The chamber is almost filled by a huge stone sarcophagus, decorated with portraits of Pacal's parents and ancestors. The body is dressed in exotic costume items, many of jade, which is associated with water and life, and maize, which represents rebirth. The central scene on the lid of the sarcophagus shows a similar scene to the Wakah Kan. Snaking into his coffin and extending all the way up the side of the staircase to the temple above is the 'psychoduct', a tube which allowed the king's spirit to travel abroad at night in the form of his 'spirit familiar', usually a jaguar. It also allowed the priests to communicate with Pacal now that he had joined the ancestors.

• http://www.virtualpalenque.com/

■ Establishing rules and models of behaviour. Most religions put divine power behind definitions of what is right and wrong. They may tell believers the 'right' way to live. Religion can be used to enforce obedience to a ruler (e.g. medieval kings) or even to justify rebellion.

■ The maintenance of social solidarity was seen as the primary function of religion by the sociologist Durkheim. His study of **totemism** (▶ p. 140) amongst Australian aboriginal societies suggested that what was being worshipped represented society and its values. By holding collective ceremonies

Figure 6.5 *Vietnam Memorial*

This stunning group of bronze statues are part of a massive complex of funerary monuments in the heart of Washington DC. State memorials to the fallen promote and legitimise values and help create identity as well as providing a focus for remembrance rituals.

people reinforce their sense of togetherness and social cohesion.

- Transmitting memory, especially in non-literate societies, by the learning of oral traditions and through repetitive rituals. The classic example of this is the telling of creation myths. Myths are explanatory narratives that rationalise religious beliefs and practices. Myths invariably are full of accounts of the doings of various supernatural beings and hence serve to reinforce belief in them. The building of religious monuments can literally set collective memories in stone.

Detecting evidence of past beliefs and practices

A standing joke amongst archaeologists has been the idea that anything that can't immediately be

explained must be ritual. While there has been some overenthusiasm in what is still a relatively new area of archaeological interpretation, most studies are based on far more than an odd shaped building or one figurine. Egyptologists have the advantage of the Book of the Dead to draw on but for other cultures different approaches are required. Analogies drawn from ethnography have been particularly useful; not for direct parallels so much as to demonstrate a range of possible options and influences and to prevent simplistic interpretation. It may appear common sense that a burial with many goods was that of a wealthy person, yet ethnography has provided examples where this is not the case. Studies have often focused on repeated patterns. These include symbols that recur in similar places or on specific types of artefact; non-random patterns of deposition of particular artefacts or animal remains and the distribution of deposits and monuments across the landscape. The treatment of boundaries in the past has also been a focus of many studies.

WHAT KINDS OF RELIGION WERE THERE?

Most known religions include a belief in supernatural beings and forces through whom appeals for aid may be directed. For convenience we may divide these into three categories: deities, ancestral spirits and nature spirits. While some societies have only believed in one of these categories, it has been common for belief in several or all of them to co-exist, for example belief in evil spirits in medieval Europe.

Major deities

Gods and goddesses are great and remote beings who are usually seen as controlling the universe. **Monotheistic** religions have one god as can be seen in later Roman Britain at Lullingstone or in Egypt at Achetaten where Akhenaten and Nefertiti worshipped the 'Aten'. In **polytheistic** religions a panoply of deities are recognised. Often each has charge of a particular part of the universe. Hinduism, the oldest major world religion, is around 6,000 years old and is polytheistic. Its contemporaries included the gods of Ancient Greece: Zeus was the lord of the sky, Poseidon was the ruler of the sea and Hades was the lord of the underworld and ruler of the dead. In addition to these three brothers there were many other deities of both sexes. Each embodied characteristics seen as typical of male and female roles; each was concerned with specific aspects of life and the workings of the world, or indeed universe. Pantheons or collections of gods and goddesses, such as those of the Greeks, were also common in non-western states such as Egypt or the Maya. Specific deities are identified from repeated images on buildings or artefacts ranging from mosaics to statues.

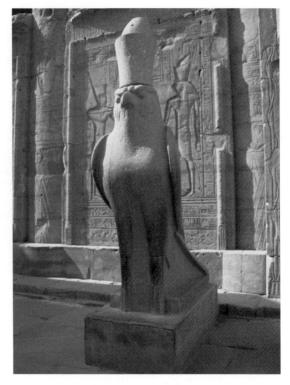

Figure 6.6 *Pharaoh as Horus at Edfu*

Kings were the earthly embodiment of the god Horus. Horus, the son of Isis, was a protector god who destroyed evil. When a king died he became the god Osiris and the new king became Horus. As Horus he could mediate between men and gods. Note the double crown worn by the falcon is the same as the falcon-man in the background. All pharaohs had a 'Horus name' as part of their title, in order to identify them with the deity.

Belief in gods, goddesses or both, often seemed to parallel what we know of the gender relationships between men and women in everyday life. In societies where women have less power than men, the nature of 'god' is defined in masculine terms. This is commonest in societies where the economy is based upon herding animals or on intensive agriculture, which would have been largely male activities. In such societies men may often have been seen as rather distant authority figures to their children. Goddesses, on the other hand, appear more often in societies where women make the major contribution to the economy, enjoy some measure of equality with men and in which men are more involved in the lives of their children. Such societies often depend on horticulture or specialised craft production, which is done by women. Evidence from Catal Huyuk (Turkey) and Karanovo (Bulgaria) suggests that pioneer agricultural societies venerated female roles. Gimbutas (1991) took up this theme in her book *The Civilisation of the Goddess* and argued that there was a kind of monotheism in the early prehistory with the 'cult of the mother goddess'. She claimed that world religions developed to legitimise the emergence of patriarchal, warlike societies in the Bronze Age. The masculine god that replaced various goddess cults amongst the Hebrews during the late second millennium BC may have helped establish gender relationships in which women have traditionally been expected to submit to the rule of men. This in turn shaped Jewish, Christian and Islamic society.

Ancestral spirits

A belief in ancestral spirits has its origins in the widespread idea that human beings are made up of two parts: the body and some kind of vital spirit, which in Mesoamerica for example resides in the blood. For example the Maya Indians have always maintained that each person had a 'spirit-companion' that could leave the body and move around during sleep. The 'spirit-companion' was envisaged as an animal. One inscription tells us that 'the watery jaguar is the "way" of the Lord (King) of Seibal'. Given such a concept, it is only a small step to believe that the spirit could be freed by death from the body and have a continued existence. It has something in common with recent accounts of 'out of body experiences'.

Where people do believe in ancestral spirits, they are frequently seen as retaining an active interest and even membership in society. For

KEY TERM

Propitiation

Making offerings or sacrifices to a spirit or deity. Giving something in advance to please the spirits or gods, usually to guarantee success such as when setting out on a new venture or ward off ill fortune of a personal or wider nature. It may involve an offering or sacrifice perhaps in a 'liminal place'. The widespread burials of human and animal remains in grain pits, as at Danebury, the bog bodies of northern Europe and Iron Age deposits in the Thames are examples interpreted as such offerings. Egyptian temple foundation deposits serve a similar function as do Roman votive altars.

example the 'ghost ancestors' of the Wape might either provide or withhold meat from their living descendants. Like living persons, ancestral spirits may be well or badly disposed towards the living, but they are often capricious and unpredictable, hence the need to appease them with offerings.

Whatever their involvement in particular past societies, belief in ancestral spirits provided a strong sense of continuity. These beliefs seem to have been particularly strong amongst early farming communities. Ancestors may have linked past, present and future generations and ownership of particular land.

Animism

One of the most common sets of beliefs about the supernatural world is usually referred to as animism. This centres on the idea that the living share the physical and spiritual world with all sorts of spirits. Animals, plants and people may all have their own individual spirits, as may springs, mountains, or other natural features.

Figure 6.7 *Sea eagle talons from the Neolithic stalled cairn at Isbister*

Totemism has been used as an explanation for such finds in prehistoric tombs. Hedges noted that Isbister Tomb on Orkney contained the remains of at least eight massive sea eagles while nearby Cuween held the remains of 24 dogs and another tomb contained deer bones. Local tribal groups may have identified with particular animals. However, these may have been food or in some cases scavengers which entered the tombs independently or as part of the excarnation process. The tomb contained the jumbled remains of 342 people including rows of skulls on a shelf. Joints of lamb had been left in the tomb while outside was a pile of deliberately smashed pots and other remains of feasting.

People who believe in animism are inclined to see themselves as being part of nature rather than superior to it. This includes most hunter-gatherers, as well as those food-producing people who see little difference between a human life and that of any growing plant. Gods and goddesses may have created the world and perhaps provided the main physical fabric of that world but it is spirits to whom one turns for the ordinary needs of daily life and whom the ordinary hunter may meet during the hunt or while out roaming the woods. Many Native Americans subscribed to this view of the world and would pray to the spirits of their 'brothers and sisters' the animals for success in the hunt. They asked animals to give up their lives for the good of people and apologised to them when they were actually caught. The Hollywood version of this can be seen at the start of the film *Last of the Mohicans*.

Totemism is a label sometimes attached to animistic forms of religion. Here animals or plants with special powers may be worshipped or there may be complex rules about their treatment.

Animatism

Some societies believe in a supernatural power that exists independently of deities and spirits. The people of Melanesia, for example, believe that 'mana' exists as a force inherent in all objects. In itself it is not physical but it can be revealed through its physical effects. When a warrior experiences success in battle this will not be as a result of his own strength but directly attributable to the 'mana' carried with him in the form of an amulet that hangs around his neck. In much the same way, in farming societies an individual may know a great deal about the right way to treat plants, about soil conditions and the correct time for sowing and harvesting, but still be dependent on 'mana' for the success of his crop. He may build a simple altar for this power at the end of the field, as often seen in the rice fields of Bali. If the crop is good, it is a sign that the farmer has in some way acquired the necessary 'mana'. The possession of objects containing such power may provide the owner with confidence. For example, in going into battle. Confidence might then lead to fearlessness and victory. This would then 'prove' the power of the 'mana'. The Sioux followers of the Ghost Dance cult provide a less successful example. They believed their magical shirts would stop bullets in their final conflict with the US army in the late nineteenth century.

Belief in magic has some similarities with animatism. Magic involves individuals influencing events through potions or chanting. It can also involve divination, astrology and curses such as those found on the walls of Pompeii. The wearing of charms to bring good fortune and ward off evil combines elements of magic and animatism. It has survived in a watered down way in societies which have been Christian for many centuries.

• Havilland 1994

RELIGIOUS CHANGE

Comparative studies over long periods often reveal changes in the evidence for religion. This can be useful as the contrasts often suggest much

Figure 6.8 *Scene from Agia Triada sarcophagus*

This painting on plaster covering a stone sarcophagus includes many aspects of Minoan funerary ritual. On the reverse a bull is strapped down for sacrifice by priestesses. Here a priestess pours liquid into a krater on an altar. This may be sacrificial blood or water or wine for lustration (bathing) of the altar or for purification rites. Another woman brings further liquid while a man plays a lyre. Birds wait for the gods, perhaps called by the lyre. To the right one of several men carries offerings of animals to a male priest.

about the nature of beliefs. The overlap between paganism and Christianity revealed in the changing grave goods and orientation of bodies from Anglo-Saxon cemeteries such as Lechlade (▶ p. 317) are well known. Many Christian churches were deliberately built on earlier pagan sites, most spectacularly at Knowlton and La Hougue Bie on Jersey. The continuing power and importance of earlier beliefs can also be seen in the reuse of some religious sites. The nature of the religious changes of the reformation can be seen in the study of structural and decorative changes in churches. This is most evident when medieval wall-paintings are revealed under Puritan whitewash as at Baunton.

RITUAL ACTIVITY

Much of the value of religion comes from religious activities. These can range from daily rituals to great cyclical events from Easter to the Egyptian festivals of Opet or Sed. Participation in ceremonies enables people to relate to higher forces; it is religion in action. Ritual involves repeated performance of religious activities, usually at a particular place. It can reinforce the social bonds of a group and reduce tensions. Participants can feel a wave of reassurance, security and even ecstasy and a sense of closeness. Although the rituals and practices vary considerably, even those rites that seem to us the most bizarrely exotic can be shown to serve the same basic social and psychological function. Anthropologists have classified several different types of ritual, a major division being between 'rites of passage' and 'rites of intensification'.

Rites of passage

Rites of passage are ceremonies to mark crucial stages in the life cycle of the individual. These might include birth, puberty, marriage, parenthood, and advancement to a higher class, occupational specialisation and death. Anthropological analysis of ceremonies, which help individuals

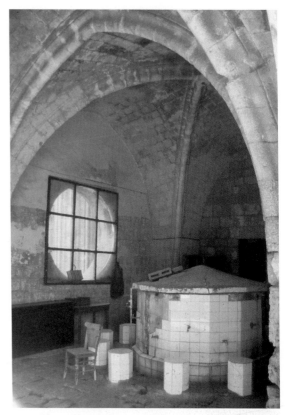

Figure 6.9 *Washing facilities at a mosque in Cyprus*

In many religions entry into religious sites is marked by ritual. This may mark a transition from the 'profane' everyday world to a 'sacred' enclosure or building. Ritual washing with its connotations of purity is a good example of this. This kind of categorisation into pure/impure and sacred/profane can sometimes be discerned through archaeology, for instance where special deposits are placed at thresholds or entrances.

through these potential crisis points, has often identified three stages: *separation*, *transition*, and *incorporation*. The individual would first be ritually removed from the society as a whole, then isolated for a **liminal** period and finally returned to society with a new status.

Van Gennep (1909) observed this pattern amongst Australian aborigines. When boys were to be initiated into manhood, elders led them to secret locations in the bush. Women cried and pretended to resist their removal while the boys pretended to be dead. In the bush the boys were taught the culture and stories of the tribe but also went through ceremonies including minor operations, such as circumcision, to teach them to bear pain. During this period the boys were 'dead' to the tribe. On returning they were welcomed with ceremonies, as though they had returned from the dead. The ceremony highlighted their new status as adults and reminded existing adults to act towards them in the appropriate ways. They skipped the ill-defined status of 'teenager', which causes problems in western society.

Similarly, female initiation rites prepared Mende girls in West Africa for womanhood. When they began to menstruate, they were removed from society to spend weeks, or even months in seclusion, usually on the grounds that their menstrual blood would 'contaminate' that with which it came into contact. There, they were trained by experienced women and

Figure 6.10 *Sacrificed object*

'Ritually killed' objects which are destroyed before being deposited 'out of this world' may be indicators of intensification rites. This elaborate shield boss was from a huge sacrifice of military equipment in a bog in Jutland.

changed their appearance, setting aside the remnants of their childhood and undergoing surgery to remove their clitoris. They returned from their initiation as fully adult women in control of their sexuality and ready for marriage and childbearing. Archaeological studies of rites of passage have largely focused on gender construction and the transition of the dead from the world of the living.

Rites of intensification

Rites of intensification mark crises in the life of the group. Whatever the precise nature of the crisis (war, disease, etc) mass ceremonies are performed to mitigate the danger. Because these rites are carried out at a group rather than an individual level, the effect is to unite people in a common effort in such a way that fear or confusion are replaced by optimism and collective action and the natural balance is restored. The ancient Greeks routinely offered sacrifices before attempting hazardous undertakings, most famously the war against Troy. In regions where the seasons differ enough to force changes in human behaviour patterns, annual ceremonies develop. (Christmas replaced midwinter festivities dating back at least to the Iron Age.) Participation in such ceremonies cultivates the habit of reliance on supernatural forces through ritual activity, which can be activated in other stressful circumstances.

Funerary ceremonies

Funerals blur this neat distinction. The death of an individual can also be a crisis for an entire group, particularly if the group is small. The survivors must readjust, take up new roles and work out how to behave towards one another. They also need to reconcile themselves to the loss of someone to whom they were emotionally tied. This can take extreme forms. One of the **funerary rites** of the Melanesians was ritual cannibalism. This was felt to be a supreme act of reverence,

Figure 6.11 *Excarnation*

Excarnation or 'sky burial' appears to have been a common mortuary rite in later prehistory. This example recreates the practice at the 'Tomb of the Sea Eagles' at Isibister (◀ p. 140). The removal of flesh may have enabled the spirit to leave the body. The symbolism of birds carrying remains into the sky may have also been significant.

love and devotion. Funerals offer the opportunity for outpourings of emotions without disrupting society. They can also emphasise that the values of the group outlive the individual. Burials are just one part of the funerary process but they are the most archaeologically visible. This does not mean they were the most important part.

Mortuary rituals

The treatment of the dead can overlap with funerals. The dead may be prepared in advance for funerals and their remains may need further ritual treatment afterwards. Much has been learnt from studying the treatment of the corpse, particularly its final disposal. This can take many forms:

Inhumation (burial) is a deliberate setting of the dead outside the world of the living. Where this occurs it may indicate attitudes to the dead. Christian cemeteries are placed apart from the living while some Upper Palaeolithic burials, as at Franchthi Cave, were kept close to the living. The orientation and position of the body – flexed, extended or contorted – may be significant. For example, foetal positions may indicate some belief in rebirth.

Cremation is more complex. Funeral pyres can leave several kilos of charred bones. The fire may destroy the body and release the spirit but these remains may have to be dealt with in a secondary ceremony. This can involve burial.

Excarnation is also likely to be part of a process. It involves exposing the body for scavengers and the decay process to clean the flesh from the bones. For example Parsees practise 'Sky burial' today. Alternatively knife marks on bones may suggest that flesh was removed to free the soul to journey to the ancestors or the underworld. Cleaned bones may be used in other rites or stored in an ossuary.

Mummification is often an elaborate process, which can involve removing some parts of the body. It may be believed that the body can be used by the person's spirit in another world or the future. The use of certain types of coffin or funeral vaults that may slow down natural decay processes may reflect similar beliefs.

Sometimes the dead are hard to find. This may be because they are totally consumed. The Yanomamö grind the cremated remains of their dead to a powder that they then drink. The dead thus remain in the living. There are also ethnographic examples of bones of ancestors being worn by their descendants.

Funerary monuments and grave goods

Both of these categories may tell us more about the mourners and society than they do about their religious beliefs (▶ Chapter 9). However, elaborately decorated tombs such as those in the Valley of the Kings or the reliefs carved on Maya tombs may provide detailed information about both beliefs and rituals.

Gravestones provide many insights for a variety of cultures, not least about the setting aside of respected areas for the dead. Goods buried with the body or which were consumed

Figure 6.12 *Late Minoan sarcophagus*

These ceramic vessels, large enough to hold a crouched body (or two), were used to bury wealthy Cretans. They are called 'bathtub style' and even include a plughole.

Figure 6.13 *Cremation in Bronze Age funerary urn*

Unlike modern crematoria, funeral pyres could not usually reach sufficient temperatures to reduce bodies to ash. The larger chunks of bone along with charred grave goods were often collected and placed in vessels for burial. Sufficient bone may survive to allow identification and even DNA testing.

Figure 6.14 *A pot being excavated from grave 5 at Empingham (◀ p. 50). Were grave goods such as these the possessions of the dead, offerings to them or the gods, or food for their journey to an afterworld?*

in a funeral pyre are suggestive of an afterlife but this is not necessarily the case. Goods may be placed in the grave by mourners as tokens of affection or because they belonged to the deceased and are considered unlucky or taboo. Tools used to prepare the dead, such as razors or tweezers, may fall into this category. There may also be important offerings of food or organic materials that have not survived. The absence of grave goods doesn't mean that there was no belief in an afterlife. It may suggest a belief in an afterlife where people are equal and provided for or it may reflect an idealised picture of society that masks differences in wealth.

IDENTIFYING RITUAL AND RITUAL SITES

Most essays on this topic rarely stray from Renfrew and Bahn's list of indicators. In most cases their key points – focus of attention, boundary zones, symbols or images of the deity, and participation and offerings – can be ticked off.

Tombs and temples are obvious places but one can also apply the list to monuments such as shrines and ghats.

However, there may be exceptions. Their indicators work best for communal rather than individual ritual acts, many of which leave no traces. They also rely on there being a distinct area set aside. Even if it is in a dwelling special zones can be identified. For example, the altar or 'lararium' mounted on the wall of Roman houses. However, there are societies today where there is no clear demarcation between ritual and the everyday. The layout and structure of houses as far apart as Bali and the Amazon jungle are determined by religious beliefs. Their orientation, where domestic activities occur and the direction particular people can move around them are all subject to religious rules. Evidence from later European prehistory suggests that people did not make a clear distinction between domestic and ritual places in that period.

Identification of objects with known religious links such as **votives** provides powerful clues.

Figure 6.15 *Graceland*

The grave of Elvis in the garden of remembrance at Graceland is one of the most visited funerary monuments in the modern world. Like many other pilgrimage sites, it is the focus for a variety of offerings.

 KEY TASK

Identifying ritual sites

This is a simple exercise designed to get you using and applying the terminology of ritual. List Renfrew and Bahn's (1991) indicators of ritual sites down one side of a piece of paper. Visit two different local centres of religion such as a church or mosque and see how well the indicators apply. Jot down what you find against each point. Next take studies of two archaeological sites from your area of study and apply the same test. You may find that this gives you almost enough material to support an essay on the subject.

These have sometimes helped identify otherwise ordinary features such as wells or springs as being the focus of rituals. Objects cannot be seen as ritual simply because they are exotic. However, the form and find sites of particular artefacts have been used to suggest ritual objects for most periods. In some cases the material is important. Amber is associated with burials from the Mesolithic onwards. Its colour of blood and fire with slight magnetic properties perhaps marked it out. Pottery vessels with particular designs

Figure 6.16 *Votives*

Ceramic models of body parts are frequently found at cave and peak sanctuaries in Minoan Crete and at temple sites in later cultures including Rome. They were left with offerings by pilgrims who were suffering in some way and hoped the deities would heal them.

Figure 6.17 *Scene from the Yaxchilan Lintels*

This huge stone slab was originally placed above the entrance to a Mayan temple. It illustrates bloodletting or 'autosacrifice', an extreme form of participation in ritual. Blood, analogous with water, was vital for the fertility of crops and maintaining good relations with the gods. It repaid sacrifices made by the gods at the time of mankind's creation. Here Lady Xoc is perforating her tongue and Shield Jaguar is bleeding his penis. Blood is collected on paper to be burnt as an offering, smoke rising to the gods. They are rewarded by the appearance of an ancestor in the form of an armed warrior dressed as the 'vision serpent'.

such as beakers or grooved ware are often seen as ritual artefacts. In some cases these have been repaired but not sufficiently to make them useable. Figurines and statues and non-functional artefacts such as copper axes are more ambiguous unless their context can link them with other indicators. Evidence of sacrifice – which literally means 'to make sacred' – might include deposits of valuable items, animals or even humans ritually murdered to invoke favours from deities.

Feasting falls into a similar category. The sharing of food is a powerful social unifier and is likely to feature in many rituals, but it can also be secular. The great halls of most castles were places of feasting for social rather than religious purposes. However, where there is other evidence, the remains of feasts can help identify ritual functions.

Evidence of other apparently waste material has also been used to suggest the embedding of ritual in the everyday. In particular Scottish and Danish middens (▶ p. 204) from the Mesolithic with their deposits of artefacts and human remains may not have been simply rubbish heaps.

Art and symbolism have also provided indications of ritual. Some, such as the example of Palenque are undoubtedly ritual, others are disputed. Palaeolithic cave art and Neolithic rock carvings have been particularly hotly debated. Other approaches to ritual symbolism have focused on repeated patterns including pairings such as left/right, male/female, in/out. This technique has been drawn from media and critical theory.

The sequential nature of the buildings at Palenque and Copan provides a good opportunity to study the continuity of ideas over time. Here one ritual structure would be ceremonially decommissioned and another structure, which was physically and iconographically related to its predecessor, would be built on top. The same rich symbolism in these temples is also found in graves below household patios, which connect commoners with the ancestors and the great cycle of heaven and earth.

LANDSCAPE, RITUAL AND BELIEF

A combination of the development of landscape archaeology and a growing awareness from ethnography of the ritual significance of landscape has led archaeologists to look beyond burials and individual monuments. Studies from Australia, for example, reveal that to the aborigines the whole landscape had a mythical dimension and they in turn inscribed it with meaning, including the use of rock carvings. Analogies based on ethnologies have been used to explore ritual use of the landscape in the Neolithic in relation to petroglyphs (rock-art) and cursus monuments.

RELIGIOUS SPECIALISTS

In all societies there are certain individuals especially skilled at contacting and influencing supernatural beings and manipulating super-

KEY TERM

Liminal

A boundary, space or time which is literally between two worlds. It may be between land and water as at Flag Fen or between the living and the dead. **Liminal** areas can be dangerous and therefore are likely to be marked by ritual. Most well known ritual sites have well defined boundaries. People, creatures and even time can be liminal – e.g. Halloween.

natural forces. They assist or lead other members of society in their ritual activities. Their qualification for this role may be certain distinctive personality traits or they may have undergone special training. A body of myths may help explain how and why they are different from those who lack such powers.

Priests and priestesses

Priests and priestesses are found mostly in complex societies that can afford to support full-time specialists of all kinds. He or she will be ceremonially initiated into a religious organisation and given a rank or office similar to those held before by others. They interpret their wishes or commands for other people but may also appeal to deities on behalf of believers. This may be for a fee or for payment in kind. The priest and recently the priestess are a familiar figure in western society. Priests may be recognised archaeologically through objects placed in burials, through special equipment and clothing, through literary and epigraphic evidence and through artistic evidence of persons involved in ritual activity. Their presence could also be inferred from the structure of monuments themselves. In most cases monuments physically divide people into those who are in and those who are out, those at the head of a procession and the followers.

Figure 6.18 *Temple complex of Srirangam at Triuchirappalli*

This is the largest temple complex in India and a major centre for Hindu worship of the god Vishnu. The huge gopurums (pyramidal entrance towers) are masterpieces of early modern Dravidian architecture. Their height dominates the town and ensures visibility at distance in the same way as European cathedrals

Shamans

There have been societies without full-time occupational specialists for much longer than those in which one finds priests and priestesses. However, there have always been individuals who have individually acquired religious power. This often happens in isolation and may involve bodily deprivation, even self-torture, to try to induce shamanistic visions. It can also involve trances induced by hallucinogenic drugs or repetitive dancing and chanting. Through contact with a spirit or power, or visits to the land of the dead these persons acquire special gifts, such as healing or divination and the ability to deal with supernatural beings and powers. When they return to society they are frequently given another kind of religious role: that of the 'shaman'. Faith healers and some evangelists in our own society are similar in some respects to this definition of the shaman.

Definitions of shamanism vary. Some writers reserve it for Siberian culture but it is widely applied, particularly to herding, hunter-gatherer and mobile **horticulturalist** societies. Shamans are sometimes characterised as magicians rather than religious leaders. In some situations they may coexist. Unlike the priest or priestess who represents deities on earth the shaman is essentially a religious entrepreneur, who acts for their client. Sometimes shamans are paid in kind but usually the increased status that their activities bring is sufficient reward.

and ventriloquism. Shamans know, of course, that they are tricking people, but at the same time most shamans really believe in their power to deal with supernatural powers and spirits.

The drama of the shaman's performance promotes a feeling of ecstasy and catharsis for the individual members of society. Psychological assurance is the key to the role of shamanism in society. The shaman may claim to be able to manipulate super-natural powers, and promise such things as protection from enemies, success in love, or a cure from some illness or mental affliction. This treatment may not be effective in any medical sense that we would acknowledge, but the state of mind induced in the patient may nevertheless play a large part in his recovery. The shaman may also help to maintain social control through the ability to detect and punish evildoers. This can backfire on the shaman. If they are believed to work evil as well as good, or are unsuccessful, shamans may be driven out of their group or even killed.

In societies without iconography shamans are most likely to be detected through burials (▶ p. 287). Siberian examples have been buried face down, tied up and covered with rocks.

RELIGION AND RITUAL IN EUROPEAN PREHISTORY 40,000 BC–AD 43

This period from the Upper Palaeolithic to the Iron Age is huge and this can only be a brief overview to introduce the range of evidence and current interpretations. Examples are largely from the British Isles except for the earlier periods. You need to be aware that in many respects, particularly monument types, there are regional differences that may be significant; and also that we only know about the mortuary practices for a tiny fraction of the population. They may not be typical. Excarnation or cremation before disposal in natural places (possibly rivers) may have always been the norm from the Neolithic onwards.

Figure 6.19 *A ritual artefact? This Neolithic flute carved from a human bone comes from the Trentino region of Italy (▶ p. 209). The anthropomorphic designs and the material itself suggest that it might have been used in shamanic rituals*

A shaman in action may put on something of a show. Frequently shamans enter a trance-like state in which they can see and interact with spirit beings (Lewis-Williams 1988). The shaman enters a dangerous contest to impose his or her will on those spirits, as in faith healing or exorcism. In many groups trancing is accompanied by conjuring tricks, including the use of elaborate masks (for example in the Pitt-Rivers Museum)

Upper Palaeolithic Europe 40,000–10,000 BP

Even before Homo sapiens arrived in Europe there was evidence of symbolism and beliefs in burials, art and personal adornments (▶ p. 336). The survival of burials from the Upper Palaeolithic is rare but two key elements are repeated. One is the use of the pigment red ochre which appears to have been sprinkled or painted on buried bodies. The second is personal ornaments or grave goods. Most commonly this involves shell, stone and ivory beads, bracelets and pendants. These elements are found in the Paviland Cave burial of a young man and most spectacularly in the group of burials at the riverside site of Sungir near Moscow. Both are dated to between 30 and 20,000 BP.

This period also saw the development of portable art. The oldest known statue, the 'Lion Man' of Stadel im Hohlenstein dates from 32,000 BP. This mythical, anthromorphic figure may represent beliefs in animal spirits or that human qualities were seen in animals. The mobile art tradition of representing women as so-called 'Venus Figurines' (▶ p. 309) ranges from the famous examples at Willendorf and Dolni Vestonice to the less familiar sculptures from Russia at Kostienki. The familiar overblown female characteristics whatever their symbolic significance are not in fact outside the physical range for normal modern European women. Interpretations range from Bonsall's Palaeolithic

Figure 6.20 *A selection of Venus figurines*

These may or may not represent mother goddesses.

'Playboy Magazine' substitutes for men on long hunting trips without their women to objects actually made and used by women in initiation ceremonies. Certainly the diminutive hands and feet, the lack of distinctive faces and the elaborate hair and clothing suggest that the artists were not depicting individuals but generic qualities of womanhood. The detail and complexity of these statues, which mainly date between 28–20,000 BP, is echoed across Europe and must indicate a degree of commonality in cultural and religious ideas.

The middle of the Upper Palaeolithic when these objects were made is often termed the 'Creative Explosion' because of the increase in the range of artefacts and the skill levels needed to produce them. The Ice Age seems to have been an extraordinary time of technological developments including musical instruments, the first textiles, groove and splinter technique and the needle, together with using different materials in one composite article. It is perhaps best known for Cave or Parietal Art on the walls and ceilings of both caves and rock shelters, some of which have a three-dimensional character. Like the tools and statues these also hint at complex ideas and rituals. Excellent examples are the three-dimensional sculptures at L'Abri Cap Blanc with its beautiful frieze of horses; at Le Tuc d'Audoubert with its magnificent bison in clay; and not least the horse at Pech Merle in the Lot region of France, carved from a sheet of stalactite with another horse painted in black and white on its surface. This is quite splendid especially when viewed in context by the flickering light of a pine torch when shadows and imagination enter the viewer's consciousness along with the image itself.

Cave art at first sight seems very appealing and accessible and a common misconception is that it consists of 'hunting scenes' which we can interpret through our imagination and appreciate in our modern way as 'art for art's sake'. In fact there are very few if any 'scenes', instead the significance seems often to be in the performance

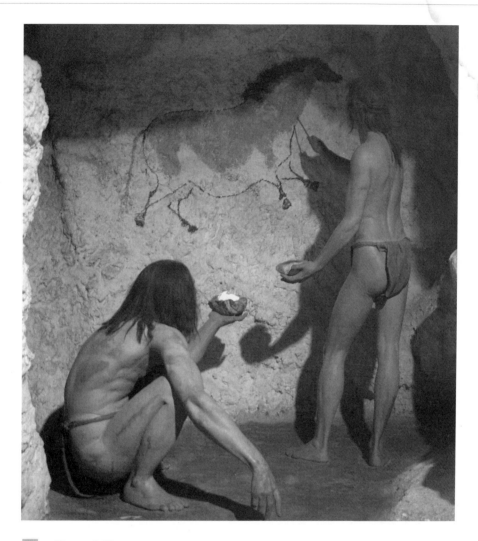

Figure 6.21 *Reconstruction of cave painting*

as much as the actual images. In most cases we cannot be sure which images on a particular wall were painted at the same time, never mind whether they 'go together' in any meaningful way. Images of animals predominate but not usually in proportion to their importance as a food source. Reindeer were often the most common prey species but not the most frequently painted. Images of human beings tend to vary hugely. They can be schematic at one end of the scale, as at Lascaux, or intensely realistic, as at La Marche. In addition to the main images there are also many geometric designs or 'signs', which some have interpreted literally as spears, nets, traps and houses.

These collections of images have been through a number of different interpretations since the discovery of Lascaux in 1940 including 'art for art's sake', 'male/female symbols' and the idea of 'caves as cathedrals'. Analogies drawn from the Pacific coast of North America suggested the possibilities of totemism or 'sympathetic magic' designed to bring prey to the hunters. The inaccessibility of the galleries also raised the possibility that they were educational, to teach hunting and tracking skills, perhaps as a rite of passage. Until recently no one had attempted to integrate the large number of abstract motifs into the overall schema. Then Louis Williams and Dowson (1988) opened up a new approach combining neuropsychology with ethnography. Many of the symbols were shown to be 'entoptic' or geometric shapes that are 'hard-wired' into our central nervous system as humans. They are images that come from within our brains rather than from what we have seen. We project them over the top of images from everyday life when in an altered state of consciousness such as a

trance. These geometric shapes are shared by all modern peoples and therefore by the people of the Upper Palaeolithic. Similar analysis has been carried out on neolithic rock art. They also drew on work in South Africa initiated by Wilhelm Bleeck who studied Bushmen art and mythology until his death in 1878. His records of these people provided the key to understanding Bushmen rock paintings. San shamans often describe themselves as feeling weightless and changing shape during 'trance dances' which they use to reach the spirit world. They record their visions and spirit travels as rock art. Palaeolithic images include a shaman transforming into his animal spirit companions. The human figure is still quite rare despite enigmatic images at Les Trois Frères, Cougnac and Lascaux which suggest that we are dealing with shamans turning into creatures that are half man and half animal – therianthropes. Trancing may have involved the shaman dancing and imitating the movements and sounds of a bird as part of his performance, perhaps dressed in a bird costume and carrying magical artefacts such as the staff. Ritual dances such as this were also described among the native Americans of the north-west coast. Some of their elaborate shaman's masks and ritual equipment can be seen in the British Museum and Pitt-Rivers Museum. Research into links between shamanism and rock art across much of African and Eurasia suggests that cave art may be shamanistic in origin. It may also mean that we can even understand elements of ancient religion as far back as the last Ice Age.

Mesolithic Europe c.10,000–4,500 BP

Animistic beliefs and shamanism appear to have continued into the Mesolithic. The antler 'head-dresses' from Bedburg and Star Carr (◀ p. 54) have been interpreted as props for ritual dancing. Human-fish hybrids are also a feature of statues created at Lepanski Vir on the Danube. Much of our data for this period comes from burials,

Figure 6.22 *Palaeolithic images which may be of shamans transforming*

particularly from the Ertebolle Culture (▶ p. 240) – the last Mesolithic people from Denmark and southern Sweden – which has particularly good preservation. Ertebolle burials at cemeteries such as Skateholm suggest a reverence for the dead, most eloquently expressed in the interment of a child on a swan's wing at Vedbaek. Grave goods emphasise natural materials including amber, red ochre, animal bone and antlers. Some of these are associated with burials as far back as the Upper Palaeolithic which may suggest some continuity of belief. Dogs were also buried in a similar way to humans. Taken together the evidence points to beliefs in a spirit world. Perhaps people saw themselves as part of nature rather than in control of it. In Britain there is some evidence for excarnation in the nature and location of human bone remains. Other human bones have been recovered from middens. These are effectively the first monuments in the landscape. A tantalising hint that places may have been marked in other ways is provided by the four massive wooden posts erected near to the later site of Stonehenge (▶ p. 168). There are also Mesolithic pits underneath some later barrows. We must never forget, however, that we are trying to interpret partial and static evidence of complex and dynamic behaviours – all that remains of human cognitive activity and the physical rituals that give us access to it.

The early to middle Neolithic c.4500–c.3000 BC

A number of major changes are apparent in the Neolithic. At one time this was put down to invasion by a new people. Increasingly archaeologists believe that in Northwest Europe, the indigenous Mesolithic people adopted aspects of Neolithic culture. DNA research shows that there has been no wholesale replacement of population since the last Ice Age. People's lives in the early Neolithic may have been similar to the later Mesolithic; herding rather than hunting but still seasonally mobile.

The most obvious changes in the archaeological record are:

- The building of circular enclosures, particularly on hill tops e.g. 'causewayed camps'.
- The building of funerary monuments containing human remains such as long barrows or long cairns. These were sometimes in use for over 1000 years.
- Widespread evidence for excarnation and the association of human remains with manufactured artefacts (pottery, stone tools) and cattle bones.
- Structured deposition. Particular bones, and artefacts placed in particular places on sites.

A range of hypotheses have been put forward about the nature of the religion of the builders of the passage graves, cairns and long barrows of Western Europe. Although these monuments are similar in some ways there are significant differences in their contents. In long barrows there was a gradual change from individual articulated burials to collections of disarticulated bones as at Hazleton or re-sorted bones as at West Kennet. However, this pattern is not universal, which suggests some regional variety in beliefs. The tombs that hold the remains of the dead are often massive while remains of the settlements of the living are more fleeting. Neolithic people may have been mobile herders so this may not be surprising. Tilley (1996) suggests that monuments were sited in particular places in relation to important places in the natural landscape. Mountains, spurs and crossing points on pathways may have already been important.

The shape of the tombs may celebrate domestication in its widest sense: houses and control over the fertility of animals. Some writers (◀ p. 139) see the swollen mound of these monuments as evidence for worship of an earth or fertility goddess. The shape of passage graves with their narrow entrances suggests a womb from which the soul is reborn. For farmers, fertility is a crucial issue and reseeding Mother Earth with

KEY STUDY

A ritual landscape in west Sligo

This sequence of pictures illustrates the way in which monument builders used natural features and also related different groups of monuments to each other in order to create a ritual landscape. The earliest monuments in the area are shell middens on the coast such as at Culleenamore (▶ p. 204). The first burial monuments in the Carrowmore Cemetery have recently been dated to before 5000 BC. The cemetery comprises largely Neolithic dolmens and passage graves. Within the cemetery there appears to be a focus on tomb 51 or Listoghil which has petroglyphs on some of its stones. There were at least 100 tombs before quarrying depleted their number.

Location of major monuments in Sligo area. Mountains are shaded
*1 Carrowmore cemetery *2 Culleenamore Middens *3 Maeve's Cairn *4 Carrowkeel cemetery
*5 Heapstown Cairn *6 Ben Bulben Mountain

Area with monuments focussed on Carrowmore

Figure 6.23 *Map of Carrowmore and related monuments*

Figure 6.24 *A ring dolmen from Carrowmore*

This may have been covered in a cairn of stones before quarrying damaged the cemetery.

KEY STUDY *cont.*

A ritual landscape in west Sligo

Other monuments were added in the surrounding countryside. From the Ox Mountains to the south to the distinctive shape of Benbulben to the north, all the high ground surrounding the low-lying farmland east of Carrowmore is marked with passage graves. These are orientated on the earlier cemetery. An enormous passage grave (Maeve's Cairn) was also built on the prominent summit of Knocknarea which overlooks Carrowmore from the west. Its position means that many of the passage graves on other hills also appear to be focussed on it. In the distribution and orientation of monuments we can therefore see connections which suggest common belief systems and understandings linked to ancestors and the seasons. If the dates are correct, megalithic tomb building may have spread out from Carrowmore to other parts of the British Isles.

Figure 6.25 *Carrowkeel passage graves looking west*

Figure 6.26 *A ring dolmen at Carrowmore looking towards Knocknarea. Maeve's Cairn is visible as a tiny bump*

Figure 6.27 *Maeve's Cairn on top of Knocknarea*

the bones of ancestors may have been a symbolic gesture to ensure good crops or plentiful livestock. Other archaeologists have noted the similarity between some of these monuments and the longhouses of the first farmers of central Europe. Some Neolithic monuments appear to have been sited at places which already had ancestral significance. Perhaps inscribing the landscape with permanent markers associated with their dead was to establish land rights. Mesolithic pits and post settings have been found underneath early long barrows and there are three huge Mesolithic post holes under the Stonehenge car park (▶ p. 356).

Not all tombs had entrances. Amongst many that did, the disarticulated bones from different individuals were deliberately mixed and sometimes re-sorted. Perhaps this was to downplay individual differences and mask inequalities amongst the living. The dead became part of a shared group of ancestors rather than belonging to a particular family. The restricted entrance passages and evidence of the transformation of skeletons through sorting hints at the possibility of ritual specialists. Recent acoustic experiments (Watson 1997) suggest that the design of burial chambers may have enabled specialists, possibly shamans, to create atmospheres and illusions through the use of sound. Similar effects have been noted at later stone circles. The mortuary rituals in tombs may be linked to activities at other Neolithic sites. At some causewayed enclosures such as Hambledon Hill, human bones appear to have been subject to excarnation. Perhaps the spirits of the dead could not be released until flesh had been removed from bones. Some bones exposed at such sites may have later been transferred to tombs.

Around barrows there is often waste from feasting and some human bones. Ethnographic evidence from the Merina of Madagascar (Parker Pearson, 1997) has been used to suggest that the remains of the dead may have been removed from time to time to be involved in rituals. While they are radically different societies there are interesting parallels. The Merina use communal, chambered tombs, to emphasis community and kinship. Skeletons are wrapped in the tomb but are periodically taken out and re-wrapped. These rituals involved both the living and the ancestors.

Figure 6.28 *The inside of a Neolithic tomb with disarticulated human remains*

KEY STUDY

Newgrange

This massive Neolithic passage grave was constructed around 3200 BC on a ridge overlooking a large bend in the River Boyne. It is part of a mortuary complex of tombs which includes the equally massive monuments of Knowth and Dowth. Clusters of small passage graves are aligned on the major monuments. Newgrange measures some 105 metres in diameter and was once encircled by standing stones. 12 of around 35 of these stones still survive. In common with other monuments in the complex it has suffered through being used as a stone quarry for road and wall building over the centuries. Around the base of the mound are 97 kerbstones, many of which are decorated with art. The south side of the monument appears to have been faced with quartz which petrology showed had come from the Wicklow Mountains, a long boat journey to the south, while the granite pebbles came from the Mountains of Mourne to the north. The entrance has a light box above it and a sinuous, gently rising 19-metre passage leading to a cruciform central chamber. This is corbelled to create a domed roof 6 metres high in the centre. The chamber contained relatively few artefacts although some items may have been taken over the millennia. Stone basins held disarticulated burials and cremations and some animal bones. On the walls is some of the most important carved rock art in Europe. These include tri-spirals, which are often mistakenly thought to be Celtic in design, zig-zags, herring bone, concentric circles and axe shapes (▶ p. 161). The chamber was possibly designed to provide particular acoustic effects. At dawn on the winter solstice, and two days either side of it, a shaft of light shines through the light box to penetrate the central chamber. This effect and the womb-like design of the monument have led many to link Newgrange to a belief in rebirth.

Newgrange was built in an area where settlement already existed. A mixture of landscapes in the local area meant that both pastoral and arable farming was practised. The sheer scale of the monuments suggests that building them was in some way competitive with a sequence of complexes stretching west across Ireland including Loughcrew, Carrowkeel and Carrowmore. At one time it was thought Newgrange influenced these others but recent dates suggest Carrowmore may have been the earliest. Certainly there were links between them with Carrowkeel style pottery found at all the

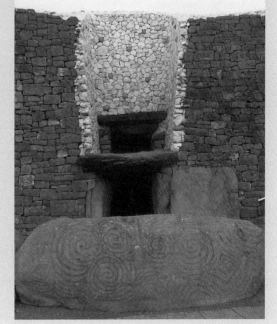

Figure 6.29 *Newgrange entrance*

Newgrange's entrance has the lightbox above the entrance to the passage and a massive blocking stone with distinctive spiral petroglyphs. The composition of the reconstructed façade, with granite 'peppering' of the white quartz is clearly visible.

KEY STUDY *cont.*

Newgrange

sites. There are also polished mace heads of a design common in Orkney. The logistical effort of mobilising and feeding a labour force to complete the project has been seen as signifying an increasingly ranked society. Certainly the design itself structures people into those who would have witnessed the chamber art and the solstice and those who would only see the kerb art. The earliest art in the chamber is incised and largely made up of lines. It is similar to that at Maes Howe on Orkney. Later, often curved, designs were created by 'pecking' and have similarities with megalithic art along the Atlantic seaboard from Temple Wood in Scotland (▶ p. 165) to Iberia.

As with many major prehistoric monuments, considerable changes took place during its use. In the third millennium the tomb may have been blocked. Certainly the façade had collapsed or been demolished. The circle of monoliths was built to create a more open type of monument, perhaps more concerned with wider rituals than burials. This is a pattern also seen at the Clava Cairns near Inverness (▶ p. 164). During the Beaker period a cluster of round houses was built next to the monument and an oval ring of pits and timber post settings were dug. There may also have been a henge, roughly the same size as Newgrange. Grooved ware and animal remains suggest that feasting took place here.

Newgrange illustrates some of the problems faced by Stonehenge. During excavation in the 1960s the decision was taken to reconstruct the monument to enable visitors to appreciate its original features. Antiquarian accounts, experiments and engineering principles were used to determine the final shape of the mound. The result has been much criticised. The controversial vertical façade would probably fall down without the concrete holding it in place while the peppering of the sparkling quartz with granite pebbles is said to make it look like a cheesecake.

A major interpretation centre was built a short distance away with buses used to transport tourists to the tomb and control numbers. Its massive popularity means visits often have to be booked ahead and a lottery system used to select those to witness the solstice. While many have criticised the 'reconstruction' of Newgrange it serves as a tourist 'honeypot' which reduces pressure on the other major tombs and other monuments in the World Heritage Site of the Boyne Valley. The equally large passage tomb at Knowth is currently being excavated while that at Dowth has not been developed.

• http://knowth.powernet.co.uk/neolithic-religion-status.htm

Figure 6.30 *Newgrange*

Neolithic Art

Lozenge and zigzag rock art from Four Knocks tomb. This art like that of nearby Newgrange (◄ p. 159) bears a strong resemblance to entoptic images. Statistical analysis has established a significant correlation between these images and entoptic images produced during trancing. This may suggest that shamanism remained important into the Bronze Age.

Figure 6.31
Lozenge
rock art

Figure 6.32
Zigzag
rock art

Graslund (1994), in a comparative study of Scandinavian tombs from the Neolithic to Viking periods, concluded that settled societies share a belief in some sort of afterlife and in souls or spirits. He identified two models. The breath soul leaves the body with its last sigh and goes to join the ancestors. The free or dream soul is active when the body sleeps. After death it remains with the body until the flesh is gone. Graslund argued that the treatment of bodies after death reflected different soul beliefs. Where excarnation or disarticulation had occurred before placing in a tomb it suggested a breath soul. The tomb served as an ossuary. Where decomposition occurred inside the tomb it was a grave. The evidence for this is the presence of small bones that would have been lost during excarnation, skeletons in

sitting positions and beads that may have come from clothing. There are also fatty deposits in the soil in some tombs. With dream soul beliefs the corpse would have to be cared for as if it were alive. This would also account for the presence of food remains and grave goods.

Evidence from the relatively small number of Neolithic houses that have been found suggests that these may not have been domestic at all. Many have odd, non-functional features and strange deposits or unusual artefacts and have been described as cult houses. The massive timber house at Balbridie appeared to have a screen just inside the door, which would have made the inside dark and restricted access. Another at Balfarg probably had no roof. It held finds of a beaker which contained possible traces of narcotic substances. Even apparently purely economic sites such as flint mines may have had some ritual functions. It seems that in the Neolithic there was no distinction between ritual and practical. Actions were informed by beliefs.

The later Neolithic and early Bronze Age c.3000–1800 BC

The veneration of ancestors, communal rituals and belief in spirits continued into the third millennium BC but very gradually a number of changes occurred. The new elements included:

- The construction of a wider range of funerary monuments with significant regional variation. These included barrows, cairns, cists and megalithic tombs.
- A wider range of ritual monuments including cursus, timber circles, henges and standing stones (rows, circles and monoliths).
- Specific artefacts which are found in association with particular monuments. These include beakers with single burials and grooved ware pottery with timber enclosures and henges.
- The positioning or structuring of monuments to reference earlier monuments, rivers and/or solar alignments.
- Development of rock art across much of Britain and Ireland.

Amongst the significant developments here are the scale and type of monument and the symbolism of the alignment and positioning of monuments.

Many of the larger monuments would have required considerable organisation and millions of man-hours to build. Engineering skills were needed to transport and erect huge timbers and megaliths.

Large, open monuments may represent a move to large scale rituals. Certainly there is evidence of extensive feasting at many, such as the slaughter of pigs and cattle at West Kennet timber enclosure. The architecture and use of space in the monuments also suggests that if they were not organised by ritual leaders, they may have created them. Linear alignments lend themselves to processions (someone always leads) while barriers, boundaries, elaborate entrances and series of concentric structures on some sites divide people into in/out. The circularity of monuments could symbolise many things. For example the horizons of their world as they could see it, the community or the sun. Some writers have suggested that monuments reflected the landscape. Henges often occur in river basins where long views are cut off.

The positioning of later monuments seems to be affected both by the landscape and earlier monuments. Loveday's (1998) work on Dorchester suggested that the cursus might have been aligned on a natural feature: a twin peaked hill known as Mother Dunche's Buttocks. Other monuments including cursuses are then aligned on it even after it went out of use. Its proximity to the Thames is surely also significant. Rivers, including their springs, do seem to be a focus for ritual activity from at least this period. Henges in particular are often associated with rivers. There are also many examples where monuments are aligned on earlier funerary monuments. The Dorset Cursus was aligned on a long barrow, the Giants Ring at Ballynahatty on a small passage grave. The new monuments are linked to earlier ancestral beliefs; perhaps to provide legitimacy. Many monuments are also aligned on solar or possibly lunar phenomena. The most famous is the reorientation of Stonehenge towards the midsummer or midwinter solstice. Equally significant are the 'lightboxes' on passage graves in Ireland and Orkney. These allow light to penetrate into burial chambers on the winter solstice. This linked ancestors to an annual cycle of death and rebirth.

Where large numbers of monuments cluster together, archaeologists have used the term ritual landscape. The idea that a whole block of land

KEY TERM

Megalith

Essentially it means 'big stone' and is applied both to standing stones and monuments constructed of large boulders. Increasingly 'megalithic' is used to describe other aspects of society such as art during the time when megaliths were erected – essentially the Neolithic and early to middle Bronze Age.

• http://www.megalithic.co.uk/index.php

Figure 6.33 *The standing stone of Clach An Truishal stands 6 metres above ground and is the largest megalith in Scotland. In France (and in Asterix books) it would be called a menhir.*

Figure 6.34 *The Ring of Brodgar*

This elemental monument is part of an astonishing concentration of ritual sites on an isthmus where a freshwater and a sea loch almost meet. This World Heritage Site also includes Maes Howe chambered cairn and the huge Stones of Stenness. Like Avebury, a circle of megaliths was erected inside a massive henge, in this case with two causewayed entrances. Brodgar is the third largest stone circle in the British Isles and 27 of the original 60 megaliths remain. It dates to the late third millennium BC and was probably associated with large-scale ritual performances. An alternative view is that the process of construction was the most important aspect, perhaps a way for local leaders to gain status through competition with monument builders elsewhere. As with many stone circles, dancing giants feature in the folklore of the site.

KEY STUDY

The Clava Cairns

This group of monuments near Inverness illustrates many of the different features of ritual sites.

This distinctive, regional complex comprising ring cairns, passage graves and standing stones had originally been thought to be Neolithic. Bradley's (2000a) re-excavation revealed that building had begun in the early Bronze Age around 2000 BC. The complex was remodelled in the late Bronze Age and funerary deposits were also made in the Iron Age.

The passage graves are aligned on the midwinter sunset. When viewed from the passage of the north-eastern cairn the dying sun disappears over the south-western cairn, thus linking the event to the ancestors. The rays of the setting sun fall on reddish sandstone boulders while the rising sun would have sparkled on white quartz. This symbolism has been found in other monuments. On Arran red boulders were chosen to face the setting sun with white granite facing the rising sun. The colours red (blood, flesh, ochre and amber) and white (bone, semen and flint) are often associated in grave deposits.

Figure 6.35 View of the south-west passage grave looking down the main alignment towards the north-east cairn from the direction of the midwinter sunset. The entrance stones, the rays and stones linked to them and much of the chamber were built using pink and reddish stones while much of the kerb and the back of the chamber were white. Note the erosion of the platform due to visitors

Figure 6.36 View of a relationship between the features of the monuments. Two standing stones on the left are linked by 'rays' to the central ring cairn. The child is standing on the first ray. This integral relationship could only be established by excavation. Note how small the kerbstones are on the back of the south-west cairn in the distance in comparison with the front ones

KEY STUDY *cont.*

The Clava Cairns

A number of conventions were adhered to in building the monument. The kerbstones of the cairns were carefully graded in height from the south-west. From an engineering point of view this makes no sense but may have symbolised the passage of the sun. Rock carvings were included both inside and outside the cairns with the same 'cup and ring' designs as others in Britain and Ireland. However, these monuments seem to represent a change in ritual practice. Excavation revealed low platforms covered in seashells and flat stones surrounding the cairns. 'Rays' or ridges of stones led out through the platform to standing monoliths. Excavation showed that these were all integral to the cairns rather than later add-ons. These monuments seem to have been a transitional stage between passage graves, where the views of mortuary rituals would have been very restricted, to stone circles, where ritual may have been much more public and perhaps on a larger scale.

• Bradley 2000a

Figure 6.37 Achnabreck rock art (petroglyphs)

This slab with its examples of classic 'cup and ring' marks, and 'stars and spirals', overlooks one of the approaches to the Kilmartin Valley, a significant ritual centre. Other examples have been found throughout north-western Europe on monuments such as Newgrange (◄ p. 159). Analysis of the abstract images suggests that they comprise similar patterns to those recorded in research into hallucinogens and trancing. If this is the case then attaining altered states of consciousness through dancing, sound, drugs or fasting may have been a feature of rituals. Possibly the distinctive pottery (grooved ware and beakers) found in ritual deposits from this period may have held more than just refreshments. An alternative function may have been territorial markers (► p. 213).

might have been dedicated to gods or spirits was first applied to Cranborne Chase where the 11-km long cursus monument was the focus for burials over several thousand years. Analysis of fieldwalking finds revealed that higher than usual proportions of exotic artefacts and human remains were found close to the cursus with little sign of everyday activity (Green, 2000). Whether areas were set aside for gods or spirits the monuments affected the way people moved around the landscape and saw the world. They probably reinforced ideas about life, death and society. Some of the monuments may have been at points where people met during seasonal movements. The massive henge at Durrington Walls may have been a place where herders crossed the Upper Avon and spread out into summer grazing lands in the spring. The site may have been important for seasonal rituals or festivals. Many monuments were remodelled several times perhaps reflecting changing beliefs. At Stanton Drew magnetometer surveys have revealed that the stone circles replaced earlier timber monuments. Recent work suggests that henges might be the final form enclosing ritual sites.

The study of sacred geography involves examining the relation between monuments and landscape and the ways in which the building of monuments affects the way in which people may have moved around or viewed the landscape. Amongst the range of techniques are studies of intervisibility, which examine whether

Figure 6.38 *Cist grave at Temple Wood*

This cist grave is the focus for the main stone circle in the Kilmartin ritual complex. It is encircled by a tiny ring of stones only 3 metres in diameter. A larger ring of megaliths (12 metres in diameter) – some with petroglyphs – may align on the winter solstice. The cist held cremation burials and had no lid, being originally covered in a cairn of stones. The monument itself dates back to the fourth millennium BC and was originally constructed in timber. The cist was added during the third millennium BC after the large stone circle was built. This filling up of an existing monument may represent particular lineages in the early Bronze Age staking a claim to a shared ancestral past. The monument was still the focus of burials 1000 years later, demonstrating the continued importance of ritual places even when their original belief system was forgotten.

monuments were sited in view of each other. This has been assisted by the use of GIS and has been particularly applied to rock art and barrows. Attempting to 'read' the way monuments structure experience of the landscape borrows from the sociological approach known as phenomenology and has been pioneered in case studies in Britain by Tilley (1994). This approach has led to a reappraisal of linear monuments. These clearly structure movement in a particular order and direction but may themselves be permanent inscriptions of earlier movements or processions. Barnett's (1998) study of the stone rows on Dartmoor noted how many lead from the valleys onto the moors, perhaps marking a route for spirits or the dead. Similar suggestions have been made for Avebury and Stonehenge with pathways linking ritual areas for the living and those of the ancestors.

There is increasing evidence that dramatic events played an important part in ritual. Some monuments appear to have been built in stages over many years so that participation in the project may have been more important that the final product e.g. the Cleaven Dyke. Others were deliberately destroyed by what must have been spectacular fires. Often timber structures were repeatedly built and destroyed as at Dunragit and West Kennet. At the latter site Whittle's (1998) excavations revealed two massive but short-lived, egg-shaped enclosures. The large number of meat bones which had been discarded without being fully processed provided strong evidence of feasting, as did large amounts of grooved ware. The enclosures were located very close to other monuments and the source of the Kennet. The concept of liminality was used to explain the special attention given to boundaries. In particular, deliberate deposits of grooved ware, bone and artefacts had been made around the entrances. This practice has been noted at other timber enclosures throughout Britain.

Beakers of course are best known from their place in a new tradition of single burials in graves and cists. As part of fairly standard assemblages

range of grave goods (decorated beaker, arrowheads, dagger, wrist guard etc) they may represent a more individualised view of an afterlife as well as a more ranked society.

The Middle Bronze Age 1800 to 1200 BC

Once again, there is great continuity from the late Neolithic. This is most obvious in the elaboration of earlier monuments such as the remodelling of Stonehenge and the way new monuments continue to be linked to much earlier ones. Key features are:

- The building of thousands of round barrows or cairns.
- A variety of burial traditions including single and multiple burials, flat cemeteries and particularly cremations.
- The final phases of major monument building including major stone circles at Stonehenge and Avebury.
- The importance of orientation for the entrance of enclosures and houses.

Individual burials occur throughout prehistory, but there seems to be a shift of emphasis in the Bronze Age. This is most marked in round barrows or cairns that were often constructed over a primary burial or cremation with satellite burials around it (and often later secondary burials). The development of a range of regional burial traditions could reflect changes in beliefs and society. The old way of life of semi-sedentary herding amongst roughly equal social groups was being replaced by a more unequal society based on control of the land. The new barrows and cairns cluster round earlier monuments and in the case of some small circular monuments, such as Cairnpapple, fill them. This surely represents high status individuals linking their families to 'the ancestors' and their rights and power. Some burials, particularly in Wessex, included rich and exotic grave goods. The 'Amesbury Archer'

KEY STUDY

Stonehenge

Any summary of the archaeology of Stonehenge cannot do justice to the immense body of material available for archaeologists, students and general readers. The focus in this section will be on the central monument within its landscape setting, introducing key aspects of archaeological importance and establishing links that those who wish to expand their investigation can follow.

The Stonehenge 'prehistoric ritual landscape' lies on Salisbury Plain in Wiltshire, an area of undulating chalk-land with the river Avon some 2 kilometres to the south-east giving links to Amesbury (of Amesbury Archer fame) and Durrington Walls, a massive contemporary henge monument a few kilometres upstream. The number and variety of neolithic and Bronze Age monuments in the area are greater in density than anywhere else in the United Kingdom and attest to the undoubted significance of the area in terms of ceremonial and funerary ritual.

A full description of all the component parts of Stonehenge and their phases of development requires a book focused on just this site such as Richards (2007). The complex of stones now visible, some standing and some fallen, belies the developmental phases and the orderliness of the monument during its active years. Care needs to be taken whether on site or pouring over site plans to distinguish different related groupings. There were three major phases in its development and several minor episodes of remodelling as well. The place seems to have been significant from the Mesolithic when a line of three pits to hold massive pine posts was dug nearby. In the earlier Neolithic a small causewayed enclosure, a dozen or so long barrows and two cursus monuments (the longer one being nearly 3 kilometres in length and just north of Stonehenge) reveal a continuing and growing involvement in the development of a ritual landscape by the local population.

The initial part of Stonehenge was a relatively small henge with two entrances built around 3100 BC. Henges vary greatly in size but have a common factor of a basically circular shape

Figure 6.39 *Stonehenge with the henge ditch in the foreground*

KEY STUDY *cont.*

Stonehenge

created by a ditch with the upcast being thrown outwards to form an external bank. This classic non-defensive format could be interpreted as providing a viewing platform from which to witness activities taking place in the central and perhaps restricted access enclosure or maybe the bank simply blocked the view from outside so one had to enter the henge to participate in the ritual. Stonehenge is atypical: its surrounding ditch and *internal* bank are not significant earthworks – many people simply do not notice them when visiting the site – something one certainly couldn't say about Avebury! Around the same time the 56 Aubrey Holes – a concentric circle of post holes were dug just inside the bank. Over the next few centuries other post settings came and went and at least 30 cremations were placed in the monument. The ditch and pits would have been dug using antler picks and cattle shoulder blade shovels. Several were left behind.

In the middle of the third millennium BC four other henge monuments had been built within 3 kilometres of Stonehenge itself; all are quite different, ranging from the small site at Fargo Plantation to Woodhenge, dominated by a circular timber construction which filled its interior, to the massive Durrington Walls at nearly 500 metres in diameter. However, the significance of Stonehenge was enhanced with a rebuilding in stone. The stone settings are formed by two quite different groups of stones. The larger stones weighing up to 45 tons are sarsens, a type of hard sandstone from the Marlborough Downs just east of Avebury about 30 kilometres away. The smaller (though these can weigh up to 4 tonnes) bluestones originate from a small area of the Preseli Mountains in south-west Wales. Both clearly required a great deal of human ingenuity and effort in terms of transportation, no doubt using seaways and waterways where feasible and rollers for overland journeys. The first phase of stone settings around 2600 BC comprised a double horseshoe of the relatively smaller bluestones set in the centre of the henge (it may have been the intention to form two concentric circles but, if so, this plan did not come to fruition). However this design was not set to last and all the stones were later removed and, presumably, stored off-site. Darvill and Wainwright who recently located the quarry for these stones argue that they may have had an association with healing. Local folklore associates both quarry and monument site with such power.

The sarsen circle of the late third millennium had 30 dressed uprights topped by a continuous ring of horizontal lintels held in place by mortice-and-tenon joints with the uprights and tongue-and-groove with each other. Within this circle a horseshoe setting of the largest sarsens (up to 45 tonnes) was made up of 5 trilithons (free-standing settings with two uprights and a lintel connecting them). These stood over 7 metres from ground level. These sarsen features were never moved once erected. The bluestones, however, 'stored' to one side, were returned to the site early in the second millennium. Two circles of holes outside the sarsen circle (the 'Y' and 'Z' holes) may have been dug to take them but the designers did not follow through on this idea. Instead the bluestones reappear as a circle inside the sarsen ring and also in an oval/horseshoe setting within the sarsen trilithon horseshoe. By this final phase the whole middle section gives the appearance of being quite tight and cluttered and is clearly unique in terms of stone circles and settings within henge monuments. Stonehenge was undoubtedly a highly complex monument designed and built by people with developed engineering skills allied to an eye for calendrical events and contemporary

KEY STUDY *cont.*

Stonehenge

religious beliefs. A number of additional single large stones can be linked to the use of the site and will feature in a complete study of the arrangements: the Heel Stone, the Slaughter Stone and the four Station Stones. During the Bronze Age several of the stones were carved with images of metal axes and at least one dagger. At one time these were thought to link Stonehenge to Mediterranean builders but radio-carbon dating demolished that idea. Today they are barely visible due to visitor erosion but have recently been recorded by laser scanning.

To understand the building of Stonehenge more fully you need to investigate the many theories about moving and erecting the stones and will need to follow arguments about:

- stone holes cutting earlier stone holes;
- silting in ditches;
- the distribution or lack of stone chips from the processing of the stones;
- C-14 dates based often loosely on single samples;
- comparative shapes of holes dug for different stone settings.

These changes which span the late Neolithic and early Bronze Age may have reflected changes in use and belief. The entrance to the inner area through the earthworks faces north-east. An earlier one (there were two originally) to the south was later blocked and the current one realigned to lead out onto the Stonehenge 'Avenue'. This linear earthwork has two banks with internal ditches and

■ **Figure 6.40**

Inside Stonehenge

In the centre of the monument the largest trilithon lies broken over an inconspicuous slab of sandstone (to the left of the person). This appears to be in a central position and may have played a key role in rituals. In the foreground is one of the Welsh blue stones while behind tower sarsen trilithons.

KEY STUDY *cont.*

Stonehenge

is about 12 metres wide overall. It runs straight for just over 500 metres before taking firstly a more easterly course and then a south-easterly one down to the river Avon. The avenue seems to focus the monument on the midsummer sunrise and most popular theories build on this. This includes ideas about an earth goddess/mother with Stonehenge representing a womb. However, the midwinter solstice is on the same axis and increasingly archaeologists see this as the real focus. Darvill has suggested that the site may have been viewed as the home of a winter god. Coinciding with the stone construction phases a major funerary landscape developed with the construction of literally hundreds of round barrows, a great many of which cluster together to form barrow 'cemeteries'. Some of these can be clearly seen to be linear cemeteries laid out in a rough line across the landscape such as the Winterbourne Stoke Crossroads group just to the west of Stonehenge and on King Barrow Ridge either side of the Avenue. Ancient long barrows were significant in these new alignments.

An influential interpretation of the change to stone has come from Parker Pearson and the Madagascan archaeologist Ramilisonina. They saw the stone as marking a permanent monument to the ancestors and contrasted the area around Stonehenge which has little sign of habitation with Durrington Walls with evidence of feasting: timber for the living, stone for the dead. They argue that the dead were taken from Durrington down the Avon and then up the avenue. The avenue itself is suggestive of processions. Parker Pearson is currently leading an exciting joint university investigation of the area on the Stonehenge Riverside Project. At Durrington Walls excavations since 2005 have revealed evidence of an 'avenue' which predates the eastern entrance to the henge and leads from a large timber circle (similar to the one at Woodhenge) for a distance of 170 metres down to the river Avon. The width of this 'avenue' compares to the Stonehenge Avenue. The excavations have also provided evidence of a potentially extensive settlement. 8 houses, very similar in layout to those at Skara Brae (and with impressions suggesting similar furniture) have been found in a small part of what is expected to be a much larger area of habitation. Several hundred houses may lie under the huge bank. Finds indicate that this settlement was probably occupied on a seasonal basis. It is a reasonable theory to suggest that these dwellings were lived in by the people who contributed to the building of Stonehenge. The remains of large numbers of nine-month old pigs suggest that they may also have been involved in midwinter feasting.

The grave goods in barrows around Stonehenge are the richest in Britain and may have been the burials of high status people. Examples include Bush Barrow with its gold lozenge and the 'Amesbury Archer' (◀ p. 79) It is highly likely that this man, or others very similar to him, were part of an elite who were influential in local society at the time of the great developments at Stonehenge. Certainly someone was mobilising and sustaining a significant labour force. Recent examination of the ditch at Durrington suggests that around 50 people worked in a section of the ditch at any one time digging with antler axes. To support them, others would have had to carry soil baskets out of the 5.5 metre-deep ditch while others must have provided food. Estimates of numbers range from hundreds to several thousand. Perhaps the process of building Stonehenge and the related monuments helped an elite of priests or chiefs to emerge.

(◀ p. 79) and the Bush Barrow burial are the best known. The size of the burial mounds may also indicate the importance of individuals but could also be to provide platforms for funeral pyres. It is likely that the funerary rituals would have been more important at the time than the artefacts which archaeologists recover.

Perhaps reflecting the increasing importance of farming, the sun and seasons seem to become more important in the Bronze Age. Most of the circular enclosures, monuments and houses are aligned to the south-east or south-west. It may imply involve solar worship. The final phase at Stonehenge was constructed so that the midsummer sun shone along the processional 'avenue' into the heart of the monument. This strongly suggests a seasonal ritual involving large numbers. Alternatively the monument may be aligned on the midwinter sunset, linking the dying sun and year to the ancestors buried nearby. Stonehenge with its complex design, avenue and restricted interior provides a good indicator of organised religion and specialists. The nearby Upton Lovell burial (▶ p. 287) suggests a possible candidate.

The Late Bronze Age and Iron Age 1200–55 BC

Some archaeologists have approached this period from later Roman accounts while others have traced developments in the archaeological record. While there is not full consensus, a number of patterns are clear.

- The abandonment of the monument building tradition.
- A move towards more extreme forms of propitiation (sacrifice) including that of people.
- The importance of deposition in natural places particularly water. These may have been seen as entrances to an underworld.
- Still relatively few burials. Most of the dead are missing.

- Evidence of ritual being part of everyday activity.
- Orientation remained important for houses and enclosures.

The impressive burials seen in museums such as the 'chariot burials' of Yorkshire and rich burials from Kent are exceptions. Most of the dead disappear. Excarnation seems to have been common with some cremation and possibly water burial. Bruck's (1995) study of human remains on sites from this period revealed that bones occurred in many locations not necessarily thought of as ritual, including huts and pits. Relatives may well have kept relics of their dead ancestors. Human bones along with animal remains were also used as deliberate deposits at entrances, boundaries, and in grain pits. 98 of the pits at Danebury contained some human remains. Studies of middens and rubbish pits have also shown that their fills were non-random. Rules structured their creation. Some domestic sites also had very patterned orientation. Hill's (1996) comparative study of Iron Age sites revealed a tendency for houses to face south-east. This may have been to do with light, although in Britain south would be the best direction to maximise daylight entering a hut. Light cannot have been a factor with enclosures. These tend to face south-west even when local topography and defensive considerations might suggest other directions. It may be that there was a 'right' direction from which to enter or perform activities. Ritual was a part of everyday life.

Society was now based on settled villages involved in mixed farming. Perhaps the domestication of religion reflects a less mobile society. The total abandonment of earlier beliefs appears to be evident in the way later Bronze Age field systems cut across earlier monuments whose faint traces had been respected for over a thousand years. Instead of monuments, natural places seem to have become significant as locations for ritual. In addition to water and pits, deposits occur on hilltops, which may well

KEY STUDY

Flag Fen

Flag Fen near Peterborough was originally situated in a coastal swamp. Over the centuries it was buried in layers of peat. Since the seventeenth century the area has been gradually drained to provide farmland but this process dries out the peat and destroys organic archaeological deposits. Flag Fen was discovered by accident when timbers were spotted in a recently cleared drainage ditch. Samples were dated to 1000 BC and Francis Prior's team of archaeologists embarked on a race against time to recover what they could before the site vanished.

What they found were rows of thousands of upright oak posts and the remains of thousands more pieces of wood. There may have been up to 80,000 posts originally. These made up a kilometre long barrier or causeway linked to an artificial platform or island one hectare in area. The site appeared to have been in use for at least 400 years from 1350 BC during the late Bronze Age and possibly into the Iron Age as well. First thoughts that it might have been a crannog (◀ p. 52) were dispelled by the longevity and scale of the site and the deposits recovered from the peat. Most artefacts were of high value, often unused and included swords, spears, jewellery and millstones. The metal items had been deliberately smashed before placing in what was then water. In addition the bones of dogs – probably valuable hunting dogs – were found on the seaward side of the platform. This kind of structured deposition is very familiar in northern Europe where deposits of weapons, prestige objects and human remains are often associated with watery places (◀ p. 115).

Careful recording of the positions of finds enabled the distribution pattern to be interrogated. The excavators also had to rapidly conserve the finds, many of which would have disintegrated soon after removal from anaerobic sediments. Their expertise led to the timbers from Sea Henge (◀ p. 119) also being sent there in the 1990s. This work has also extended our understanding of prehistoric carpentry. Construction involved the use of a variety of mortice and tenon and lap joints. Interpretation of the site

Figure 6.41 *Preserved timbers at Flag Fen*

KEY STUDY *cont.*

Flag Fen

considered the wider context of the late Bronze Age. Tree rings in this period are often very narrow, suggesting a time of climatic deterioration and wetter summers. There is evidence of settlement desertion on some of the uplands in Britain which may have become unsustainable in poorer conditions. This may have led to greater social stress and economic upheaval. It is a period also where the trade in prestige goods between northern Europe and the Mediterranean appears to have broken down and also one in which bronze swords and spearheads seem to indicate a change in the nature of warfare. Elsewhere in the British Isles there is evidence of increased deposition in water ranging from fine metals in the Thames to the artificial pond at Navan with its animal and human bones. There is another Iron Age causeway site at Fiskerton on the river Witham in Lincolnshire.

What appears to have gone on at Flag Fen were acts of sacrifice and propitiation. These rites may mark a more extreme form of religion, possibly to placate or gain the help of an underground or water god. Because of the location help may have been sought to prevent rising sea levels from swamping farms and settlements. It certainly is located at a boundary between land and sea and in a liminal sense, possibly between worlds. Northey Island, at one end of the causeway, has been suggested as a possible place of the dead in the fen with cremated remains being brought from some distance to be deposited there.

The amount of objects found and the investment to build the site suggest considerable importance and it may have been a place of pilgrimage.

Today the visitors' centre includes a reconstruction of the island and a tank holding preserved timbers.

Figure 6.42 *Shears from Flag Fen*

This perfect pair of clippers from Flag Fen shows us that Bronze Age shepherds already had technology which would be in use until the nineteenth century. They were not lost or casually discarded. These valuable items complete with their wooden case were deposited from a wooden causeway as ritual offerings. Hundreds of other valuable finds from jewellery through swords to millstones belonged to these structured deposits.

KEY STUDY

Wetwang Slack

Although this site or series of excavations on the Yorkshire Wolds is now usually referenced under the name of the parish where the more recent discoveries were made, the original archaeological activity took place slightly to the east in Garton Slack and some older articles or books may therefore use this earlier location.

Between 1965 and 1975 major excavations took place ahead of gravel extraction producing religious and ritual evidence from the early Neolithic to the end of the Iron Age. The major focus was on an Iron Age cemetery with a large number of square or rectangular ditched burial enclosures under barrows some of which covered so-called 'chariot burials'.

However the earliest funerary monument on the site was an early Neolithic earthen long barrow some 55 metres by 18 metres with some inhumations placed just behind a façade at the broader south-eastern end. Later a barrel-shaped cremation furnace was constructed to enable bodies to be burnt in a standing position. A small pit halfway along the barrow contained cremated bone. A second cremation furnace belonging to a ploughed-out barrow was discovered approximately 200 metres north-east of the first. Radio-carbon dating placed this phase at the end of the fourth millennium BC.

There were a great number of Bronze Age barrows too, nearly all without ditches. Burials often had grave-goods including beakers or food-vessels. Urn burials were in pits without covering barrows. The largest barrow contained 11 graves and a complex sequence of burials was recorded within circular re-cut ditches and a later square post-hole enclosure. A key factor to emerge was that the beaker burials clearly predated the food-vessel ones. No beakers were found in association with cremations whereas most of the food-vessels contained cremated bone. Radio-carbon dates were approximately 1600 BC.

Later in the Bronze Age two exceptionally wide pits, the first 9 metres wide and 2 metres deep and the second 6 metres wide and 4 metres deep, with graves at the bottom, were dug though neither revealed grave-goods nor were dateable finds possible because of adverse ground conditions. A ritual pit, specially dug and with filling clearly not of a domestic nature, lay next to the second pit. Carbon dates from charcoal and antler samples gave a date around 1250 BC.

A large number of Iron Age circular post-built huts were excavated but available evidence suggests they pre-date the later Iron Age barrow cemetery and no evidence of settlement contemporary with the barrows is attested.

The Iron Age burials were under square or rectangular ditched barrows, in single graves in barrow ditches or in groups of graves isolated from the barrows. There were some high status burials as exemplified by a woman with an iron mirror which had bronze mountings.

In 1971 the first 'chariot' grave to be excavated under modern conditions was unearthed. There had been 8 examples from England prior to this discovery. The grave contained the dismantled chariot, the owner (a male of about 30 who was approximately 175cm tall), his whip and all the harness fittings. Single-piece iron tyres had been fitted to the 12-spoked wheels by heating them and shrinking them onto the wheels just as wheelwrights do today. One tyre to all intents and purposes was new while the other was clearly worn and repaired. The excavators were of the opinion

KEY STUDY *cont.*

Wetwang Slack

that the coachwork of the chariot had been inverted over the body which in turn was partly resting on the wheels.

(There has been much discussion as to the best word to describe these two-wheeled vehicles. Some argue that 'chariot' conveys ideas of a fast, mobile fighting platform and therefore a more suitable term to identify what seems to have been a more prosaic form of transportation would be 'cart'. This is used as a reference to a people-carrier as opposed to a 'wagon' which is slower and carries goods. A sound solution may be to think of them as the 'trap' part of a pony and trap. They were nonetheless objects of high status and for the sake of this section they will be referenced as 'chariots').

Two rectangular ditched enclosures were found in the cemetery with pits inside and various half-circle features faced these enclosures from the north. Finds from all these features indicate deliberate placement of headless chalk figurines, pottery and animal bone rather than domestic rubbish and strongly suggest connectivity with funerary ritual.

Under a later neighbouring Romano-British farmstead an Iron Age infant cemetery was located. Each of the 33 burials in it had a small lamb or kid buried in a separate grave next to it.

By 1978 250 burials had been recovered, 150 of them from under barrows. The barrow platforms – the area enclosed by the barrow ditch – measured 9 metres by 8 metres at the largest to only a few metres each way at the smallest. All the primary burials were past puberty so it appears the full rite of barrow burial was for adults only. Many were in plank coffins and had been dressed or were in a shroud. Grave goods fall into three main types: food offerings (pork was the favourite joint), personal objects (sword, shield, bracelets, pendants etc.) and dress fastenings (31 brooches which allied to the site's horizontal chronology allowed development and confirmation of a typology of Iron Age brooches).

In July 1984 two more chariot burials were found 20 metres apart containing the remains of one male and one female respectively. The following month another male chariot burial was spotted by a quarry worker adjacent to the first two. The female grave appears richer (to us) as most of the objects, many of them horse fittings, were of bronze and so better preserved than the iron objects in the first man's grave. A significant and unique find with the female was a small round container with decoration similar to that on the Witham shield. The male was buried with, amongst other items, his sword in its scabbard, seven spears and a shield. These were the first weapons to be found in a Yorkshire chariot burial. The second male burial also had a sword and shield but no spearheads. All three barrows were clearly related with the female at the centre and one male to the north of her and the other to the south.

The most recent discovery at Wetwang Slack was made in the spring of 2001. Another adult female was found and her burial seems to date to the fourth or third century BC which would make her earlier than the others noted above. Her body had been laid in a small hollow at the southern end of the grave pit along with an iron mirror and joints of pork. The dismantled chariot had then been placed in the grave with the axle and pole across her and on top of them the body of the vehicle. The wheels were positioned a little away from her in the northern part of the grave

KEY STUDY *cont.*

Wetwang Slack

pit. Evidence again points to the chariot being old and used rather than specially made to accompany the burial. This burial of a female with a chariot, along with the 1984 discovery, raises major questions about gender and status over a substantial time frame in the Iron Age.

Wetwang is one of a number of large cemeteries where human remains have been subjected to stable isotope analysis (▶ p. 214) to determine main food sources. Of 450 skeletons tested, all have a similar isotopic profile regardless of the accompanying grave-goods. All had a terrestrial diet with a high meat content and virtually no marine food. Similar results have come from cemeteries in Cornwall. This suggests that Roman writers may have been correct when they reported taboos against the eating of fish.

Current Archaeology has regularly covered discoveries at Wetwang Slack notably in CA 51, CA 61, CA 93, CA 95 and CA 178.

■ ***Figure 6.43*** *Welwyn burial*

This rich burial documents the influence of Rome in terms of burial goods if not religion. The cremation was buried with amphorae of wine, fine table ware, games and a variety of luxury items. This is not how most people in the Iron Age were buried.

have been wooded. This is particularly the case with torcs. The Romans mentioned Druids lurking in oak groves! Symbolism was drawn from the natural world. Birds, particularly ducks, feature on some high status artefacts and bird bones are often found with human remains.

Some human deposits are likely to have been sacrifices, including some burials outside hill-forts, which were previously thought to be battle casualties. Sacrifices may have been connected with fertility but also with rites of intensification. In Britain and Denmark bodies which had apparently been ritually killed have been recovered from bogs. Throughout north-western Europe large quantities of metalwork including the very finest, were deposited in rivers and lakes. Water sacrifices may be acts of propitiation, perhaps in appeals to a water or underground deity. It may also be the case that water was always important, but that it becomes archaeologically visible at this point.

Specialists remain elusive. The Mill Hill (Deal) burials (▶ p. 299) include a young man wearing what has been interpreted as a Druid's crown because of its similarity to Roman priests' crowns. The Birdlip burial (▶ p. 310) was classified as a woman's grave but some researchers have reinterpreted the grave goods as shamanistic. From the very end of the Iron Age a handful of possible temples have been identified. This may reflect a southern elite adopting continental customs along with imported goods in advance of the Roman invasion. The Romans also gave us some names of local deities such as Sulis at Bath and of the festivals which marked the Iron Age calendar including Samhain, the forerunner of Halloween. Some wooden carvings from bogs and Roman reliefs (▶ p. 181) may represent Iron Age deities.

• Thomas 1991 Bradley 1998, Whittle 1996

A BRIEF INTRODUCTION TO ROMAN RELIGION AND RITUAL TO C. AD 476

Religion in the Roman world is a story of classical pantheons, mystery rituals and wonderful syncretisms of local and Roman deities. This creative fusion is exemplified by Sulis Minerva at Bath where Roman votives and 'defixiones' (curse tablets) were thrown into a liminal place that had been special to prehistoric Britons for hundreds of years already. This concept of 'you scratch my back and I'll scratch yours' underlies much of Roman belief. This can be seen in thousands of votive altars, plaques and miniature objects found nailed to temple doors or thrown into wells, rivers and springs all over the Empire. While much is known about Roman religion from classical texts, archaeology has been particularly useful in helping us understand less recorded aspects such as ritual embedded in everyday life.

Offerings could enable you to hedge your bets when embarking on a new business venture, going on a journey or any potentially life-changing event. Animal entrails were burnt, chickens sacrificed and the flight of birds consulted. This was a reciprocal bargain between mortal and supernatural beings and the gods were expected to perform their side of the deal by using their power (*numen*) to influence events. 'Numen' was also embedded in particular places. This was later enshrined in temples and

symbolised by statues of the *'genius loci'* (spirit of the place) such as the British goddess Brigantia and her nymphs in north-east England (e.g. Arbeia) or Sabrina Fluvius, the spirit of the River Severn. The 'numen' was everywhere in the Roman world from poems such as Horace's *Fountain of Bandusia*, 'more glittering than glass . . .' to the end of a bar in Pompeii where one glanced across the top of a wine cup to see the household deities of the owner and the place, the Lares and Penates. Rather like our custom of leaving a mince pie and glass of sherry for Father Christmas, food and drink offerings would be left at this 'altar'.

Early Roman religion was animistic with worship of ancestors and spirits who inhabited or influenced particular everyday places, events and things. From the outset, Romans borrowed beliefs and practices from cultures around them starting with the deities of the Etruscans and Greeks. They usually dealt with new ideas through a process of 'syncretism' or equating native gods and their attributes with the nearest equivalent from their pantheon as in the famous example of Sulis Minerva. Roman deities had less developed personalities and mythologies than those of the Greeks. Their powers and relationships to each other were more important. The major deities including Jupiter, Mars and Minerva had their own priesthoods, temples and festivals.

A strong thread of state ritual is equally apparent from Claudius' Temple in Colchester to the Pantheon in Rome where the state is personified and the gods that support it are extolled. Imperial expansion following the wars of the third century BC added more exotic cults from the East such as Isis. Initial Roman attitudes to new religions were generous providing that they did not suggest a political challenge to the state. One that did, Judaism, led to ruthless repression. The worship of Mithras can be seen on Hadrian's Wall where it appealed to a military audience while the more cerebral appeal of the Eleusinian Mysteries revealed itself in a series of

KEY STUDY

The Temple of Mithras

The cult of Mithras was one of the secretive and exotic 'mystery religions' of the Roman Empire. As a result there are few literary sources and the cult is best known from archaeological remains. It is believed to have been brought to Rome from Persia in the first century AD by returning soldiers who were attracted by this heroic god and only men were initiated into Mithraic rites. That the best surviving Mithraeum in Britain is one of three along Hadrian's Wall reflects the popularity of the cult amongst soldiers and traders. The values of Mithras included discipline and courage which fitted well with the demands on the Roman Army. Initiates took the title 'Invictus' which meant unconquered. The Roman cult appears to have been very different from the worship of the sun god Mithra in Persia or India amongst Zoroastrians. Strangely, although there were temples across the Empire, most evidence for the cult is in Europe rather than the Near East. There are several temples in Rome itself.

The central aspects of Mithraic iconography can be seen in the fresco or relief of Mithras killing or sacrificing a bull. This was usually sited above or behind the altar. In the scene (also called the tauroctony) Mithras is shown cloaked and wearing a distinctive near-eastern or Phrygian pointed cap. He straddles the bull and cuts its throat while a number of animals assist him. These include a scorpion, dog and raven. He has two smaller and similarly dressed helpers bearing torches. Cautes on the left holds a flaming torch while Cautopates who stands under the moon holds his torch downwards and often extinguished. The figures may represent the cycle of the sun and also the Roman planets. There is an astrological link in the signs of the zodiac which appears in one of its earliest forms at Carrawburgh. Scenes from various Mithraea have enabled the story of the tauroctony to be pieced together. Usually Mithras is shown being born from a rock or tree and after a great struggle capturing and sacrificing the bull in his cave. However, at Housesteads he is born from the sacred egg holding the sword of truth and the torch of light in his hands. Truth was another of the Mithraic

Figure 6.44 *Image of Mithras from Carrawburgh*

KEY STUDY *cont.*

The Temple of Mithras

values. By sacrificing the bull he releases its life force for the benefit of all. Plants grow from its body, vines from its blood and animals from its semen.

To reflect the story, temples were designed to look like a natural cave. Sometimes they were within other buildings or underground but most were free-standing like that at Carrawburgh. Rectangular in shape they had an entrance at one end opposite the sanctuary, but no windows. The ceiling may have been vaulted and decorated to symbolise the heavens.

Figure 6.45 Temple of Mithras at Carrawburgh

Along the side of the nave were benches or dining couches for the initiates. There is evidence that feasting took place but Mithraea were small, perhaps holding up to 30 men, so it is unlikely that bulls were sacrificed inside. There were seven levels of initiation with tests or ordeals to pass between grades from Corax or Raven up to Pater (Father). These may have involved fasting and extremes of temperature. At Carrawburgh there is an 'ordeal pit' and a bench next to a fire. The

Figure 6.46 Reconstruction of a Mithraeum

This careful reconstruction at Newcastle Archaeology Museum uses evidence from Carrawburgh including artefacts, altars and fragments of wall plaster combined with information from Temples of Mithras elsewhere in the Roman world.

KEY STUDY *cont.*

The Temple of Mithras

antechamber appears to have been screened off from the nave so the Mithraeum would have probably been quite dark which would add to atmosphere during the rites. At Carrawburgh several altars and two pots containing ritual deposits were found. There are dedications from worshippers on some columns including one from a German or Dutch prefect which reads '**To the Invincible God Mithras, Marcus Simplicius Simplex, prefect, willingly and deservedly fulfilled his vow**'.

The range of beliefs in the Empire can be appreciated just yards away to the west of the Mithraeum on the edge of a boggy patch of ground at Coventina's well. Here there was a shrine to the Romano-British water goddess Coventina. This was a simple walled enclosure surrounding a ritual well or tank about 2 metres deep and roughly 2.5 metres square which was fed by a spring. Masses of votive offerings had been deposited including thousands of coins. The polytheistic approach came to an end with the Christian Emperor Theodosius. Mithraism was banned as paganism and temples, including Carrawburgh, were desecrated. Some writers claim that Mithraic temple design, iconography and perhaps communal worship influenced early Christianity. There are also claims that Mithras was born on 25th December.

A virtual Mithraeum is at http://museums.ncl.ac.uk/archive/mithras/frames.htm

exquisite frescoes in Pompeii. The 'Ara Pacis Augusti' and the Vesta Temple in Rome show clearly how much the interests of the state were identified both with the 'royal family' and with the Vestals, the guardians of the sacred flame and of Rome's moral integrity. A marvellous array of the gods' servants peer down at us from frescoes and statues all over the Roman world: flamen Dialis, popa, haruspex, augur, vestal, pontifex, auspex, flamen Martialis – their very number showing the complexity of rituals overseen by specialists of every kind. This eclectic mixture served the inhabitants of the Empire well with its variety and multicultural appeal.

Figure 6.47 *Two of three Genii Cucullati from near Hadrian's Wall. Wearing their distinctive hooded cloaks, these Romano-Celtic gods symbolised healing and fertility*

KEY STUDY

The Temple of Vesta

Vesta is often thought of as the Goddess of the hearth but there is no image of her. Instead she is represented by the sacred fire. As well as being worshipped in the home, Vesta had her own distinctive temples. All are circular and their entrances face east towards the rising sun. The shape may represent a thatched round house which may have been the earliest shrine in the seventh century BC. The Temple of Vesta in Rome is sited amongst a complex of ancient temples in the Forum. The visible remains today are from a rebuilding in AD 191 by Julia Domna, the wife of Septimus Severus. The circular cella contained the sacred flame and appears to have been the focus of attention as there is no sign that statues were present. A cavity which could be reached from the cella may have been a secret vault. The temple was said to contain relics brought by Aeneas from Troy. Since he was the

Figure 6.48 *The temple of Vesta in Rome*

mythical ancestor of the Romans it adds to the symbolism of the sacred flame. The building was one of the first marble buildings in Rome and was surrounded by 20 Corinthian-style columns.

To the east of the temple was the House of the Vestal Virgins. These were the priestesses whose duty was to tend the sacred flame and ensure that it never went out. Originally the Vestals were the kings' daughters but were later chosen from upper class families. However, the strict rules and thirty-year service made these families increasingly reluctant to give up their daughters to the tradition. Daughters of freedmen were chosen on the basis of appearance when they were between the ages of six and ten. The girls were sworn to celibacy and became novice Vestals for 10 years after which they spent ten years as priestesses. In addition to tending the flame they would have taken part in the annual festival in honour of Vesta. Their final ten years were spent teaching novices, after which they could marry.

The life of the Vestals was very different from that of normal female citizens. For example if a Vestal had lost her virginity or let the fire burn out the punishment would be burial alive or a painful death often in front of the public. The man responsible for having sex with the Vestal would have also been executed publicly. The Vestals would have been given extraordinary privileges for their duties: they would have been able to vote, to reserve seats at the theatre and gladiatorial games, and they would have also travelled in covered carriages around Rome. The Vestals were considered to be the most prized priestesses of Rome because they protected the most sacred thing in the city: the hearth.

In AD 394 the emperor, Theodosius I, disbanded the sisterhood and extinguished the sacred fire.

Figure 6.49 *Temple of Mercury at Uley*

Mercury, messenger of the gods, was the patron of travellers (and also thieves!). His popularity in Corinium and at the nearby cult temple at Uley is evidenced by statues, votives and lead 'curse' tablets. Mercury is often shown with sheep or goats (fertility) or a cockerel (herald of the day). The bones of these animals were found in considerable numbers at Uley. The complex with the standard temple design (right) also included shops and hostels for pilgrims which can be seen to the left of the aerial view.

Temples were houses of the gods so the Romans built them on a grand scale and in prominent places. Temple layouts followed a defined plan which can be seen throughout the empire from the Temple of Apollo at Didyma (Turkey) to the Maison Carrée at Nimes (France). Each has a raised podium with access via a flight of steps, a large external altar, a temenos (boundary wall) and often ancillary buildings for priests and pilgrims. The priests (flamen) of the various cults were all overseen by the high priest or 'Pontifex Maximus' who in imperial times was the emperor. Their responsibility for organising religion came from law codes found inscribed on metal and stone in local towns. Other specialists included 'augurs' and 'haruspices'. These diviners interpreted the meanings in natural phenomena and the livers of sacrificed animals. They were consulted before important decisions. Perhaps the most well known of Roman ritual specialists were the Vestal Virgins who tended the continually burning flame on the altar of the Temple of Vesta in Rome.

Worship was not confined to temples; individuals looked to their household gods the Lares and Penates. Rich people had their own shrine

Figure 6.50 *Fresco from the Villa of the Mysteries, Pompeii*

A chamber in this Villa at Pompeii is thought to have been the site of female initiation ceremonies. In a series of frescos, a woman (wearing a scarf) is prepared for rites involving satyrs and the god Dionysus. She emerges to scenes of transformation and later appears as a bride. An alternative interpretation is that she has been initiated into the cult of Dionysus, who was popular amongst Roman women.

Figure 6.51 *Triad of mother goddesses from Cirencester*

Roman Corinium appears to have been a focus for this cult. The goddesses, carrying bread or fruit symbolised fertility. Many such deities appear in threes since that was a magical number for many Iron Age peoples. There is a close correlation between finds of mother goddesses and genii cucullati.

• www.unc.edu/celtic/
  catalogue/triplism/#genii

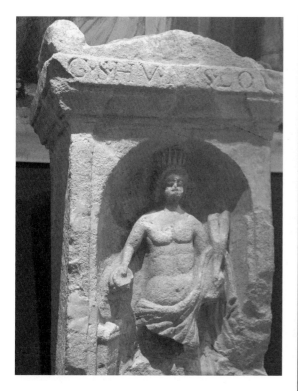

Figure 6.52 *Altar from Cirencester*

This altar is dedicated to the Genus Loci of Corinium. In one hand he holds a cornucopia with a patera (an offering or sacrificial bowl) in the other.

Figure 6.53 *Tombstone of Sextus Valerius Genialis from Cirencester.*

This cavalryman and citizen of Corinium from AD 60 is shown defeating a 'dying Gaul'. However, he was not from Rome but from Thrace. The Roman army was cosmopolitan. Soldiers posted to and often settling in Britain were as likely to have come from the Middle East or north of the Rhine as Rome itself.

built into their houses while for ordinary people worship centred around a simple lararium or set of statues. Pompeii has provided good examples. At the House of the Vettii two brothers had a very fine lararium on the wall, where a magical snake protected the household from evil forces outside. Phallic symbols performed much the same role outside many houses, including the town brothel with its massively endowed depiction of the god Priapus. More noble and richer families often put great faith in the cult of their ancestors and kept masks of them in the house to be carried in festival processions. There was also 'pietas', the sense of love, respect and duty towards both gods and their families, expressed through ordinary people's lives.

The variety of mortuary practices is equally astounding with both cremation on pyres and inhumations being common as seen in the cemeteries of Londinium. There are also pipe burials, mausolea and cremations in jars of ceramic or glass. Thousands of grave stones with their elaborate decoration and Latin inscriptions

KEY SITE

The Water Newton Treasure

This important hoard was discovered in 1975 in a ploughed field that now covers the remains of the Roman town of Durobrivae next to the A1 just north of Peterborough. The finder, a local metal detectorist (though reports at the time suggested he was walking across the field with his detector switched off), removed the archaeological material from its original context and, some time later, it was referred via a local archaeologist in the Nene valley to the coroner's court. There it was eventually declared 'treasure trove' under regulations in force prior to the 1996 Treasure Act. The hoard was taken to the British Museum where it can now be seen in the Roman gallery.

Most of the artefacts were silver but the major interest was caused by 15 out of the 27 recovered objects bearing the Chi-Rho symbol denoting their Christian affiliations. (The Chi-Rho is formed by using the first two letters of the Greek word for Christ – ΧΡΙΣΤΟΣ – placing the Rho (Ρ) across the Chi (Χ) to form the monogram). Alongside the Chi-Rho many also displayed an Alpha/Omega symbol (αω) these being the first and last letters of the Greek alphabet and thereby linked to the Christian notion of 'the beginning and the end'.

Archaeologists are agreed that the artefacts form the silver plate of a Christian community rather than being the possessions of a single rich individual. The list of finds is impressive: a two-handled cup, three bowls – two of which had inscriptions – a hanging bowl, a large shallow dish into which all the other objects had been piled, a long-handled strainer, two flagons, 17 triangular plaques – one with an inscription – and a single gold disc. The inscriptions named four individuals (one male and three female) and thus gave strong support to the objects being a part of this particular community's religious activities.

It was tempting for archaeologists to try to identify some of the larger objects with the ritual of celebrating Communion. Given that a two-handled cup might be a 'chalice', the bowls could have been used to mix wine, the hanging bowl could have contained incense or a lamp, the flagons might have held wine and thus be associated with the strainer – the possibility exists but is far from proven. Archaeologists really do not know to what extent Communion had been established in the fourth century AD. It is equally feasible to argue for ritual feasting using the collection of vessels found.

The plaques are similar to others well known in pagan contexts where they were nailed up in temples. Of the 17 discovered 7 had a Chi-Rho in relief on a central roundel and some had nail-holes too. The inscribed one read: 'Anicilla has fulfilled the vow that she promised'.

Much of the hoard is relatively plain, the most decorated items being the flagons and the hanging bowl. Compared to the Mildenhall treasure it is much more conceivable that its contents could have been produced by local craftsmen.

Dating, because of the circumstances of the hoard's discovery and the lack of any coins associated with the artefacts, relies heavily on stylistic analysis. The closest parallel is for the hanging bowl which is similar to ones from France (Gaul) dated securely to the later third century AD. The plaques have close similarities to pagan contexts immediately before the advent of Christianity. The rather plain nature of the whole hoard distinguishes it from other later fourth century AD hoards. The most likely date is therefore in the first half of the fourth century AD. It is important

KEY SITE *cont.*

The Water Newton Treasure

as the earliest group of Christian liturgical silver and may have been hidden during a time of persecution or political unrest.

This fourth century Christian centre piece to a villa mosaic contains what may be the earliest image of Christ in Britain and the Chi-Rho symbol. As at Lullingstone there were images from mythology elsewhere in the villa including Bellerophon killing the Chimera. This may have symbolised good triumphing over evil.

Key reference: Current Archaeology 54

Figure 6.54 *Mosaic from Hinton St Mary*

tell us equally about belief and the lives of the deceased. The spirits of the dead, the *'dis manibus'*, also figure largely in standard grave inscriptions. Families often visited the grave to feast beside the tomb. At Caerleon one cremation was served drinks through a spout which led down to the urn. Only neo-natal burials were allowed inside the 'pomerium' or town boundary. Cemeteries therefore were kept apart from settlement areas. In Rome burial could be in underground niches or 'loculi' but above ground tombstones were also very common. This was especially so in Britain due to the influence of the army.

By the second century AD inhumation became the norm across the whole empire. This may be associated with increasing worship of the sun god 'Sol Invictus'. At the same time cemeteries were laid out east–west and in neat rows. Inhumations were usually in the extended position but it is also quite common for the head to be cut off and placed elsewhere in the grave,

often between the knees. Grave goods include lamps, jewellery and shoes, usually surviving as sets of studded nails. One of the most spectacular graves is the 'Lady of Spitalfields'. Her unique collection of lead coffin, grave goods and high quality apparel is displayed in the Museum of London. One distinctive Roman religious organisation was the 'burial club' where people saved money to pay for their burial and tombstones. Such clubs were often affiliated to trade guilds with their own club room for meetings and dining – several of these have been identified at Ostia, the port of Rome. Unlike modern tombstones which tend to be conservative and modest their Roman counterparts often list in detail the good qualities and achievements of the deceased.

Despite bad press for their treatment of Christians the Romans were generally tolerant of other cults. However, during the first century AD we hear through Tacitus of the punishment meted out to a difficult new sect of Jews known

KEY SITE

Lullingstone Villa

The Romano-British villa at Lullingstone in Kent makes an interesting contribution to our understanding of religion in Roman Britain. It was first built around AD 75 and included a circular temple. In a rebuild of an earlier villa in about AD 190 a cult room was created below the villa with a pit containing ritual water at its centre and a niche in the wall decorated with a painting of three water nymphs. The central one of these nymphs has green leaves in her hair and water falling from her breasts. It must be presumed that the room was dedicated to the worship of these water-goddesses. Elsewhere in the villa, precisely where is not known, the owner had portrait busts of his

Figure 6.55 *Wall-plaster painting from Lullingstone*

The images are praying in the original manner of Christians before the change to clasped hands. This is sometimes referred to as the Orans posture which is similar to prayer stances in other eastern religions. It may also represent the soul.

ancestors carved from Greek marble. The cult rooms became disused and were blocked off in another refurbishment at the end of the third century AD.

In the third phase of the villa, mosaics depict mythological scenes including Jupiter in the form of a bull kidnapping Europa. A less well executed panel shows Bellerophon killing a Chimera (a Greek mythological creature combining lion, goat and snake). On the edge of the mosaic are swastikas which represented good luck. The faces of the four seasons were seen at the corners of the mosaic and scenes from Virgil's *Aeneid*. Elsewhere in the villa a mausoleum was built with the burials of a young man and a woman.

Between AD 360–370 the owner, by now a Christian, converted part of the villa to Christian use. By chance this took place in a room immediately above the earlier cult rooms. The new facility is perhaps best described as a house-chapel although no artefacts were found to support its use for worship. However, six human figures are clearly depicted in a wall painting with their arms outstretched in the pose adopted for prayer by early Christians. They wore blue and saffron robes edged with pearls. Next to them a large Chi-Rho monogram encircled by a wreath was painted as part of the wall decoration.

The villa was destroyed by fire in AD 420 and never rebuilt. It encapsulates changes in religion over the period of the Roman occupation from the adoption of native deities to the import of Christianity.

as Christians – they were burnt as torches by Nero to illuminate the parks of Rome at night. Despite this Christianity grew in importance and physical evidence of its presence grows more frequent in mosaics, wall paintings, ritual structures and even secret word squares such as

ROTAS
OPERA
TENET
AREPO
SATOR

Also symbols such as the Chi-Rho monogram became more prevalent as at Water Newton and Hinton St Mary. Finally in AD 313 Christianity was legalised by Constantine. In 391 Theodosius I declared it to be the sole state religion and many other temples were destroyed.

A BRIEF INTRODUCTION TO ANCIENT EGYPTIAN RELIGION AND RITUAL

Possibly the most important aspect of religion in ancient Egypt is the idea of 'balance' or order which has its roots in the natural world so familiar to the Egyptians themselves. The annual cycle of the Nile which provided the fertile black silt that gave the land its name – Kemet or 'the black land' – also gave a sense of regularity which it was the pharaoh's duty to maintain by appropriate behaviour, propitiation and offering. The goddess that personified this concept was Ma'at, usually represented as a seated woman holding an ankh and with a feather on her head. The ankh, symbol of life, shows the crucial gift upon which all Egyptians depended, that is the golden grain that sprang from the black silt. Only Ma'at could keep at bay the forces of chaos that daily threatened to challenge the rhythm of life by allowing the forces of evil, in the form of Seth, to encroach on the long green strip of land either side of the valley. Amun's creation was kept alive and in order by Ma'at. Ma'at also appears weighing the hearts of the deceased against her feather to determine their fate. The importance of this one goddess is summed up in the throne name of one of Egypt's greatest pharaohs – Rameses II. It appears on temple

Figure 6.56 *Step Pyramid of Pharaoh Djoser at Saqqara*

The first in the line of monumental stone built tombs from around 2700 BC. The high priest Imhotep is usually credited with the design. Originally it would have been faced with gleaming white limestone. It is the most visible element in a major ceremonial complex which appears to have been used for festivals as well as funerary rites.

columns and walls all over Egypt in very deep relief as User – Ma'at – Re – Setep – en – Re which means 'strong in truth chosen of Re'.

Early Egyptian deities were zoomorphic, reflecting animistic beliefs and the use of animals to represent particular manifestations of gods. Worship of particular deities was often very localised. Gradually a few of the hundreds of deities became more prominent. Increasingly these were depicted in human form but with animal heads. During the early dynastic period of the early third millennium BC the most prominent included Re, the sun-god, who was the creator of the earth and the sky, and the husband and wife Osiris and Isis. Confusingly, deities have quite fluid identities and often had multiple forms and names. At times some were blended together to form single deities with different aspects, a practice known as syncretism. For example Amun, the main deity of the New Kingdom who represented the hidden power of god was combined with the visible light of Re as Amun-Re.

Knowledge of Egyptian religion is heavily based on surviving papyrus scrolls. Some describe myths, others rituals. Versions of the Book of the Dead survive from 1600 BC because they were placed in tombs to provide the dead with details of the next world and instructions and spells to help them get there. In addition there are much earlier hieroglyphic inscriptions and wall paintings in tombs, coffins and on monuments. Stone built monuments containing burials of the elite have survived much better than the mud-brick houses and simple burials of the mass of the people.

The rectilinear, cult temples of Egypt were the divine power plants that gave pharaohs the moral, spiritual and economic support to maintain their own position and the whole fabric of Egyptian society that was inextricably linked to the fortune of the royal house. Kings were the earthly embodiment of the god Horus. Horus, the son of Isis, was a protector god who destroyed evil. When a king died he became the god Osiris and the new king became Horus. As Horus he could mediate between men and gods. All pharaohs had a 'Horus name' as part of their title, in order to identify them with the deity. Temples were sanctuaries which safeguarded 'the holy' behind huge mudbrick temenos walls and massive pylon gates. They were places where ritual specialists of all kinds made themselves pure in sacred lakes so as to wash, clothe, anoint and entertain the gods who in their turn would shower gifts upon humanity and maintain the natural order. Above all, they were theatres for the crucial rituals which brought humankind into contact with the gods through ritual activity.

Ritual ideas and practices are reflected in the symbolism of wall paintings and the physical structure of the temple building itself. The mound

Figure 6.57 Sequence from the Egyptian Book of the Dead

Figure 6.58 *Aerial view of the Mortuary Temple of Rameses III at Medinet Habu*

It illustrates the conventional rectilinear layout of major Egyptian temples although the whole complex is contained within a mudbrick defensive wall, protected by gates in the style of a Syrian fort. The massive inscribed reliefs on its walls celebrate the victory of Rameses III over the Sea People. From left to right can be seen the pylons leading to the open first court. Through more pylons is the Hypostyle Hall. Beyond that is the funerary chamber of the Pharaoh and eventually the shrine of Amun. The interior would have been furnished with doors inlaid with precious metal and jewels.

Figure 6.59 *Hypostyle hall at Luxor*

These massive columns represent bundles of papyrus reeds. The building, which would have been roofed, represents the swamp surrounding the mound of creation. At Karnak the central columns are carved to look like papyrus scrolls.

KEY STUDY

The Temple of Karnak at Luxor

The largest temple complex in the world, its 100 hectare area could hold more than a dozen medieval cathedrals. There are actually 3 main temples for the gods Amun, Mut and Montu and several smaller ones. There is a Temple of Osiris inside that of Amun. The layout of Karnak was designed as a microcosm of the world at the time of its creation by the god Amun. His temple is at the heart of the complex. Its high walls and huge gates or 'pylons' excluded ordinary people. Only priests could enter the temple and they, like all other things dedicated to Amun, had to be pure and clean. They shaved off all their body hair, bathed daily in the Sacred Lake in the heart of the temple and dressed in spotless robes. Rituals depicted in hieroglyphics include the journey of Amun's sacred boat from Karnak to Luxor with attendants singing and dancing. The desire for the maintenance of order is also featured symbolically in the temple reliefs. Battle scenes show foreigners as disorderly mobs until they have been conquered and brought within the civilising influence of Egypt. Then they are shown in neat lines. In the nearby Luxor Temple this contrast is very clear: the Egyptian infantry and chariots at the Battle of Kadesh are immaculately organised in geometric squads while the opposing Hittites are in total disarray. The south wall of the enormous Hypostyle Hall records the signing of a peace treaty between Rameses II and the king of the Hittites. It is the earliest record of diplomacy. Successive Pharaohs added to the temple over time to ensure their names were linked to Amun.

The myth at the heart of the temple is that of the original creation of the world from the waters of chaos. The Hypostyle Hall represented the 'Swamp of Creation' with its forest of columns whose capitals were carved in the shape of plants such as papyrus. Amun came into being in this chaos. He lifted himself out of the water and masturbated himself to produce the two constituent elements of all life: wet and dry. From this act comes the first land in the form of the 'primeval mound' (the temple) and then the sky and later the first inhabitants of that Egyptian 'Eden': Isis and Osiris. In the hidden depths of the temple was the cult statue of Amun. The exact nature of the statue is much disputed due to the damage inflicted on the portraits of Amun in antiquity and the desire of previous generations

Figure 6.60 *Entrance to the Temple of Luxor*

KEY STUDY *cont.*

The Temple of Karnak at Luxor

of scholars to play down the sexual nature of Egyptian iconography. For the Egyptians this statue was a house for the god, a place where he could take up residence to interact with mortals. Through his divine presence it became 'alive' in a very real sense. The priests would anoint the statue, dress it and entertain it each day as they would the pharaoh himself. One relief shows a group of females playing musical instruments while others clap rhythmically. They are led by a woman who is identified by the hieroglyphs as 'the Hand of God'. Many scholars believe that the statue of Amun was shown in a state of sexual excitement grasping his erect penis and that the reliefs are picturing a ritual re-enactment of the original moment of creation induced by the rhythmic music and hand clapping. The question here is whether the ritual was essentially a metaphorical act that happened in people's minds or whether it had some sort of physical reality enacted by the chief priest of the temple or by the pharaoh himself once a year.

Outside the Hypostyle Hall is a narrow court where several obelisks once stood. A pink Aswan-granite obelisk still stands nearly 30 metres high and is visible for 80 kilometres. It is dedicated to the woman pharaoh Hatshepsut. A successful ruler, she was also a self-glorifying builder including her own mausoleum, one of the first great monuments near the Valley of the Kings. There was no female version of pharaoh and Hatshepsut is depicted with the usual pharaoh beard. After her death there were attempts to eliminate her name from history but her legacy survives in stone.

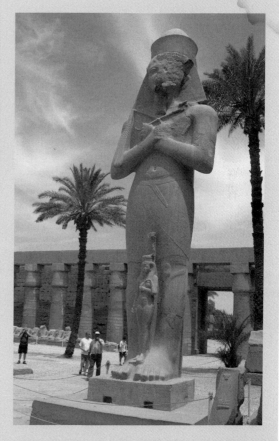

Figure 6.61 *Statue of Rameses II at Karnak*

is also symbolised in the inner sanctum of the temples. The shrine contained cult statues and was dark with a raised floor and low ceiling and decorated with reeds. It was the centre of the universe, cut off from the world of mortals by a succession of chambers, each progressively lighter. On the lower half of walls plants are shown emerging from the fertile silt while ceilings depict the stars. The pyramids too may have represented the sacred mound of the creation story from which Re emerged or on which he landed, depending on the version. Their steps represent a kind of stairway to heaven and their shape a solar symbol representing the pattern made by the sun's rays when they fell on the sacred mound. Their sides faced the cardinal points. Orientation is crucial too in the Temple of Rameses at Abu Simbel. Instead of a free-standing structure this was built into the side of a mountain. Rather like Newgrange (◄ p. 159) it was engineered so that the sun's rays would flood through the temple and right up the sculpture in the shrine. At Abu Simbel this occurred in February and October.

Temples were homes of the gods and off-limits to ordinary people. Only the priests who catered to the needs of the deities could enter the inner chambers although people might come to the temple gates for advice or oracles. The priestly hierarchy included specialists who maintained the temples, played instruments and sang hymns and the Sem priests who carried out mortuary rituals. At morning, noon and dusk a series of rituals were carried out. After purifying themselves by washing, priests would burn incense and sing to the gods before breaking the seals and enter the shrine. After prostrating themselves they anointed the effigies with oil, perfume and incense and offered food and drink. They would be dressed and have eye makeup applied. On festival occasions priests would take images out of the temple for festival processions. Festivals reflected the agricultural cycle, mythology and cosmology. The months in the Egyptian calendar were named after the cycle of festivals with times

Figure 6.62 *Relief from Temple of Kom Omba*

Sacred crocodiles basked on the Nile at this point which is the site of a temple part dedicated to Horus and part to Sobek, a crocodile god. Sobek represented the Nile and fertility. Several hundred mummified crocodiles have been found nearby.

fixed by the priesthood. Festivals were times of mass participation with pilgrimages, feasting, fortune telling, elaborate decorations and revelry. Several focussed on the Nile itself and the flooding which was vital to the fertility of the land. Osiris was worshipped at such key times since the November floods represented his renewal of life and the fall in water levels in the summer represented dying. At these times floating shrines were launched and offerings made to the river.

The most well known aspect of Egyptian religion is mummification. However, this mortuary ritual emerged gradually. It probably developed because bodies buried in sandy, desert soils in such a hot climate rapidly became desiccated and were preserved like leather. The practice of embalming began with the royal family and then gradually spread to other, rich members of society. Some animals (◀ p. xxviii) which may have represented deities were also mummified. It was a complex, specialist process involving the removal of all internal organs except for the heart and the application of a soda-ash drying agent called natron. The washed and dried body was then varnished, wrapped in cloth for protection and placed in a sarcophagus. The internal organs were embalmed and placed in canopic jars.

Embalming developed around the time that the early Mastaba tombs were being built and may have been a response to the problems of preserving bodies in them. Mummification was important because the body would be reunited with the deceased in the afterlife. Death was viewed as a gateway to another world. Grave goods were placed by the dead for their use following resurrection in the realm of Osiris. Ordinary people had simpler burials in graves, often with headrests for the body and a few personal grave goods. Mastaba tombs marked the beginning of the development of increasingly elaborate funerary monuments for the pharaohs culminating in the great necropolises of the Old Kingdom.

Figure 6.64 Sarcophagus and mummy

Figure 6.63 Canopic jars

The organs from mummified bodies were placed in jars which were usually painted. The four sons of Horus each guarded an organ. For instance Hapi (baboon head) guards the lungs while Duamutef (jackal) guards the stomach.

It is easy to forget the changes that took place in both ritual structures and the nature of religion during the three thousand years up to the arrival of the Romans in Egypt. The cults of particular deities were identified with by different pharaohs and their popularity changed as a result. Styles of ritual, styles of mummification, styles of ritual burial and accompanying grave goods all change radically over this three thousand year period to say nothing of tomb location and decoration. King Djoser would have been quite at home next to the Giza Pyramids but baffled by the rock cut tomb of Tutankhamen by which time Djoser's own 'Step Pyramid' at Sakkara was already thirteen hundred years old! Certainly there are no easy answers to dealing with the complexity of Egyptian archaeology. Complex sites and objects, such as the Palette of Narmer and the talatat from Akhenaton's Temple to the Aten at Tell el Amarna must be approached strictly in period context to avoid the dangers inherent in simplistic developmental scenarios. The physical material itself must always be the place to start.

• hthttp://www.egyptologyonline.com/introduction.htm

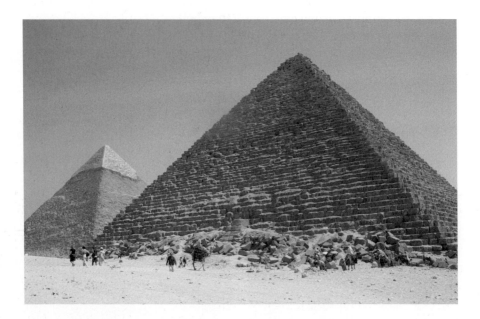

Figure 6.65 *The Great Pyramid of Khufu*

The Great Pyramid is the larger of the two standing 146 metres high and with a base of 230 square metres. However the Pyramid of Khafre is better preserved and stands on higher ground so appears larger. Probably the best known funerary monuments in the world, they were constructed with limestone blocks built up layer by layer and sheathed in white limestone. The precision of the engineering is superb. Tiny passages lead into the interior before opening out into hidden galleries and chambers which included the tomb of the Pharaoh. Robots are being used to look for hidden chambers. One of around 100 pyramids, it was built shortly before 2500 BC as part of a major complex of tombs. These include small pyramids for Khufu's wives and the Mastaba tombs of nobles. A large pit contains a boat which may have been intended for the Pharaoh to use to join Re or it may have been a barge used in the funerary rites. The Sphinx is also close by.

The Archaeology of Settlement

WHAT DOES THE ARCHAEOLOGY OF SETTLEMENT COVER?

Whether you are studying a range of different cultures or following a thematic course, settlement is likely to be a central topic. However, the term itself can mean several things.

Today, when we think of settlements we usually mean cities, towns and villages. However, for most of human history none of these existed. For periods when the population was mobile rather than sedentary, humans created a range of temporary camps and sites for processing raw materials and food. Sometimes caves or rock shelters were repeatedly used for occupation and rich deposits remain. Other sites consist of scatters of flakes from stone tool making (debitage) or animal bone remains from a butchery site. It is likely that these people identified with an area of the landscape, through which they may

have moved on a seasonal basis, rather than living in one fixed place as we do.

The term site does not adequately cover repeated activity in the same area (or 'locale') or the range of activities across the physical landscape. For many past societies, off-site areas that we sometimes detect as flint-scatters or field systems were as important as the 'sites' which archaeologists have tended to excavate. The work of Binford in particular demonstrates that individual sites can provide a rather biased picture of activity in the past and that there is a need to consider the whole settlement 'system'.

Settlement archaeology, therefore, includes the study of both permanent and temporary sites and the interaction of humans with their landscape in order to understand how they adapted to it. Human impact on the landscape from forest clearance to division by boundaries into territory

Figure 7.1 *Mesolithic tent*

Relatively few settlements in the British Isles are known before the Bronze Age. Some degree of mobility, perhaps based on herding seems to have continued from the Mesolithic into the Neolithic. Instead of the foundations of houses, typical settlements from this period tend to be a series of small stakeholes and hearths. At Mount Sandel and Morton these were interpreted as the remains of skin covered 'benders' or tents as recreated here.

KEY TERM

Site

A broad definition is useful here. The term is applied to field monuments, such as round barrows, to concealed evidence, such as cropmarks on aerial photographs, and even to towns.

A **site** is any place where traces of human activity are found. Usually these traces include artefacts but depending on the period studied they might include remains of structures, faunal remains or modification of the landscape such as a quarry. Boundaries make it easier to define sites, but many sites appear as unenclosed scatters of material. The recent emphasis on the significance of natural places in the ritual life of past peoples in the works of Bradley (2000b) and Tilley (1994) stretches the definition still further. For this reason some writers have adopted the term 'locales' for less easily defined places. The duration of use of a site might range from a few hours for a hunting site to centuries for a village or town. A settlement is just one type of site. The specific forms of site will vary according to period: kill-site, barrow, motte, mill, etc.

Structures

Interpreting the function of buildings and other structures on archaeological sites

Intra-site analysis

Discovering the spatial distribution of activities on archaeological sites

Inter-site analysis

Tracing settlement patterns and the relationship between different sites

THE ARCHAEOLOGY OF SETTLEMENT

Landscape

The impact of humans on their environment and their use of it

The meaning of settlement

Interpreting the importance of different sites and places to people in the past

Figure 7.2 The archaeology of settlement

KEY TERM

Sedentary

Essentially **sedentary** means living in one place. It used to be thought that hunter-gatherers were mobile or nomadic and that people 'settled down' with the advent of farming. Evidence from archaeology and anthropology suggests that the reality is more complex. Many cultures have existed whose settlement pattern lies somewhere between the two poles of mobile and sedentary. A wealth of terms such as semi-sedentary, radiating or tethered mobility have been used to describe these patterns. Hodder argues that in the Neolithic people became 'entangled' with artefacts which they increasingly used to mediate between themselves and their environment or other people. Just as there is a truism that the longer you stay in one place the more 'stuff' you accumulate, the decisions Neolithic people made about 'things' led to accumulations of artefacts and permanent structures. These impeded movement and they became increasingly sedentary.

is therefore a vital part of settlement study. Archaeologists also try to understand the ways in which people in the past understood their landscape through ideas such as ownership, territory and status. To do this they need to identify and explain the spatial distribution of past human activities. This might mean understanding the location of sites within a landscape or the placing of structures or other features within a settlement. At a micro level it includes studying activities within a room or living floor. The key questions asked usually revolve around identification of functions or the reasons for patterns in their distribution. Artefacts, ecofacts and features are the key evidence base in studying of distribution of ancient activities.

RECONSTRUCTING ANCIENT LANDSCAPES

Huge progress has been made in recent years in our ability to research and understand past landscapes. By attempting to reconstruct local environments, archaeologists hope to understand how sites developed and were abandoned, and how people adapted to their surroundings. To do this, archaeology uses intensive regional surveys that borrow from geology, biology and environmental science.

The land surface

Today's landscape has been shaped by human and natural activity on top of a geological base. Observing the morphology (shape) of the modern landscape is the starting point for research. Major investigations will also use GIS to produce digital maps and 3D models of past environments.

For the Palaeolithic and Mesolithic, understanding of geological changes is essential. For example, sea levels and the courses of rivers were often radically different. At Elveden in Suffolk geophysical survey was used to track ancient river channels running west-east through a series of narrow gorges. Today the land is flat and drains north-south.

- http://www.esri.com/industries/archaeology/index.html

For most periods, data on soils is essential both to understand the environment it may have supported in the past and to track changes in its composition due to human activity (◀ p. 72). For example, the soils of many upland areas, including Dartmoor, show that they were once wooded. Clearance and agriculture in the Bronze

KEY STUDY

Nunamiut ethnoarchaeology

Binford's (1978) classic ethnoarchaeological research project amongst the Nunamiut Eskimo examined the dynamics of their settlement pattern through seasonal movement from an archaeological perspective. His studies revealed the huge range of territory covered and the variable factors that influenced the location and timing of campsites. Specialist camps were established for hunting, carcass processing and sexual liaisons while non-residential sites included caches of meat and deadfall traps. While careful not to draw direct parallels between Nunamiut and Palaeolithic hunters, Binford was able to argue convincingly that since humans do not confine their behaviour to identifiable sites, we should study sites as part of a wider context. Drawing an analogy with the parts of a car engine he showed that in order to understand the activities of a mobile society we need to fit all the parts of the system together to see the whole picture, from hunting stands to skinning sites. Within the sites he put great emphasis on the spatial relationship between lithic and bone evidence.

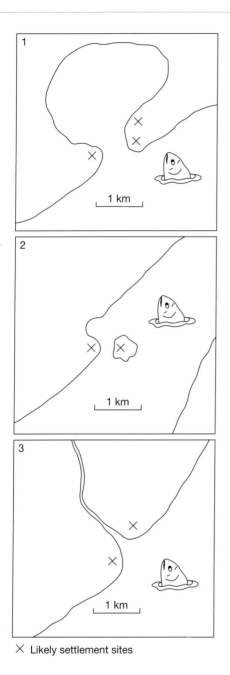

X Likely settlement sites

Age contributed to degradation of the soil and the formation of 'iron pans' which have prevented their use for crops since then. Studies of eroded layers of soil from the highlands of New Guinea around Kuk Swamp enabled Baylis-Smith (1996) to identify the start of slash and burn agriculture in the surrounding forests.

The environment

Climatic data can be obtained from international studies of deep-sea cores, varves and ice cores. These methods involve the examination of annual layers, which reflect climate at the time. In the case of sea cores the tiny organisms trapped in sediment were sensitive to contemporary oxygen levels. Strata of ice laid down at the poles reflect the temperature and salinity of the ocean at that time. Varves are layers of sediment at the bottom of lakes. Their thickness reflects the extent of annual thawing and the length of summer. Local climates can be inferred from ecofacts including animal bones, invertebrates and plant remains, especially pollen (◄ p. 84) The types of plants growing on specific soils can also provide evidence of past microclimates. For example, bluebells and oxlips indicate where ancient woodland stood. Consequently, landscape archaeology often begins with desktop research (◄ p. 4).

For more recent periods a wider range of evidence becomes available. The texts by Aston, Fleming and Muir in the bibliography provide a wealth of examples. Their research has revealed that earlier patterns of land use are often fossilised within today's pattern of fields and woods. Some boundaries may date back to at least Roman times and the hedges that mark some of them

Figure 7.3 *Finding Mesolithic sites on the seabed*

The building of the Oresund Bridge between Denmark and Sweden in the 1990s provides a good example of a model being used to locate sites. Danish archaeologists had observed a pattern in the positioning of fish traps at entrances to lagoons or where streams entered the sea. They reasoned that settlements would cluster around such suitable locations. The results of underwater surveys which had mapped the topography of submerged landscapes on the sea-bottom were used to predict where sites might be found. When divers investigated these locations their success rate was over 75% and included well-preserved settlement remains.

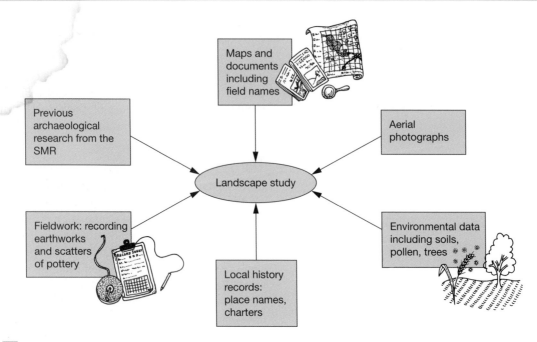

Figure 7.4 *Sources for reconstructing past landscapes*

may be almost as old. Field names provide clues to what the land was used for. For example, *assart* refers to land cleared from woodland, while *wick* and *chester* refer to settlements.

Seasonality

People in the past often exploited different parts of the landscape at different times of the year. Ecofacts have been used on many transitory sites to identify periods of occupation. The activities around the Palaeolithic sites of Ambrona and Torralba were identified by the bones of migratory birds while occupation periods of the Mesolithic midden on Oronsay were estimated from the ear bones (or otoliths) of fish. These methods are not without controversy. The antlers found at Star Carr have been used to argue for the site's use in almost every season. Seasonal mobility is not limited to hunter-gatherers. Herders (pastoralists) often follow a yearly cycle, spreading out onto higher or cooler grazing areas during the early summer and then coming together in more sheltered areas for the winter. This pattern is called transhumance.

IDENTIFYING HUMAN USE OF THE LANDSCAPE

The term 'cultural ecology' has been used to describe the relationship between people and landscape. Humans are part of the ecosystem like other living organisms and climate, environment and natural food sources impose some limits on human populations and how they live. However, unlike that of other mammals, human movement around and use of the landscape cannot be explained solely in terms of biology and the physical environment. Humans adapt to their environment through the use of cultural technology. They can extend the range of resources and territory they exploit beyond their natural biological limits by, for example, harvesting sea fish through the development of boats, traps and nets during the Mesolithic (▶ p. 240) or using irrigation to farm arid areas. To understand the

KEY SITE

Hayley Wood

Rackham's (1990) study drew on estate documents from the fourteenth century onwards and fieldwork to show how this ash and hazel woodland was managed as a renewable crop. Timbers were felled and replanted on a thirty-year cycle and coppiced on a seven-year rotation. His work demonstrates the range of evidence available to the woodland archaeologist including monuments, banks and the trees themselves. Coppiced and pollarded trees still remain from managed woodland.

Figure 7.5 *Coppices and pollards (after Rackham)*

These are two of the easiest examples of woodland management to spot. Coppiced trees are repeatedly cut back to a stool. This encourages the growth of lots of long straight shoots suitable for fences, arrows and kindling. Where animals are present which might eat the shoots, pollards are used instead. The tree is repeatedly cut back to about a few metres height (a bolling). A, B and C show the process before and after harvest then after a year's new growth. Even when management has ceased and the tree has reached normal height, the distorted trunk or broad stool is a give-away.

dynamics of human adaptation, archaeologists need to understand both the environment of the area studied and the technology available to the people living there. Humans can also modify their environment. Human fertility is not just determined by the carrying capacity of the land as the modern world demonstrates. However, the relationship is complex as archaeology can demonstrate. The collapse of the Mesopotamian civilisation at Mashkan Shapir (▶ p. 224) provides a classic example. The city prospered in a desert area through the development of irrigation and the construction of a network of canals. At one time the city was also a port. Unfortunately irrigation contributed to the rapid salination of

the soil. Crop yields collapsed and the civilisation crumbled. This process of human change provoking environmental change is referred to as feedback. Flannery (1976) identified an example of positive feedback in his study of the Oaxaca Valley in Mexico. His study showed how mobile foragers had encouraged the spread of a type of grass, which was to develop into maize. Maize flourished and as the average size of maize cobs grew, it became a major component of human diets. Maize was able to support a higher density and more sedentary human population than previously. Eventually this meant that there could not be a return to a foraging existence and dependency on maize agriculture increased.

KEY STUDY

Early medieval settlement in the Cotswolds

Between the decline of Roman towns and villas and the emergence of known villages by the eleventh century, settlement patterns in the Cotswolds are hard to detect. The absence of dateable ceramics from the archaeological record means that fieldwalking has contributed little and there has been no major excavation of a village. Reece's ongoing study (1998) focuses on the possibility that hedgerows may be indicative of past settlement locations. They would have been used to separate arable land from pasture and trackways and would be expected to occur along tracks and within a doughnut shaped zone around settlement. The idea that there is a direct relationship between the number of species in a hedge and its age is well established. Hooper's hedgerow hypothesis held that the number of species in a 30 yard stretch equalled the age in centuries. It assumed diversity increase over time as new seeds take root. However this model only really works for the last 1000 years in certain conditions.

Through examination of the species in Cotswold hedges Reece found that periods in which hedge management lapsed led to domination by a few species and the elimination of slow growing species. This means that the Hooper method may underestimate the age of the oldest hedges. Reece found that combinations of certain key species such as wayfaring tree and guelder rose were better indicators of older hedges. Through comprehensive mapping of richer (older) hedges he hopes to identify lost settlements.

Figure 7.6 *One of the Culleenamore middens on Ireland's west coast*

These huge mounds formed by the discarding of tons of oysters and other shells stand several metres high in places. Their builders were probably exploiting migrating salmon and pigs and plant foods from the surrounding woods. Middens are found from Portugal to the Baltic and represent repeated seasonal occupation by Mesolithic people to exploit marine resources. Although shells form the bulk of the finds, fish and animal bones, hazelnuts, tools and human burials are often present. Hearths and even the traces of dwellings are commonly found in middens. Middens are the first monuments in the British Isles.

KEY SITE

Head Smashed In

The UNESCO world heritage site of Head Smashed In in the Canadian Rocky mountains was in use for nearly 6000 years from at least 3700 BC by the ancestors of the North Peigan tribe, part of the Blackfoot Confederacy.

It is a place where ethnographic, historical and archaeological data have combined to give us an unrivalled picture of a society and economy based around communal hunting. It also illustrates human use of a landscape and the importance of 'off-site' areas to understanding past activity. The name of the site is a translation of the Blackfoot *estipah-skikikini-kots* which refers to the fate of a young man who chose to watch the buffalo jump from underneath the cliff.

The site comprises several linked areas over a wide area of around 600 hectares. The jump-site itself is a 300 metre stretch of cliff over which buffalo were stampeded to fall 35 metres down to the kill site. When excavated this was an 11 metre-deep stratified midden of rock and bone and produced a long typological sequence of lithics. These include blades, choppers and thousands of

Figure 7.7 *Reconstruction of main features at Head Smashed In*

KEY SITE *cont.*

Head Smashed In

points and arrowheads. The most recent layers contain metal points indicating that the site was in use when European traders first arrived on the plains. The site probably went out of use when the use of horses spread north from Spanish colonies and a new method of hunting developed.

North-west of the jump-site is the drainage basin of Olsen creek. This is a grassy area of 40 square kilometres surrounded by the Porcupine Hills with two exits leading directly to the cliff. Buffalo would be herded into this basin along the valleys of streams which fed into Olsen Creek. Within the basin are numerous lines comprising hundreds of cairns, each approximately a metre in diameter. The cairns lead towards the exits which in turn led straight to the cliffs. These are the drive lanes along which buffalo would be stampeded.

South-east of the cliffs is a flat area with many hearths, pits, circles of stones and huge amounts of smashed and processed bones. Artefacts include bone awls and beads, some pottery and lithic scrapers, butchery tools and drills. There are also huge quantities of fire-cracked rock.

To interpret these finds, archaeologists made use of historical accounts including that of Peter Fidler, an English surveyor working for the Hudson Bay. He was taken through the area in 1792 by a Peigan band and witnessed the use of a jump-site. There are also Blackfoot ethnographic records which provide detail of social organisation for the most recent use of the site.

Blackfoot social organisation was based around the family and then the band. These were relatively fluid groups of around 100–200 people living in tipis. They followed a mobile lifestyle well adapted to the climate and food sources of the plains. During the winter the Blackfoot bands were widely dispersed in sheltered valleys where there was fuel, water and some food. In the summer bands would come together for tribal ceremonies and communal hunting. The movements or 'seasonal round' of the tribe was structured around the migration of the buffalo. Bands would come together, particularly in autumn for communal hunts at buffalo jumps. The organisers of the hunts derived status, wealth and influence over the tribes. This included ritual specialists who would encourage the buffalo to come.

Young men would encourage the buffalo into the gathering areas by imitating the sounds of lost calves. Other hunters would move in upwind of the herd and scare them into the drive lanes. The cairns may have hidden other hunters or supported branches which would move in the wind and further alarm the animals. Once the herd was stampeding, the animals at the front could not stop and the entire herd would plunge over the cliffs. At the bottom, hunters would finish off wounded animals and begin the butchery process. In the processing area, meat, horns and hide would be stripped from the bones and bones were smashed open to extract marrow. Pits were lined with buffalo hide, filled with water and brought to boiling point using hot rocks from the hearths. This would render the grease from broken bones.

This vast processing operation provided for most of the tribe's needs. Bone was worked into tools and ornaments. Skins provided clothing, containers and clothes. Meat was consumed in a feast but the great majority was stored. Thin strips of meat were dried on racks by the sun or a fire, pounded with rocks and then mixed with an equal amount of fat and marrow. Sometimes flavoured with powdered berries, this 'pemmican' would be stored in hide pouches for months or even years. During the processing families would live in their tipis. The rings of stones mark where the edges of the tipi were anchored to the ground. Once the work was completed they would disperse, dragging their tipis and carrying pemmican to get them through the winter.

Site catchment analysis

In the 1970s archaeologists interested in understanding how humans exploited their environment and the extent of settlement 'territories' borrowed a range of analytical techniques from economic geography. Prominent amongst these was site catchment analysis. This assumes that settlements were not located randomly across the landscape, but were sited to maximise efficiency and minimise effort in gathering resources. In other words the point where it ceases to be worth expending energy to get to in order to forage or farm is the limit of a site's catchment. It may also be the edge of its territory. By walking and analysing the area around a site, archaeologists tried to identify the resources its inhabitants would have been able to exploit and therefore understand its location, function and the subsistence strategy of its inhabitants. Ethnographic studies of site exploitation territories were used to determine the distance people might travel for subsistence resources. For instance, foragers such as the !Kung bushmen of the Kalahari rarely walk more than 10 kilometres (about 2 hours walk) from their base with a range of 20–30 kilometres to other sites with whom they traded and areas they occasionally visited, for example for building materials, clay or summer pasture. Studies of peasant farmers suggest that their normal limit is just 5 kilometres. Although models tend to feature circular territories around sites, in reality they would reflect local topography. This was the case with pioneering studies of early farmers in coastal Palestine.

A problem with site catchments based on time-travel is that they can be difficult and time-consuming to work out on the ground. A solution is to use path-distance models. These divide up a map into a grid of cells and calculate the time and energy 'cost' of moving through each cell. Aspects of the landscape which impede movement are assigned values so for instance a cell with a steep, rocky slope covered in thorn bushes and divided by a ravine would take more effort (and 'cost' more) to move through than a flat one. Where data on terrain and vegetation is available in a GIS database these calculations can be done very quickly. This method can also be used to explore the relationship between different sites. An international GIS project on the Croatian island of Hvar explored the relationship between soils, terrain and different settlements in a number of periods. A path-cost model was used to establish site catchments for each of the major Bronze and Iron Age hillforts. Then data on land quality and water sources was compared to establish whether hillforts had been sited to maximise control of the best land. There was a strong correlation with the catchments but the actual locations of the hillforts were often on poor sites. The explanation is that these were selected as defensive positions on high ground but still close to farm land. In the Roman period however, villas are invariably sited on good land with the best climate for agriculture. Analysis of the Stari Grad plain, an area with no climatic variation, demonstrated clearly that land quality was the most important determinant of settlement location.

- http://www.arch-ant.bham.ac.uk/research/vince/index.htm

Distribution of Roman settlements in relation to land quality on the Stari Grad Plain, Hvar (after Gaffney)

Figure 7.8 Roman settlement and land quality on Hvar

Site catchment analysis provides a model, which can be compared with archaeological evidence such as food, remains, pollen and artefacts. Human remains can also provide some dietary information as to which resources were particularly exploited (◀ p. 75). Similar ideas can be used to understand settlements in the historic period. Mick Aston's study of Ashington in Somerset (1985) used the idea of site catchment to illuminate the way that medieval farmsteads organised their exploitation of the local environment. Resources needed on a daily basis were produced in or close to the settlement with less frequently needed resources located further out. He also demonstrated how the landscape could be used as a text to read off past activities and relationships.

Plants are good indicators of local environments because we know the conditions that the various species can tolerate. Analysis of plant samples from sites can provide insights into the 'catchment area' beyond the immediate locality with people bringing plants into the site which they gathered or harvested elsewhere (◀ p. 120). A good example of this sort of study was the analysis of weed seeds in the plant remains at Danebury. Weeds, like food crops, prefer specific soil conditions, such as wet lowland valleys or higher chalk pastures. From the types of weed present archaeologists were able to infer the soil conditions in which the main crops were grown before being brought into the hill fort. This information meant that the catchment area of Danebury in terms of agriculture was more clearly understood and future research could be focused on the soil types contributing to this overall assemblage.

However, site catchment analysis has limitations. It depends on accurate reconstruction of ancient landscapes, which is difficult since traces of changes in much of the flora and fauna may not have survived. It assumes that people in the past were aware of and could access the resources we can identify today. It also assumes that their behaviour was economically 'normal'. That is,

they sought to maximise returns for the least effort. Finally, it is a rather deterministic model of human behaviour. It may well be that spiritual, cultural or political considerations were as important factors in decisions about site placement as economics. Kent's (1989) ethnoarchaeological study of modern sites in the Kalahari tested the importance of site catchment in determining difference in size, complexity and period of occupation between different settlements. She compared the camps of different groups of farmers and foragers to see whether ethnicity or a major source of subsistence was critical, and was able to talk to the people themselves about their behaviour. There was a marked variability of data but it could largely be explained by social factors, for example the layout and range of features was determined by how long people expected to remain at the site. Kent's work reminds us never to overlook human choice even when investigating environmental issues. Nevertheless, site catchment analysis remains widely used in exploring potential site use and in forming hypotheses to be tested against archaeological data.

Studying spatial distribution

The distribution pattern of sites and settlements across a landscape has the potential to tell us a great deal about the interaction between people and environment and the nature of social organisation. The first stage is to plot known sites of similar dates on a map and then add aerial and surface survey results if they are available. The distribution can then be analysed for signs of patterns, clustering, and relationships between larger and smaller sites. GIS is particularly useful here. Once the data is inputted, queries can relate sites to a wide range of factors including soils, water and intervisibility.

Describing the pattern is easier than explaining it. Various types of cluster analysis have been used to test archaeological site distribution against geographical models of distribution.

KEY STUDY

Mesolithic hunters of the Trentino

Clark (2000) studied the connection between sites, environment and economic strategy in the mountains of Northern Italy. He was able to detect diachronic or gradual change over a long period in assemblages of animal bones (◀ p. 72) and lithic tools from well preserved deposits in valley rock shelters. By combining this data with comparative analysis of scattered assemblages at high altitude open air sites he traced changes in use of the landscape and hunting patterns. During the early Mesolithic, hunters

Figure 7.9 *Replica of a rock shelter in use by a group of hunters*

went up into the mountains during the summer to kill Ibex and chamois. To minimise the risk of wasted trips they developed arrow technology to maximise their chances of killing animals at well chosen ambush sites such as Colbricon. To facilitate this they had to acquire flint from quarry sites and bring it with them into the mountains. Ibex and chamois bone assemblages at the rock shelter sites suggest selected joints of meat were being brought down by the hunters.

In the later Mesolithic the high level intercept sites were abandoned and bone assemblages only comprised resources from the lower woods and river valleys. Lithics also changed in order to kill forest animals. Whole carcasses were now butchered at the shelters. This suggests that hunting territories were much smaller. These changes coincided with an extension of forest cover into the mountains. High level hunting became less reliable. To reduce risk new strategies, tools and landscape exploitation patterns were adopted.

Figure 7.10 *A Mesolithic hearth at the Grotto D'Ernesto*

A hearth from the Grotto D'Ernesto rock shelter. The positioning of artefacts and ecofacts around the hearth provides clues about the size of the group and the activities they were involved in. Charcoal and bone collagen provided radio carbon dates around 8500 BP. Most of the bones were from young male animals which suggests very selective hunting. Upper leg bones were rarely found here but were found in larger shelters which suggest that this site was not a 'home base'.

KEY STUDY *cont.*

Mesolithic hunters of the Trentino

a) Early Mesolithic

b) Late Mesolithic

Key

Flint source	Red deer	Caves and rock settlers
Wild pig	Ibex	
Roe deer (small deer)	Fish	Upland hunting camp

Figure 7.11
Economic changes in the Trentino region during the Mesolithic

During the early Mesolithic bone and lithic data from the valley rock shelters suggests that bands of hunters operated over wide areas, exploiting resources on a seasonal basis. Lithic evidence from high level sites suggests small groups from summer hunting camps ambushed ibex and red deer herds through intercept hunting strategies.

By the late Mesolithic, pollen evidence suggests that trees had colonised the high pastures, pushing herd animals and ibex beyond the reach of the hunters. Evidence from the valley rock shelters suggests a switch to broad spectrum foraging within a much more limited territory. Riverine resources increasingly supplemented forest animals killed through encounter hunting strategies.

Figure 7.13 *Part of the Jupiter Column from Cirencester*

As the second largest Roman town in Britain Corinium had massive and extensive city walls and a range of public buildings including temples, basilica and an amphitheatre. Its high status is also suggested by the lavish mosaics and frescos in opulent townhouses. Proof of its political importance comes from this massive carving which stood in the forum or market place and included carvings of several deities. On a nearby inscription stone a general (Septimius) dedicated the column to Britannica Prima. This indicates that Corinium was the capital of the South-Western province.

Figure 7.12 *Territorial models from Geography*
The effects of modelling with CPT (b) and Theissen polygons (c) on a prehistoric landscape (a).

Central place theory (CPT) based on the modelling of Christaller assumes that as the landscape fills up, settlements will be spaced evenly throughout it. Where settlements are more or less of equal size this reflects a fairly equal society. Where there is considerable variation in size it reflects a hierarchical society and one where the larger places perform central functions and provide a wider range of goods on behalf of a cluster of smaller satellite settlements. These will also emerge at regular intervals across the landscape. The most efficient pattern of spacing is a hexagonal lattice so areas for each central place are modelled by drawing hexagons around them. A study of medieval English market towns found that they fitted this model quite well. Each town was 4–6 miles from its neighbours and served a cluster of satellite hamlets and farmsteads. **Thiessen polygons** have been used in similar ways. These are created by identifying the midpoints between settlements, and joining them to form irregular shaped zones of influence and exploitation.

These methods can be used to generate hypotheses to test ideas about territory or catchment. CPT could also be used to suggest where there might be undiscovered sites. Such models have been used in a variety of regional studies including predicting the influence of Roman towns and changing social organisation in Iron Age Wessex. Cunliffe (1995) noted that a wide distribution of hill forts gave way to fewer, larger hill forts later in the first millennium. He interpreted this as representing a wider scale of social organisation with the development of tribal chiefdoms. A similar approach was used by Renfrew (1973) who interpreted the distribution of long barrows on Arran as reflecting the territories of groups of pioneer farmers. He found that the areas of land involved were similar to the holdings of modern crofts.

These idealised models tend to minimise the contribution of social and cultural influences and the influence of topography. CPT fits all known sites into one of the categories in a hierarchy of sites, which may not be realistic. A single pattern of settlement may be the physical expression of

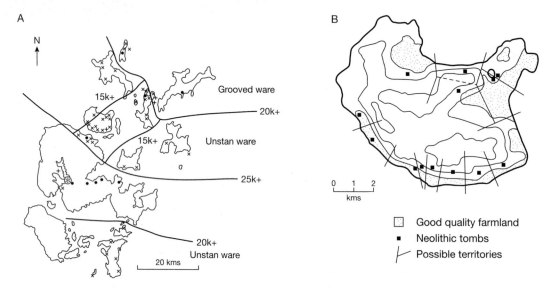

Henge
Tomb with grooved ware
Tomb with Bookan type ware
20K+ etc man-hour territories

Figure 7.14 *Territories in prehistoric Orkney*

These diagrams summarise two attempts to use Neolithic monuments and related ceramics to model tribal groups, territories and increasing social complexity. Hedges' model takes the whole archipelago and divides the major monuments according to the main pottery found in them. He also models the manpower needed to build each type of monument from small chambered cairn up to henges and stone circles. The result is several tribal groups perhaps merging under a chief for larger projects. Renfrew's work on Rousay relates tombs to arable land and takes account of more recent patterns of land ownership. He reasoned that each tomb might represent a family group who owned a strip of land going back from the sea to the rocky hills. Each unit would have some arable and some grazing land and access to the sea. The tombs marked their claim and also linked the remains of their ancestors to the fertility of their land. A similar explanation has been offered for the pattern of Brochs along the western shores of the Outer Hebrides.

many different social systems. Belief, social relations and political considerations can be significant. For example, the distribution of Roman towns could reflect administrative areas for tax and law and order as well as the influence of markets. Some small sites may also have a social or ritual importance, which means they are of major importance in their region. One has to be confident that all the plotted features are related (for example contemporary) and also that no significant ones have been omitted. If not, the analysis is of the results of archaeological discoveries rather than of decisions made in the past. The key point is that these are models. Their primary function should be in helping generate questions and hypotheses that can be tested against archaeological data rather than fitting data to a model.

The social landscape: territory and boundaries

Of course, many social territories include many sites and are not obviously shaped by geography. Spatial distribution is of little use in explaining the British Empire of the nineteenth century although another geographical model, world systems theory, is useful in helping understand its workings. For state societies, written records often exist which help to identify centres and their territories. Roman inscriptions and the stone stelae of the Maya have both been used in this way. For some states the extent of political control is indicated by physical boundaries. Hadrian's Wall and the Great Wall of China are well known from the ancient world but during the twentieth century fortified borders became the norm for nation states. The ruins of France's Maginot Line and the 'Iron Curtain' dividing East and West Europe provide classic examples. Less certainty surrounds the purpose of early medieval earthworks such as Offa's Dyke or Wansdyke. Artefacts of administration also provide clues to territories and the influence of central authorities. These include clay seals (▶ p. 263), emblems,

standard weights and measures and coinage. However, influence and territory are not identical. Well-recognised currencies were used in the past outside their area of issue just as the US dollar is today. The evidence may be

Figure 7.15 *Ormaig rock art panel, Kilmartin*

This recently discovered example is relatively unweathered and includes a unique rosette or dial motif. Like many other panels in the area it is located on poor agricultural soil near an entry point into the Kilmartin Valley. There are extensive views from the carvings but they cannot be seen from a distance. Similar arrangements of rock art have been noted on Ilkley Moor and around the Milfield Basin. Dating from the Neolithic or early Bronze Age there are several interpretations of their function. Waddington (1998) argues that they 'inscribed grazing areas'. In other words they identified secure upland pasture for particular groups which was used in summer as part of annual transhumance cycles. Bradley (1997) believes that intervisibility between the sites is more significant and that they may denote pathways through the landscape.

KEY STUDY

Isotopes, diet and territory

Bioarchaeologists use skeletal material to find out about lifestyle but it can also help us understand settlements and society. Two recent studies by Shulting in south-west Britain are shedding new light on territories and economies during the Mesolithic. Unfortunately bones have been recovered from few sites from this period and several of the best collections have been lost. Aveline's Hole in the Mendips was the largest known cemetery in Britain and may have held 100 skeletons when the cave was first opened in 1797. Most were taken by collectors and the remaining 21 excavated by 1933. Sadly most of these along with tools and faunal remains were destroyed by German bombing in 1940. Schulting's team analysed the few survivors as well as recovering bone fragments missed by the excavators from the cave. Radiocarbon dates showed that the bones had been deposited between 10,400±200 BP. Close examination suggested they were smaller in stature and shorter lived than the modern population and had not always had easy lives. One of the skeletons suffered from osteoarthritis. An ulna (elbow joint) was shiny from bone to bone contact where the cartilage had been worn away. This would be due to repetitive strenuous action such as rowing or throwing. Harris lines in dental enamel suggested childhood stress. In farming communities this tends to be caused pre-harvest when food supplies are running low; for foragers it tends to be in late spring.

The cemetery, which was not sited in an area where food would have been plentiful, suggests it was a significant location for other reasons, perhaps spiritual. It is what is sometimes termed

Figure 7.16 *Tracing diet through stable isotope analysis*

Along the horizontal axis the ratio of carbon isotopes varies depending on whether food has come from mainly terrestrial or marine sources. Along the vertical axis the level of N15 is enriched higher up the food chain. Where there are many links in the chain (or trophic levels) the concentration is most pronounced. The approximate position of each of the human groups studied is indicated.

KEY STUDY *cont.*

Isotopes, diet and territory

a 'persistent place'. Strontium isotope analysis of 8 molars and some faunal remains showed that all had grown up close to the Mendips. This suggested a relatively small annual range of movement. Carbon and nitrogen isotope analysis showed that they had a terrestrial diet. Faunal remains suggested red deer and pig were their main prey animals.

Similar tests were undertaken on Mesolithic samples from the Caldey Island and Gower areas of South Wales. The Island group had a largely marine diet; coastal samples from Worm's Head suggested a more mixed intake while inland samples were similar to Aveline's Hole. This reflects patterns in Ireland where a coastal group at Ferriter's Cove had a marine diet while burials from Killuragh Cave near the Shannon suggested a terrestrial one. This is despite large numbers of salmon in the river and being only 30 kilometres from the estuary.

Taken together, these results point to groups continually using small territories over long periods of time. This is very different from the familiar model of seasonal movement between coast and uplands which is based on Scottish coastal sites. Perhaps inland and coastal groups adapted in different ways, with different tool kits and knowledge. Their separateness may help to explain the evidence for violence in some late Mesolithic societies if territories were seen as exclusive. It may also help to explain differential adaptation to changes in the Neolithic. Schulting suggests that this evidence combined with an understanding of minimum healthy population sizes (at least 500 people) could provide insights into population levels in the Mesolithic. The dietary evidence from his study suggests each territory was approximately 25 kilometres in diameter.

contradictory in other ways. Zones of pottery and coin distribution have often not matched up. For early periods there may have been markers of territory which have not survived. These might have included totems or the appearance of peoples themselves.

On a local level, the landscape can also be used to explore power and status. The position of powerful social institutions such as churches and country houses are often prominent in the landscape. The traces of deserted villages on land cleared for sheep pasture in the later middle ages (◀ p. 21) or for deer parks in the eighteenth century provide insights into local control. Studies such as that at Shapwick (◀ p. 12) have revealed the way that the apparently natural distribution of villages nestling in the countryside was often a medieval creation. Powerful estate owners reorganised the landscape, creating nucleated villages from scattered farmsteads to

maximise control and profitability. Modern field patterns strongly reflect the enclosure movement of the early nineteenth century, which was pursued for similar reasons.

- http://loki.stockton.edu/~ken/wharram/ wharram.htm
- www.le.ac.uk/elh/whittlewood/index.htm

IDENTIFYING THE FUNCTION(S) OF ARCHAEOLOGICAL SITES

Archaeological sites are usually categorised by function. Generally this is a matter of determining the primary function since most sites have several. A castle is primarily defensive but may also have a domestic, economic and political function as well as being a status symbol. The same point could also be made about individual buildings. Archaeologists therefore try and identify what activities were carried out and whether

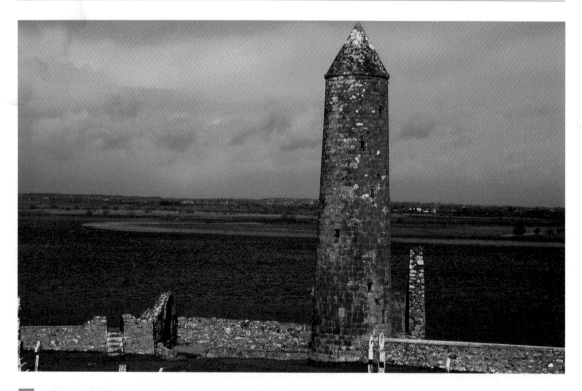

Figure 7.17 *Clonmacnoise Monastery*

This tower at Clonmacnoise overlooks the Shannon at a point where divers have discovered traces of an ancient bridge. The remote monastery was founded by St Ciaran in AD 545 and became a centre of monastic learning. However, the site was well chosen at a crossing point both to maximise influence and to gain income from travellers and pilgrims. The monastery became one of the richest in Ireland. Some of the finest medieval metalworking and manuscripts were produced there and it became the burial site of kings. The stone buildings including the twelfth-century tower testify to its success. It also attracted unwanted attention and was raided many times, starting with the Vikings. A Norman castle alongside it hints at the strategic value of such a location.

there are any significant patterns in the evidence that might indicate that those particular spaces (areas, buildings or rooms) had specific functions. For example, was food preparation separated from storage? Taken together these enable the functions of the site to be described and assessed to determine their relative importance.

Evidence of human activities varies widely according to period, degree of preservation and the resources available to the excavators. If a site is from a historic period there may be written accounts, artistic depictions, plans and for the last few centuries maps, photographs, film and even living people! This is clearly not the case with much of prehistory. While there are cave sites and rock shelters with deep deposits of cultural material that have been sheltered from erosion, these sites are not typical. Most Palaeolithic sites have been subject to the ravages of a full range of transformation processes (◄ p. 112) and any interpretation has to take these into account. The main evidence for most sites will come from the archaeological record resulting from excavation or reconnaissance survey. Archaeologists will then try to recognise and explain patterns in the data. This relies on the comprehensiveness and accuracy of excavation recording (◄ p. 44) for its validity.

KEY STUDY

Minoan settlement hierarchy

Minoan towns of the early second millennium BC are comparable in scale with all but the largest towns of the Middle East, yet are very different. No Minoan town has anything like a complete defensive wall. As a result the internal settlement pattern is not dictated by those walls in the way that cities such as Mashkan Shapir were. Apart from the palace complexes, there is no zoning of different activities or industries and little evidence of street plans being imposed. Workshops such as forges occur in the palaces or are scattered in residential areas while some houses doubled as workshops for pottery or wood-working. Mesopotamian and Egyptian cities are dominated by colossal religious and political architecture such as Ziggurats and statues or reliefs of deities or rulers. While Minoan palaces were prominent, and may have been inserted into existing settlements, they were never overwhelming and their inhabitants remain anonymous. There are no major Minoan temples either. There are some small shrines in the palaces but religious emphasis seems to have been towards remote sites such as caves and mountains.

The larger Minoan towns were characterised by extensive administrative areas and public spaces including this 'theatre' or arena. It is unclear what kind of performances took place in this arena but it is clearly linked to the high status buildings to the left and extensive storage areas to the right. The arena seems designed either for large audiences or large scale participation orchestrated by those living in the palace and controlling the resources.

Nevertheless, the palaces in the larger towns themselves seem to have served as central places. Their storage capacity (▶ p. 258) and public spaces combined with evidence for administration and specialists (▶ p. 283) mark them apart. The mountains of Crete ensured against an even distribution of larger centres across the landscape but there still seem to be patterns. Branigan identified one large town per 200–250 square kilometres. Allowing for a few discoveries in the future he suggested the ratio between large and small towns might be something like 1:5. Both had 'palace' complexes but the scale, range of public buildings, storage capacity and evidence for administration was far greater at the large regional sites than at the smaller provincial sites. There were also some small

▨ **Figure 7.18** Central arena at Phaistos

KEY STUDY *cont.*

Minoan settlement hierarchy

towns which seemed to have a specific economic function such as a port or market. Below these urban centres were villages, hamlets and individual farms. Some of these would have a 'villa' or mini-palace at their heart. Driessen argues that the towns were central places and of higher status than other sites in their region.

The quality and scale of the palace architecture (▶ p. 306) suggests an ability to mobilise labour, materials and technology while the storage capacity and evidence of seals and writing shows that agricultural surpluses of grain, oil, honey, wine, wool and figs were all accumulated there. Finds of identical seal (▶ p. 263) impressions have allowed some reconstruction of exchange networks for particular palaces. In a classic redistributive model, the palaces appear to have converted regional surpluses into ritual, exotic imports and possibly performances.

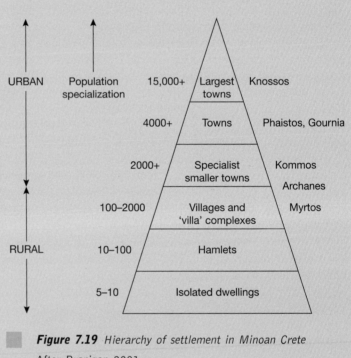

Figure 7.19 Hierarchy of settlement in Minoan Crete

After Branigan 2001

How are different types of activity identified on archaeological sites?

Boundaries such as internal and external walls, fence alignments or ditches are usually intended to separate different activities. This applies equally to a room, a farm or a town. Clear demarcation with boundaries makes detecting patterns of finds or space and comparing finds and features in different areas easier than on open sites. Where boundaries are identified, their shape, size and orientation can provide

indications to their use although analogies will be needed to interpret them. Certain shapes and patterns (for example 'four-posters' or 'church shapes') may occur frequently. This enables interpretation of features on new sites with reference to identified examples from known ones (for example, comparing Roman features with well-preserved examples from sites such as Pompeii). Shapes of buildings and patterns can also be detected from detailed aerial photographs or by remote sensing. Archaeologists use their experience and data from excavation reports to

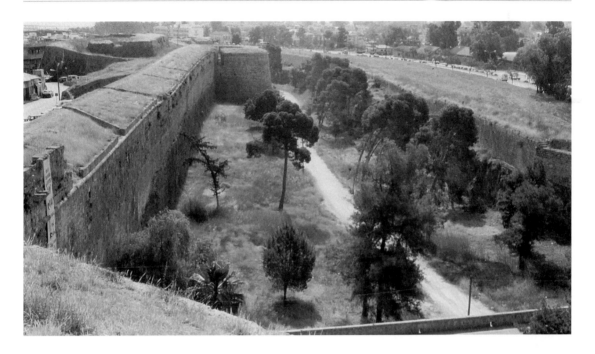

Figure 7.20 *City walls, Famagusta.*

Some city walls were meant to control trade but these massive examples from city walls in Cyprus clearly had a particular threat in mind. The 3 km long low, outer wall shields the main ramparts from artillery. Attackers then have to traverse a 46 m wide moat (which could be flooded) with vertical sides to reach the curtain wall. Projecting bastions provide a field of fire within the moat. The main ramparts are 8 m thick and 15 m high. Built by the Venetians, its 8000 defenders withstood a siege by a Turkish army of 200,000 for 10 months in 1570–1 before starvation led to surrender.

identify connected groups of features. For example, a particular group of holes might be suggested as the postholes of a house from similarities in size, depth, fill, date and because the archaeologist recognises their pattern. Other evidence will be examined to see if the interpretation can be corroborated.

• www.silchester.rdg.ac.uk/

Association of artefacts and other finds with particular areas is the most common archaeological method. Detailed three-dimensional plotting of the distribution of finds across entire excavations enables patterns of activity to be identified. Examples include clusters of hide or bone working flints or the association of

particular artefacts with particular features such as loom weights in a hut doorway. However, one has to be careful not to assign function on the basis of a few finds.

Computers make sophisticated density analysis possible such as comparing ratios of finds to area or volume of earth excavated. This can suggest which areas were most used for particular activities and may counter the bias created by large finds or raw numbers of finds. Similar analysis has been used on pits to suggest that they were not used solely for refuse disposal.

Areas with few finds present more of a challenge. The apparent deliberate clearing or 'purification' of an area can be a signature of ritual activity (for example the ditch at Avebury

KEY STUDIES

Interpreting Iron Age hillforts

Early studies of hill forts often started with classical sources and looked for evidence to support those historical accounts. Caesar had described chiefs and the warlike nature of the Celts. Evidence of violence at sites such as Hod Hill seemed to confirm this. Many had massive and complex earthworks which one might expect at the strongholds of powerful chiefs. Cunliffe's (1985) excavations at Danebury (◄ p. 120) seemed to support this view. The massive storage capacity might indicate foodstuffs being stockpiled by a chief for redistribution or exchange. Cunliffe interpreted Danebury as a central place occupied in part by a ruler, specialists and possibly a warrior aristocracy.

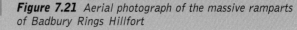 **Figure 7.21** *Aerial photograph of the massive ramparts of Badbury Rings Hillfort*

To us these concentric earthworks and complex entrances look defensive. Excavation of several hillforts has revealed military features including evidence of timber or stone facings to the ramparts and caches of slingshots.

Maiden Castle had been seen as the archetypal military fort by early excavators and there was evidence that it may have been held unsuccessfully against the Romans. However, military use in such an emergency may have been atypical. Sharples (1991) found a more confusing picture. At times defences were built up, at others they were neglected as much of the hillfort was abandoned for long periods. Like Danebury there was massive storage capacity, firstly with four-posters and later with pits. Like Danebury there was little difference in size or artefacts between the mass of huts concentrated inside its massive earthworks. The main signs of an organizing power were the ramparts and the reorganization of houses into rows during later phases. In many respects it was a giant farming village rather than a town. Outside there were few traces of the sort of farms which surround Danebury. This suggests that social organization might have been different at the two sites.

Hill (1996), in a series of attacks on Cunliffe's view of the Iron Age, undertook statistical analysis of the ratios of finds per cubic metre of soil excavated on a range of Iron Age sites. While Danebury produced more finds of loom weights, spindle whorls, ornaments and metal horse fittings than smaller sites, more soil was trowelled to produce them than on other sites. Comparison of the ratio of finds to volume of spoil suggested that Danebury was unexceptional in its density of craft tools and fine goods. Several farmsteads such as Winnall Down produced higher densities of many finds and more evidence of iron working. These sites also had their own storage and similar sheep assemblages to Danebury. Hill also pointed out that the densely packed settlements on rich farmland in the Thames Valley (within a day's ride of Danebury) were undefended. This was hardly likely if hillforts were bases for raiding warbands. Hill used this kind of data to argue for a less hierarchical and warlike Iron Age.

KEY STUDIES
cont.

Interpreting Iron Age hillforts

Collis' (1996) work provides a further insight. He views hill forts principally as enclosures and sets them into a tradition of special hilltop enclosures in southern England stretching back to the early Neolithic. Many hillforts overlie earlier monuments and Danebury in particular has a large number of ritual burials and other deposits in its storage pits. Hill also discovered that just as most round houses and enclosures faced east or south east, most hillforts opened east or west regardless of defensive considerations. Nobody is suggesting that they were never used for defence and never occupied by a powerful leader, just that those may not have been their sole or principal functions. Ritual and seasonal gatherings may also have been important.

Figure 7.22 *Even today the ramparts of Barbury Castle look defensive. The height advantage to defenders using projectiles is clear from the relative positions of the students. Topped with a palisade and with a near vertical facing of stone or timber it would be virtually impregnable. However, this interpretation assumes warfare at the scale of armies. The defences seem excessive if raiding for cattle was the main problem.*

- Champion and Collis 1996
- Cunliffe 1995
- Hill 1996

or the Zapotec temples of San Jose Mogote). However, absence of finds alone should not be taken as proof of ritual purification!

Analysis of soils or other environmental evidence has been used successfully on some sites to determine activity. Phosphate or heavy mineral analysis can indicate where animals have been penned and there is some suggestion that different animals may have different chemical 'signatures'. Other environmental data including the remains of invertebrates with specific habitats can also provide clues (◀ p. 86).

The immediate context of a site can also provide clues to its general function and the activities that may have occurred there. A site surrounded by arable fields is likely to have had areas for processing and storing crops while evidence of watercourses may help to identify the remains of a building as a mill. This is least easy to do in towns where a picture of overall patterns can only be built up over a long time through a series of 'keyhole' excavations.

There are, of course, limits to the conclusions that can be drawn about any site. Archaeologists

KEY TERM

Palimpsest

For the Palaeolithic, assemblages of artefacts and faunal remains are often the key to determining function. The 'living floors' of Olduvai Gorge and Koobi Fora in East Africa with their dense concentration of stone tools and animal bones have been much debated. Archaeologists who took these assemblages at face value tended to see these as kill sites or base home camps where groups of hunters butchered carcasses or shared meat from their prey. This idea has been challenged on the grounds that the 'sites' were unsafe for humans and that microscopic analysis of the bones suggests that humans scavenged the bones after other predators had processed them. Further studies have questioned whether we should consider these as 'sites' at all. Taphonomic studies of bone distributions from predator kills and experimental work on site formation processes affecting tools and bones in the region suggest that the sites might be **palimpsests**, that is, accumulations of material from different times caused by natural forces as well as human activity.

- Schick and Toth 1993
- Binford 1989

are usually investigating at the end of lengthy post-depositional processes and need to understand the impact of these on the evidence. For example, is it a site or a palimpsest? Partial survival, partial recovery, accuracy of find identification and the quality of sampling will also influence what is there to be studied. For example not all excavations will have recovered environmental evidence. Beyond this there is the quality of the insights and interpretations of the archaeologists. Analogies can be drawn from experimental archaeology, ethnography and ethnoarchaeology (◀ p. 125). Studying patterns of deposition from known activities may reveal signatures, which can help unravel evidence from the past. Conclusions will also reflect the values and assumptions of the archaeologists as well as their skill and knowledge. This is even more significant if one hopes to identify areas associated with particular gender, status or age groups.

THE USE OF SPACE ON ARCHAEOLOGICAL SITES

The reasons why sites within the same area differ in their internal layout have been explored by archaeologists drawing on ethnoarchaeology. Binford's work with the Nunamiut (◀ p. 200) provided insights into the complex reasons for differences. He showed that it was wrong to expect the same group of people to produce homogeneous sites. Sites differed due to their role in the overall settlement system. For example, hunting and residential sites used space differently, but even hunting camps might differ widely. The site of a successful hunt might generate many additional activities to the site of an unsuccessful one.

Ethnoarchaeology has identified some of the problems that can occur if the distribution of artefacts and features on a site are interpreted as a direct record of economic decisions and activities. Site maintenance, the practice of disposing of rubbish, may create misleading patterns in the archaeological record. Different materials are treated differently, some being thrown aside while others are recycled or deliberately taken to dumps. Some activities are deliberately sited to be near heat and light while tasks that require a lot of space are rarely in areas where people socialise. In Clarke's (1972) study of Glastonbury Lake Village he used artefactual evidence in relation to spaces marked

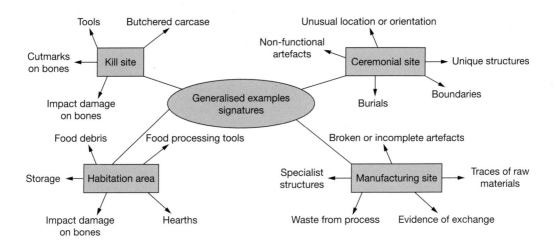

Figure 7.23 *The evidence from four different types of activities which could be used to develop a signature for each*

by boundaries to identify a series of zones which went beyond economic activity. Distinct compounds for carpentry, leather and iron working were identified and interpreted as male working areas while zones for spinning and baking were interpreted as female areas. Clarke also identified some differences in the value of artefacts in different huts, which he saw as evidence of a ranked society with differences in wealth.

The distribution of activities can be most clearly seen where buildings remain. Distinctive features such as ovens, drains and traces of fixings provide important clues. Decorative features, the size of the room and the nature of doors and windows provide hints to both function and status. Surviving buildings also enable greater exploration of the social use of space than on excavated sites. This involves analysis of what the use of space meant and how social relations were structured by the architecture. For example, the household is the fundamental organisational unit for most known societies but there are exceptions where more extended social groups live under one roof. Physical space between clusters of huts may represent social distance while a building that

physically dominates others may be the home of a social leader. For instance at Gurness (▶ p. 229) the architecture of the houses reflects this differentiation. This type of analysis has also been applied to investigations of gender relations. Gilchrist (1995) has suggested that the layout of domestic areas of medieval castles reflects and reinforces contemporary views on the differences between men and women. In the analysis of space, boundaries are of particular importance and archaeologists are careful not to see ditches and entrances as simply functional.

On a larger scale the differing size and elaboration of buildings may suggest a stratified society while controlling elites might be inferred from settlements structured along gridlines or with fixed orientations. The layout of Teotihuacan in Mexico is an example where the existence of a directing elite can be substantiated from other evidence.

The status of different sites is also determined by examining patterns. Elite sites or buildings are expected to be larger and richer in finds and decoration than humbler versions. Key features such as unusually large storage facilities and exotic finds are also indicators of status. The

KEY STUDY

Mashkan Shapir

Unlike other Mesopotamian cities which have been identified from extensive settlement mounds or tells, Mashkan Shapir, 140 kilometres downriver from Baghdad, was discovered by satellite photography. From space the traces of long filled-in waterways were visible in the Iraqi desert. At the point where they converged, archaeologists found the remains of buildings up to 2 metres in height and scatters of Bronze Age artefacts in the sand. Aerial photography was not allowed so the ground plan of the site was mapped using a camera mounted on a kite. The name of the city, which means 'encampment of the overseer', was revealed when clay cylinders covered in cuneiform writing were deciphered. From these texts it seems that the city was founded around 2000 BC by the King of Larsa (one of the larger Mesopotamian city-states) who had ordered the construction of a trade canal between the Tigris and Euphrates rivers. Holding a strategic position and controlling trade in wood, metal and stone coming down the Tigris, Mashkan Shapir grew rapidly. With a population of around 15,000 it became the second largest city in the kingdom but was suddenly abandoned around 1720 BC probably after a war with Babylon.

Because it was abandoned rather than built over, archaeologists were able to investigate the spatial organisation of the city. By mapping of the location of remains and artefacts on the surface and then checking with limited excavation, a picture began to emerge of life in the city. There were several entrances to the city for both roads and canals. Inside the fortified mud-brick walls was a large area of some 70 hectares. It was divided by

Figure 7.24 *Plan of Mashkan Shapir (and image of Nergal)*

KEY STUDY *cont.*

Mashkan Shapir

canals into zones dedicated to manufacture, administration and living areas. Canals were important for water, fish (many fish-hooks were found) and transport. Mesopotamian texts record the city as having 240 boats. Two harbours joined to canals were probably commercial areas while an empty area with some storehouses near a gate was possibly a market and another was probably a garden.

The southern zone, cut off by a wall and canal, seems to have been a religious sanctuary dedicated to Nergal, the God of death. Within the mudbrick platform which would have supported a pyramid-like ziggurat were clay effigies of people and animals. Enclosed between a wall and canal at the south-west end of the central area was a large cemetery. Here the dead along with weapons and jewellery were buried in ceramic jars. Usually the dead were buried in domestic areas so this may have been a special burial site for particular social groups.

A smaller walled-off area directly over a canal to the west is thought to be the administrative area. It included many regularly built buildings, a possible palace and unusual artefacts including clay pieces with seal marks which are thought to mark out storage areas. Many miniature chariots with effigies of Nergal or the scythe which was his symbol were also found here. The excavators believe that these were used for oath-taking.

The other zones appear to have been mixed residential areas with concentrations of buildings along the canals. Different sized houses were grouped together which suggests rich and poor were not segregated. Symbols of authority such as seals and high status metal artefacts were widely dispersed as were manufacturing sites including kilns and slag from pottery making and copper smelting. Fragments of grey-black rock were also discovered which seem to have been by-products from the manufacture of synthetic 'volcanic' rock to be used in for grindstones and building material.

Elizabeth Stone and Paul Zimansky have argued that the layout of Mashkan Shapir represents a very different kind of urban society from those recorded from excavation of palace sites. Absolute rulers tend to exercise control and centralise authority by keeping religious, political and administrative buildings close to them, sometimes within their palace complex. However, early Mesopotamian texts describe citizens exercising power through assemblies rather than being controlled by their rulers. At Mashkan Shapir power seems to have been dispersed with both rich and poor living in the same neighbourhoods. Commerce, production, administration and religion all appear to have been separate. The lack of concentration may suggest a more heterarchical society.

Other research at Mashkan Shapir has concentrated on parallel evidence for decline. The area is now desert but in the Bronze Age irrigation had brought agriculture to the area. The canals were raised above the levels of the fields so water fed into them by gravity. As it evaporated it left mineral salts behind. Ultimately the soil became toxic to plants and crop yields fell. Across the region agricultural production may have collapsed for this reason.

Unfortunately war intervened before exploration of the site could be completed. Since the second Iraq War the site has been comprehensively looted and the surface is pock-marked with hundreds of holes where artefacts have been dug up.

• http://www.savingantiquities.org/feature_iraq.php

KEY TASK

Linking signatures to sites

To familiarise yourself with the concepts and issues relating to identifying settlement function for the period(s) you are studying. Produce your own version of the signature diagram (Figure 7.23). This will provide a useful aide-memoir for when you write evaluative essays on this topic.

- Insert three or four additional, relevant categories in boxes, for example military site, port, extraction site and high status site.
- Enter one or two sites from your study in each of the boxes, for example Boxgrove as an example of a butchery site. You may find that some sites fit several categories.
- Around the boxes list types of evidence which could serve as indicators of activity on these sites.
- Finally, try to identify any problems you have encountered such as contradictory or ambivalent evidence. For example, some archaeologists have identified Neolithic houses as dwellings, others as ritual structures. It is possible that they had several functions.

Minoan capital Knossos (▶ p. 255) provides a good example of this.

UNDERSTANDING STRUCTURES

Many of the points made in relation to sites and features also apply to structures, but you also need to understand how archaeologists interpret structures from buried traces. Key questions revolve around why particular designs were selected and the technology and materials used to construct them. Structures range from traces of a windbreak around a hearth or stakeholes from a tent through to recent industrial or military buildings. Faced with pits, slots and postholes, archaeologists have to make imaginative leaps to reconstruct buildings from the past. Early examples reflected modern perceptions of people in the past or were drawn from ethnography.

The development of experimental archaeology has been particularly important in investigating structures from prehistoric and medieval times. While ground plans can be estimated from hearths and postholes or foundation trenches, the walls and roofs are problematic. However, we have developed an understanding of building and materials from sites with unusual preservation. Woodworking capabilities from the Mesolithic onwards have been informed by finds at waterlogged sites such as the Sweet Track in Somerset. They have provided insights into construction techniques, tools and the type of wood used and have hinted at the extent of woodland management. Experimental structures such as those at West Stow (▶ p. 317) and Butser Ancient Farm have used this information to test hypotheses about the design and materials used to make the walls and roofs and then about the use and function of the buildings. It is important to remember that while everyone refers to these buildings as reconstructions they cannot be reconstructions. We cannot be entirely sure what an Iron Age roof was like, so modern versions should properly be called constructs or models. Similarly we cannot know if the house was decorated or whether people slept on the ground or on platforms that lay across the roof beams. Experiment can only show what might have been and then test it to failure.

Experimental archaeology is, of course, weighted towards technological understanding. There may be social or religious reasons for particular designs and materials being used which reconstructions cannot directly address.

KEY STUDIES

The Mask site and Pincevent

Binford's observations of behaviour and the use of space around a hearth by Nunamiut caribou hunters at the Mask site have been particularly influential. He identified an irregular doughnut-shaped distribution of material. He divided this into drop and toss zones according to the way the hunters disposed of rubbish. For example, larger pieces of debris were thrown behind the hunters or across the fire. He was able to detect differences in distribution patterns caused by differing numbers of hunters. He also noted that hearths tended to be spread by people searching for food in the ashes and that when the wind changed direction, the hunters would turn around and start another hearth. Binford contrasted this behaviour with observations inside structures where hearths and resulting ash are usually surrounded by stones to prevent the spread of fire and to provide working surfaces. People also tend not to throw rubbish over their shoulders indoors.

Binford (1983) used these insights to challenge Leroi-Gourhan's (1978) interpretation of the Upper Palaeolithic site of Pincevent. Excavation here had revealed rings of stone associated with a number of hearths. Leroi-Gourhan had interpreted these as tents with the stones used to hold the edges of the tents down. Binford suggested that it was an open-air site with the stones used to hold down hides for working on. People built new hearths in response to changes in wind direction.

Figure 7.25 Drawing of the Mask site and interpretation

Figure 7.26 Drawing and alternative interpretations of Pincevent

KEY STUDY

Black Patch

Figure 7.27a *Settlement at Black Patch showing sub-divisions and land use based on surviving features and assemblages. (after Drewett)*

Drewett's (1982) excavation of part of this Bronze Age farmstead drew on ethnography and detailed analysis of different categories of finds to suggest the functions and social organisation of the site. The largest hut, which had its own compound and pond and contained finer pottery and evidence of a loom, was the home of the headman. The smaller huts were for food preparation, storage and accommodation for the rest of the headman's extended family. Detailed study of finds within the huts was related to likely sources of light to identify areas for weaving, leather working and storage.

N ↑

░ Storage ▨ Weaving

░ Hearth ⋮ Leather, wood, bone working

Figure 7.27b *Main hut at Black Patch (after Drewett) with activity areas based on clusters of loom weights, flint debitage and metal finds*

KEY STUDY

Gurness

Brochs are double-walled, drystone tower houses surrounded by clusters of other buildings. Recent studies of this Iron Age broch on Orkney by Historic Scotland have challenged the idea that it was simply a defensive site. The great tower of the broch dominated the settlement and the smaller houses were ranged either side of the single passage leading into the broch itself.

The architecture controlled movement around the site and constantly drew attention to the tower. The broch provided a home to a chieftain and protection for his followers. However, it also made his dominance of the people and the area visible. In helping to build it and living under its shadow the local people accepted his authority.

• http://www.brad.ac.uk/acad/archsci/field_proj/scat/

Figure 7.28 *The broch at Gurness looking down the entrance corridor to the central tower. This was the only way in or out and the view would have been dominated by, and observed from, the tower*

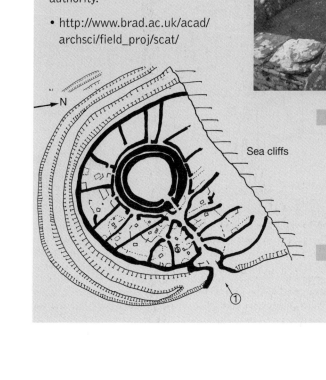
Sea cliffs

Figure 7.29 *An example of a smaller building at Gurness*

Were these the houses of the clan members of a chieftain? Note how these building are all linked and cluster around the larger tower. They all open out onto the main corridor. These houses are similar to those at Skara Brae (▶ p. 306)

Figure 7.30 *Simplified plan of Gurness to show how the tower dominated the other buildings and the access route*

The places where Figures 7.28 and 7.29 were taken from are indicated.

Figure 7.31 *An Olympic village at Roman Salamis?*

A major commercial centre for 2000 years, most of the remains at Salamis are from the Roman period. This view illustrates some of the extensive public buildings. The re-erected columns would have supported a stoa or covered walkway. It surrounds the gymnasium square or palaestra. Adjoining it are hot and cold public bath houses and a 44 seat latrine. Nearby is an amphitheatre and theatre. Much of the construction is faced with marble. This indicates the wealth and importance of this centre.

Figure 7.32 *Çatalhöyük*

This cluster of interlinked dwellings became one of the earliest towns. It was occupied from the early seventh to sixth millenia BC and the 18 layers of mud-brick dwellings housing several thousand people eventually became a tell (▶ p. 242). Unusually, access to the houses appears to have been through the roof; there are no streets. Similarities in house size and contents have been interpreted as being the result of a fairly egalitarian society. Burials under the houses and art have been interpreted as suggestive of a mother goddess cult although cattle also appear to have been an object of veneration, perhaps because of their strength. Recently, Hodder, who has been excavating the site for many years, pointed out that while images of females have been found, there are also male icons and penises. He believes men and women had equal status.

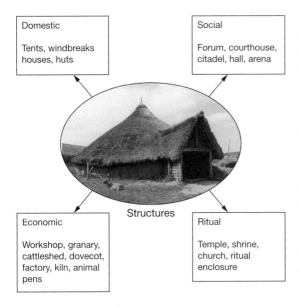

Domestic	Social
Tents, windbreaks houses, huts	Forum, courthouse, citadel, hall, arena

Structures

Economic	Ritual
Workshop, granary, cattleshed, dovecot, factory, kiln, animal pens	Temple, shrine, church, ritual enclosure

Figure 7.33 *Structures in archaeology*

Therefore other sources of analogy and analysis of the symbolism of designs are also studied. The predominant orientation of Bronze and Iron Age roundhouses and enclosures towards the south-east may be such a case. Experiment has shown that a southerly orientation would maximise light. The choice of south-east or west may reflect beliefs linked to the rising or setting sun.

Where archaeologists are investigating standing buildings a wide range of insights can be gained into the technical skills, communications and prosperity of the societies and individuals that created them. For instance, petrological examination (◀ p. 69) to identify the sources of building stone used for Roman villas or medieval cathedrals tells us about contemporary geological knowledge and hints at the nature of markets for materials and the transport system necessary to move them.

Figure 7.34 *Models of Minoan houses*

These faience miniatures along with models and illustrations have provided much information about the construction of Minoan houses. In addition to windows and chimneys we know they were often two storey and used wood as well as stone and mud-brick in their construction.

Figure 7.35 *Reconstruction of Central European mammoth bone house*

A number of sites have been excavated in central Europe and the Ukraine dating from the Upper Palaeolithic with large quantities of carefully arranged mammoth bones. Although there is some controversy over the nature of possible structures, the dominant interpretation is that modern human hunters used the tusks, long bones and skulls of mammoths as substitutes for wood in constructing huts. Skins were probably tied over the bones to provide waterproof shelter. If accurate, this provides a classic example of human adaptability in harsh climatic conditions. It may also indicate a very specialised economy.

Chapter 8

Material Culture and Economics

YOUR GOALS

You need to

■ understand, define and use the key concepts associated with these themes

■ be familiar with a range of relevant case studies for your period which each cover several topics

■ be able to synthesise ideas and data from case studies to respond to a variety of types of questions

---

Although material culture and economics are different themes, there is considerable overlap in relevant case studies. Economics is concerned with how people manage the cultural and natural resources available to them. Material culture is concerned with the things (in their broadest sense) that people made and what they signified.

Material learnt for one theme can usually be applied to the other. This chapter should be read in conjunction with Chapter 3. A grasp of analytical methods helps you understand and evaluate case studies. Other major links include interpretation (Chapter 5), particularly the use of ethnographic and experimental analogies, and the use of geographic models to interpret distribution patterns and site function (◀ p. 215).

SUBSISTENCE: HOW DID PEOPLE IN THE PAST FEED THEMSELVES?

This is a fundamental question in most periods. Many writers have assumed that the type of economic system used largely determines the nature of society. Indeed, archaeologists define many societies according to how they acquired their food. This is because there seems to be a relationship between the type of economy and the kind of society it supports. For example, hunting and gathering economies seems to support fairly egalitarian, small scale societies (▶ p. 292). Their rituals and rules focus on the group and their relationship with their environment. Agricultural societies which produce a food surplus seem to develop marked social hierarchies and laws and rituals which promote the interests of the elite.

Faced with different environmental challenges humans have always adapted to minimise the risk of starvation. Archaeologists try to identify the strategies they adopt and the reasons for those choices. If your course is thematic, you need to ensure that you have case studies from a range of societies. '**Hunter-gatherer**' is a label used to cover a wide range of societies across over 90 per cent of human history. For the earliest period humans were not hunters at all but foragers and scavengers. Hunting developed following a lengthy period of scavenging and gathering. Archaeologists are divided about when hominids began proper hunting. Estimates have ranged from over 1 million years ago to about 100,000 years ago. (▶ p. 332) The Mesolithic saw diversification into a broad range of animals, fish and marine foods. In most parts of the world this was followed by agriculture which provided the economic basis for life up to the Industrial Revolution. Societies that herd animals are called **pastoralists**. Rearing animals for food is also known as animal husbandry. Sedentary *farmers*

are usually associated with societies from the last 10,000 years. In some regions they were preceded by mobile *horticulturalists* whose pattern of farming was very different to those of **arable** (crop) agriculturalists of historic times.

Direct human exploitation of animals takes many forms. *Hunting* may be random (you kill the first animal you encounter) or selective (you take only young males or old females, leaving breeding age females and hence maintain the effective breeding population). Intensive hunting may also include human manipulation of the vegetation environment to make conditions more favourable for a particular species. Pastoralists may herd the animals and exercise some control over reproduction by selective culling of the stock. Finally, they may control all aspects of an animal's life, dictating where it feeds (by the creation of fields), dictating its mate (by creating single sex herds) and so on. Wherever an economy lies between hunting and *stock rearing* it will leave slightly different signatures in the archaeological record (◀ p. 125). Interpretation

Figure 8.1 *What a mammoth trap might have looked like. If only . . .*

of this will depend on an understanding of local taphonomic processes.

Identifying the nature of exploitation

The interpretation of the contribution of animals to the economy of a site is dependent upon the recovery of a sufficiently representative sample of the animal population and the identification of its age and sex structure (◄ p. 72). Kill ratios are indicative of particular strategies. **Catastrophic profiles** of the age and sex of dead animals, where whole herds were killed, suggests unselective hunting, for example using stampedes. Overrepresentation of particular animals provides evidence of more selective hunting. The type of damage caused to animal bones by hunting tools can help corroborate this. Natural predators tend to pick off the old, young and sick and early human hunters were probably similar. This does not endanger the survival of the herd and creates an **attritional bone profile.** More sophisticated hunters will manage herds, producing indistinguishable patterns of kills to many farmers. For instance culling young males but not the females needed to reproduce the herds. The presence of very young or migratory animals provides clues to seasonal patterns of exploitation.

Bone assemblages also provide insights into preferred food sources, although the archaeological record has a preservation bias towards larger bones. Assessing the use of invertebrates, with the exception of molluscs is much harder. Inferences about the importance of fish and birds can be made from the remains of fish traps, specialist fowling tools or even art, as in Egyptian tomb paintings. **Isotope analysis** of human bones and teeth can indicate the proportion of diet from animal, marine and plant sources. (◄ p. 214) Modern excavation techniques have also added to our knowledge. Animal fats have been recovered from Upper Palaeolithic cave sites and phosphate analysis has been used to identify stalls and paddocks. Tools, once they have been interpreted, are used to make inferences about hunting and processing animals. Use wear marks (◄ p. 125) and traces of blood on tools can also be examined. Experimental archaeology can show the capability of tools and provide insights into the ways that they might have been used. It can also indicate how the animal was processed through comparison with modern butchery practice and experimental observation of scavenged carcasses. Cut-marks near the joints may indicate butchery for meat while smashing the mid-section of long bones suggests marrow extraction. Similarly, angled cut-marks on animal skulls may indicate skinning. Assemblages comprised of particular meat bearing bones possibly indicate storage. Their absence from kill sites suggests that consumption occurred at a home base. However butchery in the past has some differences with modern practice. Experimental studies have demonstrated that many past societies smashed bones to extract marrow fat or boiled bones to get grease. Fat has far more calories than other parts of an animal and was attractive in cold climates or time of food shortage. This was particularly pronounced amongst the Vikings of Greenland. Fat also can be used for fuel, softening skins and waterproofing. Bone assemblages at 'Head Smashed In' and Stellmoor suggest that fat was extracted from buffalo, probably for pemmican making.

The direct contribution of animals to human economy takes four main forms:

- as a source of food products such as meat, blubber, fat or marrow
- as a source of secondary food products such as blood, milk, cheese, butter
- as a source of raw materials for artefact manufacture, light and fuel including antler, bone, skins, grease, dung, hair and wool
- as a source of traction, haulage and transport.

Primary products are all those which require the killing and butchery of animals such as meat or bone. **Secondary products** include all those

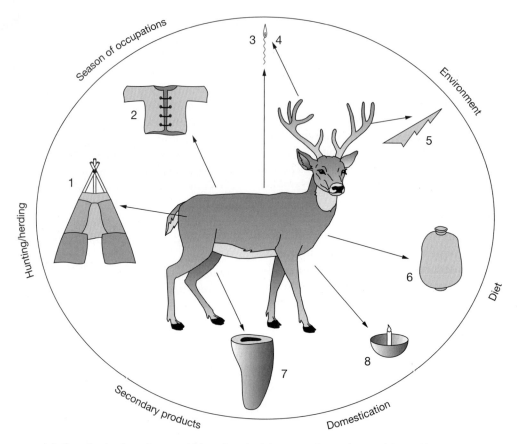

Human exploitation of animals and areas which archaeologists can explore using surviving evidence

Key to primary use of animal

1. skin for tent
2. skin for clothes
3. sinew for thread
4. bone for needle
5. antler for harpoon
6. intestine for water container
7. meat
8. fat for fuel or lamps

Figure 8.2 *Human exploitation of animals and topics that animal remains contribute to*

that involve utilising the products of living animals such as dung and wool.

Tracing developments in human exploitation of animals

Hunting or scavenging?

There has been continued debate amongst archaeologists about when hunting began. (▶ p. 332) Evidence from human bones suggests that more protein was needed as brains enlarged. On the other hand, the long digestive tract in humans is not suited to meat processing and we are slow and lack cutting teeth. This does not point to a biological adaptation to hunting. Clues to humans consuming meat include bones and tools found next to each other on 'living floors' (◀ p. 41). However, these could be palimpsests – the accumulation of materials from several

KEY SITE

Stellmoor

This Upper Palaeolithic site on the North German Plain dates from the last Ice Age of 9000 BC and illustrates the development of selective hunting. First excavated by Rust in the 1930s, the site lay in a peat deposit near a lake and had excellent organic preservation. Wells were bored to help drain the site and a huge area opened up for excavation. An occupation layer around half a metre deep was uncovered. Thousands of tanged points (arrow heads) were recovered along with axes and harpoons. The most significant finds have been 105 long flint-tipped arrows made from pine. These are the first clear evidence of the use of bows in the world. Previous shafts with points could have been thrown using atlatls (spear throwers). Bones of elk, horse, wolf, marten and water-birds were found but the main prey were reindeer. 1300 antlers were recovered, mostly from male animals. Reindeer on their summer migration to the northern tundra passed through a 'tunnel valley' where hunters used bows to kill selected animals. This is known as an intercept strategy (◀ p. 209). The survival of a pine post suggested that fences may have been used to direct animals towards an ambush – a technique also used by Native Americans. Some complete animals had been weighted down in the lake with stones. Were these offerings?

More recent surveys, excavations and re-analysis of finds have added to our knowledge of the site. Molluscan evidence suggests that the lakes were shallow with considerable vegetation on the margins but open, moving water further out. Pollen analysis shows that during the early phases the site was at the northern-most point of the tree-line with a scattering of birch and rowan on

Figure 8.3
*Stellmoor. Diagram
to summarise key
aspects and links*

Late glacial
moraine lake

Wooded
slopes

Campsite

Route of
migrating
reindeer

100 m

KEY SITE *cont.*

Stellmoor

the slopes around the lake. Above the kill and butchery site was a camp with rings of stones which may have anchored tents. Evidence of horn and antler working to make tools has been found at this and a number of other contemporary sites in the valley.

Bratlund's (1991) analysis of the lesions (impact damage) on the bones was able to determine the angle and velocity of the arrows. The hunters predominantly used head shots or shots towards vital organs, avoiding the ribs.

Figure 8.4 *As with much innovative technology, tools could also be art as this beautifully carved Upper Palaeolithic spear thrower, carved from mammoth ivory, illustrates.*

These targets were used to maximize damage and blood loss. It appeared that animals passed in front of hunters and were driven into the lake so that selected individuals could be picked off. Analysis of the sex and age of kills provided evidence for selective culling of young males. This indicates a very purposeful and organised approach to hunting in this period, and knowledge of the animals' behaviour that is perhaps to be viewed as a stepping stone towards domestication. The huge quantities of bone dumped in a nearby lake margin suggest the hunters were processing more meat than they could consume. Ethnographic analogy suggests storage practices could have included caching, drying or making pemmican. The Upper-Palaeolithic is generally seen as a time of specialised hunting of large animals such as mammoths, horses and reindeer (▶ p. 239). During this period humans domesticated the dog from Eurasian wolves as a hunting companion. The earliest examples of dogs suggest a date of 11,000 BC in the Near East. However, DNA points to 13,000 BC in East Asia as being more likely. Evidence from a number of French sites such as Roc de Combe have suggested that some human groups were almost entirely dependent on one species. In some cases 99 per cent of remains are reindeer.

Humans adapted to challenging environments using their conceptual abilities and technology. Their material culture transformed their position in the food chain to dominant predator. Knecht's (1994) study of the evolution of projectile points during the Upper Palaeolithic helps explain how they did this. She demonstrated how people used an understanding of design and the physical properties of raw materials to produce increasingly efficient and flexible spears which were easy to repair. Her experiments with a goat carcass confirm the accuracy and penetrative power of spears thrown by hand or by spear-thrower or atlatl. Technology enables humans to hunt large, dangerous prey effectively and from a safer distance than previously possible. As with much innovative technology, tools could also be art as this beautifully carved Palaeolithic spear thrower illustrates. Mesolithic arrows developed in response to smaller, fast moving prey in thickly wooded environments.

unrelated events over long periods but in the same location. Even where bones and tools did come from a single event this association does not prove whether humans were hunters or scavengers. A key indicator is the nature of cut marks on the bones when observed using a SEM. Marks from human butchery are distinctly 'V'-shaped when compared to the 'U'-shaped irregular scratches of carnivores' teeth. Analysis can show who got to the bone first. Analysis of the bones from Olduvai Gorge suggested that hominids began as scavengers.

A growing body of evidence supports unselective hunting by the Middle Palaeolithic. During that period the sea cliff above what was then a plain at La Cotte de St Brelade on Jersey had a deep cleft in it. At the foot of the 30 metre drop were the butchered remains of large herbivores, mainly mammoths and woolly rhinos and thousands of stone artefacts. The catastrophic bone profile (◄ p. 73) suggested stampeding or other form of mass slaughter. Some shoulder blades appeared to have been deliberately arranged against the wall of a small gully in at least two separate episodes. Amongst these remains were stone tools and several Neanderthal teeth.

The site was interpreted as a 'drive site' for hunting. The animals would have been carefully herded into position on the slope leading to the cliff and then stampeded to their deaths in the gully below. There they could be butchered at leisure. There is a considerable body of ethnographic evidence for similar practices involving bison in North America (◄ p. 205). This suggests a very organised and concerted group effort perhaps using firebrands to frighten the animals and groups of people or stones as guide lanes to steer them towards the cliff. The end result would have been large quantities of meat to be processed and the arrangements of large parts of skeletons against the gully wall may suggest storage practice in the form of a cache.

Selective hunting

Modern human hunts are more persistent than the charges of predators and involve human culture. Hunters often work together, exchange information and share food in base camps. Knowledge is needed, for example how to create balanced, aerodynamic spears and where to penetrate large animals to kill them. This requires communication and the debate about modern hunting is closely linked to debates about when human social attributes developed. The evidence for selective hunting includes **specialisation**. Recently there has been some criticism of the methodology behind the interpretation of single-species hunters since it could rely on differential preservation and recovery. Most existing evidence has come from cave sites because they have been easier to identify and often have good stratigraphy. However, open sites such as Le Flageolet I often have a broader range of prey species including red deer and aurochs. There is also some evidence in the sex-ratios amongst reindeer bones from cave sites that suggest these were used for seasonal hunting and may not therefore reflect the all-year economy. Migrating reindeer move too fast for humans to follow them for long and their populations tended to crash periodically. Focusing on a single species would therefore be a high risk strategy. Plants and small animal remains survive very poorly from this period and are generally absent from cave paintings. However, the existence of fishing technology and possibly textiles (impressions were found on clay models at Dolni Vestonici) during the last Ice Age suggest that a broader spectrum of food sources were exploited than previously thought. There is currently a major debate over both the extent of specialisation during this period and whether it marked a significant change in strategy. Most kill profiles are attritional while specialised artefacts indicate sophisticated hunting technology. Spear throwers, blades and bows were all developed during this period. Some aspects of this may be reflected in their art (◄ p. 153).

KEY STUDIES

Baltic foragers of the late Mesolithic

Sites in Denmark and Scania (southern Sweden) have produced remarkably well-preserved evidence of foraging peoples. Continuity in flint technology and skeletal shape suggests stable populations, while site density and the absence of much disease from human bones suggest that they were well nourished. Their 'broad spectrum' foraging economy drew on many different resources. Quantities of nuts and water chestnuts and residues of porridge made from seeds testify to the importance of plant food. However, isotopic evidence from human bone and a range of specialised equipment suggests an **intensification** focusing on marine foods.

Fishing equipment included hooks, nets, harpoons and weirs. Remains of whales and sharks in coastal middens may indicate offshore fishing although they could represent strandings. The faunal assemblages on some sites suggest some specialisation, possibly on a seasonal basis. They may

Figure 8.5 *Reconstruction of life at a lagoon site such as Tybrind Vig*

The inhabitants of the site literally built fences in the sea. This illustrates passive hunting taking advantage of tidal movements of fish through fish traps and nets as well as the use of hooks and lines. The canoe has a hearth at the stern, possibly to attract eels at night. Special three pronged eel spears called leixsters which pierced and grasped the fish have been found on nearby sites. Tybrind Vig (Andersen 1985) like many Danish sites was submerged by rising sea levels. This preserved many organic artefacts including knotted string, baskets and beautifully carved paddles such as the one illustrated. Under normal conditions most of the features in the drawing would have been archaeologically invisible.

KEY STUDIES *cont.*

Baltic foragers of the late Mesolithic

have hunted seals for their fat. Large numbers were killed and sites often had exotic artefacts that may have been traded for seal oil. Contemporary sites such as Ringkloster included the processed bones of fur-bearing animals such as pine martens. Some skulls were marked in a way which suggested the animals had been caught in traps. Analysis of faunal assemblages indicates selective hunting of deer, pig and aurochs, possibly even herd management of smaller species.

Danish data was sufficient for Mithen (1990) to use computer analysis to compare real assemblages with predicted assemblages based on different models of hunting behaviour. His research suggested that hunters were being highly selective in animals they stalked and killed and were under little pressure to bring back meat from every trip. The key sites such as Ertebolle, Vedbaek and Skateholm had hearths, pits, various structures and their own distinctive pottery. Some even had cemeteries. They could afford to become semi-sedentary and develop a rich culture because their subsistence strategy was so successful.

Figure 8.6 *Semi-sedentism in the Baltic*

Mobility is a strategy to reduce risk. However, rich coastal environments and technological innovation allowed Ertebolle foragers to become almost sedentary. This has been called tethered or radiating mobility where a band has main site but task groups might go on seasonal foraging trips for short periods. This might be to outer islands to exploit seabirds and seals in the spring or inland lakes for migratory waterfowl in the winter. The increase in investment in a site through burials and the building of traps and other structures might eventually lead to a mobility pattern paralleling that of early farmers.

KEY SITE

Tell Abu Hureyra

A tell is an artificial mound up to 60 metres in height composed of mudbricks from generations of houses combined with domestic rubbish. Their extremely long period of occupation produces a very deep stratigraphy and make them particularly valuable for archaeologists studying long term changes.

Faunal remains from the lowest level of Tell Abu Hureyra were dominated by gazelle. After several thousand years the numbers of gazelle being caught fell dramatically. Sheep and goats took their place. These two species are often lumped together and referred to as 'ovicaprids' since it is difficult to distinguish between their bones at this early stage of domestication. Later morphological changes such as horns changing from curved to curly make the distinction much easier. The change in bone assemblages coincides with a period known by archaeologists in the region as PPNA (▶ p. 244). Similar changes are evident in plant foods with a wide range of wild food being replaced with a few cereals and increasing finds of grain processing artefacts (▶ p. 244). Initially the inhabitants of the tell were specialised hunters who ambushed the Persian gazelle that migrates in herds along predictable routes. They were herded into 'desert kites', landscape features used as traps, and then killed with spears. However, the gazelle could never have been domesticated because they lacked traits of behaviour which made the ovicaprids more manageable. Gradually, in line with other local settlements the inhabitants switched to pastoral agriculture and then mixed farming. However, gazelle remained the main source of

Figure 8.7 *Tell es Sa'idiyeh*

This huge tell, site of the biblical city of Zarathan, sits at a crossroads of trade and dominates the fertile land of Canaan east of the Jordan River. Occupied from the third millennium to the 7th century AD, it began as a village of Neolithic transhumance farmers. By 2900 it was a large planned city falling under the influence of several empires, particularly the Egyptians. Despite such changes it provides evidence of long term Canaanite cultural continuity.

 Figure 8.8 *Excavations of the palace complex at Tell es Sa'idiyeh*

The great depth and the complexity of the stratigraphy is evident in this excavation by an international team of archaeologists working with Jordanians in the palace area. They revealed evidence of production on an industrial scale of wine, textile and pottery as well as extensive storage.

KEY SITE *cont.*

Tell Abu Hureyra

animal protein for 1000 years after arable farming had begun. It is only as gazelle became scarcer that ovicaprids became important. This indicates how long and complex the shift from foraging to farming was. The site is also crucial in understanding early arable farming. Seeds which were charred in fires show a sequence of wild grasses, then a break, then fatter seeds characteristic of domestication such as rye. These date to 11,000 BP. Hillman argues that local climatic records indicate a sustained drought which would have reduced returns from gathering and may have prompted the inhabitants to start cultivation.

The transition to agriculture also left traces in the bones of the human inhabitants. Some showed the signs of strain from carrying heavy weights, perhaps building material. Women in particular had arthritic knees and big toe joints caused by rocking backwards and forwards whilst kneeling to grind grain on saddle querns. This suggests a division of labour with women processing food and men hunting and perhaps cultivating. Both sexes had teeth damage caused by hard kernels and grit which got into the flour. This was less noticeable in later populations as the development of pottery allowed grains to be soaked to make a kind of porridge which required less chewing. Tell Abu Hureyra was occupied from 11,500 to 7000 BP. The tell itself is the remains of successive layers of mud-brick houses. As with most early farming settlements there is little sign in burials or houses of social inequalities. These are much more pronounced in later tell sites such as Tell es Sa'idiyeh.

Broad spectrum foraging

Humans have been hunter-gatherers for most of their existence. Today this part of our history is rarely studied and almost never below university level. In the 1960s attempts were made to explore prehistoric hunting through ethnography. One surprising finding was that even in hostile environments, hunter-gatherers spent much less time working than did farmers. Although some have questioned the romantic view of hunter-gatherers as the original affluent society (they were time-rich whereas we are rich in consumer goods), sites with good organic preservation have revealed that they often had rich diets and rich cultures. A second finding was that in most societies, the bulk of the food came from gathering. Where a diverse range of food resources were exploited, many archaeologists now use the term **foragers** to describe the economic strategy.

Foragers are not usually nomadic but often move around an area during an annual cycle. This is rarely random. It is a strategy to exploit a series of environments in turn and minimise seasonal shortages. However, not all foragers need this mobility. To try and understand decisions made by foragers, archaeologists have drawn on evolutionary biology, economics and psychology. A popular concept has been 'Optimal Foraging Theory' which sees behaviour as being based on maximising returns for the least effort and risk. Both contemporary foragers and the archaeological record were studied to understand and test predictive models. However, this approach has been criticised for minimising social and individual factors in human behaviour. There are instances where potential resources have been neglected, for example fish in the Neolithic and Iron Age.

KEY TERM

Neolithic

Archaeologists first divided human prehistory according to changes in materials used such as bronze and iron. A further refinement has been the breaking down of the Stone Age in relation to other changes. The Neolithic or 'new Stone Age' was originally associated with domestication and farming. It was identified from a 'package' of changes including domesticated crops and animals, sedentary 'village life', agricultural tools such as grinding stones and polished stone axes,

and pottery. However, reality is rarely clear. At Near East sites such as Jericho layers revealed settled villages with domesticated animals but no pottery – hence the term Pre-Pottery Neolithic Age (PPNA). Baltic forager sites (◄ p. 240) had some 'Neolithic' artefacts but not domesticates.

Figure 8.9 *Saddle Quern*

The processing of grains to produce flour led to the adoption of grinding tools which are one of the first artefactual indicators of settled agriculture. Grain rubbers or quern stones were quarried from very hard stone and became an early trade item. The effort involved to process flour was considerable. At Tell Abu Hureyra female skeletons had worn and arthritic toes, knees and lower backs. This damage had been caused by kneeling with the big toe curled under as a lever and repeatedly pushing and pulling the quern for long periods. It also illustrates division of labour based on gender and possibly age.

Intensification of hunting

Intensification means to alter a strategy to significantly increase productivity. A good example of intensification of hunting is the development of deep sea fishing. Fishing is a form of hunting. Today stocks of fish everywhere are widely seen as under threat but the long term effects of intensive fishing are poorly understood. To help address the origins of this issue researchers across northern Europe are taking part in the Medieval Origins of Commercial Sea Fishing Project which in turn is part of a global census of marine life. By researching past ecosystems and the impacts of human activity they hope to inform policy-making on sustainable fishing and conservation. Since the Roman period documents, particularly tax-records, have tended to predominate over archaeological evidence as the basis for research into economics. In the case of fishing, archaeology has been hampered by poor survival of fish bones. Analysis is focussing on archive material from sites with good organic preservation across the region including urban areas with deep stratified waste deposits such as York and Southampton to examine the rise of the world's first commercial fishery.

Researchers had expected the main change to be in the fifteenth century with the exploitation of waters in the North Atlantic. However, the team led by James Barrett of the University of York discovered what they term the 'fish-event horizon' to be between 950 and AD 1050. In the early middle ages most fish recovered from archaeological sites were freshwater species such as pike, trout and bream, but after that time cod and herring predominated. A change at this point is surprising because climatic data suggests it was warm which would have meant lower stocks of sea fish and more productive farming on land.

From written sources it is known that Viking vessels carried dried cod which were caught from the waters off arctic Norway. Dried cod can be identified archaeologically by distinctive butchery marks left on fishbones. Biochemical analysis is being used to identify trading patterns. Stable isotope ratios (^{13}C and ^{15}N) in fish vary according to factors such as temperature and salinity of their waters. These indicators are being used to identify where fish found in medieval midden deposits were caught. The size of fish, which were randomly caught, provides insights into fish population structures. In time the team hope to model past fish population levels and to measure the impact of fishing against other factors. Initial results have established that dried cod was being traded over long distances by AD 1000. The team's hypothesis is that over-fishing due to population rise and religious requirements to eat fish on Fridays led to a collapse in stocks of freshwater fish. This crisis was resolved by the exploitation of off-shore fisheries made possible by the development of seine and drift nets and square-rigged ships. As a result there was a rapid increase in fishing and trade in dried cod and then herring. By the fourteenth century herring was the most important commercial commodity in northern Europe and other trading networks grew up around its distribution.

Herding and the domestication of animals

The timing, nature, location and reasons for the transition from hunting to herding have long been debated. For areas where domesticated species were not native the dating of farming practices is relatively easy. However, care has to be taken that a few exotic food or sacrificial imports are not mistaken for farming. The same applies to cereal grains. In regions where domesticates originated, herding may have been the end point of a long period of parasitic herd management or selective hunting during which humans acquired knowledge of animal behaviour. This makes it difficult to pinpoint a turning point. Morphological (shape) changes in animals, such as reduced horns, smaller stature and less robust bones than their wild ancestors, have been used as an indicator of selective breeding. Essentially herders will kill the more aggressive animals and breed the more docile ones. However, climate can produce similar changes (most animals have reduced in size since

Figure 8.10 *Domesticating goats*

The wild ancestors of goats were strong, agile animals which would have been challenging to tame.

the end of the Ice Age) and in any case the changes take place slowly. Where archaeologists have dated domestication from changes in the size of animals or certain features such as horns they may have underestimated the date at which farming began. Art, artefacts, specialist buildings and burials of humans with animals have all been cited as potential evidence but each could either apply to wild animals or be later than initial domestication. Where large bone assemblages survive archaeologists have tried to reconstruct animal populations. Domestic flocks and herds do differ from wild groups since they tend to allow more female animals to survive to adulthood. However, bone assemblages may also reflect selective culling of wild herds.

Refinements of dating technology and DNA research on modern animals and excavated bones are revealing surprising results. New C-14 dates for sheep (from the Asiatic Mouflon) and goat domestication (from the Bezoar goat) in the Near East have been pushed back to at least 8000 BC. MtDNA sequences suggest there may have been two independent goat domestications in the same region. DNA research on pigs suggests simultaneous domestication in the Near East and China from wild boar. However the situation in Europe is more complex with domestication of wild European boars taking place once domesticated pigs were introduced from the Near East. European pigs appear to have totally replaced the imported strain fairly quickly. One study from Hallan Chemi in Turkey detected a significant change in pig bones around 9000 BC with high number of suckling pigs being killed. If this represents domestication then it predates cereal farming in the area. Most accounts still see a date of 7000 BC as more likely. European cattle (Bos Taurus) were descended from wild aurochs domesticated south of the Caucasus. Morphological changes put domestication at around 6000 BC but DNA research has pushed it back further. Aurochs were huge, strong, dangerous animals which makes them unlikely domesticates. One possibility is that they were originally captured

as status symbols or for ritual purposes. Çatal Höyük in Turkey is one of a number of sites where cattle horns are found in what appear to be ritual sites.

Post-domestication studies focus on what purpose the animals were exploited for. The 'secondary products revolution' is used to refer to rearing animals primarily for purposes other than food. This can be difficult to detect even in the bone record. Fleece, for example, rarely survives and leaves no physical trace on the skeleton. Deformity from use in traction can provide a useful indicator, but not always.

Explaining the change to food production

For many years this was not really a question. Agriculture was assumed to be superior to foraging and the change seemed a natural step in human evolution. However, while foragers all over the world had great knowledge of local plants and animals, it is only in a limited number of regions that people began farming. In much of the world foraging remained the major strategy, until recently, including some peoples who encourage particular plants to grow such as Australian Aborigines who use 'firestick farming'. The earliest and best known agricultural region is the 'fertile crescent' of the Near East. In this region at the end of the last Ice Age

Figure 8.11 *A symbol of a new world*

A Bronze Age rock carving of a ploughman from the World Heritage site of Tanum in Sweden.

there were woodlands in wetter areas, extensive areas of grassland as well as more arid environments. The ancestors of the first wave of domesticates including wheat, barley, lentils, sheep and goats were all found within this region. However, the existence of potential food does not explain why people ceased foraging and began farming. Many theories have been developed to explain what Childe termed the 'Neolithic Revolution'. They differ in their emphasis of ecological or social factors.

Childe favoured an ecological explanation. In his 'Oasis Theory' climatic change concentrated people and resources in a limited area. A more recent ecological model suggested that rising populations of foragers in the most productive locations outstripped the carrying capacity of the land, and farming and storage were developed to supplement wild foods. A related idea developed in Meso-America by Flannery drew on cybernetics theory to develop a positive feedback model. Successful broad-spectrum

Natural habitat of wild sheep and goats

●   Key early farming sites. 1 Jericho. 2 Tell Abu Hureyra. 3 Jarmo. 4 Ali Kosh. 5 Hacilar
●6   Slightly later site of Çatal Hüyük

(⌇)   Natural distribution of wild grains including Emmer and Einkorn wheat and barley. Note the crescent-shape this makes

Figure 8.12 *Map of the Fertile Crescent*

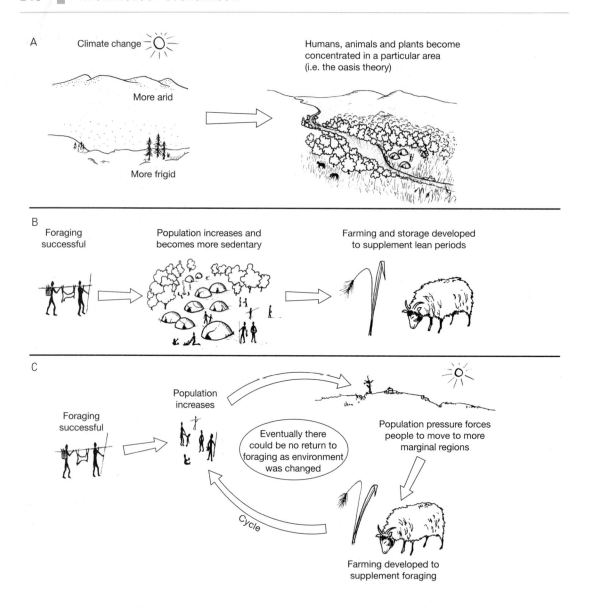

Figure 8.13 *Explanations for the adoption of farming*

A Illustrates the 'Oasis Theory' where human and animal populations were forced into restricted ranges by climatic changes and the relationships between them developed as a result.

B, 'Hearths Theory' is a similar idea but without the climatic change. In areas with good wild resources successful foragers became sedentary and began to experiment. They developed some aspects of farming and storage to reduce risk and to iron out lean periods in natural resources. Ultimately population levels rose and farming became necessary.

C. The 'Positive Feedback Model' sees successful foragers speading out into more marginal areas. They find they need to supplement their wild food sources by developing new strategies in these areas such as horticulture and animal husbandry. These are very productive and raise human populations above the carrying capacity of the land so that there can be no return to foraging. This theory works best with corn/maize in Mesoamerica.

Figure 8.14 *Loom weights*

Clay or stone loom weights and spindle whorls (◀ p. 112) are almost universal finds on Iron Age sites and provide evidence of widespread production of woollen cloth at a household level. We understand the operation of such looms from ethnography and reconstruction. Typically only the loom weights and weaving combs survive. Further evidence of rearing sheep primarily for wool rather than meat or milk comes from bone assemblages and landscape evidence. Prior's (1991) investigations of the area around Peterborough have revealed a mass of fields, pens and trackways which typify animal husbandry.

foragers spread out into more marginal regions. Food production began in these regions to supplement foraging. As population levels were raised farming spread. Eventually the environment was changed so that there could be no return to foraging. Social explanations of intensification focus on why a society might want to change its economic strategies. Hayden suggested that competitive feasting between different groups, perhaps as part of reciprocity networks, created obligations which could be met by accumulating produce. Similarly, Bender argued that developing social networks might have the same effect. Where hierarchies developed they might need to acquire prestige goods through exchange and the stored products of farming might be a way of doing so.

No one theory has yet come out on top. The feedback model seems to work best for corn (maize) and beans in Meso-America and not so well elsewhere. In the 'fertile crescent' during the Later Natufian Mesolithic culture of 12,500–10,000 BP some people lived in permanent mud-brick settlements. While they foraged they also developed tools for processing the seeds of wild grasses including sickles. This coincided with a dryer climatic spell (Younger Dryas) which may have reduced wild food supplies although not all researchers are convinced. This could have led the Natufians to encourage particular grasses through watering or planting. A change in harvesting methods may also have been a factor. Wild grass seeds break off easily if shaken. Collecting using a swinging basket is easy but scatters seed which enables new plants to grow. Using sickles to collect nearly ripe seed heads will scatter less. Within those collected there is a higher proportion of seed heads which don't shatter. If some of those seeds are replanted then that genetic trait is encouraged and becomes more common. After several hundred years the plant ears will not shatter and are reliant on human planting. The first recognisable arable crops included rye, lentils and then wheat, barley and beans. Some of the earliest samples come from Tell Abu Hureyra (◀ p. 242).

Identifying human exploitation of plants

For foraging peoples, research has focused on identifying which plants they used from plant remains and specialised artefacts such as digging sticks and grinding stones. Site catchment analysis has been used in conjunction with environmental data to suggest possible resources. Glimpses of the range of non-food uses of plants have been obtained from sites with exceptional preservation. Nets, boats and clothes (▶ p. 280) have been recovered from later prehistory and probably represent only a fraction of plant uses. With the development of pottery, twisted cord was used for decoration, suggesting that the use of rope was well known. In the historic period, the economic importance of agricultural produce means that there is considerable historical documentation of various sorts and artistic sources that provide information on techniques, organisation and productivity.

Most attention has centred on the transition to agriculture because of the impact it has had on social development. Almost all civilisations have been based on wheat, barley, millet, rice, maize or potato.

Identifying the change to food production

Much early research on farming tried to identify where the first domesticates appeared. The Near East is generally acknowledged to have been the first, with wheat, barley, goats/sheep and cattle as its staples. However, it seems that a number of 'hearths' appeared in different parts of the world based on a different range of crops including maize in Mesoamerica and rice in East Asia.

Horticulture involves modifying the growth cycles of plants, most simply by weeding, to increase productivity and usefulness. **Arable agriculture** is associated with a specialised and systematic approach to crop production, ultimately including fields. However, in its early stages agriculture involved minimal changes in the toolkit of late Mesolithic peoples, which makes its detection difficult. Many foragers for instance developed grinding tools for processing grains. At the submerged site of Ohalo II in Israel a grinding stone used to process cereals was found in a hut next to a primitive oven. Calibrated radiocarbon results suggest it may have been in use around 23,000 BP. Amongst over 90,000 plant specimens were the remains of toasted grains. These foragers appear to have been making some kind of flatbread or porridge. Recent reports on the development of non-shattering ears of grasses suggest that the process may have taken 1000 years. This means stone sickles would have been ineffective for harvesting and would therefore be poor indicators of early domestication. Most of the plant evidence comes from seed crops, which can give a somewhat distorted view. Cereals are genetically malleable and domestic varieties eventually became morphologically different from wild varieties. For example, domestic maize cannot disperse its seeds. The way they were processed meant there was more chance of grains being preserved through carbonisation than other plant foods. Furthermore, other crops such as legumes (peas and beans) seem to have changed more slowly while root crops are almost archaeologically invisible. Recent Australian research in Jordan has provided evidence of barley grains from around 7500 BC that were larger than wild varieties but not the same as domesticated examples found in higher levels.

Figure 8.15 *The Neolithic package*

The classic assemblage associated with the introduction of agriculture included domesticated plants and animals, a new range of tools including polished stone axes, and pottery. The 'package' for Southern Scandinavia is shown here. There are slight regional variations but the essence is similar. For Southern England substitute Windmill Hill Ware, Polished Axes and Long Barrows.

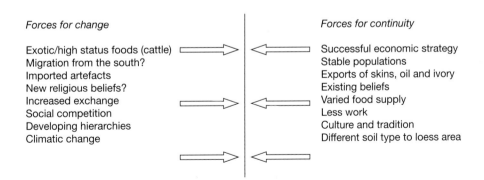

Figure 8.16 *A force field diagram to illustrate the different pressures and motives which influenced the 'Neolithic standstill' in the Baltic. A shift in the strength of some of these eventually led to a very rapid conversion*

KEY STUDY

Ceide Fields

This Neolithic field system (pronounced K-Ja) on the coast of Mayo in Ireland was found by peat-cutters who discovered dry-stone walls underneath the peat. Excavation revealed a landscape of rectangular, enclosed fields, houses and tombs all buried beneath today's blanket bog. It is the oldest field system in Europe and dates from the early fourth millennium BC. While some features have been excavated, the site is too large (around 20 square kilometres) to open up. It is too wet for resistivity so researchers have used 2-metre probes to trace the buried walls. When the pole hits a wall a cane is placed in the hole and the walls can be traced from the canes. They form coaxial patterns with the main axis running north down the slope towards the sea and other walls coming off at right angles. This suggests that the walls were planned and were roughly contemporary rather than gradually built up over time.

The extensive field pattern demonstrates considerable social organisation and must have involved a sizeable community to clear woodland and build and maintain the walls. Bone and environmental evidence suggests the fields were mainly pasture for cattle rearing. With a warm climate in the fourth millennium, grass for grazing would have grown for 11 months a year. Archaeologists' interpretations of the main function of the fields include protecting herds from wolves or rustlers, controlling grazing patterns, separating animals to ensure selective breeding and keeping cattle and crops apart. Indeed there is also evidence for arable farming. Ard marks have been found along with the stone point of an ard and pollen analysis has revealed that wheat was grown. Buried mineral soils from this site and others nearby were compared with earlier Mesolithic soils. Organic phosphate was higher in all cases than the Mesolithic soils and highest in those fields with ard marks. The same fields showed a high level of bile acid from cattle dung when subjected to lipid analysis. This suggests that farmers were manuring the soil to enrich it.

Figure 8.17 *Probing the Ceide Fields*

KEY STUDY *cont.*

Ceide Fields

Integrated within the field systems are domestic enclosures and the postholes and hearths remaining from small circular huts. These occur roughly once for every strip of land. Relatively few artefacts have been recovered but pottery and lithics, including arrowheads and quernstones, have been found. There are also stone-built court and portal tombs spaced out evenly across the landscape every 1–2 kilometres. This suggests that family groups lived amongst the field systems and may also have been buried there. The lack of differentiation suggests a relatively egalitarian society. Currently the dominant model of the Neolithic in Britain is that people were mobile, moving with their herds on a seasonal pattern, but Ceide is very different. It seems that people here were firmly anchored to a relatively small area. Cooney argues that people would have had a much stronger sense of

Figure 8.18 Map of the Ceide Fields

place and a community identity. Furthermore he argues that there is evidence elsewhere in Ireland, the Northern Isles and the Atlantic seaboard of Britain for long-lasting sedentary settlements. Certainly other field systems with similar relationships between tombs and round or rectangular houses are known elsewhere along the Mayo coast. It is likely that many more are hidden under the bogs that cloak much of the region. A growing number of durable, oak-built houses have also been discovered in Ireland including one at Ballyglass close to the Ceide Fields. In other words, the Neolithic took a number of forms and we need to be careful not to extend a model from one area to everywhere else.

By 3000 BC the fields were abandoned and the bog developed. Current evidence supports the idea of environmental damage as the key reason. There is an iron pan under the topsoil on the site which is caused by rain water leaching nutrients from the soil. The reasons for this may lie in the clearance of forest cover by the farmers for fuel and building material. Eventually the iron pan restricted drainage and the soil became waterlogged. Annual vegetation died but did not decay because of the anaerobic conditions. Their remains piled up year on year to form a blanket-bog several metres thick in places.

They interpreted the inhabitants of the permanent site as foragers who hunted and gathered wild food such as figs and pistachios but who also encouraged wheat, barley and legumes to grow. This might include some weeding and spreading seeds of favoured species on good, well watered soil. They argue that farming was preceded by a period of up to 1000 years where wild plants were cultivated. The spread of arable farming is easiest to track in regions where the species were not native as long as original distributions are known.

In Britain but not Ireland there was a lag of hundreds of years between the appearance of the first sign of arable crops and evidence of widespread farming. Most of the early finds of cereals and cattle come from ceremonial sites, (◄ p. 155) suggesting that economics may not have been the main reason for importing them. Relatively few settlement sites have been excavated before the Middle Bronze Age which has led many writers to suggest that the population was mobile rather than sedentary and that wild resources were still important.

Once arable agriculture was established, its traces are relatively easy to detect archaeologically, particularly through changes in pollen sequences. Field and irrigation systems, storage pits and specialist equipment from ploughs to sickles become common from the late Bronze Age. Interest then shifts to the productivity and use of agricultural products. For classical civilisations, art and written sources have provided data on consumption and types of crops. For other areas, experimental archaeology has been valuable. Butser Ancient Farm has demonstrated the kinds of yield possible with ancient crops and explored their response to a range of growing conditions. Detailed analysis of plant assemblages to examine weed types and ratios of weeds to grain and grain to chaff enable archaeologists to identify whether crops

Figure 8.19 *Roundhouse from Archaeolink*

Although the first farmers in central Europe lived in massive rectangular longhouses, the preference in Britain when arable farming became common during the Bronze Age was usually for roundhouses. These are the commonest large structure on sites up to the Roman period. Their universality suggests that similar sized groups of extended families were the basic building block of society and probably of production and consumption too.

were grown and processed on-site and suggest where the fields were (◀ p. 120).

Most early works on the origins of agriculture assumed that a sedentary, farming life was superior to foraging. Certainly the wave of pioneer farming which spread (diffused) through south-eastern and central Europe at a steady rate seems to support this view. However, recent work on successful foragers (◀ p. 240) provides an opposing view. For up to a thousand years the Mesolithic peoples of north-west Europe did not adopt farming in what is termed the 'Neolithic standstill'. There were farmers to the south with whom they occasionally traded so the ideas and crops were available, but they chose not to adopt them. Why should people give up economic strategies that produced a wide variety of foodstuffs and other resources and may have provided surpluses? Farming is hard work and would have produced a monotonous diet.

Eventually agriculture did spread and this raises another question, why then? Theories include environmental change, the prestige attached to cattle and grain and even religious conversion. What is clear is that the transition to farming was not a simple process and that a variety of economic strategies were selected by people according to social requirements as well as ecological pressures. Increasingly, archaeological studies have examined the social signifi-cance of different models of food acquisition including gender relations and social structure.

The introduction of dairying

The application of new scientific techniques is revolutionising our knowledge about past human diets. Humans are naturally lactose intolerant and this is still the case in parts of Africa and the Far East where there is no tradition of dairy foods such as milk, butter or cheese. Partly for this reason archaeologists have tended to see dairying developing much later than initial domestication of cattle. Sherratt's idea of a Secondary Products Revolution has been particularly influential, seeing dairying as part of a process of intensification and change in the early Bronze Age which included horse riding, rearing sheep for wool and the use of animals for traction. Until recently the main evidence base has been typologies of ceramics and faunal assemblages. During the third millennium BC there does appear to be a spread of particular new forms of drinking vessels and other containers from the Balkans and eastern Europe westwards and the use of horses certainly followed that path from the area of original domestication on the Russian steppes.

Faunal evidence has been more ambivalent. Modern dairying herds are made up of adult

Figure 8.20 *Wild and domestic cattle and sheep*

Tracing domestication and changes in the exploitation of animals has generally been through artefacts and faunal remains. Morphological changes between wild and domestic animals are clear over a long period of time but can be hard to detect over short periods. Assemblages have also been analysed to determine whether they are similar to modern examples, for instance a dairy herd. Organic residue analysis and DNA (◀ p. 246) offer a whole new range of insights.

female cattle. The archaeological signature might be a disproportionate number of calves, young male animals and much older females. The neolithic causewayed enclosure at Hambledon Hill has a high proportion of calves and older female cattle in its faunal profile which may suggest dairying and veal production. However there are other possible interpretations and many sites lack the quality of faunal remains to be certain.

Pioneering work led by Professor Evershed of the Organic Geochemistry Unit at Bristol University has established indicators of dairy fats in residues preserved in the walls of unglazed pottery vessels. Stearic acid and palmitic acid are fatty acids which are both found in prehistoric pottery. Stearic acid is more commonly derived from animal fats and palmitic acid from plants. The real breakthrough has been the use of gas chromatography to separate different isotopes to differentiate preserved stearic acid in ceramics. Meat fats from cows and sheep (ruminants) have a lower proportion of ^{13}C than fat from pigs, horses and humans. Milk fats have an even lower ratio of ^{13}C. Samples with very low ^{13}C ratios therefore suggest dairying.

Initially analysis was undertaken on nearly 1000 archived pottery samples across a range of prehistoric sites in southern England including Maiden Castle, Danebury, Trethellan Farm, Windmill Hill and Hambledon Hill. Milk fats were found in ceramics from every site and from over half of the samples overall including 25 per cent of the neolithic sherds. This suggests that dairying arrived in Britain with the introduction of domesticates. Lactose intolerance may have been initially overcome initially through the milking of sheep rather than cattle or by consumption of products such as cheese or yoghurt. Ceramics which have been interpreted as milk strainers or cheese moulds in Europe support this particular model. Many of the neolithic sites are unusual, possibly ritual centres, which may mean that their evidence is not typical of everyday consumption but it does prove that dairying was taking place by the fourth millennium BC.

This work has been extended to try to discover the origins of dairying. In the largest ever organic residue survey so far, over 2000 samples have been analysed from early farming sites in the Near East and the Balkans. Around 14 per cent contained milk fat. The earliest date so far is 6500 BC with north-west Turkey emerging as the possible area where dairying originated.

STORAGE

Storage is an economic strategy. It may be used to overcome fluctuations in supply or to collect a surplus to use in exchange. Storage can be linked to social power (▶ p. 298) perhaps used by an elite to control the distribution of resources to gain prestige or power. The concept of storage can be used to include energy, information, and even the dead. Archaeologists study both the methods of storage and the social and economic reasons for it.

Direct evidence of storage comes from the containers or other features used to hold produce. Many ancient civilisations developed central storage facilities (▶ p. 258) to hold food and other agricultural produce. At the Inca site of Huanuco Pampa, circular, ventilated warehouses which were once used for freeze-dried potatoes still survive. The same is true of many medieval tithe barns. Sometimes they contain traces of their former contents or illustrations on their walls. Dumps of raw inorganic materials such as coal or stone will also leave at least small traces of minerals in the topsoil. Similarly, features such as pits or silos of arable farming communities are frequently recognised and contain pollen or carbonised grain which indicate their uses. On a smaller scale, storage vessels including pottery and glass can be examined in the same way for external decoration or residues of former contents (◀ p. 65). There may also be written or artistic sources that illustrate storage, including tax records and tomb paintings. Other traces of

Figure 8.21 *Storage of water*

This is just one of three massive cisterns built by the Romans at Aptera. The function of the vaulted underground cisterns could simply be to feed the baths on the site, to ensure supply for the town or to enable the hilltop city to withstand a siege. Either way it is an impressive example of public works and civil engineering.

Figure 8.22 *Roman granary from Corbridge*

Built to similar plans, military granaries were raised to reduce damp and allow dogs to hunt rats underneath. They testify to the economic organisation of the Roman Army who did not just rely on local food sources. Grain surpluses were transported to bases and stored to ensure a constant supply for the troops. This is a good example of redistribution (▶ p. 268).

KEY SITE

Knossos and the Minoan palaces

Europe's first civilization developed in early Bronze Age Crete around 2000 BC. It was centred on large 'palaces' of which Knossos is the most famous. Palaces were complex groups of buildings often two or more storeys high. The public areas include a large central courtyard and often huge stepped areas that may have been for ceremonies. The west wings of the palaces were high status areas. Some had wall paintings, columns, bathing or ritual pools and light-wells which brought sunlight down through the building. Exotic artefacts including fine pottery (◀ p. 65), jewellery (▶ p. 283) and imported Syrian seals and Egyptian scarabs were also found in these areas. There were also magazines or storerooms. Some held huge ceramic jars called pithoi, others had lined vats in the floor. Elsewhere at Knossos were huge silos which may have been granaries. This huge storage capacity identifies the palaces as redistributive centres. Their fertile hinterlands provided a surplus including grain, wool, olive oil and wine. Palace accountants used Europe's first written language – Linear A to record stores and transactions. Palace workshops produced fine pottery, metal and stone artefacts often using imported materials such as ivory and copper. Cult rooms housing ritual artefacts and figurines provide evidence of other specialists. Clustered around the central buildings were more ordinary dwellings. Populations in these 'proto towns' were quite high. Estimates for Knossos reach 20,000.

The nature of the social organisation which ran the palaces is less clear. Elite rooms, exotic goods and some of the paintings suggest a ruling class, perhaps an aristocracy. Ritual evidence, images and the repeated symbolism of bulls and the double headed axe or labrys suggests a priesthood, possibly dominated by priestesses. While weapons have been found there is no sign of defences. Perhaps the population was controlled through ideology or perhaps the elite were genuinely benign – distributing good in times of hardship. In the countryside around each palace were villas: rich houses which also had storage areas. Perhaps a local elite controlled the farms and supplied the palaces with their craftsmen, architects, masons and administrators.

Figure 8.23 *Reconstructed multi-storey building at Knossos*

KEY SITE *cont.*

Knossos and the Minoan palaces

The reason for the emergence of the civilisation is also unclear. Apart from the myth of the Minotaur and labyrinth (probably a palace) the Minoans were unknown till archaeologists discovered them. Possibly ideas spread from Syria or Egypt but it is not impossible for indigenous development to have occurred. The introduction of crops such as vines or olives created regional diversity and may have encouraged redistribution. The long term investment in such crops or the development of craft skills may have led to inequalities in land holding or wealth. Continuity of tomb use and of sites such as Knossos suggest that these 'early states' emerged from prepalace society rather than arrived from outside. Increased archaeological focus on rural settlements rather than palaces may help answer this in time.

Once established, the palaces established links all over the eastern Mediterranean. Fine Minoan pottery has been found from Egypt to Greece and luxury items and raw materials from those societies flowed into Crete. Shipwrecks such as the Ulu Burun (▶ p. 272) provide further evidence of these exchanges while the discovery of a Minoan port at Kommos tells us something of the scale of trade.

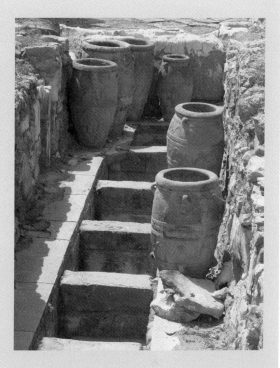

Figure 8.24 Storage magazine at Knossos with pithoi and lined vats

Figure 8.25 Entrance to palace complex from central courtyard at Phaistos. The columns, facings of gypsum and construction from ashlar (sawn stone) blocks indicate a prestigious building

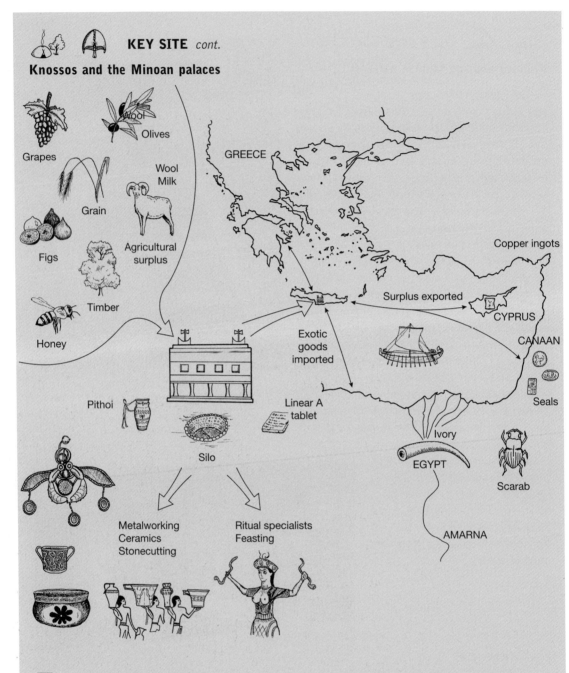

KEY SITE *cont.*

Knossos and the Minoan palaces

Grapes

Olives

Wool

Wool
Milk

Grain

Figs

Agricultural
surplus

Timber

Honey

Pithoi

Silo

Linear A
tablet

GREECE

Copper ingots

Surplus exported

CYPRUS

CANAAN

Seals

Exotic
goods
imported

Ivory

EGYPT

Scarab

AMARNA

Metalworking
Ceramics
Stonecutting

Ritual specialists
Feasting

Figure 8.26 *Minoan palace economies and Mediterranean trade.*

This diagram illustrates the relationship between the palaces in the centre which centralised agricultural surpluses from rural areas and used this to trade for luxury items and provide redistribution through ritual, entertainment and manufacturing. The map also identifies key sites mentioned elsewhere in this chapter

Economics
Peace
Quantity
Surplus
Trade
Redistribution
Accounting – Linear B

Settlement
Transport and
Communication
Inca roads
Internal storage
External
Elaborate architecture

Social organization
Accumulation of
surplus wealth

**Analysis
of plants**
Maize
Potato
Einkorn
Emmer
Weeds
Environment
Processing stages
of wheat

Religion and ritual
Danebury ritual deposits
in pits

Documentary
Linear B tablets

Pits as 'rubbish bins'
After primary use

Material culture
Technology of storage
Ventilation
Oxygen exclusion
Ceramics

Figure 8.27 *The archaeology of storage*

storage need greater interpretation. Drying racks and off-ground structures will only be represented in the archaeological record by postholes.

Landscape features may represent very different types of storage. Millponds, for example, may be stores of power, fish and water. Dense clusters of posts or ditches may represent corrals or stockyards for storing food on the hoof. Phosphate analysis is useful in confirming their function (◄ p. 14). Herds of animals are a form of storage in themselves. It is important to

remember this because there is a tendency to associate storage with sedentary societies, yet ethnography has shown many examples of storage practised by mobile pastoralists.

Other forms of storage leave only indirect evidence. Salting is often traced through distinctive containers, known as briquetage, used to transport it. On some sites inferences can be drawn from the nature of the food remains. The restricted range of bone types at La Cotte de St Brelade suggested the 'caching' of meat. At

KEY STUDIES

Early writing systems

The first writing dates from the fifth millennium BC in the Balkans and has proved impossible to decipher. The earliest writing systems were pictographic. This is where ideas are transmitted through images. We use pictographs today to sign toilet doors. The most well known pictographic system was Cuneiform which emerged in Mesopotamia after 4000 BC. It was inscribed on clay tablets

Figure 8.28 *The sedge (plant) and bee represented the Nile Delta and Upper Egypt respectively. Shown above the two original mounds of land these hieroglyphics announced the Pharaoh as ruler of both kingdoms of Egypt*

using a wedge (Latin – cuneus) shaped stylus. An ideographic or logographic system developed from this, using an abstract symbol to signify a word. For example 4 symbolises 'four'. Early Egyptian hieroglyphics were ideographs but from about 2000 BC other characters began to be used which represented the phonetic sounds of an alphabet. Modern European alphabets from the Romans onwards are based on the Greek alphabet. That in turn can be linked back via the Phoenicians to the Semitic language of the Egyptian alphabet. Greek included vowel sounds and from 1500 BC used a linear writing style – Linear B. The Mayan writing system used glyphs as both ideographs and to represent phonetic sounds. It developed in parallel to Eurasian writing systems.

Egyptian tablets and inscriptions potentially offered a vast amount of information to scholars. The problem was that nobody could read them. The breakthrough came in 1799 when Napoleonic soldiers found a stone with inscriptions built into a wall in Rosetta in Egypt. The Rosetta Stone dates from 196 BC when the Greek dynasty of the Ptolemies were the ruling Pharaohs. It was written by priests to praise the Pharaoh in three scripts:

- Egyptian hieroglyphs – the script of the priesthood
- Egyptian demotic – the linear script used by ordinary people
- Greek

Since they all said the same thing it was possible for the French scholar Champollion to eventually work out how hieroglyphics worked and decode what they said. Unfortunately we cannot be sure of Egyptian vowels, which is why there are alternative spellings for many words and names. For instance Imen/Amen/Amun.

Not all languages have been deciphered. The clay tablet in Figure 10.20 is in Linear A, the writing used by the Minoans. Although it has not been decoded there is sufficient similarity between it and the later Linear B (the writing of the Myceneans) to establish that it was used by palace accountants to record agricultural produce entering and leaving the storerooms. The tablet is an example of preservation by fire. The tablets were soft clay and could be reused. Normally they would decay over time. However, when the Palace of Zakros (▶ p. 306) burnt down, hundreds of tablets were fired and thus able to survive.

KEY STUDIES *cont.*

Early writing systems

When explorers discovered the ruins of Maya cities in the jungle in the mid 19th century they realised that the glyphs which covered the monuments were the remnants of a lost language. Until recently little progress was made with the translation. It was assumed from the little that could be read that the Maya were a society of peace-loving astronomers with an obsession with mathematics and a complex calendar. Recent breakthroughs have allowed most glyphs to be translated. Unfortunately few Mayan texts survive because Spanish priests burnt them. However the carvings survive and the stories of gods, wars and rulers such as Pacal at Palenque (◄ p. 136) and the kings of Copan (► p. 284) can be read. The glyphs provide us with information about real, named people. This is impossible for periods without writing.

Writing probably developed due to trade. Merchants needed to ensure their goods arrived at distant destinations. They made tokens shaped like each of their goods such as cattle or jars of oil. These were enclosed in a hollow ball of clay which was sealed using their unique cylinder seal. The recipient could be sure who had sent the shipment from the seal. The tokens inside would tell them how many of each item should have arrived. Writing developed from the tokens and the symbols on the seals.

• http://www.omniglot.com/

Figure 8.29 *Linear A*

Balam   Ba-la-m(a)

Figure 8.30 *'Jaguar' in Mayan glyphs*

Figure 8.31 *This merchant's cylinder seal from Crete had been rolled on wax to display the inscription. Cylinder seals themselves provide strong evidence of trading systems*

Stellmoor the sheer quantity of meat was indicative of pemmican making. Insects associated with particular foodstuffs also provide clues, for example grain beetles from Roman York.

Finally there are forms of storage which leave no trace. Woodpiles constitute one of the commonest types of stores but are usually archaeologically invisible. Organic containers such as baskets and skins only survive in exceptional circumstances. The same is true of some agricultural produce, particularly tubers.

Symbolic or abstract forms of storage are visible in the archaeological record from later prehistory. Instead of raw materials themselves being stored, they are exchanged for something which is widely accepted as symbolising a value in those materials. Coins are a particularly sophisticated method of symbolically storing value. They can be converted into goods at a later date. They have the advantage of being easily transported and concealed. Jewellery, cattle, carpets and cowrie shells have been used in a similar way. The concept of **social storage** should also be considered under this heading although it is much more difficult to recognise archaeologically. This is where one person stores value in others. In simple terms, if I give you a gift of a cow, at some point in the future you will give me something of at least equal value. (▶ p. 267) In practice, social storage is often highly complex and can encompass marriages, feasting and military alliances. Social storage blurs economics with social and political affairs. However, for most of human history these areas have probably been inextricably linked.

INTENSIFICATION OF FARMING

In a general sense intensification can describe any strategy which re-organises economic activity to increase production. It could be applied to the development of traps to catch animals or the use of two-piece moulds to speed up the manufacture of bronze axes. The greatest physical impact of intensification can be seen in evidence for increasing control over the productive capacity of the land. It is often associated with population pressure or social control.

The first traces of intensification of the landscape can be detected from the soil and pollen evidence for forest clearance and pioneer farming. The intensification of production including the exploitation of stock animals resulted in the construction of elaborate field systems and land divisions such as the Dartmoor 'reaves'. Environmental evidence can often establish the ebb and flow of human impact. For example, around Avebury cycles of forest clearance and later regeneration in association with fluctuations in the intensity of agricultural exploitation have been traced. Medieval attempts to intensify production by extending the area of arable land can be identifed through place names and earthworks such as strip lynchets where hillsides were ploughed. Manuring to increase yields is generally recognised from the halo of pottery scattered in the fields around settlements (◀ p. 12). The countryside has also been the scene of other forms of intensification, particularly extraction. Traces of quarrying, smelting and mining can often be seen, particularly in upland areas.

Some of the most dramatic evidence of intensification comes from areas of the world where artificial ways of supplying rainfall to crops were needed to raise yields. Tomb paintings supplement the archaeological evidence for irrigation schemes in Ancient Egypt. Here, canals had been used to extend the area watered by the annual floods of the Nile and so intensify production. Records survive of the technology developed to lift water from canals to fields including the shaduf and later the Archimedes' screw, an early bronze version of which may have been used to water the famous 'Hanging Gardens of Babylon'. In the Oaxaca valley of Mexico, field survey at Arroyo Lencho Diego located 20 metres of sediment which had accumulated behind a vanished dam. The inhabitants had used the dam to irrigate the whole of the valley in an

Figure 8.32 *Sail-wing windmill from Crete*

Windmill technology arrived in Europe by way of Persia in the twelfth century. Unlike their Islamic predecessors, European mills had a horizontal axis. This may have been because that was used in existing watermills. Mills such as this were used to pump irrigation water and grind corn.

area of otherwise unpredictable water availability. The canals and terraces that watered the fields supplying the major town of Monte Alban still survive as landscape features. Elsewhere in Mexico the Aztecs developed an intensive system of agriculture based on floating gardens or 'chinampas'. Rafts were covered in weeds and mud and anchored in rows. Over time more mud was added and the root systems of trees bound the rafts together as fertile islands. They could be cropped two to three times a year. The Aztec capital Tenochtitlan received most of its food from chinampas. Sometimes irrigation schemes are not immediately visible. In the third millennium BC a network of canals supplied water from the rivers Tigris and Euphrates to the fields and the port of the Mesopotamian desert city of Mashkan Shapir. Today they are buried under sand but were detected by satellite imaging (◄ p. 24). In other instances there was too much water for successful cultivation. At Kuk Swamp in New Guinea a huge network of drainage ditches was first revealed by aerial photography, showing as lines several kilometres long in modern tea plantations. Excavation revealed that early farmers had built them to drain the swamp in order to intensively cultivate the fertile soil and grow taro and other crops. (Bayliss-Smith 1996)

Communications

One aspect of economies, which generally develops in conjunction with intensification, is transport. The remains of permanent tracks and roads such as the Sweet Track or Roman and Inca road systems can indicate increasing traffic on routes. Intense use of these features can sometimes be inferred from wear such as rutting and evidence of frequent repairing.

The development of vehicles can be traced from burials, such as the four-wheeled carts in burials at Ur or the 'chariots' from Garton Slack, and through art and figurines. Evidence for the use of animals for riding and draught purposes can sometimes be determined by bit-wear marks on teeth or artefacts associated with harnesses. Artistic sources and shipwreck evidence (▶ p. 272) provide evidence of the evolution of shipping.

TRADE AND EXCHANGE

Early archaeological studies tended to largely interpret the movement of artefacts and materials as trade or the movement of peoples. Ethnographic examples have provided a much wider range of options with which to interpret archaeological evidence. There has also been recognition that exchange does not just involve goods and that its aims are often social rather than economic. Often the relationship is of more value than what is exchanged, as with modern Christmas cards. The exchange may involve social obligations which help bind society together.

Exchange in its widest sense includes any transaction between people. This can include exchange of information, services and people. For instance, the spread of bell beakers throughout Europe and North Africa in the third millennium BC was due to exchange. Archaeologists have been divided over the mechanism for this exchange, whether it was through movement of people or the spread of ideas, drinking culture or religion. Trade is just one form of exchange.

Three main categories of exchange have been adopted by archaeology from economics. These are **reciprocity, redistribution** and **market exchange**.

Figure 8.33 *Relief from Rievaulx*

This carving encapsulates several key economic elements. Market trade in wool from the extensive sheep farms of the Cistercian monks helped pay for the great monastic establishments of the Middle Ages. Bulk goods such as wool were transported to river ports by packhorses. The windmill represents the intensification of energy production. Human and animal muscle was replaced by machinery harnessing wind power. In this case probably to grind grain for flour. The contrast with grain rubbers (◀ p. 244) is stark.

• http://www.windmillworld.com/windmills/history.htm

Figure 8.34 'Agia Triada' market

A market place would seem to be the clearest evidence for a market economy. While some are easily recognisable, the evidence for others is ambivalent. In this example there appear to be shops and storage containers with a public area between. It is also situated between the town and the high status buildings which might have controlled trade. However, the same evidence can be used to argue that it is another variation on Minoan central storage depots (◄ p. 258).

Reciprocity

This involves transactions where a gift from one person creates an obligation to return something at a later date. We do this when we buy a round of drinks. Many societies have used it as the basis for social stability. In some cultures marriage involves payment of bridewealth from the husband's family to the bride's family. This is to compensate for their loss of a fertile worker. Payments may be in goods and may take place over time. Such exchange also cements the relationship between the two families. Feasting and the sharing of food with others are often a powerful example of reciprocity. It creates an obligation to return the favour at a later point. It can also be seen as an exchange of food for social prestige. A popular example for archaeologists has been the Big Man feasts of highland New Guinea where status is acquired by throwing huge feasts at which party-goers are given generous gifts of meat or livestock. A related concept is social storage. Here a gift or favour is given which stores up future gifts or assistance for times when they will be needed. Extreme examples of this are provided by ethnographic accounts of the Potlatch and Kula Ring (Orme 1981). Reciprocity can involve an equal exchange (balanced reciprocity) but can also be positive or negative if one partner does better. Ethnography once again warns against imposing our values on the evidence. Islanders on Yap in the Caroline Islands used to gain prestige by spending their savings on huge stone discs, which they then buried under their homes.

Historical sources such as Homer and Egyptian tomb paintings have provided insights into prestige goods exchange. High status individuals established and cemented relationships

Reciprocity

Gift exchange

Redistribution of resources

Down the line exchange

Polished
stone axe

Figure 8.35 *Some types of exchange identified by archaeologists*

through reciprocal exchanges. This continues at a symbolic level amongst leaders of state today. These exchanges used to involve marriage partners and exotic goods or creatures. Archaeologically this sort of exchange may be recognised where special artefacts such as gems, amber, jade and ivory move long distances. In these cases archaeologists have talked of '**prestige goods chains**'. A classic example is the movement of amber from the Baltic to Mycenae during the Bronze Age and some of the fine metalwork that travelled in the opposite direction from central Europe. Grave goods and special votive deposits have often been the source of such material for

archaeologists. The rich graves at Varna (see front cover) contained bracelets of spondylus, a Mediterranean shellfish. One interpretation is that these were exchanged for gold from sources close to Varna. However, some prestige goods such as furs, slaves, silk and feathers may be archaeologically invisible.

Redistribution

This model involves a central authority collecting together resources and then redistributing them. Our welfare state is a giant version of this, while harvest festivals symbolise it. In the past redistribution tended to be operated by individual rulers to whom it gave both prestige and legitimacy. Ethnographic studies have tended to emphasise this as a feature of chiefdoms, particularly in areas of economic diversity. Redistribution shares out particular resources to areas that lack them, for example fish to farmers and crops to fishers. Historic accounts such as Celtic histories suggest that rulers would use redistribution to reward their followers with weapons, cattle and exotic goods in order to secure their loyalty. As with reciprocity, the social aspects of the exchange may be important and as before, feasting may be the vehicle for the exchange.

Archaeological evidence includes sites with central stores as at Knossos. Some interpretations of hill forts such as Danebury (◄ p. 120) have reached similar conclusions although there is less agreement on this. Patterns of distribution where valuable goods have been widely distributed are also potential evidence of redistribution to local leaders from a central chief. The distribution of Bronze Age swords may be such a case. The clearest evidence comes from those sites where records have been recovered as at Vindolanda and Pylos.

Market exchange

In its simplest sense 'a market' suggests a recognised place where bargaining takes place. The easiest to identify are those where defined

Figure 8.36 *Late Minoan marine style stirrup jar*

Cretan potters made some of the best ceramics in the early Bronze Age. Eggshell thin Kamares wear and fine Marine style vessels with their entire surface covered in sea creatures have been found across the eastern Mediterranean and as far up the Nile as Aswan. They provide evidence of widespread trade in luxuries.

Figure 8.37 *Minoan 'ship-sheds' at Kommos.*

Kommos was protected by an offshore reef and became a major port in Minoan Crete. Six large sheds probably housed seagoing vessels during the winter months. Stone anchors found here have been sourced to Syria and copper ingots from Cyprus. Pottery which once held wine, oil and incense came from all over the eastern Mediterranean. It includes Canaanite Amphorae (▶ p. 271). The site had considerable storage capacity and was probably involved in importing and exporting on behalf of the nearby palace of Phaistos.

http://www.fineart.utoronto.ca/kommos/kommosIntroduction.html

areas or buildings exist. The agora of Greek towns is an example. Another signature is the development of mechanisms to regulate amounts or to make exchange flexible such as weights and coinage. Of course, not all market exchange happens in a fixed place and not all currencies are archaeologically visible. Blankets and carpets have been used as standards against which value can be measured. Identifying these instances of trade in perishable goods is difficult. The well-preserved Pazyryk 'Ice Maiden' from the Altai Mountains provided such a clue. Pazyryk tribes were known to have trade links with China. When silk in her clothes was analysed it was expected to have been made of yarn from cultivated Chinese silkworms. To the experts' surprise it turned out to be characteristic of wild Indian silk. This indicated that the Pazyryk traded to the south as well as in China.

Concentrations of artefacts from many areas would be expected at a port or market. The Iron Age settlement at Hengistbury Head, with its modified harbour and apparently defensive wall, may be such an example. Finds included imported pottery, glass and figs, with evidence of metals and perhaps hides and corn being exported. However, in some cases the pattern of finds could equally represent a religious or high status site. The many interpretations of Neolithic causewayed enclosures typify this sort of ambivalent evidence. Although markets today are almost entirely about buying and selling, they too have had social functions. Ethnographic studies have noted their role in information exchange, tax collection and as places for social gatherings. Historic and artistic sources are again useful. Spanish accounts of the use of quetzal feathers and cacao beans in Mexico are supported by the images of merchants and their backpacks from the rather earlier site of Cacaxtla.

Identifying the signatures of different modes of exchange

The origins of materials used in exchange are tracked using characterisation studies (◀ p. 64).

For example. Roman documentary sources tell us very little about trade, but amphorae are very common finds on excavations and in shipwrecks. The fabrics of the millions of Roman amphorae that were traded all over the Empire have responded particularly well to petrology, with the result that we now know where most types were manufactured. As a result it is possible to study the sources and distributions of important agricultural products such as Italian wine, Spanish fish sauce or North African olive oil. Seals or other marks on the objects themselves may indicate their place of manufacture. For example, many Roman amphorae have potters' stamps and some even have handwritten inscriptions, written in black ink, giving details of their contents and origin. Artistic sources can provide considerable detail. Some Egyptian tombs from the second millennium have pictures of Minoans bearing goods from Crete.

Distribution patterns of artefacts from their place of origin are plotted on maps to see whether they match models for particular types of exchange. For example, clusters of Lava quernstones at centres of manufacture and ports such as Dorestadt and Ipswich have enabled the trade to be traced.

Trend surface analysis turns plots of finds on a map into contours to smooth out distortion caused by chance finds. This has been used to map the distribution of Neolithic stone axes from their source.

Fall-off analysis is used to examine the rate at which finds diminish the further one gets from the place of manufacture. A sharp fall suggests very local exchange, a smooth decline suggests 'down the line' trade while a pattern with several blips in the curve indicates secondary trading or exchange centres. This technique has been used to identify the nature of trade in copper, obsidian and pottery.

The context in which particular artefacts are found provides some clues. Shipwrecks provide

KEY STUDY

The Canaanite Amphorae Project

Amphorae – large pottery storage vessels – have been found on Bronze Age sites across the Middle East and eastern Mediterranean. Through typology and petrological study of clay fabrics, several styles of vessel have been linked to particular areas of origin. In this particular case it was the area of present-day Israel, Lebanon and Palestine known in biblical times as Canaan. They have a particularly wide distribution, appearing in the cargo of the Ulu Burun off modern Turkey and in great quantities on Egyptian sites up the river Nile. To understand what was being carried in the amphorae and provide insights into trade, this project involves data collection and residue analysis from across the region. An early focus has been on sherds recovered from the Egyptian cities of Amarna (capital of the Pharaoh Akhenaten) and Memphis (Capital of New Kingdom Egypt).

Researchers began by establishing a detailed typology of the amphorae based on visual attributes using material from the current Amarna project and collections held in museums. Binocular microscopes were used to classify fabric types. These were checked using petrology and NAA (◀ p. 90) and compared with reference material on pottery and geology from across the region. Amongst inclusions in the clays were limestone and quartz which indicated the Lebanon coast and basalt and chert which only occur together in the Israel's Jezreel Valley. Identical pottery was found in Bronze Age settlements in this area.

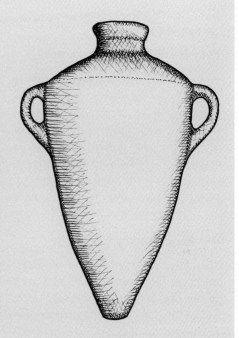

Figure 8.38 *Drawing of a Canaanite amphorae*

The archaeologists now knew where the amphorae had originated but not what they held. A few had inscriptions including honey and oil but most did not. Organic residue analysis was not very successful with the honey or pinpointing the vegetable oil. This was probably from olives which were produced on a large scale in Canaan and one particular amphora type was linked to this trade. A considerable quantity of resin was also found in broken amphorae or extracted from the fabric with solvents. It was also found on textiles and local bowls which are known to have been used for incense burning. The nature of this incense has long been debated. The Egyptian word *sntr* has been translated as incense and generally thought to mean frankincense, a gum resin from trees grown further south in Africa. However, this resin came from pistacia trees, probably Terebinth. A similar resin was found on the Ulu Burun (▶ p. 272). Traces of beer were found in a few vessels.

As a result of this research there is now a detailed reference collection of vessel and fabric types which will enable identification of ceramics and their origin using hand lenses or microscopes. There is also a reference collection of biomarkers which will help researchers identify products more easily in the future. Finally, they have been able to identify part of the Bronze Age trade network across the region.

KEY SITES

Four Mediterranean shipwrecks

Four wrecks excavated near to Turkey by teams led by George Bass over the last forty years provide a glimpse of developing trade patterns in the ancient world. They also document changes in shipbuilding techniques over time in response to social and environmental factors. In each case the ship is named for where it was found.

Ulu Burun, Turkey c. 1400 BC

The oldest sea-going ship in the world was 50m long with a short mast and square sail. It was a slow, heavy vessel similar to those depicted on Egyptian reliefs with at least 15 tons of goods onboard. These were painstakingly excavated and raised in it by lifting balloons and nets. Cargo included a 'sumptuary' range of exotic goods from across the eastern Mediterranean. The wreck was dated from Egyptian rings and seals. Also from Egypt were scarabs, gold artefacts and elephant tusks along with seals (◀ p. 262) from Mycenae and Mesopotamia, 6000 Canaanite and Mycenean swords and Baltic amber. Hundreds of copper oxhide ingots (◀ p. 91) were sourced by lead isotope analysis to Cyprus while tin ingots probably came from Turkey or even Afghanistan. Amongst organic finds were African ebony logs, pistachios, almonds, figs, olives, spices and grain. Most of the 130 amphorae contained terebrinth resin used to make perfume. Fine pottery came from Canaan, Cyprus, Mycenae and Syria and there were murex shells (used to make purple dye) and thousands of glass beads. A wooded, wax-covered writing table and balance weights suggested someone on

Figure 8.39 The decay of the Kyrenia wreck

Figure 8.40 The Ulu Burun Ship

KEY SITES *cont.*

board kept records. The personal effects suggested a Greek or Canaanite crew. Bass interpreted this as a royal cargo. Contemporary inscriptions and tablets document gifts sent as tribute, dowries or to seal alliances between rulers. On route the ship had put in to many ports and bought, and probably sold, different goods. This wreck demonstrates how long-distance trade could have developed on the back of reciprocal exchanges.

Kyrenia, Cyprus c. 300 BC

This wreck was a small merchant vessel with a cargo of 400 amphorae from the island of Rhodes, identifiable by their seal stamps, and millstones. There were very few personal possessions, only a few bone eyelets from a sandal and some fig seeds. Underneath the hull a collection of concretions were recovered. When opened and used to produce resin casts they proved to be iron javelins, some of them bent from impact on the hull. Since there are no natural hazards in the area, this evidence led the excavators to believe that pirates may have sunk the Kyrenia. The vessel had settled down onto the ocean bed, and gradually became covered in silt. As its mast and rigging rotted away, the lower part of the hull was forced outwards by the weight of the cargo and broke apart. Protected by the silt, which choked off oxygen and killed the marine worms that infested it, the remains of the hull were preserved. The ship was built in the traditional way of the classical Greeks, which is 'hull first'. Planks are carved by eye to fit along a keel, with timber selected for its natural curvature as appropriate to different parts of the vessel. The sculpted planks were held together along their edges by thousands of mortise and tenon joints which gave a very strong hull braced only with frames at a later stage. The pine frames were clenched together with treenails, fastened with copper nails. This process wasted 70–80 per cent of the wood used and required a high standard of craftsmanship from the shipwright. It would only be possible in a society which valued craftsmanship, where raw materials were

Figure 8.41 *Cargo of the Kyrenia wreck*

This partial reconstruction shows the amphorae densely packed in the bottom of the vessel. It is not clear if it had a deck over the hold but the pottery was probably packed in thorn branches to protect it. The millstones are also visible. There may have been textiles on top but no trace of them could survive.

Figure 8.42 *Construction of the Kyrenia*

The freeze dried hull of the ship reveals structural elements and construction techniques. The degree of carpentry skills which went into building the vessel is clear.

KEY SITES *cont.*

abundant and where time was no problem. The man who built the Kyrenia ship was probably a slave and his time was his master's. Over its life, the 90 year old vessel had been much repaired and partly sheathed in lead to remain watertight. It was engaged in what has been called 'tramping': sailing (usually within sight of land) between ports on a long circuit of the region, taking on and selling cargoes as she went.

Yassi Ada, Turkey *c.* AD 625

This wreck was dated by coins recovered from the wreck to the reign of the Byzantine Emperor Heraclius. An elaborate 'steelyard'

Figure 8.43 *Ships from the Byzantine period*

with the head of a boar at one end and a sliding bust of Athena at the other declared itself to be the property of 'George senior, sea-captain'. Historical documents suggest he was one of a growing class of merchants who financed their own ventures and often captained their own ship. The vessel itself was partly constructed in the old classical 'hull-first' style, with logs sculpted to fit. However, this time the mortise and tenon joints were less carefully executed. They were fewer in number and often nails were driven through them once the plank was located. The upper section of the hull was built by the new 'frame-first' method. Many flat planks were cut from a log and twisted against internal frames as they moved forward along the hull. This more economical use of materials and time suggests that social conditions had changed from the time that the *Kyrenia* was built. The Byzantine shipwright was a free man contracted to do the job. His employer would have been concerned to save time and timber and therefore money. The skeleton first building is a shift to a more modern approach and meant that much of the vessel could be built by semi-skilled workers rather than expensive specialists. Byzantine society still used slaves but only in the household and not in an industrial context. In seas full of pirates, this freighter was built for speed. With its varied cargo of 9000 old amphorae full of low grade wine, olives and lentils it may have been a supply ship for the Byzantine Army.

Serce Limani, Turkey *c.* AD 1024

This medieval Arab merchant vessel was found to contain a cargo of glass. Eighty intact pieces from the ends of the ship possibly represented personal possessions or items of merchandise but the centre of the ship held several tonnes of raw and broken glass. The raw glass or 'cullet' would have been added to new batches to improve quality and the broken glass seems to represent the sweepings from a glass factory. Many of the pieces were twisted or malformed in the process of blowing or moulding and had been discarded. The excavators classified the millions of pieces of glass by sorting them according to attributes such as colour, pattern and location on original vessels, for example rim sherds. By following this process meticulously a large number of pieces were eventually re-assembled. The cargo demonstrates craft specialisation and the technology of production, but the fabric of the ship itself is equally rewarding. The Serce Limani ship was built entirely by the 'frame-first' technique. First the keel was laid down. Frames were attached to it and planks bent around

KEY SITES *cont.*

the frame to form the hull. The technique is still used in shipyards around the Mediterranean and gives a strong hull while being economical in use of wood. Many hull planks can be cut from a single log. This development clearly happened between the building of the Yassi Ada and the Serce Limani wrecks in the early medieval period when historical scholars tell us that there was considerable conflict between the expanding Arab world and the Byzantine Empire. Historical records describe massive losses of ships through warfare. It is easy to visualise a cycle of forest clearance to feed an ever-increasing demand for ships creating a situation where there was pressure to budget-build new ships. The Serce Limani vessel shows signs of compromise on quality but it was also 'armed to the teeth'. In addition to the glass, large numbers of spears and a cache of fine swords were discovered. These wrecks demonstrate diachronic change in technology over a thousand-year period, the evolution of trade and a range of economic specialisation (▶ p. 283).

• http://www.diveturkey.com/inaturkey/projects.htm

insights into the nature and scale of exchange and who was trading what. **Hoards** may also provide such evidence although the motives for deposition could be more varied. A deposit of axe heads could be a votive offering, a store of scrap for manufacturing or a cache of trade goods.

Problems with exchange

Despite all these tools the nature of the movement of artefacts or exchange is not always clear. Not all of the possible types of transaction leave clear traces in the archaeological record and different processes can look remarkably similar in their spatial distribution. Sometimes only one side of an exchange can be found. The fourth-century site at Gudme in Denmark has revealed many hoards of gold which originated in the Roman Empire. Whether these represent tribute, booty, mercenary pay or religious offerings is unclear. There are also cases where there was no exchange. In some cases people moved, taking artefacts with them. More commonly, people collected local materials themselves. This is thought to be the case with the movement of obsidian from Melos, which has been found in nearby settlements.

KEY TERM

Material culture

This term is used in a general sense to mean the artefacts and structures produced by a given people. There are two major approaches to studying them. A 'biographical approach' is the most familiar. This might involve asking what raw materials were used, how they were obtained and worked and how the finished products were used. The second approach involves 'reading' the symbolic meanings embedded in artefacts and structures. This is based on the idea that the beliefs and values of a culture are expressed to some extent in the material things it produces. People's actions are 'structured' by the beliefs, ideas and knowledge of their culture. These actions in turn shape the things they create.

To 'read' artefacts as texts, archaeologists study artefacts and the contexts in which they are found and look for repeated patterns. They also explore the way that material things symbolised values and in turn structured the way in which people thought about and interpreted their world. For instance certain artefacts (for example beakers) may have been used to express social identity.

STUDYING MATERIALS

Many of the methods used in studying materials have been discussed in Chapter 3 and they should be referred to for further detail. This section provides some additional pointers for various stages in the use of material. You need to be familiar with a range of materials, particularly metals, ceramics and stone, and how they were used for the periods you are studying. This should include at least one example of **diachronic change** and the development of technology. For example, the gradual improvement in the efficiency of stone tools from Oldowan pebble tools through Acheulean and Mousterian types to the 'creative explosion' of the Upper Palaeolithic and blade technology.

Acquisition of materials

Extraction of clay, stone and metal ores up to the point where the material is ready to be used are most frequently studied. Aside from sourcing materials the remains of extraction sites such as mines and quarries provide insights into technology and scale of production. The process of extraction can usually be understood from marks and tools left at the mine or quarry site. At the Neolithic flint mines at Grimes Graves 350 vertical shafts were dug 10 metres down

Figure 8.45 *The unfinished obelisk, Aswan*

Lying in the quarry where it was abandoned thousands of years ago, this monstrous chunk of red granite has contributed much to our understanding of stone working in ancient Egypt. Tools left with the obelisk and markings on the stone enable an understanding of the technology used. At around 1200 tonnes and 40m in length it would have been the largest obelisk erected. However a crack in the rock led to work being stopped.

Figure 8.44 *Diachronic change: the development of axes*

Lithic axes evolved to polished stone axes such as (1). The first metal axes were flat copper. Later developments included a stopridge (2), flanges (3) and sockets and loops (4).

KEY SITE

The Sweet Track

The only areas of higher ground on the area of peat wetland known as the Somerset Levels are slight sandy knolls. These have been used for settlement since the Neolithic. The surrounding swamp would have provided rich wild-food resources including fish and wildfowl while higher areas made good grazing land. Prehistoric people faced the problem of ensuring effective communication between settlements and they solved it by constructing sophisticated trackways. They invested considerable communal effort into ventures that in some cases lasted only a few years. The 'Sweet Track', named after the farmer who discovered it while clearing a drain, was an 1800-metre artificial wooden walkway through the swamp. Anaerobic conditions had preserved the structure which has been dated by dendrochronology to the Neolithic period around 4000 BC. This makes it earlier than most of the megalithic monuments. Its construction reveals considerable woodworking skill and woodland management. The planks of the walkway were split from tree trunks using wedges, and other components were made from coppiced wood from oak, hazel and alder. This implies sustainable management strategies and forward planning. The line of the track had been staked out with wooden posts. Construction involved creating a series of X- shapes using posts that rested on a submerged wooden rail. The planks were laid on the X-shapes to create a walkway above the water level. Items found alongside the track, such as jadeite axes from Europe, suggest far-reaching exchange contacts. Environmental evidence such as spiders and rodent-gnawed hazelnuts provided

Figure 8.46 *A replica of part of the Sweet Track at the Peat Moors Visitor Centre. The various construction methods are clearly visible*

KEY SITE *cont.*

The Sweet Track

much detail about the surrounding wetland. Precise dating of the timbers suggests that the Sweet Track was built fairly quickly and only lasted some eleven years before going out of use, probably due to rising water levels.

• Coles and Coles 1976

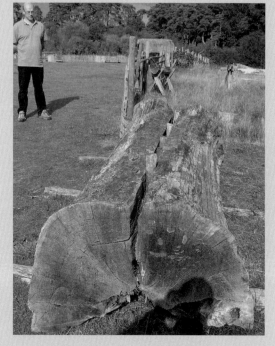

Figure 8.47 *Splitting wood*

Marks on prehistoric wood such as from the Sweet Track have enabled archaeologists to identify and replicate carpentry techniques. In this instance wedges are being driven into a trunk to split it into planks. This technique enabled planks to be produced before saws were invented.

through chalk and flint to seams of dark floor-stone flint. This was prized for its colour, purity and ease of working. Recent dating evidence suggests the whole site was in use for hundreds of years with 1–2 shafts dug each year, so a relatively small amount of people were involved at any one time. From the bottom of the shafts, galleries radiate out following the flint seams. Antler picks, shoulder blade shovels and stone axes were used to dig the mine and extract the flint. Some were left behind by the miners and the marks made by these tools can be seen on the walls. Pillars were left in the galleries to prevent roof collapses and baskets and ladders were probably used to get in and out with the flint. Smoke stains from burning animal fat on the roofs of some galleries show that the miners were using

lamps or a textile soaked in fat to provide light. However this was not just an extraction site. There are hearths and evidence of feasting in some chambers. There are special deposits of unusual artefacts and animal bones and also some human remains. This combined with the fact that miners did not need to dig this deep if they just wanted flint for tools suggests that ritual may have been involved as well. The distribution patterns of polished stone axes during this period in northern Europe suggest that materials with unusual colours and that were extracted from dangerous sites on mountains were particularly sought after. Many of these were deposited without being used, e.g. Greenstone axes from Pike of Stickle in the Lake District, one of which was found in a gallery at Grimes Graves.

Waste material also provides a signature for particular processes whether it is chippings from roughly dressed stone or slag from smelting iron. Waste can be subject to microscopic and analytical procedures similar to those for artefacts. Cyprus is well known as a source of copper from the Bronze Age onwards. Ingots of Cypriot copper were found in the Ulu Burun and at Minoan sites. In one of the letters (on a clay tablet) found at El Armana in Egypt, the King of Alashiya apologises to the Pharaoh for sending a smaller shipment of copper than expected. The mountain of Alashiya was recorded across the Middle East as the major source of copper. Characterisation of the minerals in the tablets has located the clay source to south-west Cyprus. However, the richness of the copper seams means that much archaeological evidence has been destroyed by more recent mining. As was the practice throughout the region, most excavations on the island have also focussed on urban areas. These have revealed much about the final processes of artefact production such as casting and trade, but little of the smelting process. To discover more about the technology and development of this industry, archaeologists have undertaken extensive field surveys to identify 'off-site' activity areas. One such example is the early smelting workshop of Phorades (1600 BC) which was built into a stream bed close to the source of ores. 3.5 tons of slag and much furnace debris was discovered but little copper, almost certainly because its value meant that every drop was removed. Pieces of furnace debris enabled the design of the smelting furnace to be re-created while well-preserved tuyères (ceramic pipes) revealed how high temperatures were reached.

The lack of mauls or other crushing tools suggested that initial processing and roasting of copper-bearing rock took place at the mine site. This seems to have been a pattern at other early copper mines including Great Orme in Wales. The furnaces at Phorades were cylindrical and about 44 cms in diameter. Scorching on the tuyères suggests they were inserted into the mouth of the furnace from above. Their role was to force air into the chamber to raise temperatures above 1200°C in order to smelt the copper. At some other sites ceramic bellows have been found but none were present at Phorades. This may be because they were organic or because workers simply blew down them, a method depicted in some Egyptian wall paintings. Despite the large slag heap, Phorades was a small scale operation. Only around 300 kilos of copper would have been produced which would have been enough for only 10 oxhide ingots (◄ p. 91). Other work-shops would have been scattered across the area. Other smelting sites elsewhere in Cyprus such as Almyras seem to have also covered the first parts of the production process. Final production took place in specialised workshops in the urban centres on the coast such as Enkomi which grew rich on the trade in ingots and finished artefacts. There may also have been some large scale production although no such sites have been found yet. Lead isotopic analysis of 78 ingots found across the Mediterranean found that they could be linked with the Apliki mine in northern Cyprus.

The distance materials have travelled can be significant. Materials which have travelled far from their source and which are relatively rare in the context where they are found are referred to as 'exotics'. This term also often implies a high 'value' for the material in the eyes of the people using it and consequently its possession may suggest high status. Such materials include gold in burials, for example Bush Barrow or Roman amphorae in Late Iron Age burials. Exotic materials often have their own inherent symbolism.

Manufacture

Analysis of materials and finds of tools and processing features such as kilns are vital in understanding production. Our understanding of Bronze Age metallurgy combines chemical and physical analysis of ores, interpretation of moulds

KEY STUDY

Bushcraft Mesolithic style

The recent growth of bushcraft as an activity and a subject for television programmes has led to an increase in interest in the aboriginal peoples of Europe. However, poor survival of organic materials from the Upper Palaeolithic and Mesolithic has meant that much of our understanding of past skills draws heavily on ethnographic examples of other people in the modern world who exploit wild resources for food and technology.

Lithics survive best and dominate assemblages from the end of the last Ice Age. However, across northern Europe there are sites, usually water-

Figure 8.48 *Fishtrap from Agerod made from cherry and alder*

logged, which provide insights into what was more a 'wood age' than a 'stone age'. As with plant food, plant technology is under-represented in most assemblages when in reality it probably predominated. Plant fibres made from nettles or bast were used as binding, thread and to make mats. The survival of large numbers of fish-hooks tells us that they were also used to make fishing line. Plants are likely to have also been used for fabrics, impressions having been found on ceramic material from Dolni Vestonice during the last Ice Age. Wood was crucial to Mesolithic technology and there is growing evidence of the use of large quantities of coppiced wood which might suggest that woodland management preceded farming in northern Europe. The fish-trap at Nekselo in Denmark for example was constructed using around 7000 3–4-metre long rods of hazel and many longer, straight poles. Wood was carefully selected for different properties. Lime was favoured for canoes, possibly because it does not crack as easily as other woods with repeated wetting and drying while paddles were ash. Lime bast was used for nets while hazel, and to a lesser extent willow and cherry, were used for fish traps. Willow was used for wicker baskets while birch-bark provided alternative containers. Elm was the favoured wood for Mesolithic bows with hazel and perhaps wayfaring tree. Points were secured

Figure 8.49 *Mesolithic fire lighting kit. Flint, pyrites and tinder fungus*

KEY STUDY *cont.*

Bushcraft Mesolithic style

using pine and birch resin. In addition to knowing their trees, Mesolithic people knew their fungi. Examples of tinder fungus which is used in fire-lighting and to carry embers have been found on Danish sites while the neolithic 'iceman' (◄ p. 93) was carrying several types of fungi.

Figure 8.50 Net made from lime bast fibres

Figure 8.51 Container made from birchbark

Figure 8.52 Antler harpoons

Figure 8.53 *Manufacture of stone axes*

Carefully selected stone or flint was roughed into a rectangular blank with a hard hammer of stone. Softer hammers and pressure flaking techniques were used to refine the shape and smooth the surface. Finally a laborious process of grinding and polishing with progressively less coarse materials produced the axe shape. A very fine abrasive would be used to give it the final polish. Such axes were prestige items and may never have been intended for use. However hafted examples have also been found.

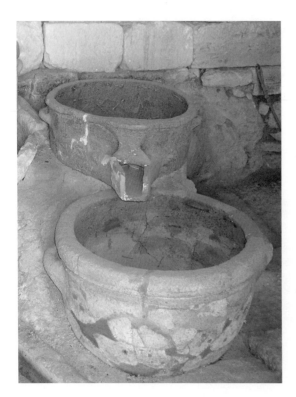

Figure 8.54 *Wine press from Archanes*

This example from a Minoan villa demonstrates the variety of uses of ceramics but also the method of processing grapes and olives for wine and oil respectively. Their wide distribution suggests processing of agricultural produce occurred in the countryside with finished products being taken to the palace sites.

and finished artefacts, and analogies drawn from ethnography and experimental archaeology. Each stage in the process leaves its own distinctive signature in the archaeological record. Similar approaches have been applied to stone tool manufacture and ceramics production. For example ethnographic studies of discard patterns, experimental knapping and refitting have been used to interpret lithic scatters from the Palaeolithic. These insights have to be balanced against awareness of the impact of differential survival of materials.

Our knowledge of ancient woodworking, for instance, largely comes from exceptional wet sites.

SPECIALISATION

Specialisation is often used as an indicator of social complexity. It demonstrates a degree of interdependence within a society and often between that society and others. The more complex a society becomes the more interdependent its members become. If the production of artefacts is concentrated in the hands of a few people it also implies skills are not available to all members of society. It may indicate age and gender differentiation. There are two main types of specialisation:

- *Attached specialists* are craftsmen who live in close proximity to a high status person. They may be part of their extended family and related by birth or marriage.
- *Independent specialists* produce goods to market for their own profit. They are not controlled by anyone else but may still be interdependent.

Identifying specialists in the archaeological record

Very often archaeology concentrates on the finished products as evidence of craftwork, for example mosaics, figurines, swords or ships.

█ *Figure 8.55* Malia bee pendant

This exquisite gold pendant from a burial at Malia is evidence of professional metalworking. A new technique – granulation – had been developed by Cretan goldsmiths in order to produce realistic images such as these bees on a comb of honey. It is evidence of sufficient food surplus to support craftsmen since it would take years of training to develop the skill required here. It also suggests an elite who wanted such artefacts. Palace workshops suggest that the goldsmiths were attached craftsmen with raw materials provided by their masters.

However, manufacturing debris can be important, as can the very names of locations where craft workers concentrated, which may have survived, albeit in altered form, over time. Both of these sources are illustrated in Viking York where there is much waste material from leather working and trial pieces for carving in bone, together with the name of the most famous excavation site in York – 'Coppergate' – which comes from the Old Norse for 'Street of the Barrel-Makers'. Burial evidence has often been interpreted as evidence of specialisation, where particular tools are found in graves. The Sutton Hoo burial contains several examples of craftsmanship from all over the Anglo-Saxon world, in particular a tiny pyramidal jewel that had been originally attached to a sword hilt. Each

KEY STUDY

Copan

Close to the House of the Bacabs in the elite residential area of the city a stone built room with a stone bench along one wall was discovered. The room had been buried quickly by an earthquake leaving artefacts where they had been used. Ceramic vessels on the bench contained tools. Some were wrapped in a leather 'quiver' rather like a chef's knife holder. Tools included antler drills which would have been used with sand and water to perforate bone and antler (◀ p. 128). They also drilled the teeth of nobles so that prestigious jade inserts could be set in the teeth. Obsidian blades were used for cutting material. Although obsidian is as strong as surgical steel it is very brittle so the blades would have been glued into wooden handles for support. Evidence of their use came from a flat cutting stone scored from the action of blades and saws. The workshop was littered with exotic raw materials and with incomplete artefacts. One outstanding find was a 'star gorget' made from conch shell similar to examples worn by statues of the Bacabs – the gods who held up the sky. This prestige item was probably made for a high status person, possibly the owner of the elite residence in whose compound the workshop stood.

So who were these craftsmen and what was their status? As in most early societies the very existence of craft specialists indicates an economic surplus can support people who are not engaged in food production. The fertile Copan Valley provided a huge quantities of maize and other crops. In the essentially closed economic system of the Maya, these resources were not used for large-scale trade, but rather to enhance the prestige of the elite by allowing them to support an ever-growing number of 'retainers'. Many of these people would have been close relatives, members of the elites themselves. These people could not be expected to carry out menial tasks but seem to have become specialists including scribes and priests. They also included craftsmen who produced jade, jewellery, featherwork and other exotic items for their lord and relative. Archaeologists call this 'attached *specialism*' as their output was devoted to their master rather than being sold or exchanged. Confirmation of these ideas came from underneath the floor of the workshop itself where several skeletons were discovered in stone cists. One of these bore the telltale signs of elite status. The Maya used cranial deformation to distinguish elite children. This left them with a high-domed head and flat forehead.

The elite position of craftsmen is corroborated by a burial behind a staircase in an elaborately decorated chamber at the heart of the acropolis. The floor of the tomb was littered with decomposed pieces of bark codices – the books

Figure 8.56 *View from the acropolis at Copan towards the ballcourt*

KEY STUDY *cont.*

Copan

of the Maya. Rich grave goods and the sacrificed body of a young slave had also been provided. It was clearly a royal burial but whose was it? The ages at death of the kings of the time did not match the skeleton. Ceramics in the tomb provided clues. Some of them were clearly associated with painting. Indeed one carried a human portrait of a man wearing a special monkey headdress and with scribes' brushes in his mouth. He represented the patron god of scribes. The body was probably a son of King Smoke-Imix , a royal scribe whose duty was to paint the books containing the history and mythology of his dynasty, and who performed a vital role in sustaining his family's power and status. In another link the façade of the houses of the Bacabs includes figures of scribes holding conch 'ink pots'.

• Schele and Miller 1986

Figure 8.57 *Gold hoard from Brangstrup*

Hoards can be interpreted as evidence of unstable times, theft or storage, perhaps by itinerant metal workers. It is tempting to assume that Viking hoards such as this were the result of raiding. However, the material – most of which is from outside Scandinavia – could have been acquired by trading, payment for mercenaries or even to make the Vikings go away as happened in England with Danegeld.

face is a plate of gold with tiny 'cells' built up on it with gold wire in the technique known as *cloisonné*. Each cell is fitted with its own individually cut prisms of garnet and some are provided with chequered metal foil underneath to enhance the glitter of the stones. The precision and exquisite craftsmanship of the worker at such a small scale is breathtaking. That so much time and effort was lavished on what is really a tiny detail of the king's burial goods is also a testament to his status.

ART

This term is applied to images and objects which show appreciation of aesthetic qualities. It may include decoration on functional objects or decoration that forms part of a system of **iconography**. The *meaning* of art is culturally embedded and may prove difficult to access. Meaning is usually studied as part of the archaeology of religion or society. Studies of art under material culture should concentrate on the technology of their execution rather than on interpretation. Thus if the context of study is Palaeolithic cave art, the focus should be on skills of draughtsmanship, paints used and the techniques of painting.

While there is debate about the meaning of cave art (◄ p. 153) we can be more certain about the techniques. Research has discovered the use of ferrous and manganese oxide for paint, chewed twigs and fingers as brushes and stone lamps with animal grease or pine torches for light. Experiments have established that paint was blown through leather stencils to create handprints. Examples can be seen at the Chauvet website.

• http://www.culture.gouv.fr/culture/arcnat/ chauvet/en/

Higher levels of study will require you to grapple with definitions of art and material culture. Pottery provides a good example of the sort of issues you might want to consider. Ethnographic studies suggest that both the production and the

Figure 8.58 *Leaf people*

Although they had no written language, an insight into the culture of northern European foragers is provided by these abstract, anthromorphic carvings. Many wooden and ceramic objects were decorated in this style.

KEY SITE

Upton Lovell

An early Bronze Age bowl barrow excavated by antiquarians in 1802 is possibly one of the earliest examples of a specialist in Britain. Whether he was a shaman, goldsmith or both is unclear. Across his chest and by his feet were rows of drilled bone points. He also had several boars' tusks and bone buttons or toggles. These have been interpreted as decoration or fastenings on his clothes.

Figure 8.59 *Artefacts from Upton Lovell*

To the left are 3 stone axes in front of 3 hollow flints with a fine stone axehead at the back. To the right are whetstones in front of smoothing stones and hammers.

These were unusual in themselves, but the stone artefacts were even more fascinating. On the chest of the extended skeleton was a large highly polished flat round stone and a high quality stone battle axe. At his feet was an array of different stone artefacts.

The exotic battle axe suggested the man may have taken part in ceremonies where his bone-tasselled clothes would have been very distinctive. The polished stone was also unique. Some shamanic cultures use polished, reflective surfaces as an aid to divination. (As with a crystal ball.)

The other stone tools were more of a puzzle. An A level student who happened to be an amateur goldsmith commented on the similarity of the burial assemblage to his own tools. He was able to suggest how each of the smooth

Figure 8.60 *The Upton Lovell burial as a Shaman*

This interpretation at the excellent Devizes Museum where the artefacts are displayed explains the possible use of the bone artefacts, the battle axe and polished stone. The significance of the latter two is enhanced because they were placed on his chest.

KEY SITE *cont.*

Upton Lovell

stones might be used to produce the hammered gold trinkets visible in several of the other cabinets. The flint nodules could be tiny crucibles. The only thing missing is the gold. Historically gold workers have often not owned gold. It has either been supplied by their patron or in the case of independent specialists, by the person commissioning an artefact.

It is possible that the man was both goldsmith and shaman. In many cultures, metalworkers' ability to magically transform material has classed them with other 'liminal' roles such as midwives, musicians and diviners. Metallurgical analysis of the tools in 2004 did find traces of gold. The resuls of the re-excavation of the barrow in 2000 are awaited with interest.

Figure 8.61 *Modern gold worker's toolkit*

As with the grave goods an array of hammers and tiny anvils is used to produce sheets, cones and circular artefacts from gold.

form of pottery are often determined by cultural rather than purely material considerations. A pot can be functional in terms of its ability to hold its contents and withstand heat but other aspects are more to do with its social use than its functionality, particularly decoration and colour. Beliefs and values determine the 'right way' for things to look even when that way is not the most functional. In Middle Saxon Southampton, imported pitchers became popular. They were more functional for pouring liquids than existing pots, yet local potters did not copy them. Instead they continued to turn out traditional vessels. Another instance where symbolism may have outweighed practicality was the use of flint as temper in some prehistoric pottery. There are usually alternative tempers available and flint would be painful to work in.

KEY STUDY

The Basse-Yutz flagons

A pair of bronze flagons, now in the British Museum but originally from Alsace, illustrate a number of points about the nature and role of craft specialists. They are from the Iron Age and yet they are made of bronze in common with most decorative objects from that period. They were decorated with inlaid enamel and coral that must have come from the Red Sea. While the wolf handle is a classical idea, the artist linked Celtic mythology with classical ideas in the iconography of the pieces. He also had a sense of humour. Ducks appear to swim down the stream of liquid as it is poured from the spout. These jugs were almost certainly used to serve wine, a novel drink in central Europe at this period, which was imported from the classical world to the south. Although the grave they were found in was not properly recorded we know that two Etruscan wine-mixing vessels were also found there. The mixture of native and classical ideas in the art shows clearly that classical culture was having a great impact on the Celtic world long before the Roman conquests. The Celtic craftsman exploited exotic materials and iconography to enhance a vessel used to serve an exotic drink at an institution which classical writers tell us was central to Celtic society – the feast. We have to imagine the gleam of polished bronze, lifted high to pour the dark red wine in a glittering stream into the goblets of rival chieftains. The ability to procure the fashionable wine and outface others who still relied on the old beer or honey mead was a powerful way to mark status.

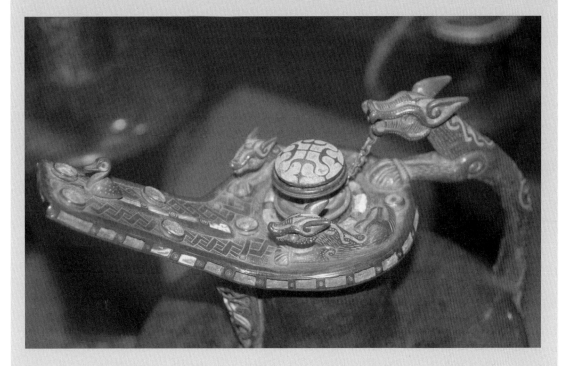

Figure 8.62 *Close up of the spout of a Basse-Yutz flagon*

KEY STUDY *cont.*

The Basse-Yutz flagons

In Celtic society craftsmen were regarded as part of the elite. They were on a par with bards and druids, in view of the 'magical' processes that they controlled, turning dull ores into functional objects like chariot fittings or superb works of art like these flagons. They had a much wider social role than the purely functional at a time when kings began to advertise themselves through coinage and the iconography it carried.

Figure 8.63 *Panel from the Gundestrup Cauldron*

This silver cauldron from the first century BC was recovered from a bog in Denmark. However, the chased style of manufacture suggests it was made in Romania and influenced by ideas from much further east as this panel suggests. SEM analysis of punchmarks suggested that 4–5 toolkits were used which may mean a group of specialist metal workers worked together on it. It provides an indication of the extent of communication and prestige good links in Iron Age Europe.

Chapter 9

People and Society in the Past

YOUR GOALS

You need to

- understand the main concepts used
- use case studies to apply and test the key concepts
- grasp the strengths and weaknesses of the techniques used by archaeologists to reconstruct society from physical evidence

Hawkes (◀ p. 134) identified the archaeology of past social systems as a difficult topic for archaeologists. Despite this, most archaeologists have written with confidence on the societies they have studied and used a wide range of models (particularly from ethnography) to help interpret their sources.

Since this is the last thematic chapter of this coursebook there is danger of repetition. Where possible, we have cross-referenced issues here to studies in earlier chapters. We have also tried to include critical points in each subsection to help you write evaluative essays.

WHAT IS SOCIAL ARCHAEOLOGY?

Social archaeology can usefully be divided into three main subsections: How societies organise themselves ranges from the basic units of family, kin and **bands** to the political organisation of states; Divisions within society include different treatment based on age or gender and also stratification according to wealth, power or status; Social action and change includes phenomena like warfare, immigration, and how and why societies transformed themselves.

For non-literate societies, archaeologists have relied heavily on evidence from burials to understand social organisation. Burial evidence has also supplemented historical records for the classical period. In addition, information has been drawn from settlement patterns, artefacts and art. Since the strengths and weaknesses of these sources are similar for each topic, we have tackled them more fully for status and gender and avoided repetition on the other topics. Where you are writing evaluative pieces you should ensure that you refer to status and gender in your reading.

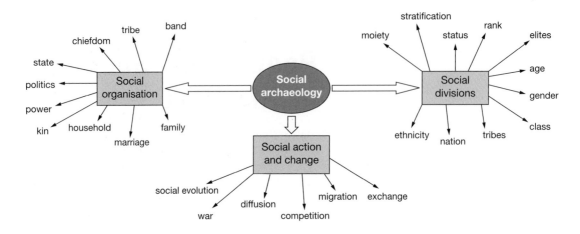

Figure 9.1 *What is social archaeology?: some key topics*

FORMS OF SOCIAL AND POLITICAL ORGANISATION

Archaeology developed in the early twentieth century when evolutionary ideas were being applied in the social sciences and when much of the world was directly ruled by colonial powers. It is understandable then that evolutionary models of social development were applied to the past. As societies became increasingly 'advanced' and 'civilised' they were expected to develop along similar paths. Much archaeological research sought to trace this development and identify reasons for particular regions being more advanced than others. Although western ideas of superiority have been challenged in recent decades, what are now termed neo-evolutionary models of social development are still commonplace.

All of the terms used to classify social organisation conceal considerable variation. However, we need to use such concepts as our starting point when comparing and contrasting social groups and talking about them. Households or families are the basic building blocks of all human societies. This is not to say that any particular model such as the nuclear family always existed in the past. However, from the

point that humans began sitting round campsites or living in tents or huts, evidence about the form of early family groups accumulated. Perhaps the most significant social aspect of a house is that it defines the living arrangements of one group by excluding others. Any internal divisions tell us something about differences within this basic group (▶ p. 306).

Kinship is also important in most societies although the significance attached to blood or marriage ties varies widely. In the past they may have been the most important form of social organisation, for example the Scottish clan system. Although their relevance in modern western society has declined there are still exceptions, notably the Mafia. Other divisions, which may cut across simple group definitions, are age or moiety-based groups. Their existence means that individuals may have several different affiliations.

Bands are self-sufficient groups of a few families numbering up to 50 individuals. They are linked through kinship or marriage. To some writers bands looked like an egalitarian society although ethnographic research has shown that inequalities exist in many modern bands. Leaders are likely to have emerged because of experience or personal qualities but may have been

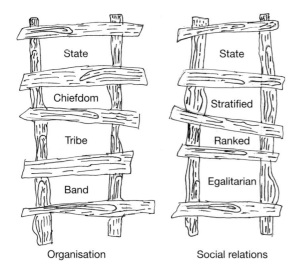

Figure 9.2 *Two social evolutionary ladders*

These model the linear development of society. One focuses on organisation (Service, 1971) the other on social relations and access to resources. (Fried, 1978). There is a close match but some overlap.

temporary. Bands were probably fluid, with families or individuals moving to join other groups. They may also have only lived together during particular seasons. The term is most frequently used in archaeology for the Upper Palaeolithic and Mesolithic.

Tribes are larger than bands but with kinship still linking the group together. Numbers can range between a few hundred to thousand or several bands. Tribes often have activity leaders who are recognised as having skill and authority

in particular areas such as hunting or ritual. Potentially most adults may achieve leadership in some areas and therefore none may stand out overall. Of the models of political organisation and leadership that have been borrowed from anthropology for tribes, the most influential has been the **Bigmen** of New Guinea. These are individuals who rise to prominence through their skill in key areas of economic and social life such as herding or hunting. Their position as Bigmen allows them to conduct trade and alliances on behalf of their group of several hundred people. Their position is cemented by their ability to provide generously for their followers. They accumulate wealth, usually pigs or another food source, and redistribute it at major feasts. The position is not hereditary and others who are better placed to dispense generously often replace Bigmen.

Both bands and tribes are sometimes referred to as **segmentary societies**. This is where society is made up of lots of similarly sized groups with little difference in wealth, status or power between individuals. This contrasts with the more ranked and unequal chiefdoms and states. Tribes are usually associated with horticulturalists or pastoralists rather than foragers. Larger tribes and less complex chiefdoms are sometimes referred to as ranked societies. This means that a hierarchy is beginning to develop with different groups being ranked in terms of prestige but not really in terms of access to resources or power.

Chiefdoms are more formally organised and ranked than tribes. Within ethnographic literature there is a huge range of different forms of

Figure 9.3 *Segmentary social divisions. These are some of many ways of organising society horizontally which don't necessarily result in a permanent hierarchy*

A moiety is the division of society into two halves (or moieties) which was common in North America. People are born or are inducted into one or the other. Depending upon the society's rules they must either marry within the moiety or marry someone from the opposite moiety.

chiefdom with numbers of followers ranging from around 1,000 to 10,000, so we must assume the same is true of the past. Chiefdoms are usually hereditary, with an individual holding some central power over the group although the role may alternate between a group of families rather than remain in just one. As a result usually chiefs and their relatives are viewed as different from the rest of the social group. They usually have an important ritual role as well as re-distribution, law giving and organizing labour. Their permanent position and high status may result in other differences including more marriage partners and more or different posses-sions. Social hierarchies in chiefdoms can be very elaborate and at least one of their settlements is likely to be a ceremonial centre. More complex chiefdoms may be stratified. That means that the hierarchy is more fixed with each strata having different levels of prestige and often access to resources and power. People will tend to be born into a strata or class, for instance nobles and commoners.

Kings can differ from chiefs simply in terms of scale. Kings will usually preside over several social groups, each with their own sub-king or

Figure 9.4 *Cahercommaun*

This early medieval fortified settlement had a triple ring of defences and was perched on the side of a very steep ravine. It looks defensive, a view that was strengthened by the discovery of underground passages (souterrains) under each of six houses, one of which came out on the cliff. One interpretation is that it is the base of the representative of the King of Cashel and its function is to collect tribute. Alternatively it is the high-status, fortified farmstead of a local clan chief who depended on cattle-raising supplemented by raiding. Around 40 people would have lived in it. It fits the model of a ranked society where kinship remains important. Thousands of such ring-forts once existed in Ireland.

chief. The term was used for nineteenth-century Africa as well as for the classical and medieval worlds so variation is considerable. The position is hereditary with some, although not all, being seen as divine. They are likely to have a larger than usual household and may have permanent social and economic organisations based close to them, for example a permanent guard. Their need to display their position through exotic goods and provide gifts to supporters may mean that their household includes attached specialists.

States are political systems where permanent institutions develop independent of individual leaders. Central authority is likely to include formal laws, weights and measures and specialists associated with justice, warfare and taxation. All modern societies are nation states. Key features are likely to include permanent borders, currencies, armies and centralised bureaucracy. Developed states are very complex with a tendency to increasing specialisation. In some states kinship remains important, particularly

Figure 9.5 *Hermitage Castle*

Built in Liddesdale to dominate what has been called the 'bloodiest valley in Britain' Hermitage Castle represents a struggle between states and allegiances rooted in kinship which is still familiar today. In the late Middle Ages the English–Scottish border zone suffered frequent invasions and rival kings encouraged local clan groups to raid across it. By the thirteenth century, raiding in these 'debatable lands' had become endemic. The exploits of the closely knit 'reiver' families (so significant that they gave us the word 'bereave') are well known from songs and stories. At times their action provoked military action in reprisal. To attempt to control Liddesdale and prevent war with England a Royal Warden was appointed and Hermitage was built first in wood then in stone. The earthworks are ruined but the main building survives. It contains a prison tower and would have had wooden fighting platforms around the upper walls. Ultimately Hermitage was unsuccessful. Reiving continued until the Union of the Crowns in 1603. With the border gone, James I used arbitrary execution and exile to impose his will on the Armstrongs of Liddesdale and their neighbours.

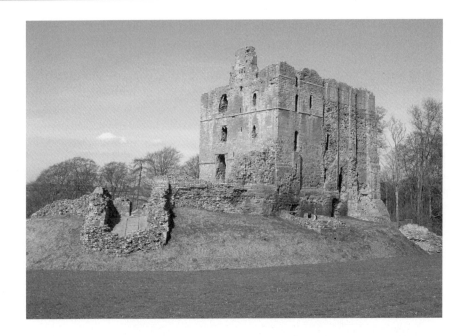

Figure 9.6 *Keep of Norham Castle*

Defensive borders are a common feature of states. This royal castle on a natural strongpoint high above the River Tweed formed part of a chain of strongpoints defending the northern borders of England against Scottish invasion. The scale of the defences and size of the bailey indicate that it was designed to hold a large garrison and hold off an army. This contrasts with the many smaller castles in the area which were designed for protection against raiding (◄ p. 295). Norham repeatedly did its job, only falling to James IV's guns in 1513, days before the decisive battle of Flodden (► p. 327).

those kingships which are also states, but this need not be the case. State societies are hierarchical with ethnicity, wealth and class some of the common divisions. States are associated with large urban populations supplied by agricultural surpluses collected from the countryside. States first emerged in the Bronze Age.

SOCIAL COMPLEXITY

A common approach to understanding societies is to see them as a system or organism. In a simple system, the various social units, be they families or bands, are undifferentiated and perform similar roles. In a complex system there is a much greater degree of specialisation in terms and

functions and a much greater variety of social units. Nevertheless, these different elements are integrated into one social system.

The study of social complexity has been closely related to questions about the emergence of civilisations or of states. In particular, growing social complexity has been used both to differentiate levels of society and to explain the emergence of chiefdoms and states. The social-evolutionary models of Service and Fried provide examples. This can lead to a perception of human development always moving in one direction and also the idea that the highest form is superior. A common explanation for the emergence of more complex societies is the development of hierarchies who wield power in order to integrate

KEY STUDY

The Palette of Narmer

This cosmetic artefact excavated at the Egyptian city of Hierakonpolis dates from 3000 BC, the period just before the First Dynasty when the rules and icons of kingship were being established. It is considered a classic example of the manipulation of iconography in support of an individual's status. It is also one of the first examples of hieroglyphics (◀ p. 263).

The king's name is written at the top, surrounded by a frame which is reminiscent of the architecture of the royal palace. The catfish (Nar) and chisel (mer) spell out the Horus name (◀ p. 138) of the king, Narmer. The king stands, left hand clasping the topknot of a kneeling captive, with a mace in his right hand. The hieroglyphs tell us that the prisoner's name is 'Wash'. The design immediately above him shows a falcon on papyrus plants pulling back the head of a figure who looks remarkably like Wash and the location is the Nile delta. The main figure is wearing the white crown of Upper Egypt and a flywhisk, early symbols of kingship. Below are defeated enemies and a sign that represents a fortified town. We are clearly being told that the king has won a victory over an enemy in the north, the delta.

On the right-hand side of the palette the king, carrying the mace and flail, and this time wearing the red crown of Lower Egypt, is explicitly labelled and accompanied by standard bearers called 'The Followers of Horus'. They march within a panel that represents the gate of the royal palace, towards two rows of bound and decapitated prisoners. The dead prisoners are now powerless and reduced to order, compared with the figures on the other side who have spread-eagled limbs. This may be symbolic of the Egyptian concept of order. In the central panel are two mythological beasts with their long necks entwined to symbolise harmony and perhaps the unification of the two lands of Egypt. This is echoed by the two crowns, which would later be incorporated into the 'Double Crown', indicating that the pharaoh was 'The Lord of the Two Lands'. At the bottom right is a raging bull, representing the king's anger, trampling a man and a walled city. There is a balance in the composition, with harmony offsetting the violence, but the message is abundantly clear. The enemies of Narmer can have been in no doubt as to what lay in store for those who defied him.

Figure 9.7 *Smiting scene from Medinet Habu*

In a strikingly similar scene, Pharaoh Rameses II is shown about to dash out his prisoners' brains with a mace. The iconography for depicting a powerful ruler had become standardised over 3000 years.

• www.ancient-egypt.org/kings/0101_narmer/palette.html

society. A variant of this is to see power distributed amongst a number of agencies in a society. This is known as heterarchy. Not all archaeologists would accept such a focus on politics as the reason for changes but it remains a dominant model.

Either way there seems general agreement that complex societies tend to be larger scale, more stratified and with more permanent institutions. Alternative causal explanations include responses to environmental change or exchange, agricultural intensification, population growth above a particular threshold and developments in ritual practice. Some prehistorians discuss social complexity in terms of changes in palaeolithic or mesolithic society, for example the apparent emergence of specialists and the 'grandmother revolution' of the last Ice Age.

Urban settlements such as Jericho and Çatal Höyük first emerged around 7000 BC but it was in Mesopotamia that states arose during the fourth millennium BC. Here a number of factors came together to produce the Sumerian civilization and the first city-states. Population levels had risen in the region with the development of irrigation systems and this led to growing social differentiation. Amongst the new specialist bronze workers, brewers and potters were priests. Temples became the focal points of towns and played a key role in the economy and politics. Clearly there were also those who organised the building of canals and public buildings, supervised redistribution of food surpluses and led raids to surrounding areas to acquire slaves. These early urban centres are sometimes referred to as proto-states because not all the features of full-blown states were present.

By 3000 BC city-states such as Ur, Uruk and Tell Brak were very different. Most were walled with massive defences, indicating a growth in warfare rather than raiding and perhaps the need of rulers to show their power and control their population. Small, hereditary elites now ruled, generally with no limit to their power and frequently controlling religion, law and commerce as well as armies and the first government bureaucracies. Religious monuments, such as the Ziggurat of Ur, were massive. So too were the palaces, statues and reliefs of the rulers whose deeds were preserved for posterity by their scribes. Similar states soon emerged throughout the Middle East and in Egypt, China and India. Rather than looking for one 'prime mover' such as war, land shortage or the need to organise public works and religion it is likely that there were multiple, interrelated causes for the development of states.

Some writers add Empires as a fifth evolutionary stage where one state becomes dominant over several others. It is also worth noting that bands, tribes and chiefdoms still exist today in many parts of the world.

POWER AND SOCIAL CONTROL

Power, the ability to make others do what you want, can be approached via status or via evidence of social control. This can be inferred, but not proved, from the apparent organisation of labour for large communal monuments such as the henges of Neolithic Wessex. In some cases such as Egypt or the Maya the religious control exerted by the Pharaohs or Maya shaman-kings is illustrated in art on artefacts and temple walls.

Typically the more powerful figures are larger and wear more elaborate costumes. Their subjects, or those they have defeated, are smaller and sometimes depicted naked and bowed or lying face down.

THE ARCHAEOLOGY OF RANK AND STATUS

These terms are often used interchangeably but do have slightly different meanings. Status is associated with social prestige; rank implies a position within a hierarchy. Both status and rank may be inherited or acquired during life by an individual. **Ascribed status** is where an individual inherits social position, usually at birth,

Figure 9.8 *Skull and crown from Deal Iron Age cemetery*

This discovery of a young man wearing a crown has been interpreted as evidence of royal families. It is unlikely a man would have achieved kingship by around twenty so it is more likely that the role was inherited. However, the crown bears an uncanny resemblance to the headgear of later Romano-British priests. This raises the possibility that the young man might be a priest or druid.

for example being born into royalty. **Achieved status** is where the individual earns or obtains position due to their own efforts, for example qualifying as a doctor. Rich burials of children are often interpreted as evidence of ascribed status.

Evidence of societies based on ascribed status is usually easier to find partly for this reason. In societies where status is more fleeting, evidence may not enter the archaeological record. In bigman societies fame is achieved by giving away wealth. A successful bigman might be buried with very little. Not all marks of status are easily preserved. Clothing, tattoos and tribal scars would have been very significant in life but are usually invisible to archaeologists.

Archaeologists employ a number of sources of evidence in their attempts to recognise status in past societies. In a few cases such studies are text-aided but in general they have to rely on material culture to provide answers. All of the main approaches try to isolate particular variables that will allow differentiation between sectors of a society and between individuals: The origins of status differences lie in way humans mark themselves out both individually and as members of groups. Personal adornment (▶ p. 336) was probably the first manifestation of this including body paint and jewellery. During the Upper Palaeolithic material culture was used in other ways to express individuality or position in society. This includes grave goods and

Figure 9.9 *Status and the archaeological evidence for it*

figurines. Clothing may also have been used to create identities. Researchers at the Max Planck Institute for Evolutionary Anthropology in Germany have established that the human body louse mutated from the head louse between 42,000 and 72,000 years ago. A key difference is that while head lice lay eggs in hair, body lice lay them in clothes. This suggests that humans started wearing clothes somewhere between 50,000 and 100,000 years ago. DNA may also explain other identity-related aspects of human behaviour. For example, unlike most of the world,

most northern Europeans do not have very dark eyes or hair. For these traits to have arisen naturally it would have taken around 800,000 years. For it to have occurred since humans arrived in Europe after 45,000 BP social selection must have been the key driver. Anthropologist Peter Frost claims that blonde hair allowed some women to stand out, be more valued in some way and thus gain a competitive edge in competing for mates. Through their success, more blonde children were born leading to the greater variety in eye and hair colour in Europe. A similar argument has been applied to the question of why modern people are relatively hairless. However, German researchers have extracted DNA from Neanderthal bones and have identified a gene that produces light skin and reddish hair. Rather than arguing that Neanderthal males preferred redheads they claim that light skin would have provided an evolutionary advantage because it is best able to generate vitamin D in European climatic conditions.

Figure 9.10 *'Mrs Getty'*

This 6th century burial of a woman aged 25–30 from the Lechlade cemetery (▶ p. 318) got her nickname from her exceptional grave goods which included 500 beads. Unlike most, she had a wooden coffin concealed under stone packing. Inside, her possessions came from far beyond the Anglo-Saxon world. Along with Baltic amber and metal bowls from the Rhineland were cowries from the Red Sea, garnets from India, Spanish glass and an ivory purse mouth. Her bronze brooches and silver spiral rings were also rare. Despite the humble spindle whorl in her coffin she was a woman of high status. Forensic reconstruction of her face along with detailed excavation records has enabled the Corinium Museum to present her as she looked at her funeral.

Burial evidence

Personal status is often suggested on the basis of grave goods. Rich burials such as those at Sutton Hoo, Varna and the 'Amesbury Archer' are usually interpreted as being the graves of high status individuals. Sometimes there is additional evidence to confirm this, as in the cases of Tutankhamun and the royal scribe burial at Copan (◀ p. 284).

In the Royal Cemetery at Ur, mortuary practice involved the sacrifice of attendants with royalty. The grave of Pu-abi included a 40-year-old woman who is identified as a queen on a sealstone buried with her. She was accompanied by exotic objects, including a lyre with a golden bull's head decoration, gold and silver vessels, a magnificent headdress of golden leaves and rosettes and twenty-three of her courtiers. These 'victims' seem to have gone to their deaths willingly as there was no sign of coercion. Human sacrifice to accompany the dead may be aimed

Figure 9.11 *Sutton Hoo*

This recreation of the burial inside a ship allows one to see the paraphernalia of status in its context. The carefully laid assemblage of rare, symbolic and everyday artefacts provides an insight into the reality and the image of early medieval kingship. Compare these artefacts in terms of craftsmanship and the distance items travelled with those from ordinary Anglo-Saxon graves.

KEY STUDY

Branc

Shennan's (1975) study of over 300 rectangular pit graves in a Bronze Age cemetery in Czechoslovakia adopted a systematic approach to evaluating the social significance of grave goods.

Gender differences were evident in the way bodies had been laid out. Males lay on their right sides and females on their left. In addition, some individuals had more valuable assemblages than others. The interpretation was that wealth and status was inherited (ascribed).

Instead of assuming that what we might value, for example gold, was of most value in the past she used other measures. The key one was energy expenditure. In other words, artefacts that required more skill, effort and resources from long distances were likely to have been most prized.

at establishing the power and status of an individual. Equally there are many instances where such behaviour is a ritual full of meaning for the whole community in terms of the fertility of the earth or the continuity of cyclical events.

However, we need to take care that we don't impose our values and assume that certain materials held the same value and prestige in past societies as in our own. In some cases symbolic associations may be an equally important factor in the choice of raw material, such as jade in Mesoamerica. Even the gold at Varna (see cover) may not be what it seems. Some of the richest graves there are empty 'cenotaphs'. It may be that the gold represents offerings from the living rather than the belongings of the deceased. A further complication occurs with vessels such as beakers. Their contents may have been the material of greatest value rather than

the pottery. Other organic materials such as textiles, food or wood may have been placed in what to us appear to have been 'poor' graves, but these rarely survive.

• Parker-Pearson 1999

Status is only likely to be represented *in* death where the person held that status *at* death. In cases where status or rank did not stay with the individual for their whole life it may not be visible. Similarly, where beliefs dictate that people should appear equal in death (as in Christian burial), indicators of status may be absent. In general, ascribed status is more likely to be visible than achieved status. The position of burials, their orientation and any funerary monument associated with them can also be used to examine status.

Settlement evidence

Status can also be inferred from settlement evidence. Segmentary societies are associated with lots of small, scattered, similar settlements. A mix of small and very large settlements suggest a more unequal society with large settlements expected to be the residence of powerful individuals. The palaces at Knossos and the hill fort at Danebury have both been interpreted in this way. High status individuals might be expected to have different houses from other people. The energy expenditure model can be applied here too. Houses may simply be bigger because the inhabitants have more to store or may have larger household units. They may also occupy a prominent position. Eighteenth-century landowners chose to build in prominent positions in the landscape to emphasise control over land. Rich merchants in earlier periods clustered in central positions in towns. In many cases their houses will be larger, more elaborate and built of better quality materials – part of a general display of wealth and status, which might also include dress and visible forms of consumption. Romano-British villas, for example Chedworth,

KEY STUDY

Military technology and organisation – The Illerup Hoard

If you have seen the film *Gladiator* you will have seen the Roman General Maximus defeating Germanic tribes in a battle of AD 180. The nature and equipment of the Roman army is well known, but what of the 'barbarians'? Often the impression we get is of a mass of recklessly brave but disorganised amateur warriors. The army hoard from Illerup is one of a number of finds which challenges that view.

The site was discovered in the 1950s when land drainage of a bog on the site of a prehistoric lake had to be stopped because of the numbers of swords and spears being churned up. A detailed survey and re-excavation of 40 per cent of the site in the 1970s revealed a 200 metre by 400 metre area packed with finds. These finds extended well out into the lake – too far to have been thrown. Rope and

Figure 9.12 *The Illerup Hoard*

Some of the sacrificed war booty from the defeat of a Scandinavian army of 500–1000 warriors.

textile impressions in the rust on the weapons suggested that bundles of weapons had been taken out by boat and deposited. Many different groups of weapons could be linked where pieces of one artefact occurred in two or more heaps. These deposits were contemporary with one another. Excavating these remains, which were structured like a giant game of pick-up-sticks, was a tremendous challenge. Everything had to be kept wet while detailed recording was made prior to removal. For complex 'heaps' a box was dug in around the finds and a wooden base pushed underneath. This enabled micro-excavation in a lab and x-raying of the soil matrix to locate tiny finds.

Over 15,000 items of metal, wood and bone have been recovered. They date to around AD 200. In Scandinavia this was the later Iron Age, whereas in Britain this was the Romano-British period. These finds and others demonstrate considerable contacts with the Roman world. Glass, bronze and silver reached Scandinavia with amber, fur, textiles, slaves and mercenaries probably travelling in the opposite direction.

Amongst the weapons were hundreds of spears, all smashed but uniformly made from split and planed ash heartwood. A concave shaft-plane for repairs was also found. 748 iron lances and 661 barbed spearheads were recovered. The design of these throwing and thrusting weapons tended to change every 30 years or so. This enabled separate deposits to be relatively dated. No warrior seems to have been using old 'inherited' weapons and the forging technology used to produce them was complex. Two of the spear-blades were stamped 'Wagnijo', a name that has been found on blades elsewhere in the Baltic. Was this the name of a war-leader or a manufacturer? Although the Romans

KEY STUDY *cont.*

Military technology and organisation – The Illerup Hoard

banned the export of high quality weapons they frequently recruited 'barbarians' to their armies. Was this evidence of someone who had served the Romans and brought the knowledge of their smiths back with him? Over 150 of the swords were two-edged Roman-style weapons designed for both cutting and thrusting. Several were inlaid with images of Mars or Victoria and some had Roman makers' stamps. One of them bore the words 'Nithijo ordered made' in the earliest Norse writing yet found. While most sword blades had locally made hilts including some of ivory, there were some with ornate Roman hilts including one made of gold and silver. For each sword there were 3–4 sets of throwing weapons.

Figure 9.13 *Spearhead stamped with the name Wagnijo*

Survival of over 400 wooden shields enabled a TPQ of AD 207 to be established. Shields were manufactured from thin boards of alder or oak with metal rims and boss. They may have also had an organic backing but this has not survived. Many had been painted red and often had silver or gold inlay. Although leather has not survived, the position of metal fittings enabled the reconstruction of over 300 military belts. These were worn outside tunics and fastened with large iron buckles. Impressions of cloth match the weave on contemporary woollen trousers and tunics found at other sites. Mountings on the belts attached daggers, fire-lighting equipment and bags with personal possessions. Their contents included beads, coins, razors, repair kits, tweezers and combs. Danish

Figure 9.14 *A warrior's possessions*

Hanging from a belt around a tunic would have been the essentials of campaign life. These included a knife, fire-starting kit, tools for repairing things and a leather purse. This contained the most personal possessions. There was usually a comb and tweezers but also lucky charms.

KEY STUDY *cont.*

Military technology and organisation – The Illerup Hoard

combs tend to be made from deer antler, but most of those found were elk or reindeer and of a design more common in Norway.

There are several similar examples of such hoards in Scandinavia and the Roman Orosius described a similar ritual in Germany. Booty was stripped from the bodies of a defeated army and sacrificed by ritual destruction before being deposited in a lake. The sophistication of the weapons and the degree of standardisation suggests that some war leaders had their own arsenals with specialist weapon smiths and professional soldiers. The scale of the battle suggests that it was not opportunistic raiding but part of a regional power struggle in which a largely Norwegian army was defeated. These conflicts were made possible by the development of sea-going vessels in the Baltic and can be seen as precursors to later raids on Britain by what were in later centuries called the Vikings.

A common conception of Dark Age armies is that they were undisciplined raiders. However, the Roman view of these barbarians was somewhat different. Tacitus described clear lines of authority amongst the Germans and the control of weapons by powerful leaders. Analysis of the artefacts also seems to support a hierarchical, specialist organisation. Amongst these finds there were clear signs of a specialist, military hierarchy. There were 60 highly decorated baldrics or sword belts, 16 of which appeared to be Roman. Fittings were either bronze or silver. There were also 12 sets of military equipment for horses. Only six shields have gold or silver bosses and ornamentation, around 40 were bronze while the majority were iron. There were similar proportional differences in the quality of weaponry. It seems that there were a handful of leaders, a second rank of around 40 well equipped soldiers and 300–400 warriors with fairly standard kit, spears and other weapons.

Figure 9.15 *Military organisation at Illerup*

■ **Figure 9.16** *Skara Brae*

This cluster of cell-like houses dates from the Neolithic. The site was buried under sand for 5000 years which partly accounts for the amazing state of preservation. The other factor is the use of local flagstone for building. Even furniture has survived. All but one house follows the same pattern with a central hearth, box-beds and storage areas. One other building may have been a ritual area or workshop. The architecture and finds suggest a tight-knit, egalitarian community of farmers. The real division is between the band inside and those outside, separated by thick walls and a build up of midden material.

■ **Figure 9.17** *View of Zakros palace from the north*

Looking from the town area the central courtyard is top left. To the right is a colonnaded ceremonial hall and behind that archive rooms, 'lustral basins' for ritual purification, treasury and shrines. Bottom right are the storage magazines while top right are the craft workshops with more to the south of the courtyard. Immediately left of the courtyard are the 'royal' apartments or megarons backing onto a hall with a cistern and other water related rooms. Off to the left are more courtyards and some industrial buildings on the road to the port. The ashlar walls cut into blocks with two-man saws indicate the scale and size of the buildings. Attached workshops included stone cutters, perfume making and ivory carving. The palace was destroyed by fire but the boxes of clay archives (◄ p. 262) on shelves survived as a result.

KEY TASK

Investigating status and rank in your settlement

Identify some useful criteria for identifying status and rank in your community. House prices may be one guide; local information on occupation and earnings by electoral ward may also be available. Focusing on the built environment (houses, gardens, enclosures, not cars), use observation to compare different areas. Identify whether there are visible indicators of rank and status and what they are. Present this in diagrammatic form.

surpluses to trade on behalf of their communities. At the far end of the European gift chain was Ancient Greece. Homer's epics were based in this period and feature heroes who 'spent' the agricultural wealth of their communities on gifts of fine weapons and feasts for their followers. Perhaps similar warbands developed elsewhere in Europe.

Artefactual evidence

Concentrations of valuable finds can be used to suggest locations used by important individuals. Evidence of long-distance trade in exotic or prestige goods or of the craft workshops of attached specialists can also be important. Their skill and effort is not easily duplicated and means

and palaces, for example Fishbourne, can be compared to see the relative differences in status between them. The layout of a site may reveal individual status through the control of space and therefore the way people relate to each other. Higher status people are also more likely to enclose their property in a more visible way than are others. These aspects and the control of space and access can clearly be traced in medieval castles and monasteries and in earlier sites such as brochs (◀ p. 229).

The development of large ceremonial and defensive sites from the Bronze Age has been seen by many archaeologists as evidence of the emergence of chiefdoms in the British Isles. Grogan's (1999) regional level study of Irish hilltop enclosures showed that these very visible, although not always defensive, sites were established at regular intervals across the landscape. Finds from these enclosures (◀ p. 294) suggest they were of high status. Certainly the Bronze Age saw increasing control over land in many areas such as Dartmoor (Fleming, 1988). The intensification and extension of farming coincides with evidence of prestige goods (◀ p. 289) exchange over long distances. This suggests that powerful individuals were amassing

Figure 9.18 *Battersea cauldron*

Large and elaborate items of feasting equipment suggest feasts and elites capable of supplying such hospitality. We know from classical and medieval literature of the crucial importance of feasting as a way of binding leaders and followers together. Rewarding followers through redistribution seems to have been a key element in the emergence of chiefdoms from the late Bronze Age. Food and drink were dispensed (with the order of serving reflecting rank) along with gifts of weapons, animals and exotic artefacts in return for loyalty. This may explain why fine goods, harness equipment and swords are often found across many sites rather than concentrated in places where one might have expected rulers to live.

such artefacts are rare and thus valuable. Sherratt (1997) interpreted bell beakers (◄ p. 64) as part of a drinking culture, perhaps in imitation of the metal drinking and feasting vessels of classical Greece. The association of elite warriors and feasting has echoes in the archaeological record of the Iron Age, the Saxon and Viking period and until well into the Middle Ages.

Of course value does not only come from the skill of the craftsmen and the rarity of the materials. Objects gain prestige from their own histories. A relatively ordinary sword associated with a great hero becomes an object of value. Tolkien was well aware of the biographical value

Figure 9.19 *Gold fastener*

This gorgeous Bronze Age fastener for holding a cloak or similar garnment can reveal far more than just clothing style. The quality of metalworking could only have come from a specialist goldsmith. The gold itself could only have come from someone with great wealth in a ranked society. The choice to display such wealth in personal ornamentation rather than other possessions or buildings suggests that society may not have been stable and that people kept and displayed their wealth with them. The symbolism engraved on the item would surely also have been significant, perhaps to the identity of the wearer. The fact that it was deposited in pristine condition in a bog testifies to the importance of deities in the lives of people at that time.

of objects when he wrote *The Lord of the Rings*. This aspect is difficult for archaeologists to recover.

THE ARCHAEOLOGY OF GENDER

Archaeologists usually distinguish between sex, which is biologically determined, and gender, which is regarded as a social construct. Gender is the identity assigned to different sexes. In any human society there is at the very least some difference between the roles of men and women. This stems from the fact that women give birth and that there are obvious anatomical differences between male and female. Gender explains these differences and specifies what is to be done about them. There is tremendous variation from one society to another. In the early stages of hominid development, males were up to twice the size of females but this distinction had largely disappeared by the time modern humans emerged. Paradoxically, gender differences were far more extreme in late nineteenth- and early twentieth-century west European societies, than they were among historically known food-foraging peoples.

Assumptions about 'natural' roles and their significance profoundly influenced the development of archaeology up to the 1970s. In particular, males were portrayed as the active sex in human evolution. For example, hunting was seen as the key humanising activity in evolution. Since then the importance of scavenging and the likely role of women in the transition from gathering to horticulture has been recognised. Even among the !Kung bushmen, often seen as archetypal hunters, women actually contributed more protein to the daily intake of the group than did the men. Hunting was very hit and miss, while gathering of wild plant foods made up 60–80 per cent of the !Kung diet.

As with most areas of archaeology, ethnographic study has been employed to gain insights into task differentiation between males and females. One weakness in this approach has been that most anthropologists have been male. This

Figure 9.20 *'Venus' figurine from Willendorf, Austria*

Upper Palaeolithic carvings of female figures have been found across Europe and are fairly uniform in character and style. Most appear to be associated with hearths and home bases. They are made from a range of materials including baked clay (Dolni Vestonice), mammoth ivory (Lespugue) and limestone (Willendorf). They have widely been interpreted as evidence of veneration of a mother goddess deity by the first modern humans in Europe. Others see them as fertility symbols or primitive pornography. Either way they provide insights into Ice Age hairstyles.

• http://www.arthistory.sbc.edu/imageswomen/

has led to criticism that they are more interested in male activities and have failed to observe female tasks and behaviour. If this is true then we need to be particularly cautious in transferring such observations to archaeological material. A further point to be borne in mind is that gender is rarely just two opposite identities. If we are to avoid stereotypical responses we should treat gender as a continuum – a curve along which individuals are placed from female to male, according to the norms of particular societies.

Studies of gender have relied heavily on burial evidence including human remains and grave goods. Settlement and architectural analysis and artistic sources, where they survive, have supplemented this.

Human remains

Differential evidence of disease can be used to identify gendered patterns of activity or consumption. Canadian Inuit hunter-gatherers from the 1890s show osteoarthritis in the right hand

and jaw of women, combined with tooth loss. These women spent considerable time preparing skins and sewing. They made the thread by rolling sinews against their cheeks. Areas most pressured by this activity reveal damage. The men hunted with harpoons, which sometimes caused disease of the right shoulder and elbow, while kayak paddling also resulted in distinctive wear of the bones. Other studies of damage and wear have identified gender-specific activities as diverse as basket-making, fighting and grinding corn.

These patterns are echoed in the skeletons from Tell Abu Hureyra (◄ p. 242). Wear grooves in the sides of women's teeth were caused by drawing fibres through them to work and soften them as a prelude to making baskets. Male skeletons had lesions and strain injuries to their arms as might be associated with spear throwing. This fits with faunal evidence for hunting gazelles.

The quantity and quality of food consumed may relate to status. Chemical analysis of prehistoric Native American skeletons show that women have a higher strontium:calcium ratio than men in the same community. This may indicate that they ate a smaller share of the available meat. However, strontium levels also alter when a woman is pregnant or breast-feeding. Differential care and nutrition of female and male children might also show up in X-ray analysis of bones. Lines of increased bone density, known as Harris lines, reflect periods of malnutrition during growth.

Graves and grave goods

The association of male and female burials with different ranges of grave goods has been noted in many cultures. At Tell Abu Hureyra women were most often buried under the floor of the house, suggesting strongly that this was their area of activity and their domain in life. From the Neolithic onwards arrowheads, daggers and

other weapons are frequently found in male and not female burials, which seems to confirm that these activities were male-dominated even by the prehistoric period. From the Bronze Age women were regularly buried with a variety of ornaments and jewellery such as pins, necklaces and bracelets. While this may indicate different roles in life there are problems with this analysis. Until recently, sexing of burials often relied on the grave goods. Jewellery without weapons was expected in female graves so these finds were used to define female burials. Today there is less confidence in this interpretation. A rich Iron Age burial from Birdlip illustrates this problem. The burial from the middle of three barrows contained a mirror, a range of jewellery including amber and shale objects, and some bronze bowls. It was interpreted as a rich woman's grave and some speculated that it might even be that of

Figure 9.21 *The Birdlip Mirror*

Boudicca. However, recent examination of the skull has shown that it has masculine traits. The assemblage is also notable in that the artefacts have all been broken and one of the vessels was placed over the face of the skeleton. Could it be the burial of a male shaman rather than a princess? Another burial was discovered in 1999 in the Scilly Isles with similar characteristics. DNA analysis at West Heslerton (▶ p. 317) showed that some females were buried with weapons and some men with jewellery. Many museums are currently reviewing their labelling of burials. Whether beautiful objects are just jewellery and whether daggers are always indicative of fighting has also been questioned. Spear-throwers have been found in some female burials of the mid-western Indian Knoll culture of the third millennium BC. Were they just ceremonial or to do with inheritance, or did women as well as men hunt?

• http://www.glos-city.gov.uk/Content.aspx?
  URN=1279

Rich male graves are often interpreted in terms of what *he* earned or won, whereas when a woman is found with elaborate grave goods they are often attributed to her husband or father. For example, if women over a certain age have certain grave goods and younger ones do not, it may be argued that these represent goods transferred at marriage. The possibility that women have achieved their own wealth is rarely considered. Examples of high status Iron Age female burials include those at Wetwang Slack, which features a 'chariot' burial surrounded by rich grave goods, and the Vix Burial at Saone, which has a gold torc, huge Greek bronze krater (wine-mixing vessel) and decorated metal bowls. A different kind of status may be visible in the female graves at Khok Phanom Di where craft specialisation seems to have played a role in achieving higher social ranking. The Pazyryk 'Ice Maiden' also suggests high status based on a particular talent.

 KEY STUDY

The Omaha

O'Shea (1981) was able to compare eighteenth- and nineteenth-century ethnographic descriptions of the Omaha by European explorers with burial evidence to test the visibility of status and social grouping in mortuary data. Where social divisions were vertical or ranked, there tended to be evidence in the grave goods. In addition, while rank was concentrated in particular age and sex groups in the population it was more archaeologically visible than horizontal divisions which were more equally distributed. Horizontal social divisions based on clan, moiety and age tended to be archaeologically invisible. From the historic accounts it was clear that some of these identities had been celebrated during the funerary rituals while a person's ranking had not been emphasised. This may indicate that the horizontal divisions were more significant in life. It also tells us that we cannot hope to read all status from burials.

• www.pbs.org/wgbh/nova/icemummies/

Differential survival can be an issue when studying gender differences. In the Mesolithic period men, and especially older men, appeared to receive special treatment, being buried with ochre, antlers or stone artefacts. However, if women had grave goods of organic materials, perhaps offerings of plant foods and medicinal herbs rather than joints of meat, and tools or ornaments of wood, these would not have survived.

Settlement evidence

Studies which have used differential distribution of artefacts to identify male and female activity areas, such as Clarke (1972) at Glastonbury or Flannery and Marcus at Guila Naquitz, could be criticised for making assumptions about gendered tasks. For example, the complete absence of men's large fingerprints on pottery at Khok Phanom Di might argue against the involvement of adult men in potting. However, while small fingerprints could have belonged to women potters they could also be those of young assistants. More recently, studies of architecture have been used to explore the way in which societies structured gender in the past. Gilchrist's (1995) study of the relationship between ideas of chivalry, gender roles and the different zones of medieval castles is a good example.

Artistic sources

Depictions of males and females in scenes on pottery, reliefs, wall paintings (◀ p. 184) and metal artefacts have been quarried for information about gender roles. Some appear fairly straightforward and provide evidence for a division of labour. Pottery from Sopron, Hungary, from the sixth century BC shows figures which seem to be women engaged in weaving and spinning: one is dancing or praying while another figure, which may also be female, is playing a lyre. Men in comparison are riding horses, herding animals and leading horse-drawn wagons. Other material is more ambivalent. A depiction of a person gathering wild honey from a tree at Bicorp, in Spain, from 7000–4000 BC has been interpreted as both male and female by different commentators. The majority have assumed it is a woman due to the size of the buttocks and the flowing hair.

Even where artistic images are clearly of females or males, they cannot always be taken at face value.

However, representation cannot in itself be taken as evidence of high status, nor can we

Figure 9.22 Male and female images from a Classical Greek vase

assume that the women depicted are typical. Until recently, sexuality in the past was rarely considered by archaeologists. Indeed, in several countries collections of artefacts with sexual imagery are often kept from public view. In 1999 the British Museum faced a dilemma over whether to display a rare Roman vase that depicted homosexual sex. A survey of sexuality in the archaeological record appears in Taylor (1997).

POPULATION AND ETHNICITY

Demographic information about past populations is largely obtained from human remains. Where there are large collections from cemeteries they can reveal information about the age and sex structure of the population, average height and life expectancy of adults as well as common illnesses and injuries. DNA offers the opportunity to explore relationships between people and to determine how homogenous any population was.

Figure 9.23 *Minoan procession*

At Knossos (◀ p. 255) a series of figurines of bare-breasted women with full length skirts have been found. They frequently have snakes twined round their arms. There are also frescoes which show women and men involved in various activities. They are easily distinguished as the Minoans adopted the convention of painting the skins of women white while those of men are painted brown. Women are depicted more commonly than men. Taken at face value it seems that elite women may have had more status and the right to participate in a wider range of activities than women in many other societies. Some writers have gone further. These images and an absence of fortifications, male statues, temples to gods or boastful inscriptions might be evidence of a matriarchal (headed by women) society. This fresco (produced by painting with plant and shellfish dyes onto wet plaster) apparently shows young men processing towards a priestess.

It has also been critical in tracing the evolution of humans. Artistic sources and preserved bodies can fill in details of appearance.

A range of additional methods have been used to estimate population sizes. For periods where burial evidence is sparse, including most of prehistory, population estimates can be based on the carrying capacity of the land. This method was originally used to work out likely population levels of animal species within a given environment. It relies on accurate reconstruction of past ecosystems and transferring ethnographic patterns of population. Archaeologists model different strategies such as foraging or horticulture to work out what maximum density of human population could have been sustained. An alternate model is to try and project backwards from historic periods. The earliest figures are guesstimates based on the impressions of travellers or soldiers and may be exaggerated for impact back home. Early historical estimates of population are notoriously unreliable because they are usually based on tax assessments which focused on those elements which might be taxable rather than numbers of people e.g. the Domesday Survey. In addition many surveys have only partially survived.

For urban areas researchers usually multiply area of settlement by an average figure for density. This is simple but subject to a wide variety of errors. There have been attempts to produce standard multipliers such as 10 square metres per person based on ethnographic averages. However, different cultures vary hugely in their use of space and household size which can all impact on density in any particular

KEY STUDY

You are what you eat

Developments in organic chemistry in the last few decades have opened up many exciting new areas of potential evidence for archaeologists including the re-examination of archived finds. In particular applications of stable isotope analysis have exploded in number and breadth including diet, origins, economic strategies and forensic archaeology.

Every living thing and every mineral is composed of material drawn from the earth or atmosphere. The atmosphere contains elements such as carbon, oxygen and nitrogen; the earth is the source of elements such as lead and strontium. In many cases these elements occur in several different atomic forms called isotopes. Carbon isotopes include ^{12}C, ^{13}C and ^{14}C. Some of these isotopes such as ^{14}C are unstable which mean that they decay over time – this is the basis of radio-carbon dating. Others are stable. They don't change over time and behave in similar ways. For instance both ^{12}C and ^{13}C can combine with oxygen atoms to make carbon dioxide. Each has a slightly different atomic weight due to its composition. ^{12}C has 6 neutrons and 6 protons in its nucleus while heavier ^{13}C has 7 neutrons and 6 protons. Around 99 per cent of atmospheric carbon is 12C with most of the rest being ^{13}C. The normal ratio in which the two isotopes are found is 100:1.

Plants absorb carbon into their cells during photosynthesis. However, they store it in slightly different ways which means that the ratios of ^{12}C and ^{13}C vary. Those originating from hot and dry parts of the world with long growing seasons store carbon in compounds with 4 carbon atoms. These are called C4 plants and include maize, sugarcane and millet. They absorb ^{13}C faster than plants which originate from wetter areas or forests and have a slightly higher ratio of ^{13}C to ^{12}C than this second group. The latter originate in more temperate regions and are called C3 plants because they store carbon in compounds with 3 carbon atoms. They include rice, wheat, barley and potatoes. Plants in the sea store a higher proportion of ^{13}C than terrestrial plants. When plants are eaten by other creatures the carbon passes up the food chain but the ratios between the isotopes remains very constant. Carbon from the remains of animals can be analysed using mass spectrometry. The ratio will determine the type of plants which originally provided it. This knowledge has been used to trace the spread of maize in Mesoamerica because it increased the ratio of ^{13}C to ^{12}C in human remains.

The two stable isotopes of nitrogen (^{14}N and ^{15}N) are also absorbed by plants but in differing rations. As nitrogen passes up the food chain the lighter isotope is gradually excreted in urine and proportionally more of ^{15}N is stored. Consequently a top predator would have a higher ratio of ^{15}N to ^{14}N than a plant eater. A breastfed baby would have a higher ratio than its mother. One potential area for confusion is where manuring has taken place. This can boost ^{15}N so that a diet based on manured plants appears similar to a meat-based one.

Nitrogen and carbon isotope analysis have been used in tandem to determine whether human populations ate terrestrial or marine food. Samples are extracted from bone, tooth enamel, hair and collagen. Although collagen is replaced over time, analysis of bone collagen does provide a broad guide to the individual's main source of food.

KEY STUDY *cont.*

You are what you eat

Recent applications of this method are shedding more light on the introduction of domesticated plants and animals into Britain during the Neolithic (◀ p. 244). Opinions about the pace of that change range from several decades to taking more than a millennium. Isotope evidence points to a rapid and complete shift from a marine diet to a terrestrial one at the point where domesticates first appear. Isotopic analysis of food residues also informs dietary studies (◀ p. 255).

Isotopes and origins

A second major application of isotopes has been in identifying the sources of minerals. Particular combinations of isotopes are only found in specific geographic areas. Variations in oxygen isotopes, which humans acquire from local rainwater during childhood, were used to determine that the Amesbury Archer originated somewhere between Switzerland and southern Scandinavia. Using oxygen in conjunction with isotopes of sulphur and heavy elements such as strontium has also proved useful in tracing origins. Research is currently underway using this technique to determine the impact of crusader settlement on populations in the Near East.

case. In addition there are many urban areas where the full size of the town is not known. A second method is to multiply an estimate of the number of houses with an average household size. This excludes unoccupied space but can still be distorted by different uses of dwellings (are they also workshops?) and family size. In some urban centres, particularly those in walled medieval towns where building space was limited, much housing was very crowded with subdivisions being common. This produces a much higher occupation density than average. Excavation bias is also a factor. Archaeology has tended to focus on high status buildings at the centre of ancient towns and these may not be typical. Understanding specific local and cultural factors is likely to be the key to successful estimation.

Figure 9.24 *Gournia*

Figure 9.25 *Plan of Gournia*

In trying to estimate the population of Minoan Crete, Whitelaw noted that similar sized houses were a feature of the smaller towns such as Gournia. He inferred from this regularity that nuclear family units of 5–6 people were the residential norm. In the central areas of the larger towns such as Knossos, large dwellings clustered around the palaces. Even with the addition of servants, these would not be as densely settled as Gournia or the outlying districts of Knossos. He also found that there were fairly consistent ratios between the amount of space devoted to public buildings (the palace complexes), streets and open areas and residential areas. Using this data he created average densities appropriate for this civilisation of up to 225 people/hectare and estimated the population of Knossos to be 14–18,000. Branigan used a similar model to project a population for the whole island of Crete. His figure of around 80,000 in rural areas and 58–78,000 in urban areas gives a figure not far below the 175,000 counted by the Venetians in the first attempt at a census in AD 1534. Branigan

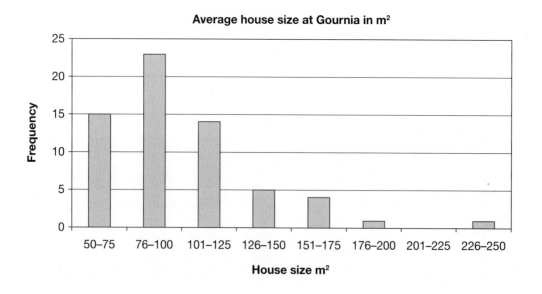

Figure 9.26 *Minoan houses by area*

KEY SITE

West Heslerton and Lechlade

Historical and linguistic sources suggest that Anglo-Saxon invaders slaughtered or displaced native Romano – British people from much of England in the fifth and sixth centuries AD. On the assumption that 'Germanic type' artefacts equalled Saxon invaders, archaeological material was used to trace the arrival and spread of migrants across the country. Similarly, areas where Saxon pottery or metalwork was absent were identified as places still held by Britons. Excavations of these two settlements present a rather different picture.

At West Heslerton in the early 5th century some distinctive Anglo-Saxon grubenhauser (▶ p. 319) were built in what had been a typical Romano-British settlement. Around AD 450 this site was abandoned and a large, new settlement replaced it a short distance away. This too combined Romano-British and Anglo-Saxon elements but was a very different settlement. It included post- and plank-built buildings and a long hall. The whole site was laid out in an ordered way with distinct zones for agricultural processing, housing and industrial activity. This included bone and metal working and the manufacture of pottery and textiles. Imported pottery, metal work and lava quernstones suggest some of this may have been for trade. The evidence of buildings and pottery suggested much continuity of population but the degree of planning and Scandinavian origin of the larger buildings suggested that the site had new, foreign leaders.

Burial evidence also appears to favour a mixed population. Amongst over 300 burials were many with weapons. Some of these seem to be female graves while others are individuals who do not have 'warrior' builds. This may support Härke's (1990) 'warband model'. His study of Anglo-Saxon cemeteries suggested that many included Romano-Britons, thus indicating co-existence. Male burials with swords were on average 1–2 inches taller than those without. This was not due to different diets and suggested two distinct ethnic groups. By the seventh century this distinction had disappeared, probably through intermarriage. DNA analysis of several cemeteries revealed two models of Anglo-Saxon immigration. In some, complete kin groups were represented, which suggests entire communities settled here, while in others, males with weapons existed alongside female skeletons which showed continuity with the Romano-British period. Härke terms this the 'warband' model. Over time, DNA evidence supports a mingling of the two populations into 'the English' while the dominant culture remained 'Anglo-Saxon'. This might suggest that weapons had a symbolic value rather than identifying male warriors. Oxygen and strontium isotope analysis of teeth enamel have also identified two distinct population groups, one with similar profiles to prehistoric burials from the area, the other with more distant origins. This suggests that many of the Anglo-Saxons buried there were first generation immigrants.

The longevity of the site and the excavation of over 200 buildings means that changes in construction techniques can be traced over time. A massive assemblage of 750,000 animal bones offers the possibility of understanding the economy and diet.

The evidence from Lechlade covers another change in British history. This cemetery was both early and long lasting. Between 450 and AD 800 over 200 people were buried and at least 29 cremated. Analysis of the feet from these burials by Jackson (1995) pointed to great local population continuity.

KEY SITE *cont.*

West Heslerton and Lechlade

The early burials were classic pagan burials with grave goods including many with weapons. However, several of these were militarily useless and in one case an 11 year old was buried with an adult spear. Weapons may have been more symbolic than a sign of warfare. Although the Battle of Dyrham (577) is supposed to have occurred a few miles away, only one burial had died of trauma related to fighting. The richest burial was nicknamed Mrs Getty (◀ p. 301) but finds of valuables did come from several other graves which attested to exchange networks reaching far beyond England. The artefact traditions indicate that these people were ethnic Saxons rather than Jutes or Angles. In the seventh century the alignment of the graves shifted from NE/SW to NW/SE. This suggests they had converted to Christianity yet they continued to have grave goods. This is clear evidence of continuity and possibly people hedging their bets.

A few years after this excavation, the homes of these people were found in a nearby field. This settlement too was longlived. Its economy was based on mixed farming of cereals, beans and flax along with cattle and sheep. There was evidence too of metal working, weaving and leather working. This pattern is common on contemporary sites such as West Stow (▶ p. 319) but also is very similar to the picture we get from Iron Age settlements in the vicinity from 1000 years earlier.

Part of the problem with attempts to study ethnicity through material culture is the material itself. In some areas such as East Anglia or Oxfordshire it can be difficult to differentiate Saxon from Romano-British greyware or Iron Age pottery, unless it is decorated. Where it can be identified, it sometimes turns up well before historical sources say the Saxons arrived, for example at Eynsham Abbey. This may illustrate the point that ethnically distinctive material may be used by other groups. Exchange, trade, small-scale migration or adoption and copying by indigenous people would also spread material.

Figure 9.27
Grubenhaus
from West
Heslerton

KEY SITE *cont.*

West Heslerton and Lechlade

Houses may be a better ethnic marker than pottery. Particularly since there is some evidence that Saxon settlers used containers made from wood and animals along with coarse grass-tempered wares which have not survived. These are very common finds on sites in the east of England from the mid 5th century onwards. It seems unlikely that native Romano-Britons would have adopted these small structures out of fashion. The same might not be true of Saxon metal jewellery. Experimental archaeology has established that these buildings had suspended floors (rather than being 'pit dwellings') and produced several models of the house superstructure.

Figure 9.28 *Reconstructed Grubenhaus at West Stow*

and other researchers all project that 40–60 per cent of the population lived in urban areas.

Estimates for world population levels at the end of the last Ice Age range from 1–10 million with 150–250 million by the late Iron Age. Agriculture was the key to sustaining higher levels.

Ethnicity and race have the same relationship as sex and gender. One of each pair is in our DNA, the other is in our heads. Racially we are all Homo sapiens but ethnicity consists of cultural norms and values that differentiate one social group from another. Physical differences are sometimes, but not always, used to distinguish different ethnic groups.

Until the later twentieth century cultural approaches to archaeology tended to dominate interpretations. In some cases they were used to

support racist political ideas, such as Nazi archaeology (▶ p. 363). Such approaches also led to a diffusionist 'invasions model' of social change in Britain with successive waves of invaders bringing developments and their own special pottery, for example, Windmill Hill Folk or Beaker People. This idea fitted with colonial experience of worldwide progress flowing from more 'civilised' to 'backward' peoples, but it has been shown to be deeply flawed by the application of scientific techniques. Stonehenge is the most famous case. A generation of classically trained archaeologists had shown how the people of Bronze Age Wessex built monuments in imitation and with help from advanced Mediterranean civilisations. Yet radiocarbon dating has shown that Stonehenge pre-dated the Mediterranean monuments it was supposed to have been influenced by. This cultural model of social change tends to undervalue the achievements of indigenous people as in the case of Iron Age brochs (▶ p. 229).

Even where we know invasions took place, the archaeological record is not always helpful. For example, there is little evidence for the Norman Conquest in sequences of medieval ceramics. Some evidence is ambivalent. Belgic coins found in South-east England from the late Iron Age have been used to support Caesar's description of immigration into the area from Gaul. However, there are other mechanisms by which the coins could have got there. As with other forms of identity, where ethnic allegiances were expressed in organic material such as textiles, evidence may not always survive.

DNA AND THE ORIGINS OF MODERN EUROPEANS

The transition from foraging to farming ranks as one of the most significant changes in human history. The way in which farming spread across Europe and the fate of the foraging people who lived there is a key debate amongst archaeologists. Agriculture originated in the Near East from around 9500 BC and first appeared in the Balkans around 7000 BC. The settlements of the first farmers in that region appear to have been very similar to those across the Bosphorus in modern-day Turkey. This suggests that these pioneer farmers were immigrants. (◀ p. 246)

The spread across Central Europe took a different form. The crops and animals were essentially the same but the material culture was novel. Key indicators include massive, timber-built longhouses, new types of stone tools and the pottery with incised bands of abstract decoration which led archaeologists to name the culture the Linearbandkeramik (LBK). Spreading out from the Hungarian basin around 5500 BC and up the river Danube into central Europe, by 4500 BC the LBK settlements were scattered from France to the Ukraine. In most of Europe there

was little sign of domesticates on forager sites before the LBK settlements. The uniformity and the dating sequence from different sites led to a widespread view that LBK farmers were immigrant settlers who displaced the indigenous foragers. By extension, the rest of Europe was colonised by later waves of farming immigrants such as the 'Windmill Hill Folk'. For many years the reasons for this were not explored because it was assumed that farming was obviously superior to foraging.

The way in which population movements occur can vary considerably. Colonisation implies deliberate organisation of movement, for example British nineteenth century settlement in Australia. Migration suggests large scale movement of people to a particular area as with European settlement on the American prairies in the late nineteenth century. A third model is Demic Diffusion. This is where one population expands faster than another and ultimately disperses till it occupies most of the available land. This is not deliberate but may lead to the culture of the successful group becoming dominant. In this case the thinly distributed foraging population was gradually squeezed out. Using settlement dates and computer modelling, Ammerman and Cavalli-Sforza outlined a series of 'waves of advance' averaging 1 kilometre per year whereby agriculture and LBK culture spread out with each successive generation of farmers. Renfrew used a similar model to argue that these farmers had spread an Indo-European language from which most modern European languages are descended. An alternative explanation was that cultural diffusion had occurred. That means the idea of farming and particular languages moved rather than the people.

LBK settlements spread onto the northern European plain but not as far as the Baltic or Atlantic seaboard. Dating evidence suggests that there was a lull of up to a thousand years before farming began to develop in these areas. When this change came the form it took was very

Figure 9.29 *A Linearbandkeramik settlement*

Earliest agriculture in Europe
    Mediterranean expansion of farming
    Linearbandkeramik

Figure 9.30 *The wave of advance theory*

different and much less clear. (◄ p. 255) A range of theories have been developed to explain why this halt occurred. Several of these focus on the limitations to the type of farming practised by the LBK. Many LBK settlements are on fertile bands of loess (soil eroded by glaciers during the Ice Age and deposited by the wind). Perhaps they were reluctant to risk farming on heavier clay soils which may have been more thickly forested. It is also argued that since frost-free days decline as you move north, arable farming was limited by the length of growing seasons. However, while loess does 'run out' in the coastal areas of north-western Europe, that region has successfully grown cereal crops since the Bronze Age. Other approaches have focused on the foragers of that region. Evidence suggests that they were thriving without farming and may have not needed to change. Perhaps they were hostile to incoming farmers. There is some evidence of violence and some LBK sites were fortified.

Increasingly archaeologists studying the eventual transition to farming around the Baltic and Atlantic seaboard have rejected the idea that agriculture developed solely as a result of immigration by farmers. Instead they believe that the successful foragers of this region chose to adopt aspects of the 'neolithic package'. The key evidence is that in this region there is continuity in some aspects of material culture and ritual practice, little evidence of houses and fields and the appearance of a variety of new ritual monuments including long barrows. The full transition to an economy based on sedentary farming appears to have then taken around another thousand years. This does not rule out some population movement but suggests that there was not a replacement of population everywhere either.

Developments in genetics which have enabled study of the DNA of past populations seem to support this view. Populations in northern and western Europe seem to be both relatively similar and markedly different from populations to the south east. This applies to research using both M+DNA and Y chromosomes. Many, but not all, researchers now believe that modern Europeans, particularly in north-west Europe are directly descended from the first modern humans to arrive on the continent around 40,000 years ago. In the most famous account Sykes presents the 7 main European haplogroups (particular sets of genetic variations) as being descended from 7 'clan mothers', the 'Seven daughters of Eve'. His research into mitochondrial DNA suggests that over 80 per cent of modern Europeans are descended from these women who lived during the Upper Palaeolithic, most frequently from 'Helena' (Haplogroup H). While this suggests that cultural diffusion (movement of ideas) was the key to changes it still allows some room for the movement of people. Descendents of the middle eastern 'Mother', Jasmine, are found in south-east Europe, the Mediterranean coast and along the Danube.

If there has been no major population replacement since the Ice Age then 'what happened to the LBK farmers?' In 2007 research was published

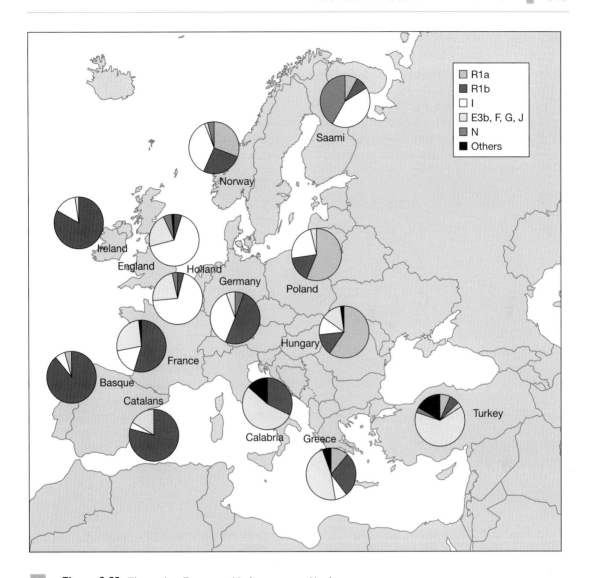

Figure 9.31 *The major European Y chromosome Haplogroups*

Only the major Haplogroups are shown. The variations can be explained in two ways. During the peak of the Ice Age human populations were concentrated in 3 main 'refuges' and some slight genetic differences developed between them. These groups then repopulated Europe after the Ice Age. The markers of near eastern immigration from the Neolithic are E3b, F, G and J. Some subsequent movements can also be traced including the spread of R1a, the so-called Viking gene.

by Burger at Johannes Gutenberg University in Mainz which challenged the idea that even modern central European populations are descended from the pioneer farmers. They analysed bones and teeth from 57 individuals buried at 16 LBK sites in Germany, Austria and Hungary. 24 of the skeletons produced sufficient mitochondrial DNA for sequences to be constructed. 6 skeletons had DNA type N1a. This is found in only 0.2 per cent of modern populations in the area but is associated with middle-eastern populations. This surprising discovery led the researchers to conclude that there was some migration by some pioneer farmers but they made little genetic impact on the population of the region. This may be because they were not very numerous since the chance of any one group passing on its genes over a long period is not high. Modern populations appear to be descended largely from the earlier foragers.

Although it is possible that the samples did not come from typical farming groups, the spread of sites analysed makes this unlikely. Computer simulations have also largely ruled out the N1a type being lost through chance or other immigration since the Neolithic. It is possible that incoming male farmers took forager wives since the study focused on mtDNA passed through the

Urban zone (core)   → Raw materials

Mature Bronze Age Societies (buffer zone)   ⇒ Exotic manufactured items ideas

Area outside agricultural Europe

Newer Bronze Age Societies (periphery)

Figure 9.32 *Core and periphery*

The relationship between richer, more technologically advanced areas is sometimes understood in terms of a core-periphery model. In this instance the urbanised palace civilisations with advanced manufacturing techniques provided a market for raw materials and luxury items from a much wider region. Some of this would have been acquired through trade or exchange networks, some from raiding. The periphery is seen as a source of minerals, slaves, textiles and semi-precious materials such as amber or ivory but is little influenced by the core. The intermediate region benefits from the exchanges and is also influenced by the core. This has been used to explain the rise of warrior chiefdoms, raiding and feasting in central Europe. The danger with such models is that it can lead to assumptions about innovation only going in one direction and that the periphery is somehow backward as in early theories about the origin of Stonehenge (◀ p. 168). As the diagram illustrates, there were other influences besides the Mediterranean including corded ware culture and burial practices and the Atlantic bell beaker culture.

female line. Either way, it looks as though some or all of the indigenous population rapidly stopped foraging and adopted the farming culture once it became available. Greater certainty could come from analysis of forager DNA. Unfortunately forager bones are rarely found. Nevertheless, DNA research is already having a significant impact on debates about the movement of peoples during European prehistory.

SOCIAL CHANGE

Most periods will have examples of social changes to which you will be directed. The kind of evidence discussed in this chapter and those on economics and settlement will provide the focus for work on this area. Studying social change is likely to require you to discuss a range of different models to account for change. Essentially these will fall into two groups. External factors include immigration, diffusion, conquest and environmental change. Internal factors include evolution, competition and innovation. You need to ensure you examine and appraise an appropriate range of these. The adoption of agriculture exercise provides a good topic for discussion. In examining change don't forget the opposite: stasis. For much of the time things remain as they are, and that needs explaining too. A useful tool for examining forces for change or stasis is the force field diagram (◄ p. 251).

SOCIAL CONFLICT

Not all social conflict is violent. Probably its most common form is competition in either display or consumption. Our society is no different in this respect. Various attempts have been made to trace this sort of competition from the Neolithic onwards. Tilley (1996) suggested that

Figure 9.33 *Ruthven Barracks*

These barracks formed part of a chain of roads and forts built by the British Government to pacify the Scottish Highlands after the 1715 Jacobite Rebellion. The site on a glacial feature was a natural defensive point dominating a junction of the new military road north to Inverness. The barracks initially held up to 120 infantry and a cavalry unit. Their function would be to patrol the area and suppress local problems whilst helping to give warning and delay more serious threats. However, cost cutting led to troop numbers being run down. By the time of the 1745 rebellion there were only 13 'redcoats' based there. They successfully drove off an attack by over 200 Jacobites who lacked the artillery needed to break through the defences. They surrendered in 1746 when retreating Jacobites with cannons arrived. The fort was reoccupied by Hanoverian forces soon afterwards but became the focus for thousands of regrouping Jacobites after their defeat at Culloden. When they heard that their leader, 'Bonnie Prince Charlie' had fled they burnt the barracks down before dispersing.

KEY SITES

Nimrud and Nineveh

The Assyrian Empire dominated present-day Iraq in the ninth to seventh centuries BC. The huge reliefs from the palaces of its great cities of Nimrud and Nineveh are interesting both as early propaganda and as evidence of early Iron Age warfare.

The use of sculpture to glorify kings in war had been common practice in the region for over 2000 years. As a result the imagery is highly stylised and intended to impress and intimidate. Rulers are shown larger than other people and they depicted the king as high priest linked to the gods. Other high ranking people have squared off beards and net skirts. The strength of rulers was emphasised through scenes of them hunting lions. Ashurnasirpal (reigned 883–859 BC) boasted in inscriptions to having killed 450.

The fate of those who displeased them was depicted in scenes of flaying, impaling and beheading. The cartoon strip style reliefs of their campaigns were also subject to conventions. No Assyrians were shown dead. The sculptures all show well equipped Assyrians trampling their foes under their chariots, beheading their leaders and bringing booty back to Assyria.

Despite all this there is unwitting evidence – that is evidence that was not deliberately distorted – about clothing, technology and warfare amongst other things. We see evidence of chariots, siege towers and inflatable skins being used to cross a river. We can see the lightly armed Aramaic forces who fought alongside the Assyrians and some of the different types of military units. The range of weapons including bows, spears and slings is evident as are some of their tactics. One panel shows a soldier holding a tall shield of wood or reeds as cover while others fire slingshots and arrows from behind it. The origin of the phrase 'taking a head count' is suggested in depictions of the aftermath of victory.

Figure 9.34 *Assyrian cavalry trampling their vanquished foes at the Battle of Til Tuba*

developments in the design of Swedish passage graves might have been the product of local competitive emulation. Other writers have come to similar conclusions about the henges of Wessex, an idea that was taken up by Cornwell in his 1999 blockbuster novel, *Stonehenge*.

Warfare

In literate societies, warfare is one of the first things to be documented. It seems likely that in societies with oral traditions it forms a major part of their history too. From Homer we know something of the wars of Bronze Age Greece while medieval recording of Irish and Icelandic sagas may provide insights into Iron Age warfare in north-western Europe. Tomb paintings and inscriptions in most of the classical civilisations of Eurasia and Mesoamerica provide graphic depiction of the nature of battles.

However, these very stylized accounts tend to concentrate on key heroic individuals and just tell the victor's version of events. Consequently, we approach them with some care as exact records of evidence. However, their unwitting evidence of equipment and organisation can be valuable. Trajan's Column in Rome provides a superb example. It commemorates the victorious campaigns of the Emperor Trajan against the Dacians. Scenes show in tremendous detail the equipment and organisation involved in the campaign. The battle scenes depict the tactics used by the legions and their effectiveness. The key events of the campaign are included and its effects, allowing for some bias, are also illustrated.

Figure 9.35 *Memorial to the dead at Flodden*

Rather unusually for a British battlefield we know exactly where the site of Flodden (1513) is from historic sources. This collective funerary monument overlooks it. In other cases these sources are less useful. Towton (1461) for example is being plotted through metal detection and fieldwalking. In the case of Tewkesbury (1471), disputes about the location between archaeologists went to the High Court when development was being planned. The sites of many key battles such as Brunaburgh (937) are completely unknown.

Apart from historic and artistic accounts, the physical evidence of weapons and fortification usually provide the main sources for identifying warfare. In some cases actual battles become visible. For instance, the 'war grave' at Maiden Castle with its famous iron arrowhead embedded in a defender's spine, or the mass grave at Towton. This was subjected to the same tests as a murder enquiry by forensic archaeologists. They were able to identify what happened to the individual soldiers and how each injury was caused. The exact location and sequence of the battle is also being revealed by archaeology. Towton shows how archaeology can add to and test historic sources, many of which are vague or unreliable in the accounts.

• http://www.brad.ac.uk/acad/archsci/depart/ resgrp/archpros/Towton_Landscape/

Of course, not everything that looks military may have been. Both weapons and fortifications can be symbolic. Early metal daggers and 'rapiers' were relatively fragile. While they could have been used to kill, they would have been less effective than flint-tipped spears or stone axes. The swords that emerge in the Bronze Age are

Figure 9.36 *Iron Age coin*

Not all coins may have been used as money, some may have been used as tokens or symbols of power.

quite a different matter. Their shape and balance suggest that they were ideal for slashing at opponents in fighting at close quarters. Analysis of their edges has shown that many have damage associated with metal-on-metal contact. Fortifications can also mislead us about the nature of warfare. 'Hill forts' with their massive circuits of ramparts suggest sieges. There is evidence of attack at a few, such as flint arrowheads around the entrance at Crickley Hill, but these are exceptions. Warfare in the Iron Age is more likely to have looked like a cattle raid than pitched battles between rival armies, at least until the Romans arrived. A similar bias would occur if we looked at the major physical evidence of warfare between France and Germany in 1940. The Maginot Line, bypassed by the Germans, is still visible while traces of mobile tank and infantry formations are harder to discern.

HUMAN ORIGINS

Of the many issues in human evolution, three major questions stand out. How did humans evolve, at what point did our ancestors start to behave in a way we would consider' human' and in what circumstances did our own species, **Homo sapiens**, develop? Before we consider these, an introduction to the developing, and rather confusing, terminology and evidence used by palaeo-anthropologists (scientists who study fossil humans) is required.

Hominids are members of a family of primates sometimes referred to as the 'Great Apes'. A sub-group or tribe of this group are called **hominins** and include humans and chimpanzees. Humans and their extinct ancestors are termed **hominans** with the term **human** applying to both our species and extinct members of the genus **Homo**. **Humanoids** are encountered by aliens.

What are the bases of evidence?

Survival of evidence from several million years ago has always meant that information has to be

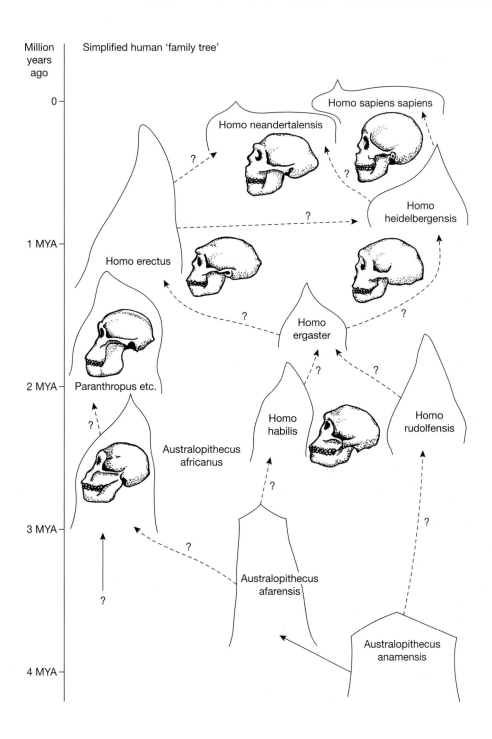

Figure 9.37 *Human family tree*

squeezed from very fragmentary remains. Hominid skeletal remains have been used to track differences between different species. Detailed anatomical study has been able to reveal details of locomotion, diet and behaviour. The advent of DNA analysis has had a tremendous impact on evolutionary studies for instance identifying that around 5.4 million years ago (mya) the hominan lineage diverged from that of chimpanzees. They are our closest living relatives and our DNA is 98.4 per cent identical. Stone tools have been seen as one of the markers of more intelligent hominans. Until the dating of tools from Gona in Ethiopia to about 2.9 mya it was thought that only the Homo genus was capable of making tools. However this date would make it likely that they were made by Australopithecines. This highlights the problem that so few remains have been discovered that timelines for different species are only approxi-

mate. A new discovery is quite capable of overturning established models and sequences. Analysis of wear marks and experimentation are key areas of research into tools. It is only with the advent of stone tools that researchers can be sure that butchery evidence on animal bones is due to hominan activity. Key sites are where both tools and faunal remains are found. The issue then is whether the collections of stones and bones at sites such as Olduvai and Koobi Fora were deposited there through water action and other taphonomic factors or were they actually 'living floors' or 'home bases' representing hominins sharing food and working cooperatively.

Density of lithics and debitage		
High	Low	
'Workshops' or quarry sites	Temporary camps	Low
'Home base' Camp or occupation area	Kill or butchery sites	High

Density of faunal debris

Identification of site function from bone and lithic assemblages after Isaacs 1971

Figure 9.38 *The homebase model*

Issacs interpreted different assemblages of animal bones and lithics as being indicators of different types of human activity.

Figure 9.39 *Binford vs Isaacs*

Binford and Isaacs disagreed over interpretations of faunal and lithic assemblages in East Africa. Isaacs saw such sites as home bases where early humans lived. Binford rejected this because of insufficient evidence and the vulnerability of early humans. He saw the assemblages as stemming from animal kills and human scavenging activities.

This may illustrate the danger of archae-ologists projecting modern behaviour onto past species. The contributions of ethnographic research, begun by Lee and De Vore, plus the acerbic questioning style of Lewis Binford, led to a more rigorous approach and more openness to the use of alternative approaches or analogies to fill in the considerable gaps in our knowledge. This has included primate studies and experi-mentation to understand potential economic strategies and site formation processes. Progress still relies on sharp-eyed discovery in the field followed by reassembly of thousands of bone and stone fragments.

What is the earliest evidence for complex social behaviour?

Humans are usually differentiated from other species by complex social behaviour, control of technology and creation of culture. In particular the ability to communicate large amounts of knowledge including abstract concepts is absent in other modern species. Indicators from the past which have been considered as indicative of human-like behaviour have included brain size, meat eating, hunting, child rearing and evidence for communication. It is not thought that early hominins differed hugely from other apes except that they successfully adapted to seasonal grassland areas as rain forests began to shrink. The Australopithecines had ape-like features including a brain about the same size as a chimpanzee (400cc) but skeletal evidence such as the famous Lucy and the footprints at Laetoli suggests that they were bipedal and had opposable thumbs. This meant that they could see predators and food sources over tall grass and hold things like tools and infants as they moved. Several different species co-existed in Africa and from one of them, the Homo lineage developed. Homo habilis (handyman) and Homo rudolfensis emerged in East Africa 2.4 mya and this area is associated with the earliest definite stone tools of the Oldowan Industry. A key transition is from using a rock or a stick as a tool to deliberately creating a tool by using one material to shape another. These were mainly used for cutting and pounding food. Tools may have developed as a response to the need to seek food underground or from animal carcasses. Their larger brains (660 and 775 cc) and skills combined with assemblages of lithics and broken animal bones suggested to Leakey and Isaacs that they might have hunted and had home bases. However, most archaeologists accept that while they might have scavenged kill sites they were not advanced enough to establish and protect base sites.

The Homo lineage has become more compli-cated with the discovery of Homo ergaster in East Africa so there was clearly a range of early Homo types plus late Australopithecines around in Africa between 2–1 mya. The origin of Homo seems therefore to spring from a bush with several branches rather than from a single stem. The larger and more intelligent (1000cc brain) Homo ergaster and Homo erectus developed after 1.8 mya. Scientists are divided over whether Homo erectus developed from Homo ergaster or if they were parallel species. Their tall leaner bodies would have been better suited to the warmer, drier climate of Africa at that time. Both used a more sophisticated, standardised set of tools chipped on two sides called **Acheulean**, including the classic hand-axe. These required planning to make. They may have been the first to definitely use fire and use a form of language. Their large brain meant that, just like modern humans, babies had to continue development outside the womb because the birth canal was too narrow for females to give birth to babies with fully developed brains. Since babies would be helpless this meant that a parent would have had to look after them and probably would rely on others to bring food. This suggests the development of parental roles in order to ensure the survival of offspring. The large brain also needed more calories to supply it. It is possible that they progressed from scavenging to hunting, particularly of small animals, but there is no evidence of weapons. Analysis of animal bones by Shipman has found examples of Homo erectus processing bone before other scavengers which does suggest that they may have moved up that particular pecking order. However they lived, they were a very successful species for over a million years during which they colonised much of the world.

OUT OF AFRICA I

The most prevalent view sees Homo erectus leaving Africa at around one million years ago and replacing all other species in a migration as far as China to the east and Europe to the west. This is marked culturally by the spread of the

Lake

0	5 m	10 m

▨ 'Huts'

▨ 'Paved area'

Ⓢ Anvil of stone or bone

▤ 'Hearths'

◯ Interaction areas or performance spaces

ubiquitous biface or handaxe (though not east of India). It is generally thought that early finds such as 'Java Man' and 'Peking Man' were variants of Homo erectus although some still see them as different species. Erectus may have coexisted in some parts of the world with other species including Homo sapiens. The most recent dates from Java are only 50,000 BP. Confusingly, there are also early, small Homo specimens outside Africa e.g. Dmanisi in Georgia. It is possible that Homo ergaster also migrated out of Africa, perhaps even earlier since some scientists have identified possible tools and Homo fossil teeth from as early as 1.7 mya in Asia. Erectus and ergaster developed into a number of different species in different parts of the world including Homo heidelbergensis in Europe and **Homo rhodesiensis** in Africa. Remains from the bottom of a natural shaft at Atapuerca in Spain from 800,000 may suggest the first evidence of ritual. Scientists are divided over whether this was heidelbergensis or an intermediate species called **Homo antecessor.** A calcified skeleton of heidelbergensis was recently discovered at Altamura in Italy and dated to 400,000 BP. Some heidelbergensis sites such as Bilzingsleben appear to have been structured and have the first hearths. Movement out of Africa may have been because of climatic changes or because our ancestors were intelligent enough to adapt to new environments. Low sea levels may have enabled them to spread as far as Indonesia using land bridges.

How early did hunting begin?

Dates for the origin of hunting vary widely from 2.5 mya to perhaps 400,000 years ago. Smashed

▋ **Figure 9.40** *Bilzingsleben*

A range of deposits including stone tools, animal bones (including elephants and rhinos) and some human remains were preserved under sediments by the side of an ancient lake. Mania interpreted patterns in this assemblage as being the remains of a camp site with distinct activity areas (main drawing). Gamble used a statistical model to challenge this view, arguing that the apparent patterns were the result of successive visits to a 'locale' and that the circular patterns were not the outline of huts but areas around trees. Gamble's gathering places are marked with circles on the plan. These two radically different interpretations offer very different verdicts on the sophistication of Heidelbergensis society.

animal bones including many with tool cut-marks have been found as far back as 1.8 mya but these could have been from scavenged carcasses. The most convincing evidence comes from the later dates with yew spear tips from Lehringen (found within an elephant rib-cage) and Clacton and 7 complete javelins from Schöningen found alongside butchered horses. There is also indirect evidence of tools with animal remains at Torralba and Boxgrove. At the latter, lesions caused by a fire-hardened wooden spear were found in the scapula of a horse and also a skeleton of a rhinoceros showing carnivore tooth marks overlying knife cuts from a flint knife – probable evidence of successful hunting of large and dangerous prey. It suggests that hominins at this time could scare off other predators, secure a carcass and dissect it in a leisurely fashion. These are likely to have been the work of Homo heidelbergensis who lived in Europe from around 600,000 to 250,000 mya. Taller and more muscular than modern humans their brain was only 50cc smaller than our own. Despite these discoveries some archaeologists believe that really secure evidence for hunting doesn't emerge until the Neanderthals or Homo sapiens during the Ice Age. This view sees humans having to develop hunting in an environment where there was little plant food for much of the year.

The Neanderthal Enigma – did they become extinct or were they absorbed into European Homo sapiens populations?

From around 250,000 BP as Europe and Western Asia underwent a series of Ice Ages, a new species, Homo neandertalensis adapted to this environment with shorter limbs, squat, muscular bodies and thicker facial features. These were all ideal for preserving heat. Brain sizes have been estimated to be as high as 1500cc which makes them comparable with the 1350cc average for Homo sapiens. They developed a new technology called Mousterian with a range of scrapers and small hand axes produced by using the Levallois technique. This involved preparing a stone core to form a standard 'blank' and then striking flakes away with soft hammers to create the desired shapes. This is a more controlled technology but one which required more skill and planning. One of the reasons there is more evidence about the Neanderthals than earlier species is because they used cave sites where remains were more likely to survive. They also buried their dead. An example from Shanidar, where flowers appeared to have been buried too, suggests they had rituals

Figure 9.41 *Blade technology*

This technology was a key to the success of modern humans during the last Ice Age. Prepared pyramidal cores were struck repeatedly around the edge of the flat platform to produce long, thin blades. With a backing these could be used as knives but they could also be incorporated in composite tools or broken to produce points for projectile weapons. They were very efficient because they maximised the cutting edge produced from a given piece of flint.

and may have had beliefs. Archaeologists are divided about whether they could speak and use projectile weapons for hunting. Neanderthal skulls with cut marks have been interpreted as cannibalism or defleshing rituals. Their skeletons show frequent signs of injuries due to accidents and stress due to poor nutrition. Neanderthals appear to have lived in small family groups and may have been nomadic within limited ranges. Their population density is likely to have been low, perhaps reflecting the difficulty in existing in such a hostile environment. At some point after 40,000 BP they were joined in Europe by Homo sapiens, sometimes called Cro-Magnons after a rock shelter in France where remains were dated to 32,000 BP. After a period of co-existence, Neanderthals gradually disappeared with the last pockets in the Crimea, Balkans and Iberian Peninsular around 30–24,000 BP. Archaeologists are divided over whether Homo sapiens out-competed them for food, exterminated them or whether they interbred. DNA results have led most scientists towards a replacement theory but not all are convinced. Trinkaus points to the 1998 discovery at The Lagar Velho rock-shelter of a Neanderthal child from 24,500 BP with Homo sapiens traits as evidence of some inter-breeding. There is also evidence of Neanderthals producing tools copied from Homo sapiens. However, there is less evidence that they copied their sewing kits. Australian research suggests that Neanderthals were well adapted to cold but the peak of the last Ice Age may have proved too much for them without the layered clothing worn by their rivals.

'Out of Africa II' vs multiregionalism

The origin of Homo sapiens remains one of the greatest debates in archaeology. The oldest fossils dating from up to 130,000 BP have been found in East and South Africa and 90,000 BP in Israel where they overlap and even may predate Neanderthals. They differ anatomically from all other species with lighter bones (gracile), flatter faces, high foreheads and a rounder skull. Scientists are (often bitterly) divided over our exact lineage. The mental differences were equally striking. Homo sapiens probably had language, ritual and art from an early stage. The oldest recovered art from Blombos Cave dates to 70,000 BP and Venus figurines to 30,000 BP. They developed an extensive range of stone tools and the pace of technological change seemed to increase after 40,000 BP suggesting greater communication.

Apart from the usual discussions of archaeological evidence such as stone tools and various types of site, this area of study has been dominated for the last twenty-five years by the contribution of genetic studies of ancient DNA. The pioneer of this work was Stoneking who, supported by Cann in her studies of mDNA, found that the greatest genetic variation amongst modern humans is in Africa. In other words they had more time to accumulate the mutations that signal differences between populations which suggest that they have been evolving there the longest. More recently Sykes has built on these foundations to produce a new synthesis of the genetic data which contributes to all of the major debates. The two extreme positions are as follows.

THE MULTI-REGION OR CANDELABRA MODEL

This model, championed by Wolpoff, suggests modern humans evolved from regional Homo erectus populations that exchanged genes through communal gene pools. Some of the minor differences in skeletal appearances between people from different parts of the world seem to reflect differences in earlier species. Homo sapiens therefore developed in parallel in Africa, Asia and possibly Europe. Thus it is claimed that modern Chinese populations share with ancestors earlier than 500,000 years ago certain physical traits such as shovel-shaped incisors.

Figure 9.42 *Ice Age hunters*

Modern humans adapted to terrible climatic conditions socially and technologically rather than physically. Larger aggregations may have led to greater efficiency through a division of labour and cooperation. The development of tents, layered clothing and storage techniques such as drying fish or meat was also significant. More efficient projectile weapons such as stone-tipped darts launched from an atlatl enabled large prey to be killed at a distance.

KEY STUDY

Beads

Beads are currently at the centre of a debate about when modern human behaviour began. This is because beads are an example of a symbolic medium through which humans express their individual identity and communicate with others. Unlike clothing, tattoos and hairstyles, beads made from stone or shells are much more likely to survive in the archaeological record. Beads are found in the ethnographic record for virtually every culture. They have a variety of functions including social markers to denote ethnic or tribal group, ranking and marital status. They are used for self-expression and in courtship and can also be gifts or media for exchange including counters. Particular beads may also be used to ward off evil or have ritual connotations. What these uses have in common is their symbolic nature. They are used to communicate with others who have the ability to interpret or 'read' them. This shared understanding also implies language.

Beads have long been associated with developments amongst modern humans in Europe. The burials at Sungir in Russia from 28,000 BP with around 13,000 beads are the best known example. In particular beads have been associated with creative developments including art and new lithic technologies during

Figure 9.43 *Native American beadwork*

the Upper Palaeolithic. The creativity and communication of modern humans are widely seen as reasons for the replacement of Neanderthals in Europe and the success of our own species. Finds at Castel Merle in France of large scale soapstone and ivory bead production have been used to argue for the emergence of specialists and a division of labour during this period. The need for a technology of ornamentation might be part of a response to increasing populations which involved communication with strangers.

• http://www.castelmerle.com/

However, recent discoveries in Africa have rekindled the debate about when modern symbolic behaviour began. At the cave site of Grotte des Pigeons in Morocco beads made from Nassarius shells have been found with traces of red ochre and microscopic wear patterns which suggest they were hung from cords. The shells had been transported 40 kilometres from the coast and were

KEY STUDY *cont.*

Beads

used around 80,000 BP. Very similar shell beads were found in Blombos Cave, South Africa dating to around 75,000 BP. Dr Marian Vanhaeren examined archive collections at the Natural History Museum and found examples of Nassarius beads from Skhul Cave in Israel which could be securely dated to around 100,000 BP. These suggest that symbolic behaviour originated much earlier, possibly soon after modern humans first appeared. Vanhaeren has pointed out that the range of early beads is much narrower than those from upper palaeolithic Europe and may have had a more restricted range of functions. She argues that their use may have been in gift exchanges between groups to establish reciprocity networks.

Figure 9.44 *Beads and identity*

Beads are frequently found in modern human burials. These examples are from a beaker period burial from Wiltshire and a Mesolithic burial from Vedbaek. In both cases the beads are fashioned from unusual – perhaps wild – materials including boars' teeth and amber. The beads themselves are therefore expressing an aspect of the deceased's identity.

THE REPLACEMENT MODEL AND NOAH'S ARK THEORY

This theory suggests that modern humans originated from a single small population in Africa. mDNA studies also predict that all modern people share their mDNA with one woman, the so-called African 'Eve' who lived c.200,000 years ago. After evolving in Africa the Noah's Ark theory championed by Chris Stringer and others, sees a complete and comparatively rapid replacement of earlier species throughout the world by fully modern people. This may have been through competition for resources, genetic assimilation through inter-breeding or annihilation through conflict or the spreading of new and deadly diseases. They extended their range into the arctic zone and into the Americas (from 15,000 BP) and Australia. The Oceania evidence is particularly contradictory. The recent date for 'Mungo Man' puts the colonisation of Australia around 78,000 BP but DNA research suggests Homo sapiens had only got as far as India by 65,000 BP.

A recent entrant to the debate is the diminutive hominin from Flores in Indonesia dating from 18,000 BP. The jury is out on whether this was a Homo sapiens suffering from dwarfism or a separate species. Bednarik claims that these islands were colonised as early as 850,000 BP and would have involved a sea crossing. There is also some possible human evidence from Australia which has been dated to 115,000 BP. If correct this would be too early for Out of Africa and suggests Homo erectus developed sea-faring skills. The same may apply to evidence of early colonisation of Indonesian islands. As well as the differences in interpretation of and weight given to various categories of evidence (DNA or anatomy) there are some underlying political ideas involved. These relate to the way people would like to look at our modern population. Multi-regionalism has been portrayed as racist or nationalistic by its critics while Out of Africa II has been called overly religious (Genesis and Eve) or politically correct. Part of the problem in arriving at a conclusion is that no DNA research is accepted universally. The fossil evidence base remains small and every year new discoveries are hailed by either side as proof of one theory or the other. It also seems that the modern human evolutionary sequence and links with and between earlier humans appear to be more blurred than once was thought.

How early was the 'Creative Explosion'?

At some point after 50,000 BP there seems to have been a rapid blossoming in human culture. This involved a much greater variety in tools, including those carved from bone and antler. The development of art, music, symbolic behaviour and structured open-air settlements are all associated with the arrival of Homo sapiens in Europe. This has been ascribed to the way humans had to adapt in that Ice Age world. Some archaeologists put the date as late as 30–15,000 BP and the extraordinary cave paintings, portable art and blade technology of the last Ice Age. Caspari and Lee's investigations into comparative ages of death of humans revealed that at this time up to five times as many people were surviving into old age than previously. This may have given Homo sapiens an edge in terms of accumulated knowledge or the 'Grandmother Revolution' which may have freed up younger adults from childcare to specialise including manufacturing and exchange. This period is also associated with a rapid growth in population. Others see a more evolutionary path or in the case of Bednarik highlight evidence for the use of symbolism by earlier humans. He argues for the possibility that organic materials were a medium for expression and cites rare survivals such as the Schöningen spears and of probable wood-working in support. There is increasing evidence of personal ornamentation, art and possibly ritual from much earlier. There is evidence of red ochre use for decoration from 164,000 BP even a possible carved figure from Israel dated to 250,000 BP.

Part Three
Issues in World Archaeology

Chapter 10

Managing the Past

YOUR GOALS

You need to understand

■ the key threats to our archaeological heritage

■ the nature and effectiveness of current protection for archaeological remains

■ the roles of the key agencies involved in archaeology and managing heritage

■ the key debates about the preservation and ownership of archaeological remains.

THREATS TO ARCHAEOLOGICAL REMAINS

Natural processes (◄ Chapter 5) account for the decay of most archaeological remains once in the soil but the overwhelming threat to surviving monuments, from field systems to buildings, comes from human activity. More has been lost in the last few decades than in the rest of human history. As a result, most excavation since 1960 has been of sites just prior to destruction by development. The rapid growth of towns and road networks since 1945 combined with declining pasture land and more intensive forms of agriculture are largely responsible. Even seemingly minor changes can have significant impacts. For example in the aftermath of 'mad cow disease' many farmers in the upper Severn valley ploughed up old pasture to grow maize which is much more destructive.

Between the 1960s and 1980s most excavation was of sites about to be destroyed through development. Despite the efforts of some government agencies, many volunteer groups and the charity Rescue, only a small proportion were recorded. This was the key factor behind the introduction of the government policy and planning guide PPG 16 (► p. 347).

Development continues and debates about the destruction of archaeological remains are rarely out of the media for long. The battle to save the Thornborough Henge landscape and the ongoing debate about Stonehenge are frequently reported. Government plans to relax some planning restrictions on house building and new infrastructure projects such as roads and airports will all have a significant impact.

• http://www.savestonehenge.org.uk/

Roads

Development

Cultivation

Housing

Threats to Archaeology

Quarrying and mining

Visitor erosion

Weather

Forestry

Natural processes

Figure 10.1 *Examples of the threats to archaeological remains*

Some high profile sites are simply threatened by increasing public interest in our past. Hadrian's Wall and Avebury are two high profile sites that have suffered badly from erosion caused by walkers. As World Heritage Sites (▶ p. 352) detailed management plans have been drawn up to try and resolve the conflict between access and preservation.

Naturally public attention focuses on threats to famous monuments and exciting discoveries. However, a massive amount of our visible archaeological heritage continues to disappear with little protest. A glance at aerial photographs from the 1940s will reveal how many hedges, water meadows and medieval field systems have vanished. To landscape archaeologists they provide key evidence about landownership,

settlement and use of the environment. Medieval field systems also provided a protective blanket over earlier sites that would otherwise have been eroded.

Nor is the problem limited to human agency. Climate change appears to be having a growing impact. Examples include erosion due to both rising sea level and the drying out of wetlands while human responses such as building new flood defences also threaten archaeological remains. Upstanding earthworks can be devastated by burrowing animals such as rabbits. English Heritage currently has a research project looking at ways to prevent badgers, whose numbers are increasing with our warmer climate, destroying round barrows through tunnelling.

Figure 10.2 *Natural destruction of a Bawdsey pillbox*

The Defence of Britain project tried to record our fast-disappearing legacy of wartime structures. In the case of this pill box at Bawdsey that recording came just in time. Sea erosion of East Anglian cliffs is rapidly demolishing coastal defences. Since this picture was taken several monuments have disappeared into the sea.

Global threats to archaeology

The pace of development across the world means thousands of archaeological sites are lost each year. Few countries have the resources to record what is lost. For many, archaeology comes an understandable second to feeding and housing their people. In extreme cases, monuments are sometimes deliberately destroyed for political reasons, as has happened recently in Bosnia and Afghanistan. A growing global problem is the looting of archaeological sites to feed the demand of western collectors for artefacts and artwork. Britain has its problems with 'nighthawks' (▶ p. 359) but looting in much of the world is on an industrial scale. At ancient temples in Meso-America and Cambodia power saws have been used to remove statues and reliefs which are then trucked over the border for export. In Iraq museums were looted following the Second Gulf War and many ancient sites have been devastated by robbing excavations. In the west, the blame is often placed with corrupt local officials and the army for colluding or even controlling the trade. However, UNESCO has highlighted the one-way traffic in artefacts from poorer countries to the art auction houses in the west and Japan which dispose of stolen antiquities.

On a much lower scale sites throughout the world are routinely looted for coins, pottery and other portable artefacts by local people. They supplement low incomes by selling to tourists and dealers. Other tourists join commercial metal detecting tours to help themselves to artefacts.

KEY STUDY

The Monuments at Risk Survey of England (MARS), 1998

Bournemouth University and The Royal Commission on the Historic Monuments of England (RCHME) combined to survey the condition of a 5 per cent random sample of England's 937,484 recorded archaeological sites. The study, which was funded and published by English Heritage, provided a census of the nature, distribution and state of England's archaeological resources. The study started by examining archive records, such as RAF aerial photographs, of the state of monuments in 1940 and then surveying to measure damage since then. Their key measures were loss of horizontal area and loss of height.

The study discovered that the South-east had lost the highest proportions of monuments with best survival in the West Midlands. Standing buildings and field systems are most at risk while those protected by legislation are at least risk. In total, 95 per cent of monuments had suffered some damage. Since 1945 23,500 monuments have been completely destroyed, an average of one site a day. Over 2 per cent of recorded sites have been lost since the survey. MARS drew on existing records plus its own surveys but inevitably will have missed many buried sites. Therefore the numbers of all sites destroyed and at risk will be higher. The table below summarises the key causes of destruction.

Cause of destruction	Wholesale	Piecemeal
New building and urban growth	27	9
Building repairs, alterations, demolition	20	19
Mineral extraction	12	3
Cultivation	10	30
Road building	9	4
Natural processes, visitors, vandalism	5	24
Unknown	17	11

Figure 10.3 *Key causes of destruction to archaeological remains from the MARS Report.*

• http://www.csweb.bournemouth.ac.uk//consci/text_mars/marsint.htm

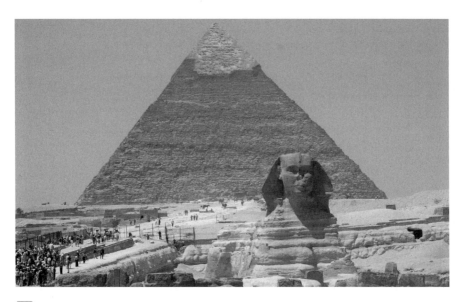

Figure 10.4 *Climatic damage to the Sphinx*

The Sphinx and many other ancient Egyptian monuments are threatened because irrigation schemes to allow all-year farming are contributing to rising water tables in Egypt. Water and the mineral salts it carries weaken the soft sandstone foundations and walls causing them to crumble.

THE PROTECTION OF ARCHAEOLOGICAL REMAINS

By the time this book is published, the shape of protective legislation in England, Wales and Northern Ireland will have changed. During 2008 a series of related Bills will come before Parliament. These include a Heritage Protection Bill, a Marine Bill and a new Planning Act. The resulting legislation will replace the 1979 Act and much of the planning guidance including PPG16. The key aims are to speed up and simplify the heritage planning system and provide better protection for archaeological remains. However the proposed changes build on and extend existing practice rather than making a complete break with the past.

Scheduled monuments

Legal protection for archaeological remains in Britain has never been comprehensive and is also fragmented between different types of remains and the various parts of the United Kingdom. What follows here applies to England although similar measures exist in other parts of the UK. The cornerstone of legal protection for nearly 30 years has been the **Ancient Monuments and Archaeological Areas Act 1979 (AMAA)**. This required owners of scheduled ancient monuments to seek the *consent* of the Secretary of State responsible for Heritage before they could make changes to sites. Fines and other penalties could be imposed for damaging scheduled (listed) monuments. It subsequently gave English Heritage the task of recording, assessing and monitoring monuments. EH could also recommend other endangered sites and the land around them for scheduling to the Secretary of State if they were deemed to be of national importance. Under the Monument Protection Programme the number of scheduled sites has risen to over 25,000 although this is still less

Figure 10.5 *Altar Q at the Mayan city of Copan showing the baton of power being passed between a whole dynasty of sixteen kings. Each is represented symbolically by a sacrificed jaguar underneath the altar. On this panel the baton is passing from from the founder Yax K'uk Mo to the last king Yax Pasajh. Despite World Heritage Site status, Copan like many similar monuments, is regularly threatened by looting. Gangs of well-organised (and sometimes armed) looters have removed stone reliefs and statues, sometimes with power-saws. Much of this material is bought by wealthy 'art collectors' in the west*

than 2 per cent of all the known sites in the country.

AMAA did provide legal protection to some visible monuments after years of destruction. It also established the use of mapping as a tool to protect sites. Developers were 'warned off' sites where their plans might be slowed down or halted. Increasingly, landowners have signed management or 'stewardship' agreements to protect sites in return for funding. However, it also had serious limitations. Sites which were discovered during development were not protected. Nor were those in areas where permission for gravel extraction had already been given. Landscapes and most marine sites were not covered and ploughing was allowed to continue on sites where it was already taking place as long as the depth of ploughing was not increased.

An example is the Roman town of Verulamium. One of the most visible failings of the Act was the way it only protected the upstanding (earth-work) element of monuments. The mounds of many long barrows survive as islands in ploughed fields while their ditches, pits and post holes are still being destroyed. Enforcement was variable. Landowners could plead ignorance as a defence for damaging sites. The cost of protection fell on local or national government for whom it was never a top priority.

Other protective legislation for sites

Laws to protect particular environments or to regulate planning have also benefited archaeology including providing some protection for unscheduled sites including archaeological

KEY TASK

Assessing local monuments

Either of these tasks would make a good personal study project or group task.

- Visit a sample of local monuments to record their condition and threats to them. Compare your findings to the MARS study.
- Investigate the impact of PPG 16 in your area. This could involve interviews with some of those involved and examination of the role of local organisations such as units, SMR, etc.

You may be able to obtain a list from your local SMR.

landscapes. The designation of some areas as national parks, 'Areas of Outstanding Natural Beauty' or Sites of Special Scientific Interest (SSSI) has been primarily to conserve landscapes or habitats but also served to protect archaeological remains better than undesignated areas. Similarly, measures to encourage landowners to manage their land for the benefit of nature or tourism through tax breaks or stewardship schemes have also brought some measure of protection. There have also been attempts to list important sites as a first step towards conservation, for example the Battlefields Register. However, none of these provide secure protection and none ensures funding for archaeological work.

PROTECTION THROUGH THE PLANNING PROCESS: PPG16

The **Town and Country Planning Act 1971** *allowed* local authorities to take archaeology into account when considering planning applications

and *required* them to produce structure plans for future development. Further legislation in 1990 created conservation areas. This did not guarantee that archaeology would be preserved or even recorded. However, a 1990 government guidance note to local authorities called Planning and Policy Guide note number 16 (PPG16) had a much more significant impact. Although PPG16 is not law, planners need to have good reasons for not following its advice when they consider applications to develop land. It advises planners to consider archaeology at an early stage of the development process and to favour the preservation of archaeological remains where possible. PPG16 advises that the developer should be responsible for funding any archaeological work deemed necessary. It also provides guidance on appeals that can be made to the Secretary of State. Another guidance note, PPG15 (1994), deals with changes to buildings of historic interest.

The effects of PPG16

PPG16 has had an enormous impact on archaeology in England although there is considerable debate amongst archaeologists about its positive and negative effects. Its underlying philosophy is that the past is a finite resource, which requires management and conservation. Preservation *'in situ'* therefore is preferable to excavation. Where excavation is deemed necessary then archaeology is 'preserved by record'. In order to consider archaeology when planning applications are lodged, most local authorities documented and mapped known archaeological sites in their Sites and Monuments Records (SMRs). A key principle was that where excavation was required by the planning authorities then the developers had to pay. For the first time this provided an alternative to public or charitable funds for excavation. Essentially this was a tax on development.

PPG16 broadly divided archaeologists into two groups, as follows.

Curators

Local authority (LA) archaeologists advise planners on the archaeological sensitivity of proposed development sites. Following a desktop survey which draws on information held by their SMR they draw up the brief for any archaeological work needed and check that it is done to required standards. Most of the finds from development work are usually deposited with the LA museum service.

Contractors

Developers put out a contract for exploratory work or excavation to competitive tender. They may also hire archaeological consultants to contest the local authority positions. Independent archaeological trusts or commercial 'units' do most of this work. LA units or amateur groups carry out some work in a few areas but this is becoming increasingly rare.

The language of PPG16

PPG16 has generated a new range of terminology which needs to be understood in order to follow archaeologists' discussions:

Deskbased assessment: The initial stage of assessing the risk to archaeology involves checks with the SMR and other archives. It may also involve a very brief look at the site.

Field evaluation: Where deskbased assessment suggests a potential risk there would be a survey of the site, which usually includes trial trenching to establish the depth, nature and condition of remains. The sample size is usually 2 per cent.

Following assessment, the planning authority, advised by LA archaeologists decides whether remains are of sufficient national importance to warrant preservation or whether a *mitigation* strategy will suffice. They then draw up a brief for the developer's archaeological contractor. This includes any post-excavation requirements.

Preservation in situ: Excavation is destructive so PPG16 advises that archaeological remains should be left where they are (*in situ*) if possible.

This can mean resting buildings on piles driven through deposits. This method is controversial. In Norway, piling, which damages and interferes with the drainage and stratigraphy of sites, is viewed as destruction rather than preservation. An alternative is to lay a 'raft' of concrete over remains and then build on that. Some archaeologists have questioned the extent of preservation of this nature. Development can alter the water table and chemical composition of the soil. It is difficult to see how the long term effects can be monitored and even if they can, what could be done to 'rescue' a site 'preserved' under a housing estate.

Mitigation strategies can range from full excavation to a *watching brief* with the objective being '*preservation by record*'. A *watching brief* is literally that. An archaeologist will watch as the machines go in to see if any archaeological remains are unearthed and to report on them.

PPG16 did provide much needed funding for rescue excavation. While developers have to meet archaeological costs it has not prevented development. Very few planning applications are refused on archaeological grounds and 'preservation by record' is the outcome of most positive assessments. There are at least three times as many excavations annually as there were before 1990 and around 90 per cent of all archaeological work comes through the planning process. One unforeseen benefit is the greater range of sites and periods than earlier research-driven excavation which tended to have a monument-bias. For example more early medieval and neolithic sites, which would not have been easily detected from the air or surface survey, have been discovered. Partly this is because development is occurring in areas which had not been intensively explored including brown-field sites in towns, the Thames Valley and major infrastructure projects such as Heathrow Terminal 5 and the Channel Tunnel Rail Link.

PPG16 has also had some negative impact. Initially the commercially inexperienced

CONTRACTORS

CURATORS

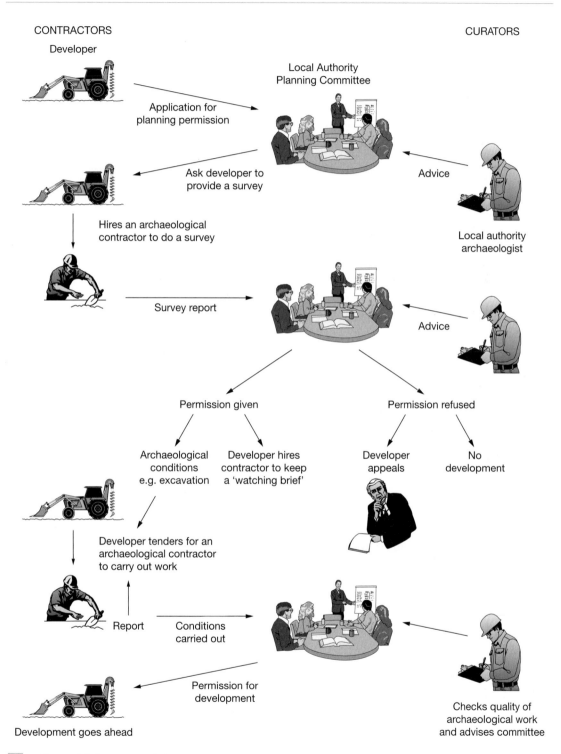

Figure 10.6 Simplified diagram to show how archaeology is involved in the planning process

Figure 10.7 *PPG16 in action*

Deposits from the area around the Forum in Cirencester lie around a metre under the surface. Rather than excavate a large area of Roman Britain's second city planners preferred a mitigation strategy. Test pits and a minor excavation down to the top of the Roman road in the foreground established the depth of deposits. In the picture these are being covered in a concrete raft before houses are built on top. Depending on your viewpoint, this is a wasted opportunity or precious remains preserved in situ for a future generation.

archaeological units tended to bid too low for contracts during the early 1990s. This meant that many struggled to pay their staff well while the cycles of the building industry also affected the amount of work there was for diggers. As a result there is a high turnover of field archaeologists. Some local authorities have used PPG16 as a way of reducing spending on archaeology. LA archaeologists often spend most of their time on planning matters. At the same time, the 'professionalisation' of field archaeology has limited opportunities for amateur enthusiasts to become involved. Similarly, the costs of post-excavation work, including the use of specialists and storage of remains, was often under-estimated. As a result, this work may have suffered and some museums are now 'full'.

There have been arguments about the quality of contract archaeology but that is a charge that has been levelled at archaeology of any type or period. If there are shortfalls then the planners do have the power to address it. Perhaps a more relevant criticism is the limitations of the system. Pressure from developers on contractors may limit the use of the most expensive dating and analytical techniques. Some researchers claim that 5 per cent trenching would provide a more indicative sample of archaeological remains than the recommended (and cheaper) 2 per cent. Perhaps the most persistent criticism has been the fragmentation of archaeological knowledge. Completed excavation reports belong to the developers. They do not have to publish them. As a result it can take a while for reports to get

KEY STUDY

The North Sea: a new frontier in Heritage Management

It might seem unlikely that Palaeolithic and Mesolithic archaeology survives under the North Sea. The destructive power of that sea is visible in England's crumbling eastern coastline. However, Danish archaeologists have demonstrated that extensive survival of sites and organic artefacts is possible in the right situations. They also pioneered the use of seismic mapping and core-sampling of the seabed to reconstruct past landscapes and identify sites. A number of studies of finds from the North Sea bed – including material recovered during oil prospection – suggested that stratified remains might still exist in areas which had been rapidly flooded by rising sea levels but were sheltered from high-energy water movements. These potential deposits are now threatened by the development including off-shore wind farms and gravel extraction. Gravel is needed for the building industry but mineral companies are finding it harder to get licences for new gravel pits on land. Much of the North Sea bed is covered in gravel washed down by glacial rivers during the Ice Ages.

In 2002 English Heritage commissioned projects funded by the Aggregates Levy Sustainability Fund (essentially a tax on gravel extraction) to research, map and assess the state of preserved landscapes in coastal waters and under the North Sea. They hope to identify both ancient terrestrial sites and potentially up to 500,000 more-recent shipwrecks. Key sites will then be scheduled to protect them.

A range of methods are used including records from oil-exploration companies. High resolution bathymetry uses lasers to record and provide images of seabed topography. 3D seismic research records sound waves 'bouncing' back off the seabed from low frequency pulses generated by airguns. This reveals the geological nature of the seabed. Coring and grab sampling provide data on sediments including environmental remains.

Figure 10.8
The destructive power of the North Sea

KEY STUDY *cont.*

The North Sea: a new frontier in Heritage Management

Some of the most spectacular results have come from the area known as Doggerland between the east coast of England and Holland. Before this was finally flooded in 5,500 BC this had been dry land. Researchers at Birmingham University have mapped and produced images of the old land surface and reconstructed vegetation and fauna. Most people think of this simply as a 'bridge' over which Mesolithic settlers walked to Britain. However the great plain of Doggerland with its broad river valleys and low ranges of hills (today's Dogger Bank) was inhabited. Some writers have suggested that this area with slowly rising sea levels bringing marine food would have been a more attractive area for forager settlement than thickly forested parts of the mainland. Professor Gaffney, the project leader, has called it "the best preserved prehistoric landscape in Europe if not the world". At the same time, researchers from Wessex Archaeology have explored the seabed of the English Channel. This has included tracing the valley of the river Arun under the sea and the discovery of several Mesolithic settlements.

Figure 10.9 *Doggerland*

• Star Carr

into the public domain and the amount of detail can vary. Work in a given geographical area is often undertaken by a range of units which means that it is difficult to obtain an overall picture of local archaeology.

International protection

Increasingly decisions taken at the UN or EU are likely to impact on archaeology in Britain. The United Nations Educational, Scientific and Cultural Organization (UNESCO) has drawn up a World Heritage (WH) list of over 850 sites of outstanding international value. These range from the Pyramids to the City of Venice. Most governments including the UK have signed up to protect these sites. In itself this provides some protection since it would be embarrassing for a government if a WH site was damaged. The scheme also enables funds to be channelled to conservation and restoration projects on endangered sites in poorer countries. However, designation does not guarantee preservation and only covers a fraction of sites worldwide. It does guarantee increased tourism which presents both

Figure 10.10 *Developer-led archaeology. A major excavation in Cheltenham by Cotswold Archaeology. This was the result of a contract tendered by the developers as part of planning permission for a new superstore. The small team of professional archaeologists dressed in safety gear, worked to tight deadlines through the winter. This is the face of most modern archaeology*

an opportunity to raise funds but also an additional problem to be managed. The UK currently has 24 WH sites including Neolithic Orkney, industrial Blaenavon and the City of Bath.

The Valetta Convention (1992)

This European Charter for the Protection and Management of the Archaeological Heritage came into force in March 2001. It is based on the principle that heritage throughout Europe is threatened by development and needs to be protected. It requires governments to protect monuments and regulate archaeology to ensure the proper conservation of excavated sites and the recording and safe-keeping of finds. It also covers the use of metal detectors, the trade in artefacts and the need to raise public awareness of and access to archaeological heritage. Although much of it is similar to existing UK measures (particularly the emphasis on preservation '*in situ*'), Article 3, which called for all work to be authorised and carried out by suitably qualified people, caused considerable debate. This was because of fears that it could be used to limit the involvement of amateurs in archaeology.

Heritage Protection Reform

Three Bills which should be passed by summer 2008 will shape the protection of archaeological remains for the next decade. The **Heritage Protection Bill** will enhance the role of English Heritage as the key conservation agency. EH took over responsibility for administering listed sites in 2005 and this role will be extended to listing both buildings and monuments in a single combined Register. This will also cover shipwrecks, historic landscapes and battlefields. These will be termed 'Designated buildings and sites'. English Heritage will consult owners before listing and there will be a right of appeal, but interim scheduling will also be used to prevent destruction while debate continues. More protection will be provided for World Heritage Sites. Current levels of protection will be extended to sites on agricultural land, under the sea and early human sites where there are no visible structures. The **Marine Bill** will provide further protection for maritime archaeology. For terrestrial sites, the setting and context of the visible site also can be protected.

Planning consent for development and management agreements for existing sites will be simplified. Local Authorities will administer the planning process and with EH will extend 'Heritage Partnership Agreements' to a greater range of sites. These enable work to take place without repeatedly seeking consent once management of a site or complex of sites has been agreed. In parallel, a new **Planning Act** will put the proposals in the 2007 White Paper **'Planning for a Sustainable Future'** into law. One of its main objectives is to streamline the planning process to reduce bureaucracy, delay and confusion. The second is to locate planning decisions at the 'right' level. This means that decisions about nationally important infrastructure projects will be taken at national level.

Some archaeological groups have already expressed concern at the lack of new resources to enable proper policing of an increasing number of listed sites and those under the sea or the plough. It remains to be seen whether legislation addresses this. A much broader range of environmental groups have formed the **Planning Disaster Coalition** to oppose the Planning Act because they fear it will favour large scale development and remove the right of local people to influence major projects.

The latest developments in these debates can be tracked at

• http://www.heritagelink.org.uk/

Protection of artefacts

Legal protection of artefacts focuses on those few examples of high monetary value. The old laws on treasure trove in England and Wales were replaced by the **Treasure Act** (1996). It defines objects and coins as treasure which are over 300 years old and either over 10 per cent precious metal or at least ten in number. In 2003 'treasure' was extended to cover all prehistoric metal finds. Items substantially composed of precious metal and less than 300 years old are treasure if it can be shown that they were deposited with the intention of recovering them. Finds of treasure have to be reported to a Coroner within 14 days and become the property of the Crown. Rewards are generally paid to the finder or landowner. Apart from general legislation on theft and trespass, the law neglects other materials (for

example pottery) which may be of greater archaeological value. This means that assemblages that include treasure can be broken up.

To improve the recording of artefacts which fell outside the scope of the Treasure Act the **Portable Antiquities Scheme** was introduced in 1997. The Government and the Heritage Lottery Fund financed pilot schemes to encourage the recording of all archaeological objects found by members of the public at any site. The scheme extends to all of England and Wales. 'Finds Liaison Officers' provide advice on finds and run 'finds roadshows'. They provide a link between the public, metal detector users and archaeologists and museums. The scheme has been very successful with over 300,000 objects reported by 2007 including an increasing amount of 'treasure'. A considerable number of new sites have been located as a result of this work. Accurate recording enables details to be added to an online database.

• www.finds.org.uk/

There is considerable support amongst archaeologists for the United Nations sponsored **UNIDROIT Convention on Stolen or Illegally Exported Cultural Objects**. This requires the return of stolen or illegally excavated artefacts to their owners and provides a way of checking the provenance of imported objects. It also sets out a minimum standard for the art trade. It would not affect existing collections. The UK has not yet signed up to this convention but may do so in the near future. In the meantime the Portable Antiquities Scheme has reached voluntary agreements with some organisations, notably eBay, to ban the illegal sale of treasure through their service.

WHO ARE THE ARCHAEOLOGISTS?

Within archaeology in the UK there is increasing debate about who should engage in practical archaeology. Archaeology's roots lie with the work of enthusiastic amateurs but it has become

KEY SITE

Stonehenge

Britain's most famous archaeological site presents a whole series of problems in balancing access against protection. A landmark for centuries, its visibility on Salisbury Plain ensured it attracted a road junction. It now exists in a traffic island, cut off from its landscape and surrounded by tourist facilities which make few concessions to the nature of the site. Recently the government has accepted that Stonehenge is a national disgrace and in breach of World Heritage conventions and have pushed through plans to redevelop the site. One of the roads will be grassed over and another will run through a tunnel. Visitor facilities will be moved over a mile away, out of sight of the monument. There is much support for reuniting Stonehenge with the ritual landscape of which it is an integral part. Visitors will be able to follow the avenue to the stones, which is probably the route taken in the Bronze Age. However, consensus ends there. There is much opposition amongst archaeologists to the tunnel because it will cut through archaeological deposits and the entrances are near other monuments. Others are unhappy about the 'land trains' which

Figure 10.11 *The point where the avenue reaches the stone circle. Two fences and a busy road block the Bronze Age entrance and cut across the monument.*

Figure 10.12 *World class visitor facilities are promised*

Figure 10.13 *The view of Stonehenge from the cursus round barrows*

KEY STUDY *cont.*

Stonehenge

will be used to bring 150 visitors per trip to the site. These pictures illustrate other problems. Look at English Heritage's vision for the site and make up your own mind. You may like to compare with Newgrange (◀ p. 159) and consider the case for 'reconstruction'. Sadly and perhaps predictably, the mismanagement of Stonehenge is set to continue. After much delay, the tunnel option was dropped on grounds of cost in December 2007 although solving the problem of the A303 remains a government 'priority'. You can follow what happens next at

• www.thestonehengeproject.org/

Figure 10.14 *This is how you currently enter this world heritage site*

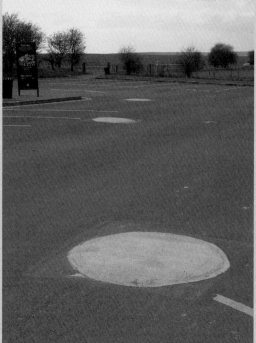

Figure 10.15 *Not the most imaginative interpretation of the three huge Mesolithic postholes close to Stonehenge. These may have made the location important long before Stonehenge was built*

increasingly professionalised. Excavation began with the antiquarians from the seventeenth century onwards. Archaeology provided a hobby for landed enthusiasts right up to the 1950s. Some early diggers were little more than grave robbers. However in the twentieth century a new breed of more informed and influential practitioners, such as Sir Mortimer Wheeler, pioneered modern excavation techniques.

Learned and excavation societies

By 1900 most parts of the country had societies devoted to gathering archaeological information and communicating it to their members and to the wider public. Most undertook excavations and began journals, many of which continue to this day. Some established museums where their collections could be displayed. This too was largely an upper-class activity, undertaken by those who could afford the time to take part in research excavations. The societies did, however, include more of the public by the 1950s. One of their strengths was their focus on particular localities so that expertise in identifying artefacts, especially lithics and ceramics, was developed. Some of these groups such as the Prehistoric Society continue to be leaders in funding and publishing research archaeology.

The rescue era

The massive urban expansion and road building programmes of the 1960s and 1970s saw a rapid rise in rescue archaeology.

The term was coined in the 1960s when so much development was occurring that the earlier pattern of amateur and university summer excavations could not cope with the volume of archaeological sites being threatened and destroyed. Rescue, a charitable trust, dramatised the threat to Britain's archaeology by using as

Figure 10.16 *How it used to be: amateur involvement in archaeology. The Empingham excavation (◀ p. 50) involved a small number of professionals working alongside volunteers. Since the 1970s, amateurs have been gradually squeezed out of much excavation work by professionalisation and the terms of developer contracts*

its logo an image of Stonehenge being scooped up in a giant earth-moving machine's bucket. While that icon itself was never really endangered, it drew attention to the scale and pace of development and the way valuable evidence was being lost unless it could be excavated and recorded. Excavation teams were needed all year round.

• http//www.rescue-archaeology.freeserve.co.uk/

Teams of volunteers or low paid diggers sought to record what they could before machines or ploughs destroyed remains. Some teams were centrally based within government agencies including universities and local authorities while others were formed locally to combat specific threats. Often these groups comprised a mix of professionals and amateurs. The M5 Rescue Committee is a good example of a group founded with a clear but essentially time-constrained focus. From these late 1960s/early 1970s teams most of today's archaeological **units** have developed.

Rescue Archaeology coincided with a rapid expansion of adult and higher education provision including the development of new archaeological departments in universities. These two developments provided many opportunities for the public to get involved in archaeology and to follow that interest academically. However, excavation was poorly resourced. Rescue teams would identify potential threats to archaeological sites from planned developments such as road building, gravel extraction or pipelines, and submit bids for public funding to excavate before development began. However, much of the funding still came from charitable efforts. As a result it was difficult to find full-time paid work in archaeology. In the 1980s some funding did come through government job creation schemes at a time of high unemployment but pay remained very low. Despite all this a pool of skilled excavators did develop amongst diggers who moved from site to site.

Archaeology today

Since 1990 planning authorities, guided by PPG16, have required developers to prepare impact assessments and may also demand a formal site evaluation. Depending on the findings there may be excavation in advance of development and/or a watching brief during construction. On the principle of 'the polluter pays' the cost is passed on to developers. Developers were expected to hire qualified workers and commercial standards of health and safety were to be applied. Commercial units of professional archaeologists developed in response. Unit archaeologists had to compete for business to survive. This left little time for the traditional professional role of supervising and training volunteers. Opportunities for amateur involvement in digging began to decline as a result. At the same time archaeology became more specialised. The application of scientific techniques for prospecting, recording and analysing was in most cases beyond the resources of rescue committees and enthusiastic amateurs. An emerging trend is for some commercial companies to offer a full range of environmental consultative and fieldwork services to developers including archaeology.

• http://www.edp-uk.co.uk/

Most excavations now fall into the following four categories:

- Assessments and rescue excavations in advance of developments. These are largely carried out by professional archaeologists in the contracting units. Over 90 per cent of excavation falls into this category.
- Seasonal research excavations run by universities. These are largely open to their own students although some take paying volunteers as training excavations.
- Occasional research excavation by specialists from government heritage agencies.
- Research excavations by local societies or amateur enthusiasts.

A frequent comment on the dominance of developer-led archaeology is in relation to research. Unlike the other three categories, sites are not selected primarily to ask a question and in some cases the results are not always fully published or easily available. In addition, the fragmentation of records makes it difficult for researchers to piece together information from large numbers of 'keyhole' excavations in particular areas. Nevertheless many of the leading commercial units are involved in research, often in conjunction with universities and English Heritage. Some of the larger ones such as the Oxford Unit and Wessex Archaeology are able to support sizeable post-excavation sections. It is increasingly common for major research projects to involve them in partnership with Universities and Government Departments, for example the Shotton Project which is bringing together information on palaeolithic sites across the Midlands. In addition many developer-financed excavations can and are linked to wider research agendas. A groundbreaking attempt to synthesize the results of both research and developer led work was Richard Bradley's three year study of findings from rescue excavations leading to the publication of a new overview of later prehistory in the British Isles. In it he highlights the ways new discoveries from commercial archaeology have led him to revise his perspective on this period in the past.

Amateur archaeology is still thriving in pockets throughout the UK although it is not as widespread as it once was. It does have the advantage of being able to look at local sites and questions without the pressure to complete work quickly. The excavators are also often able to become experts in the particular periods they investigate for their area. The Council for Independent Archaeology offers support for amateurs and has pioneered the development of affordable geophysics equipment for amateurs. The journal *Current Archaeology* often covers amateur projects and provides a critique of 'official archaeology'. Undoubtedly amateurs have been squeezed out

of practical field archaeology in many areas although many museums rely on them for finds and cataloguing work.

- http://www.archaeology.co.uk/cia/default.htm
- http://www.archaeology.co.uk/gateway/thinktank/who/welcome.htm

Metal detecting

The gradual exclusion of amateurs from field archaeology has coincided with an increase in metal detecting. Some professionals remain hostile to all detectorists because of damage that has been done to sites or looting by organised gangs of 'nighthawks'.

However, most detectorists are not intentionally destructive or members of criminal gangs but simply people interested in the physical past. Increasingly there have been moves by county archaeologists to work with detectorists. The Portable Antiquities Scheme has provided funding for liaison and recording work. The success of the scheme testifies to the desire of many metal-detectorists to contribute to archaeological understanding.

- http://www.britarch.ac.uk/detecting/index.html
- http://www.ukdetectornet.co.uk/

CULTURAL RESOURCE MANAGEMENT

This US phrase can be used to describe the role of what are sometimes called curatorial services or Heritage Management in the UK. It encompasses those employed directly or indirectly by Government and whose role involves protecting, administering and managing archaeological sites, landscapes and collections on behalf of the public.

The best known examples are local SMRs and museum services and national agencies such as CADW and English Heritage. Most of those working for such agencies will not be directly involved in either excavation or post-excavation

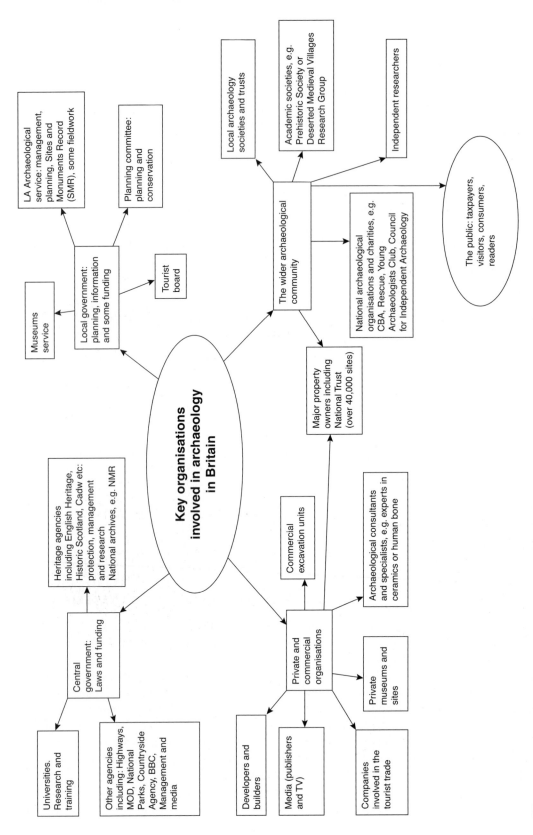

Figure 10.17 *Key organisations involved in British Archaeology*

The popular view of archaeologists is that they spend their time digging. While many do, there are at least an equal number who do not. For those of you who are considering archaeology-related careers, this chart may provide helpful in identifying opportunities.

KEY SITE

Castell Henllys

This small Iron Age hill fort in south-west Wales provides an example of a long-term research excavation. It was bought in 1980 by the co-founder of the London Dungeon, who worked to develop it as a tourist attraction with reconstructed Iron Age houses. Subsequently it has been taken over by the Pembrokeshire Coast National Park, which has established a visitors' centre on the site.

It was necessary to excavate the site and recover the evidence on which to base the reconstructions. Students and paying volunteers have helped in the excavations each summer. Over twenty seasons, archaeologists have studied the defensive circuit, the complex phases of the gateway, and almost the whole of the interior of the fort. Reconstructions of four major roundhouses and smaller constructions have been completed.

This research has provided a much fuller understanding of the archaeology of this period and provided a link via its marketing style between archaeologists and the general public.

• *Current Archaeology* 161

• http://www.castelhenllys.com/

Figure 10.18 *An area excavation to reveal the 'chevaux de frise' an Iron Age 'tank trap' protecting the entrance to Castell Henllys, West Wales. Compare with the interpretation*

Figure 10.19 *The excavator's interpretation of the 'tank traps' at the Iron Age settlement at Castell Henllys.*

research; their primary function is to manage what has already been recorded. Increasingly their archaeological remit is linked with management of other aspects of culture or the environment.

SPECIALISTS AND SCIENTISTS

There is a long tradition in archaeology of specialising in one aspect such as ceramics, animal bones or environmental evidence. The structure of archaeological reports reflects this with different specialists each writing a chapter on their findings. Usually specialists work with excavated material sent from digs all over the country although the larger units will have some in-house specialists. For lab-based scientific analysis university departments and a small number of national or commercial companies are used. Many of those working in these areas will not be archaeologists but increasingly are at the forefront of archaeological research. For example the Europe-wide study into the spread of dairying is largely being carried out by biochemists.

Campaign and lobby groups

A range of independent organisations, charities and learned bodies such as the Council for British Archaeology (CBA) and RESCUE provide information and campaign on behalf of archaeology. This includes lobbying politicians, using the media and providing advice for developers and farmers. There is also the Institute of Field Archaeologists which promotes (but cannot enforce) high standards amongst those engaging in excavations. It acts as a professional body for a core part of the sector.

Presenting the Past

WHICH PAST?

Before considering how archaeological remains and knowledge might be best communicated we should reflect on what the social and cultural implications of explanations about the past might be. Archaeological knowledge and the images of the past created by archaeologists are not value free. As with history and literature, the selection of what is significant and how it should be interpreted partly derives from the political and social values and structures in present-day society. Archaeology and history have both been used either consciously or unconsciously to justify particular values and social structures.

The political use of archaeology

Extreme cases are fairly easy to identify. A succession of rulers have sought to justify their regimes and their territorial ambitions by claiming precedent from the past. Archaeology was used for propaganda purposes by the Nazis. During the 1930s and 1940s it was commonplace for archaeologists to associate pottery styles with distinctive ethnic groups and to identify racial differences from skeletal remains. The Nazis used this confusion of race with ethnicity to draw up racial maps of Europe and identify 'superior' races. Their excavations 'revealed' artefacts of Germanic origin in occupied Poland including bowls marked with swastikas. Overlooking the fact that the swastika is an ancient Indian symbol, archaeologists gave these forgeries a scientific stamp of approval. They helped justify Nazi conquests as retaking land which had always been German. Mussolini, the Fascist dictator of Italy (1922–45), claimed to be following in the footsteps of the Romans with his plans for an

Figure 11.1 *Saddam and his use of archaeological heritage*

From the 1980s Saddam Hussein in Iraq drew parallels between his regime and the Assyrian Empire, which dominated the region in the first millennium BC. His regime drew prestige from association with that once mighty empire which originated in the area where Saddam's tribe lived.

Italian empire in Africa and to turn the Mediterranean into an Italian lake. Israel, Bosnia and the Indian city of Ayodhya are three of many places where archaeology has recently been involved in violent political conflicts. In each case the ability to control what is known about the past is used as a tool to legitimise political, social or economic power.

It is not just dictatorships or extremist political parties which have used archaeology for political ends. In Britain current political priorities influence the nature of public archaeology. Promotion of 'community engagement' and of 'diversity' are two of the key issues which organisations currently need to address when bidding for public funds. While it seems only right that public archaeology should try and involve the public when spending public money there is always a danger that priorities or interpretations may be too closely tailored to fit the current views of those controlling the purse-strings. Definitions of heritage and therefore what should be preserved and presented are never value-free.

Disputes over the ownership of cultural remains are usually political. Sometimes claims for the restoration of artefacts is an element in nation building or simply nationalism. The debate is not simply about stolen materials as in many cases artefacts had been legitimately bought in the past. Those resisting the return of materials ask whether current states are the heirs to past cultures in the same region. The quality of conservation and whether materials will remain accessible have also been raised. A new way of looking at this has been to consider whether some materials should be considered world cultural heritage – for all people – rather than for a particular nation.

Archaeology and land rights

In South Africa during the colonial period, a myth was created by Dutch settlers that they had occupied an empty land. Archaeological finds proved that to be false. In Australia, aboriginal groups have been able to use archaeological evidence to prove that their ancestors inhabited particular regions and to demonstrate their right to the land or to compensation for its use by others. In Israel archaeology is always politically charged as it is seen as key to legitimising rival claims of Palestinians and Jews.

Increasingly, native peoples in many parts of the world are using archaeology to reclaim rights lost in previous centuries. According to historical records, the Pequot Indian tribe of Connecticut died out following a war with European settlers in the seventeenth century. However, archaeologists working with descendants of the Pequots were able to establish cultural continuity between the original tribe and survivors of the war whose descendents continued to live on reservations in the area until recent times. The Pequots were able to use archaeological data to gain recognition as a sovereign nation from the US government in 1987. A treaty was signed and some of their land was returned to them.

In some cases disputes involve claims for the return of cultural artefacts taken from them by foreign museums or art collectors. Increasingly there are also disputes over the disturbance of burials by archaeologists and for the return of human remains to their place of origin for burial. Usually at the heart of these conflicts are two fundamental issues:

■ Should (usually western) archaeologists have the right to excavate cultural remains of another culture or are their actions simply a continuation of colonialist exploitation?
■ Do excavated remains from the past provide evidence which can be used to sustain claims on the rightful ownership of land?

Archaeology and identity

In Britain, there are also political struggles about rights and identity which involve archaeology and assumption drawn from it. In Wales, the selection of sites for preservation and particularly for promotion has generated debate about which version of the past should predominate: the past of English conquest and castle building or the tradition of Welsh independence and resistance. More generally, the way archaeologists have interpreted the past can lead to certain values and arrangements being seen as unchanging and therefore 'normal'.

Until the late twentieth century, many archaeologists associated particular artefacts with homogenous ethnic groups and attributed social changes to the arrivals of new peoples, for example 'the beaker people'. This fitted the assumptions of many classically educated people that social and technological developments had originated in the Mediterranean and then were spread by colonists into the barbarian lands further north. It also fitted the way in which Europeans viewed their empires in the rest of the world and to some extent justified their role in spreading 'civilisation' to inferior 'races'. Recent advances in archaeology and genetics have undermined the idea that pure ethnic groups existed in the past, while radiocarbon dating has shown that indigenous Neolithic and Bronze Age peoples had achieved a great deal well before the arrival of Mediterranean influences. The building of Stonehenge and the brochs of Scotland and the Northern Isles (◀ p. 229) are two cases where the achievements of indigenous populations are now recognised.

In a similar way, early archaeologists often identified burials of male and female on the basis of their assumptions about gender roles. For example, a skeleton buried with an axe *must* have been male because men fight and chop down trees. A burial with a mirror or domestic artefacts *must* be female. (◀ p. 310) This kind of analysis has, in turn, tended to reinforce

KEY STUDIES

Kennewick Man

Perhaps the most famous example of a conflict between indigenous peoples and archaeologists has been in the USA. By the 1990s the civil rights movement for Native Americans had won a series of legal and political victories. One of these addressed what Native Americans considered to be the 'vulture culture' of archaeologists who had desecrated burial sites to recover artefacts for analysis and display in collections. To some, archaeology was simply grave robbing by an occupying power. The 1990 Native American Graves Protection and Repatriation Act (NAGPRA) provided for the return to tribes of the skeletons and religious artefacts of their ancestors. Since then over 100 collections have returned remains. This has created problems for archaeologists who want to study the prehistory of the continent. The discovery of human remains at Kennewick on the Columbia River in Washington State in 1996 has re-ignited the conflict.

Originally examined as a potential murder case, the burial of 'Kennewick Man' dated to around 9300 BP; thus the remains were some of the oldest and most complete found in North America. There were significant anatomical differences between the Kennewick skeleton and

Figure 11.2 *The Museum of the American Indian*

This stunning museum close to the Capitol in Washington is representative of a shift in public policy in the late twentieth century USA. The Museum presents the Native American story from their perspective and combines archaeology, historical artefacts and oral history. This particular display stresses the Native American role in managing the environment, another topical political concern. The state of the art displays include video, motion sensor-activated displays as well as dioramas and more traditional displays. Downstairs you can eat Native American food.

modern Native Americans. Early suggestions were that he appeared to have originated in Europe or more likely, Japan or Polynesia. This contradicted the dominant explanation for the origins of human populations in the Americas. This is that the 'Clovis' people (named from a type of spear-point) crossed the frozen Bering Straits from Siberia after 11,500 BP and spread throughout both continents. Two later waves of migrants were the ancestors of most North American peoples. Why Kennewick was so explosive is because the claim to land ownership by native Americans has rested on their identification with cultural remains and burials found there. In addition the oral histories of many tribes say that they have lived on their traditional lands since the start of time. Fears were expressed that if Native Americans were simply seen as one of a number of immigrant groups then their claims to land rights would be undermined.

The Umatilla, Yakama, Nez Perce and Colville tribes who inhabit the Columbia Valley demanded that the remains should be repatriated to them for burial under NAGPRA. Attempts to perform

KEY STUDIES *cont.*

Kennewick Man

rituals near the bones led to claims that their DNA was deliberately being contaminated. The US Army then dumped rubble over the find-site but were unable to prevent the dispute spreading. It quickly went to court and reached the US Senate where debate continues. Scientists formed the organisation Friends of America's Past to lobby for the right to carry out research and finally in 2004 a Federal Court allowed them to do this. However challenges continued including a halting of DNA research because it destroys bone and would therefore be desecration. Meanwhile a proposed (2007) amendment to NAGPRA backed by Native American groups will give officially recognised tribes the right to claim ancient remains even if there is no tie to their group. Some scientists claim that this will be a heritage disaster. Although the debate is now polarised, opinions do cover a wider spectrum. There are Native Americans who welcome some research and there are also major differences about appropriate disposal rites since burial was never a universal custom.

Meanwhile the Clovis model continues to be undermined. Remains from Monte Verde in Chile at 13,000 BP are too early to be Clovis while date ranges for stone tools found at Topper in South Carolina have been estimated to between 16 and 50,000 BP. DNA research on American and Asian populations suggests a more complicated process than the Clovis model and perhaps starting as early as 15,000 BP.

Figure 11.3 *Stone and obsidian points*

Typologies of lithic projectile points have been the key element in tracing the populating of North America. The Clovis point, which has some similarities with Solutrean points in Europe has been a key element. The version of events constructed on such evidence is now threatened by DNA analysis and dates for recently discovered sites.

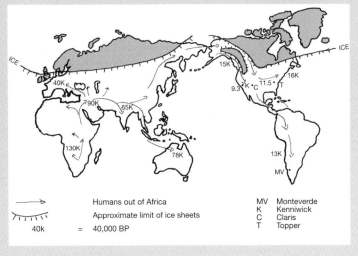

Figure 11.4 *The spread of modern humans out of Africa*

stereotypes about natural roles for men and women. Once again, recent discoveries such as the Pazyryk 'Ice Maiden' and DNA analysis have tended to challenge the traditional view (◄ p. 308). Some museums have begun to re-label displays where the earlier sexing of skeletal remains is in doubt.

New Age and pagan beliefs and the issue of access to ancient monuments

Most books on Stonehenge feature a picture of the Druids, a nineteenth-century order who developed their own ceremonies at the monument based on their interpretation of Iron Age beliefs. Since the 1960s many other groups have also sought to use ancient monuments for rituals and festivals. Pagans have claimed the sites as sacred according to their beliefs and want the right to worship there. For others their demands to hold festivals at the sites symbolise a struggle against an oppressive state. Either way, these demands have led to conflict with those responsible for managing the monuments and archaeologists concerned about damage to remains. In the case of the West Kennet Long Barrow this includes sarsen stone being damaged by candles. In the case of Stonehenge disputes over access have led to public order offences and occasionally violence. More recently the authorities have realised that those wanting to celebrate at the sites do not usually want to see them damaged. This has lead to more inclusive management

Figure 11.5 *The Elgin Marbles*

Perhaps the most famous dispute between nations over archaeology is that of the Elgin Marbles. Bought by Lord Elgin from Ottoman Turks who ruled Greece at that time, the sculptures were brought to London and are in the British Museum. The Greek government wants them back to put in a new Parthenon Museum. Should they stay or should they go?

Figure 11.6 *'Charlie'*

The exhibit at Avebury of the skeleton of a child known as 'Charlie' which was excavated by Keiller from Windmill Hill has attracted controversy in recent years. Some archaeologists believe that it is wrong to exhibit human remains to the public. This is either due to wanting to treat remains with more respect or the idea that exhibiting it is in some way sensationalist. The Council of British Druids, a modern group which seeks to rekindle the pre-Christian nature-based religion of the British Isles have also called for the re-burial of the child's skeleton.

Figure 11.7 *A pagan summer solstice at Avebury. This circular gathering at dawn includes both Druids and followers of Wicca*

KEY STUDY

The Corinium Museum Cirencester

There has been a revolution in museum design over the last few decades. The Corinium has had a complete makeover courtesy of the National Lottery and exhibits many state of the art features. Families and primary school children are the target audience and little previous knowledge is assumed. Heavy use is made of recreations to explain burials, buildings and technology including hands-on replica clothing and artefacts. Interactive displays allow exhibits and the museum's catalogue to be interrogated at several levels. A particularly innovative feature uses video, sound and lighting in conjunction with tombstones to 'bring the people to life'.

Developments in IT and communications technology have offered archaeologists the opportunities to transform the way they communicate. As a result, the range of methods and modes of communicating archaeological information is rapidly expanding and there is considerable diversity in the way they are used.

Rather than cover all periods, the Corinium has chosen to major in Roman Corinium with a minor in Anglo-Saxon Lechlade (◀ p. 317). This specialisation is a growing feature of British museums.

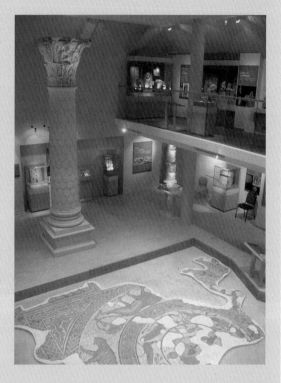

Figure 11.8 State of the art displays at the Corinium Museum

In Figure 11.8 the Jupiter Column has been re-erected to give a sense of scale. In the foreground is one of the mosaics for which the town was famous and in the background a range of different types of display.

plans and more emphasis on education about potential threats to the monuments. Many New Age websites provide excellent visual records of sites.

• http://www.themodernantiquarian.com/home/

The common thread that runs through all of these disputes is control of the past. Those who control access to sites and artefacts are best placed to interpret the past for the wider public. It is their values which will be reflected in accounts of the past and their values which in turn are supported by those accounts.

KEY STUDIES

New modes of communication

A Time Team excavation on television

Some professionals despair at the idea of a three-day excavation against the clock but they are not the intended audience for this programme. Its main function is to provide entertainment to a general audience whilst educating them in some aspects of archaeological methods and inter-pretations. The format of a time-limited challenge to a group of personalities is well established through house and garden makeover shows. Technical language and ideas are communicated simply through computer-generated images while the routine or time-consuming aspects of excavation and post-excavation work are edited out in favour of action involving celebrity diggers. Its entertain-ment value is attested to by its high ratings. In addition, its website and publications provide opportunities for people to develop their understanding and explore links to educational sites. However, the programme may raise unrealistic expecta-tions about archaeology and the possibility of public involvement that may ultimately frustrate its audience.

* http:///www.channel4.com/ nextstep/timeteam/

Figure 11.9 *Tony Robinson of the Time Team*

His programmes have been outstandingly successful in raising public awareness of and interest in archaeology.

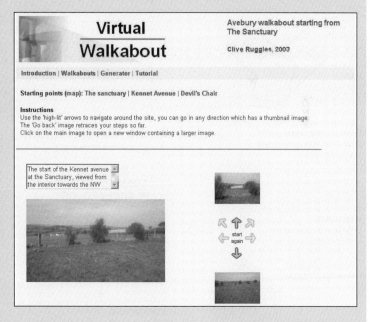

Figure 11.10 *A virtual site visit*

The growth of broadband and digital photography have enabled a range of new site presentations to be developed. One of the most exciting is the virtual tour which lets people explore sites remotely and study relationships between features. Increasingly such sites are interactive with 'visitors' able to decide the depth and level they want to investigate to. In this example created by Clive Ruggles you navigate around Avebury and see (on photos) the views you would actually see. The package from ADS (▶ p. 415) enables you to create your own walkabout – this is likely to become a popular coursework inclusion.

COMMUNICATING ARCHAEOLOGICAL KNOWLEDGE

Before 1990, most archaeological knowledge was communicated via lectures, museum galleries and the printed word. While these are familiar media, it is expensive to produce reports and books and there is often a considerable timelag before new ideas and discoveries are widely disseminated.

Increasing diversity reflects the differing audiences for archaeology and the way their requirements vary. Consider how your requirements of a site or museum might differ from those of a researcher or of a class of 5 year olds. As a result, what is a perfectly adequate mode of communication for one person may be inaccessible or too shallow for another. The contrast between a specialist pottery report and an episode of Time Team illustrates this point well.

This is because archaeological reports follow a scientific format. A series of experts present evidence as accurately and precisely as they can. There is often only limited interpretation and rarely speculation. Often only a few hundred are printed and increasingly they are owned by developers. This makes them inaccessible to a general readership. However, they are essential reading to others in the same field who rely on them to provide data for them to compare findings and detect patterns.

Cutting edge technology such as virtual reality displays and GIS systems (◀ p. 8) are still expensive but digital photography and basic websites are now accessible to most people. This

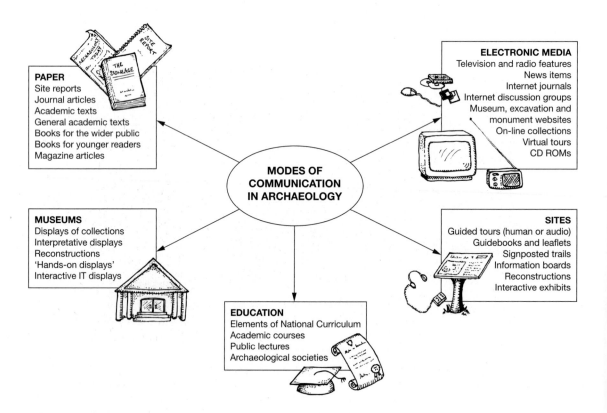

PAPER
Site reports
Journal articles
Academic texts
General academic texts
Books for the wider public
Books for younger readers
Magazine articles

ELECTRONIC MEDIA
Television and radio features
News items
Internet journals
Internet discussion groups
Museum, excavation and monument websites
On-line collections
Virtual tours
CD ROMs

MODES OF COMMUNICATION IN ARCHAEOLOGY

MUSEUMS
Displays of collections
Interpretative displays
Reconstructions
'Hands-on displays'
Interactive IT displays

SITES
Guided tours (human or audio)
Guidebooks and leaflets
Signposted trails
Information boards
Reconstructions
Interactive exhibits

EDUCATION
Elements of National Curriculum
Academic courses
Public lectures
Archaeological societies

Figure 11.11 *The communication of archaeological information*

has enabled a much wider range of people to produce and disseminate archaeological information. In the future 'electronic' site reports may enable people to interrogate data at very different levels.

• http://www.u.arizona.edu/%7Emlittler/

The time between recording and presenting to an audience is much reduced. Many excavations now offer daily diaries or webcams on their websites. The numbers visiting most site websites far exceed the numbers of site reports sold. Moreover, the audience is now global rather than largely national.

Hyperlinks embedded in text offer the chance to satisfy more than one audience at the same time. A basic account can be supplemented by detailed discussion in linked documents. Similarly, this can be built into maps and site plans (point and click options) as at Kilmartin.

• http://www.kilmartin.org/

Not only do digital images readily offer high quality colour photographs where their use was previously rationed, but they can also go beyond the limitations of two-dimensional illustration on A3 paper. Maps and plans can be presented at a larger scale and three-dimensional modelling is possible.

The online journal *Internet Archaeology* is exploring the wider potential of the internet for academic archaeological publishing.

• http://intarch.ac.uk/

Finally you can discuss ideas and seek help from fellow archaeologists through discussion groups such as the CBA's lists for archaeologists and teachers.

• http://www.jiscmail.ac.uk/lists/britarch.html

Figure 11.12 *Reconstructed tomb at Carrowmore*

Reconstruction is always controversial as we have seen at Knossos and Newgrange. At Carrowmore the central tomb 'Listoghil' was fully excavated recently. Instead of restoring it as a cairn it was decided to leave the table-like tomb exposed so that visitors could see it. Mesh boxes held the stones of the cairn back. It has been widely criticised on aesthetic, religious and archaeological grounds but it is accessible.

KEY STUDY

The 'reconstructed' Anglo-Saxon village of West Stow

West Stow in Suffolk uses a variety of different means to present an excavated and recorded site to the public.

Excavation of this site revealed traces of a number of features including rectangular sunken featured buildings (SFBs), still commonly called grubenhauser. The materials used had not survived in the sandy local soil but postholes, pits and beam slots were preserved, as were a range of inorganic artefacts and animal bones. The site report catalogues and interprets the finds for the archaeological profession. It also discusses the problem of interpreting the above ground structure of the buildings.

Rectangular pits with domestic rubbish are common on early Anglo-Saxon sites. These grubenhauser had previously been interpreted as pit dwellings. In part this reflected the view amongst classically influenced archaeologists that their inhabitants really were barbaric. With increasing knowledge of Anglo-Saxon carpentry and construction techniques, experimental archaeology has developed alternative models.

Figure 11.13 *An excavated grubenhaus at Lechlade (◀ p. 317)*

At West Stow several versions were constructed over the excavated features. It is now thought likely that grubenhauser had suspended floors with the rubbish entering the pit after the building's abandonment.

There is also a debate about the internal decoration and use of buildings. The site, which includes a display centre through which visitors enter a recreation of the settlement, addresses these issues and the problem of multiple audiences in a number of ways.

- Several different versions of the buildings were built on the sites of the originals so that visitors could enter each and judge them against the plans in guidebooks and the visitors centre.
- Artefacts are displayed in the visitors centre with pictures and reconstructions alongside to show how they were used.
- Activity areas allow visitors to see how artefacts might have been made.
- Demonstrations by experts in fields such as green woodworking are available to those interested.
- Video presentations show how Anglo-Saxons lived.
- Publications are available at a variety of levels ranging from infant school to professional.

KEY STUDY *cont.*

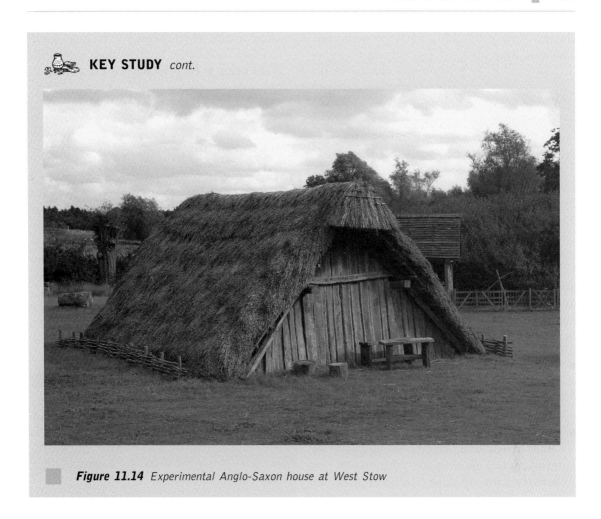

Figure 11.14 *Experimental Anglo-Saxon house at West Stow*

An extensive list of suggested websites to follow up many of the issues and sites in this book are on the companion website.

Problems with using the internet for research

There are, of course, some drawbacks to the new technology. The sheer volume of material available means that you have to be selective but it is often difficult to immediately see what might be relevant. A particular problem for students is that referencing conventions are not applied to the same degree as in printed material. It is often hard to tell what is opinion, fantasy or based on evidence. Often there is no way of checking. If you cite internet sources in essays at undergraduate level, be sure to appraise them thoroughly. A further problem is plagiarism. It is easy to cut and paste someone else's work into your own. Resist this temptation. If you are caught, the penalties can be severe.

Applying communication issues on your course

By now you will appreciate how hard it is to successfully communicate in ways that reach all possible audiences. Some sources will have clearly targeted particular audiences. Others, such as sites or museums, will probably have changed their methods to reach wider audiences. This may have involved diversifying the types of presentation or a wholesale change in the way collections or a site are displayed. If you wished to follow up this topic as a major project on a particular site you should be able to find one of their staff who can explain their thinking on this.

A second approach is for you to consider how to present a site which may currently be inaccessible, or has little existing display material. This might typically include sites under excavation or a site that has no upstanding features. In these cases you need to not only draw on your knowledge of different types of communication and their suitability for particular audiences but understand some of the other issues facing museum and site management staff. These include:

- *funding*: the latest high-tech displays might be nice but how realistic is a budget to provide, maintain and secure them? What could be done on a lower budget?
- *impact*: modern interactive displays take up more room than traditional displays of exhibits. In a finite space, what would you remove from display? Visitor centres and display boards may be useful, but will they ruin the visual impact of a site?
- *accuracy*: reconstructions are popular with the public but may be misleading. It may be possible to reconstruct the wooden handle of an iron tool with a reasonable degree of accuracy but rebuilding a Neolithic structure

from a mass of postholes will be more problematic. Is it better to show how something was used, even if it may be inaccurate, or provide the evidence and ask people (who are not specialists) to try to make up their own minds?

- http://www.archaeolink.co.uk/home.htm

The world heritage site at Lascaux provides a good example of what can be done with a large budget. The very presence of visitors in the caves was damaging the delicate Palaeolithic wall-paintings there. The response has been to close the cave but to construct a copy nearby for visitors whilst producing an interactive website to enable virtual exploration of the real thing.

- http://www.culture.gouv.fr/culture/arcnat/ lascaux/en/

▌ **Figure 11.15** *The Romans were small people*

In order to be commercially successful many ventures have to try and combine education and entertainment. At Archaeolink small children dig in a sandpit for artefacts while adults have a choice of excavated remains, reconstructions, workshops, books and New Age presentations. Those in between can dress up as Romans and throw javelins.

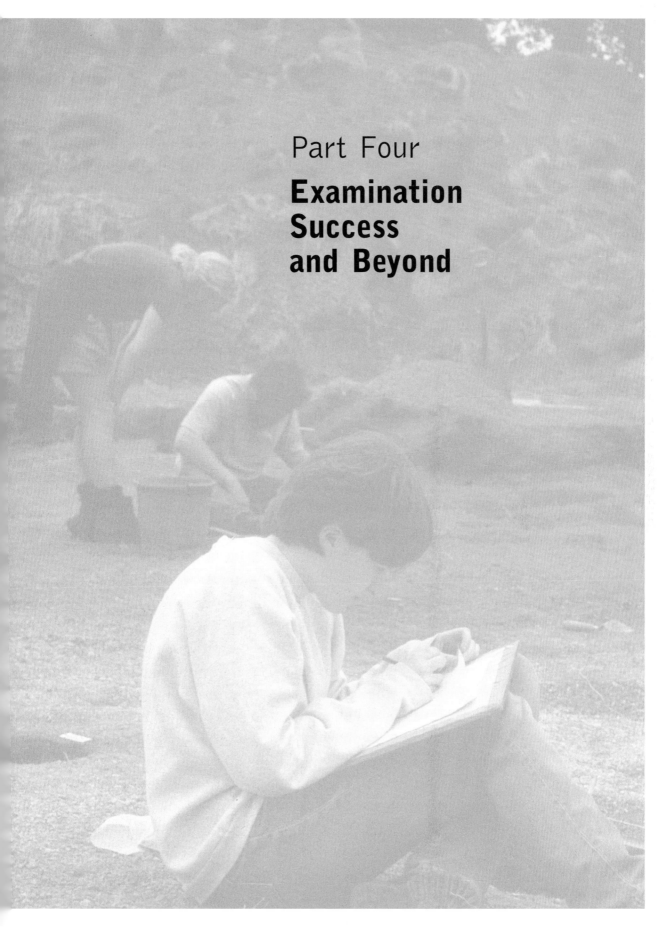

Part Four

Examination Success and Beyond

Studying for Success in Archaeology Exams

MAKING USEFUL AND WELL ORGANISED NOTES DURING YOUR COURSE FOR YOU TO REVISE FROM

Whether you are taking A Levels or are an archaeology undergraduate, the chances are that you will not have studied the subject before. In addition to developing generic academic skills such as locating and analysing sources, evaluating arguments and constructing arguments, you also have to understand archaeological terms, methods and case studies. In other words the content of this book and your course. Your first step should be to find out what you need to do to succeed on your course. All syllabuses list content in at least outline but how much detail and understanding will you need? Looking at past question papers and mark schemes often provide the best indicators. These are also of great use in determining **how** you should answer

questions. Most courses provide assessment objectives but often these are difficult to translate. It is usually easier to understand what a good answer looks like from a past example or mark-scheme. Most questions worth more than a couple of marks and essays are usually marked to 'levels of response' mark schemes where the levels are defined by set criteria. If there are five levels in a 25-mark essay you will not score high marks unless you write to suit the criteria for levels 4 and 5. Shorter structured questions are typical of schemes of assessment for AS level and larger structured questions and essays for A2 and degree level.

Successful note-taking

Right from the first day of your archaeology course you should be taking and filing notes on what you have learnt. You have probably already

You need to:	In order to:	Examples:	By:
Learn definitions	Understand questions and explanations	Mortuary, excarnation	Memorising and testing
Understand concepts	Understand explanations and argue	Characterisation, relative dating	Using them and testing
Understand processes	Assess the limits of evidence	Taphonomy, organic preservation	Using diagrams, explaining
Know case studies	Support your answers	Danebury, Sutton Hoo	Using mind maps, noting
Link methods, themes and examples	Maximise the use of your material	Boxgrove–usewear–hunting-tools	Practice
Apply understanding	Interpret sources	Aerial photos, plans	Practice

Figure 12.1 *What you have to learn to be successful*

developed your own style of note-taking but it is worth considering alternative forms of note-taking depending on what is required of you and the purpose of the information you are recording. For example, the type of information you need to record as the raw material for a major essay is likely to be very different from what is required to remind you of the meaning of a concept. It is as easy to accumulate too many notes as too few. The acid test is whether they are useful for their purpose. As Figure 12.2 makes clear, different styles of notes are appropriate to different situations.

Detailed written notes may be necessary when you are working from library texts on a major project. If you take notes from texts you always have access to, such as *The Archaeology Coursebook*, then you are wasting your time. What you want instead are brief notes which remind you of key points and direct you to places in your texts where the detail is. Try to experiment with a range of notes when preparing for discussion, revising and planning. Many people learn better from visual notes than they do from dense

written passages. You may be one of them. We have used these types of notes throughout the text. You can find examples on the following pages:

▶ Spider diagram p. 3
▶ Force field diagram p. 251
▶ Mind map p. 292
▶ Picture or concept notes p. 260
▶ Flow diagram p. 63
▶ Keyword notes p. 381
▶ Grids p. 383

When taking notes on methods bear in mind that the questions you will use them for will probably ask you to either select the most appropriate for a given situation or ask you to evaluate them. It is a good idea to structure such notes in a way which helps you to do this, for example geophysical techniques (◀ p. 15).

Similar grids could be used to bring together your understanding of types of dating or which analytical methods would be used on different materials or the most appropriate excavation

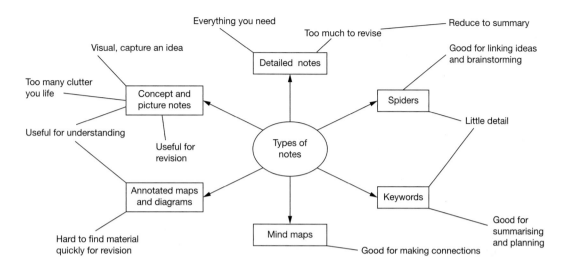

Figure 12.2 *The strengths and weaknesses of different types of notes. Always try to supplement the notes in this book from other texts and websites*

Method	Strengths	Limitations	Example
Resistivity			
Magnetometry			

Figure 12.3 *Comparing methods*

approach for particular situations. The following example of an AS level-type question illustrates the way you might apply these notes.

Examine the aerial photograph on p. 382.

1a Explain why these markings are showing up in the fields. (8 marks)
1b What would be the most appropriate non-invasive methods archaeologists could use to identify these features? (12 marks)

For many courses you will also need to know some case study examples of archaeological fieldwork. This can be approached as any other case study using written or visual notes. The key elements should include:

- Name of site
- Was this a research or rescue excavation?
- Who funded it and why?
- Prior knowledge of site and survey methods employed prior to excavation
- Style and strategy of excavation
- Key finds
- Post-excavation scientific activity
- Dating methods employed
- Value of this particular fieldwork

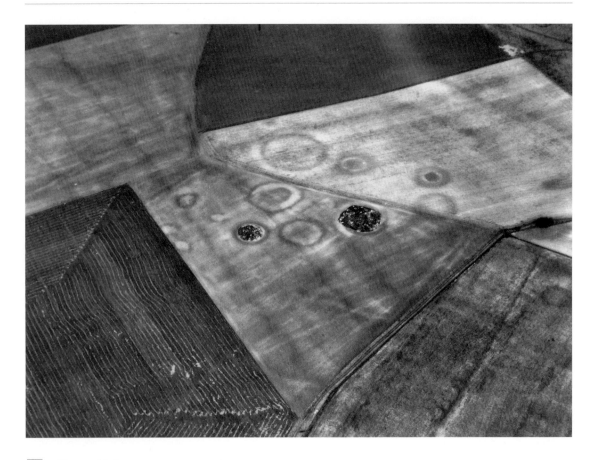

Figure 12.4 *Aerial photo of Wyke Down*

If you share your research with others who looked at different sites then you will have valuable comparative data to help you discuss key issues relating to current practice in archaeology. In addition to site reports, articles in Current Archaeology, British Archaeology or Rescue News could provide examples.

Visits to sites will also provide good opportunities for making brief notes that will help with your course. Their major value will be to help you understand artefacts and sites better but they can also help with issues related to management or presentation of the past. This is a focus of vocational GCSE history and a number of BTEC Nationals and could be the prelude to creating a presentation for visitors of a particular site.

Assessing particular modes of communication and display is usually done in relation to specific case studies, for example 'How might archaeologists best communicate the results of a particular excavation?' or 'How could a specific site be better presented to the public?'

In order to address these issues you should consider the following four As:

- *Audience*: who is it for and what might they hope to get from it?
- *Accessibility*: does its design and location enable it to reach its intended audience(s)?

■ *Adequacy*: is it useful for that audience?
■ *Alternatives*: would another mode of communication be more effective?

Start by considering the list of possible modes from Figure 7.6. Then select several examples such as a local museum display, a TV programme or a site report. Copy out the grid below on a large sheet of paper and complete it, using yourself as a student on your particular course as the intended audience. Pay particular attention to your reason for using the sources and why they were useful or not.

Now repeat the exercise for the same examples but considering a different audience. For example a tourist visiting the area or a primary school group. You should start to gain an awareness of the difficulties of meeting diverse needs within one mode of communication. You could rate the different sites you have visited on your course.

Getting useful case studies together

Whichever course you are on you will need some detailed case studies of particular sites or artefacts to discuss and to support your answers.

The key sites and key studies used throughout this book are case studies which indicate the amount of detail you might be expected to provide. To reach the higher levels in any mark scheme you must use case studies. They are usually the difference between getting grade D or grade B at A Level. You should build up a portfolio of case studies throughout your course, covering each of the major topics.

Finding case studies

Your teacher will provide you with a basic set of case studies but you should supplement this through your own research. Museums, television and archaeological magazines are all rich sources of case studies as well as the texts and websites we have listed. Select those which interest you and cover your course.

How to note case studies

Avoid copying down large chunks of information and keep in mind your purpose. You will find case studies as you research one piece of work, but need to consider what other questions you might be asked in the future which they could

Examples	Audience	Accessibility	Adequacy	Alternatives
	Research for my essays on . . .	Could you get in and understand it?	How did it meet your needs or was it of limited use to you?	What alternative mode might have worked better?
Local museum				
A local site				
Site report on X				
An academic text				
A website				
A guidebook				

Figure 12.5 *Assessing modes of communication using the four As*

also help with. It is sensible to adopt a thematic approach such as the way we have used icons in this text e.g. although the Stellmoor case study appears in the economics section it could equally be used under settlement as an example of a kill and butchery site. It could also be used in the debate about hunting and modern humans in the origins section of 'People and Society in the Past' There are many other ways to do this from simple highlighting keywords and concepts to elaborate cross-referenced, illustrated and colour-coded separate notes. Use which-ever system you find the most effective for retaining useable data. Experience has shown that the following work well:

- Condense the factual content to one third or less of the original, emphasising keywords and concepts. These will trigger recall of data in an examination situation.
- Extract phrases and quotations but keep them punchy and brief.
- Use illustrations and diagrams where possible. They can convey a concept more effectively than you could do with words.
- Use the 'list' or 'brainstorming' method to give consistency and information at a glance.
- Use highlighters sparingly in your own notes and never on the original!
- Use colour to code for methods and big themes. Limit yourself to six colours.

Managing case studies

As your folder grows it is easy to lose track of material. You should catalogue your studies by using a grid such as the one below. Enter the name of each site in the left-hand column and then indicate key aspects of the site which relate to the themes you are studying and which you may be examined upon. This grid is set up for A Level. It could serve as an index in your folder and help you to make links between themes.

Handling contradictory accounts

At A2 and undergraduate level you will increasingly encounter disagreements between different archaeologists. Your task now is to consider the merits of each argument in order to reach a conclusion. Most students find evaluation challenging and may find it more approachable by breaking down the key elements in each argument. A table is a simple way of structuring these sort of notes (Figure 12.7).

Having done this you may now be able to distinguish between the arguments. Are some of the points in them contradictory? Are some points unsupported or supported by evidence that you feel is unsound? Is the difference one of belief or opinion which you can only decide on a moral basis? You may find that the two archaeologists agree on certain aspects or that you think they are both sound in different ways.

Study	Methods	Material culture	Economics	Settlement	Society
Gudme	Typology	Metal working	Exchange Manufacturing	Trade Ritual site	Status Specialists
Boxgrove	Box grid Use wear	Lithics	Hunting	Kill site	Band

Figure 12.6 *Using case studies effectively*

List the key points they make	What evidence do they give to support this point?	Do you find the evidence acceptable?	Does this point support their overall argument

How strong do you think this argument is?

▌ **Figure 12.7** *Taking notes from contradictory sources*

This is the kind of information you will need to write down when you move on to discursive essays (▶ p. 388).

What you will probably find is that different archaeologists are

- using different data which will produce conflicting results
- disagreeing in their interpretation of what the archaeological record actually shows
- using different analogies to interpret data
- writing at different dates and there have been new developments in the intervening years.

Your task will be to explain the difference and then reach a conclusion about which of the explanations you consider most valid. For example, you could argue that some data is better than others for the particular question in hand or you could consult other sources to see which side they tend to support. Two classic examples of debates are:

- Binford vs. Freeman over whether there were elephant hunters at Torralba (Binford 1989)
- Cunliffe (1995) vs. Hill (1996) on whether Celtic chieftains ruled during the Iron Age in Britain

Where you are faced with lots of different views and competing evidence it can be difficult getting started with organising your work. This is a simple idea to get you moving and help you reach a judgement.

1 Draw a large pizza shape with a circle of 'topping' in the middle.
2 Take an issue you have been studying where there is considerable debate and at least five different theories. For example, 'What happened to towns in Britain in the fifth century?' or 'What sort of social change were the Anglo-Saxon invasions?'
3 Put each theory into one of the inner sections of the pizza.

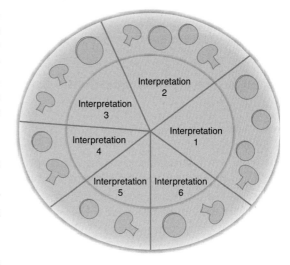

▌ **Figure 12.8** *An archaeological pizza diagram*

4 Research supporting evidence and enter it in the tomato or mushroom in the outer sections of the relevant slice.

5 Adjust the size of the slices so that the most convincing argument is the largest slice and so on.

6 If you have done this as a team exercise, each team has to argue for their version.

Command words

All questions have key words or phrases which tell you what examiners expect you to do. They will vary in their frequency at different levels of study. You need to know all those you may encounter and how to respond to them.

Understanding command words

All questions contain words or phrases which let you know what the examiner expects of you. It is important that you become familiar with the words and phrases used by archaeology examiners. The list in Figure 12.9 is roughly ranked in order of difficulty. Words in the top half of the list are usually used only for short or structured questions. Those in the lower half are used for essays. The marks allocated will provide you with further clues. For example, for two marks the examiners will want a couple of words or sentences, for ten marks at least a paragraph.

Tackling Interpretation questions

At AS and sometimes undergraduate level you may have questions which require you to interpret sources. In any event you will need this skill to understand archaeological reports. In almost every case you will be looking at tables, plans and illustrations to find patterns and trends. You should always start by noting these and any anomalies you can detect. In some cases sources will be selected for you because there are anomalies in them. When writing responses always cite figure numbers and use the scale,

key and orientation in your description. You may also have to criticise sources or a conclusion drawn from them. Think about the uses and limitations of different methods, the scope of the investigation and whether the methods were appropriate.

You will usually have several sources to work with at the same time. These will be drawn from archaeological plans, sections, illustrations, tables, maps, photographs and reports. Four common areas are outlined below. Two essential pieces of equipment (which you can also take into exams) are a ruler and a magnifying glass. Be sure to use them.

Interpreting plans

Begin with an accurate description of the relevant sites, features and artefacts in order to build up a picture of overall function or changes. Always refer to context numbers where they are given. You should consider:

- size and orientation
- spatial distribution of features
- phases of use: discuss any stratigraphic evidence for different periods of activity
- assess individual features to identify site function
- boundaries: are they defensive or just a demarcation line – a physical or a spiritual barrier?

Interpreting aerial photographs

Read all the questions concerned with these first. They will probably ask about method as well as interpretation and you need to match the right response to a question. For interpretation start by describing what you can see. Is it a cropmark, soil mark or shadows? What size and shape is it? Is it a boundary, structure or some other type of feature? How is it aligned?

Only when you have done this, suggest specific site or period. This way you will get some marks even where you get it wrong. Questions about methods usually require an account of

Command words	What they mean	Examples
List	Simply write down names or examples.	List three methods of dating.
Describe	Say what something looks like using scales	Describe the feature shown at A.
Define	Give a precise meaning. (An example helps too.)	Define taphonomy.
Illustrate	Provide examples to support a definition or point.	Illustrate your argument.
Explain	Show how something works or give reasons.	Explain how the source of artefact A could be identified.
Outline	Describe with reasons.	Outline how an archaeologist might survey the field at X.
Account for	Explain clearly with supporting reasons.	Account for the lack of surviving evidence of X.
Compare (or Compare and contrast)	Identify similarities and differences.	Compare the sections of pits 23 and 46.
Synthesise (or summarise)	Reorganise materials to create a new version.	Synthesise the data in tables A to D
Analyse	Break down into parts, find patterns and links. Order the factors identified.	Analyse the data provided in tables B and C.
Justify	Give reasons for and provide supporting examples.	Justify your selection of method in question 2a.
What can archaeologists learn from . . .	This is a list type essay but it is not just a list. You have to provide examples and assess	What can be learned about societies in the past from the way they disposed of their dead?
Assess (or discuss)	Identify strengths and weaknesses to reach a judgement.	■ Assess the reconstruction drawing in source A. ■ 'Nucleated villages were a medieval development from the eleventh century onwards.' Discuss.
Evaluate	Assess and reach judgements about the relative value of some items.	Evaluate the evidence for industrial use of the site in source C.
How far (or to what extent)	Present both views, assess and reach a judgement.	■ How far can archaeologists be sure about when hominids began hunting animals? ■ To what extent does archaeology support historial views of the Vikings?

Figure 12.9 *Understanding command words*

why features are visible and can be recorded and why they do not show up in all areas (◄ pp. 19–24).

Appraising methods

You need to understand the basic techniques for each type of material you are likely to be tested on, for example stone, pottery, metal, and what it can tell us. Ensure you know the main principles and some of their strengths and limitations. In the case of dating and reconnaissance methods it is sensible to test yourself on their application to different types of material and sites. In all cases, one good example is useful.

Interpreting organic remains

Questions will focus on what could be learned from the remains. You need to be familiar with common ways of presenting such data and what terms such as **MNI** mean. Always consider the sample size. Are there sufficient examples to say much at all? Also comment on their survival: why have they survived and how might they have been transformed by taphonomy (◄ p. 115)?

Examples of data sets and how to interpret them are on the companion website.

Starting to construct arguments

Putting together arguments is a key element in higher level essay writing. One way to approach this is to organise your notes into pro and con lists. Try this for the following question. It would work equally well as a small group task.

Outline the case for and against amateur involvement in excavation

Aim to write three sides of A4. You might like to consider the following points as starters.

- Most archaeologists start out as amateurs.
- Professionals are 'better' than amateurs.
- Can standards be ensured without professionalism?

Tip

Writing pro and con assignments usually leads to one of the following structures.

A
Introduction and outline of issue
Points and examples for
Points and examples against
Weighing up to reach a judgement
Conclusion

B
Introduction and outline of issue
Point by point for and against
Weighing up to reach a judgement
Conclusion

A is easier to write than *B*, but *B* ensures that you compare for and against on each point. *A* can become descriptive while with *B* you have to be analytical. Whichever you select, try to provide a range of points and support each with a specific example. If you only consider a few points it is difficult to reach the higher levels of mark schemes, however much detail you have included. It is also vital that you say at the end how far you agree with the arguments for and against. Don't worry about what you conclude as long as it is supported by the judgements you make in the body of the assignment.

Alternative assignments:

- Consider the arguments for and against metal detecting.
- Consider the strengths of research archaeology against developer-led archaeology.

The ability to reach supported conclusions is expected at A Level and above. Learning how to reach judgements takes time and requires confidence building. One way of doing this is through short exercises where you get used to quickly summing up strengths and weaknesses. A simple task is to take three or four methods and list their advantages and disadvantages for particular tasks or in general. If you present the information in graphical form you are more likely to remember it. Adapting the scales of justice is a popular version. Try this as preparation for the next piece of work you have on methods.

Developing extended arguments

When faced with an open-ended question it is useful to break it down into manageable chunks. A title such as 'How far is it possible for archaeologists to identify ritual for your period of study?' provides a good example. First, you might want to distinguish between periods that have written sources and those that do not, although it is a good idea to ask about the reliability of sources. For the rest, you could

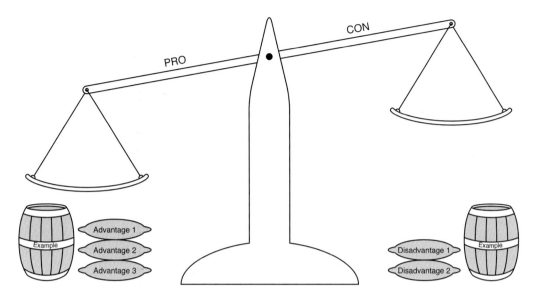

Figure 12.10 *A scales of justice diagram*

subdivide using sub-questions based on the '4 Ws':

■ *What*: can we identify the kind of ritual, which took place (for example, feasting, sacrifice)?
■ *Where*: can we identify places where ritual took place, how, what evidence and examples?
■ *Who*: can we identify who was involved (for example, individuals, groups of pilgrims)?
■ *Why*: can we identify the purpose of the ritual (ancestor worship, rite of passage, etc.)?

In each case you will come up with an answer somewhere between yes and no depending on the techniques used and the quality and survival of evidence. This provides you with a structure and, taken together, the basis of an argument about the extent to which it is possible to detect ritual.

In writing up each section you need to argue. If your tutor keeps writing 'assertion' on your work then you are not doing this. You must support each point you make with evidence from relevant studies. There are several models or gambits for integrating supporting material:

■ Using authorities to support statements: '. . . as Prior (1991) demonstrated at Flag Fen'.
■ Cross-referencing: 'The possibility of the Dorset Cursus being used to structure movement was enhanced by Green's (1990) discovery of avenues of postholes leading from it to later round barrows. Analysis of the Stonehenge landscape by Parker Pearson (1998) also suggested movement along the avenue between the zones of the living and the ancestors.'
■ Using evidence to choose between competing versions: 'Renfrew (1978) suggested that long barrows might have been territorial markers. Recent studies by Tilley (1998) and Barnett (1998) suggest otherwise. They found that . . .'
■ Juxtaposing evidence to assess it: 'Deposits of cattle bones and smashed pottery near many entrances may suggest feasting but similar evidence inside is more ambivalent.

Is it debris from feasting, gifts to the ancestors or the remnants of food the dead took with them?'

It is useful early on in your course to build up a vocabulary of *link words* and phrase such as 'however', 'for example', 'on the other hand'. These will prevent you from becoming repetitive and remind you to always back up your statements.

Finally you need to conclude. You should revisit the conclusions of each sub-question and see what the balance of your argument was. Use this to make a tentative judgement (try to avoid certainty) in response to the main question.

Writing essays

Today essays are generally marked according to 'levels-of-response mark schemes' (▶ p. 398). Generally, speaking, the first third of the levels are for descriptive accounts or essays that make assertions but provide no evidence. These are fails. The second third start to combine these two elements and are low to middling passes. For the upper third the same essential rules apply to essays in all subjects. Accurate statements and logical arguments which are well linked to the question and supported by relevant examples will score highly. It is more important in Archaeology than in subjects such as History to include detailed case study material at this level. The commonest reasons for underperformance are not supporting your statements and being irrelevant. To avoid this, most successful students plan their essays.

A plan can help you to:

- remain focused on what you need to do
- ensure you cover all key points
- prevent you wasting time on irrelevant points.

There are many different ways of planning. No one method is better than any others. During your course you should experiment with different methods and choose the one which suits you. The three most common models are:

A bullet point lists
B structured or tree diagrams (▶ p. 392)
C brainstorms, mindmaps and spider diagrams (◀ p. 381)

Often people will start with C to identify possible material and connections and then use A or B for finer planning. If you think of your essay as a body then the plan should enable you to reconstruct that body from its constituent parts:

Skeleton
Basic structure
Order of points
Levels of importance

Muscles
Paragraph content
Major ideas
Links backward and forward

Flesh
Depth and detail
Content from case studies
Theoretical concepts

Having planned what you need to include, you then need to choose a logical and appropriate structure. You should respond to the command words (◀ p. 387) in the title to identify the type of essay you are being asked to write. The most common are:

- List-type essays ask you to focus on a process or methods. For example, '**What can** archaeologists learn from human soft tissue remains?' You need to detail a range of techniques with examples and try to assess their relative value.
- Evaluative essays (▶ p. 392), ask you to weigh up how far something can be supported by

evidence. For example, '**How far** is it possible to identify settlement in the Mesolithic?' This is the most common kind.

- Comparative essays usually ask you to explore a theme in relation to two or more major case studies. You need to select examples that you know in depth which give you scope to discuss similarity and difference.
- Discursive essays (▶ p. 392) ask you to explore all sides of an issue and reach a conclusion. They are often posed as a quotation followed by the instruction 'Discuss'. For example, 'Aerial photography has contributed more to our knowledge of Iron Age settlement patterns than excavation. **Discuss.**' You can respond to these with an argument but you do need to consider other interpretations as well as your own.

While these require different structures in the body of the essay, they have common features, which you could use as a checklist.

1 Introduction

- Define terms mentioned in the title.
- Outline types of sources to be used.
- Make a statement about the issue in the question, even if it is pointing out that there are several dimensions to it.

2 Main body of the text

- Generalised answers are not appropriate and will not score high marks in essay questions. You must root your response firmly in archaeological contexts, selecting specific data and explaining how it is relevant to the original question.
- Link your answer to relevant theory.
- Do not be afraid to use anthropological or geographical terms and concepts where appropriate, for example Christaller, kinship, reciprocity.
- Explain conflicting or opposing theories which account for the same phenomenon where appropriate.

- Select the relevant parts of some of the bank of case studies you have at your disposal.
- It is usually better to use fewer case studies in depth than to attempt a broader approach, which runs the risk of being superficial.
- Length matters – it is difficult for your ideas to develop sufficiently or for the examiner to be able to reward you fully if your essays are very brief. You should aim for at least three sides of A4 for a formal essay.

3 Conclusion

- Don't just repeat what you have already said.
- Sum up your main arguments.
- Express a view where appropriate.
- Answer each part of the question. It is acceptable to give different responses to different aspects of a question. Most conclusions will be a variation of 'to some extent'.

A) Example using a list-type essay

'How can archaeologists differentiate between attached and independent craftsmen?'

Introduction Define attached and independent craftsmen (◀ p. 283) and provide an example for each. Hint at the range of possible evidence and techniques. If you are going to limit yourself to 2 or 3 case studies then say so.

Body Text each point could be a paragraph.

- What kind of societies and economies are associated with each type.
- The emergence of specialists – Upton Lovell
- Patronage and kinship at Copan (◀ p. 284)
- Palace workshops at Knossos
- Craft areas in towns – Jorvik
- Shipwrights and social change
- Metalworkers and the Gundestrup Cauldron.
- Other sources including art.

Conclusion: Focus on qualifying judgements:

- Is one sort easier to spot than another
- Does it depend on society, materials used
- Is some evidence more reliable than others

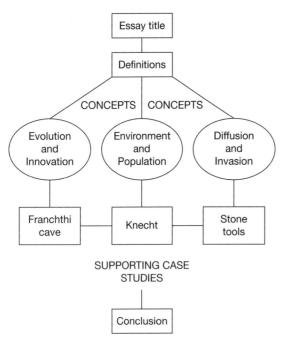

Figure 12.11 *B) Example using a tree diagram for the question 'How does material culture change over time?'*

Writing evaluative essays on concepts

These are often the types of essay which students find hardest. Questions on this theme often take the form 'To what extent can archaeologists recognise X?' X could be status, gender, chiefdoms or war. Whichever it is, you need to deploy several relevant case studies to explore the concept and its archaeological visibility. The nature of the topic means you need to be very aware of bias in interpretation and of the strengths and weaknesses of models, particularly ethnographic ones, which archaeologists have employed. You need to be comfortable with the terminology and to construct a coherent argument.

The following exercise includes examples from different periods. Try producing your own version, using examples from your studies.

Q: To what extent can archaeologists recognise territoriality?

1 Discuss what territory is. Is it the same as site catchment or the hunting ranges of Mesolithic foragers?

2 Discuss the modern idea of territory, as static and rooted in ideas of the sovereignty of nation states. It is marked by physical borders, coinage distribution, flags and other symbols.

3 Discuss some possible archaeological examples of territory:

- *Bronze Age:* land divisions on Dartmoor or Fengate – territories, or ranches?
- *Iron Age:* distribution of hill forts, coin distribution, Roman accounts of tribal areas
- *Roman period:* coinage, public buildings, Hadrian's Wall (a border?)
- *Medieval period:* boundaries (for example Wansdyke), coinage, charters, siting of castles

4 Discussion: does territory mean the same thing in all periods? Is it a dynamic or static concept? What types of evidence are the most/least persuasive? What are their strengths and limitations?

5 Conclusion: which of your examples provides the strongest evidence and why? Is this because there is more likely to have been territory in those examples or is it to do with survival of evidence? Use these points to explicitly address the 'how far' element in the question.

Referencing

For undergraduate essays, adhering to referencing conventions is mandatory. On other courses it is good practice to reference properly with longer written assignments and is usually required for major projects at A Level and BTEC. Details on how to reference are given on ▶ p. 422. In exams you are not expected to remember this level of detail. Where you have used an idea or major case study, try and mention the name of the archaeologist. That is the approach we have taken with this text although we have listed the main sources in a bibliography at the end.

Improving your essays

Some people seem naturally very good at essays, others struggle. Everyone can improve.

A comment frequently seen on student reports and returned work is 'your style could be improved'. It is often difficult to work out what this means and harder still to do something in response. Sometimes the comment actually refers to structure and sometimes to written English. Generally speaking it is about how you knit the essay together. Here are three mechanical things you can do to help yourself in your next piece of work:

1   **Use words and phrases which lead you to consider several pieces of evidence and reach judgements**

    Include all of the following at least once:

    for example   however   therefore
    an alternative   potentially   extent
    on the other hand   nevertheless

2   **Gobbets and gambits**
    One way of looking at your notes is that they represent lots of chunks of knowledge. These are your gobbets. In responding to a question you need to join these together as seamlessly as possible. The linking phrases which join up explanations or examples are gambits.

3   **Vary your sentence length**
    At secondary school you may have been encouraged to use longer words and more complex sentences. Sometimes this can lead to rather turgid writing. To make your work more 'punchy', experiment with alternating sentence length. Short sentences can give your

work more impact and are often clearer. Never use a complex word if a simpler one does the job just as well.

SUCCESSFUL REVISION

The key to successful revision is to be proactive. Start early and take charge, don't wait until the last moment. However, it is also possible to waste time revising ineffectively. Focus from the start on what you actually need to do to revise actively. The key is to ensure that you understand your subject and can communicate that understanding in the format required by the examiners.

Cataloguing your portfolio

Ideally you will have been cataloguing and cross-referencing your notes as you went along. If you are like 90 per cent of students you won't have even thought about this. This should therefore be your first task.

■   Start by putting your notes into an order. You may have a course content list supplied. If not, then you could organise your notes chronologically or by theme. The key is to get them organised.

■   Now see what you have got. One way of doing this is to write out lists or grids. The latter are preferable because they will enable you to make connections and use the same material in several ways.

■   Compare your lists with course or syllabus details. Are there gaps? If so then your next task will be to copy up notes from a friend or make some from a key text.

■   Cross-reference your notes. You may be examined on methods, sources or topics so you need to have flexibility about how you use material. There are several ways of doing this such as colour coding, using Post-its or producing grids. A particularly useful way is to use index cards.

What do examiners

want to see?   **not want to see?**

Paragraphs	Poor spelling
Clear structure	Long descriptions
Argument	Irrelevance
Detailed supporting evidence	Few examples
A range of relevant case studies	Woolly sentences, e.g. 'the first
Conclusions	chapter of the human story'

Figure 12.12 *What examiners want to see*

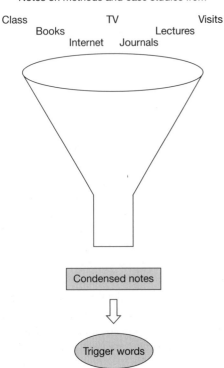

Notes on methods and case studies from

Class   TV   Visits
  Books   Lectures
       Internet   Journals

Condensed notes

Trigger words

Reducing information onto cards

Many students find index cards useful for learning and condensing essential knowledge and to help them apply their understanding. To produce good cards you have to decide what is the essence of each topic, case or method you need to learn. This is a useful discipline in itself as it forces you to consider relevance to exam questions and to be selective. How much you write on each card will depend on your confidence in your ability to remember. Some students go through a process of reducing notes in this way several times until they are left with keywords or phrases. This process in itself helps with revision of knowledge. Because *you* have had to process the information it lodges in your memory much better than if you had just read or underlined notes. The words or phrases themselves will work as prompts and suggest additional material to you.

Figure 12.13 *Condense your notes*

Geophysics *Survey*	Star Carr *Settlement*
Resistivity: Deviation of electrical conduction due to resistivity of ground. Generally due to dampness. **Magnetometers:** Deviations in the magnetic field, caused by heating of hearths, kilns, filling in of pits, and solid features. **Metal Dectectors** **Radar and Sonar** **Remote Sensing:** Radar, infrared **Dowsing**	**Mesolithic** JGD Clark (1949–51) • Platform on swampy lake side. Birch and moss • 3–4 families, 20 people • Flint and antler tool making • Faunal remains indicate summer occupation • People probably based on the coast • Dogs kept for herding?
Head-Smashed-in *Kill Site* >5,500 BP	**Trade and Exchange** *Economics*
• Southern Alberta, Canada • Blackfoot Indians • 50 hectare animal processing area • Plains bison • Cairns to channel animals • Skin-lined boiling pits, drying, fires, • Seasonal kill site, feasting and storage	**Gift Exchange and Reciprocity** • *Kula network of Melanasia (Solomon Sea)* **Redistribution** • Tribute or appropriation • Central organisation • *Knossos, Danebury* **Market Exchange** • Internal or port-of-trade • *Ancient Greek Agora*

Figure 12.14 *Examples of revision cards. The process of selection involved in making these will help you remember the detail*

REVISION ACTIVITIES

Mix and match

This is one of several ways in which you can use the cards you have just made. It can be done individually or turned into a game with other students. Divide case study cards and themes or aspects of themes into two separate piles. Turn over one card from each pile and then try to make a connection, for example Boxgrove and Technology. This can be done with both sites and methods.

Make up mnemonics

Mnemonics are usually made by taking a number of linked words and then trying to make a new word from the first letter of each, for example Trench, Area and Box makes 'Tab'. Or develop formulae such as RIQI: recover, identify, quantify, interpret. This can work as a prompt when you need to remember a list of detailed points.

It is probably best for methods or 'what can be learned from . . .?' type questions. Use it sparingly. There is a limit to the number you will recall and exams are increasingly about applying understanding rather than remembering lists.

Mindmaps

A creative way to remember connections is to create a visual map of a subject in our minds. This works on the principle that we remember key images better than keywords. Start by placing a major concept, theme, site or method on a page. Identify four or five main aspects you wish to learn and mark them in bold on lines radiating out from the original word. Next draw something which each word suggests to you at the other end of the line. The more personal your choice of image, the more likely you are to remember. (It doesn't have to be sensible.) From here other connections can radiate out much like a spider diagram. ◀ examples on pp. 292 and 381.

Figure 12.15 *Example of visual cue notes. If you are a visual learner, this may work for you*

Visual reminders

For archaeological methods, visual cues can be useful in revising and checking your understanding. One method is to produce your own sketches such as the examples in Figure 13.4.

Playing games

Many students find that games help them to remember and also encourage them to make links between areas of knowledge. They also break up the revision process. Many popular games can be adapted. These are just four you could try.

Archaeological dominos

Two archaeological words are put on each domino (card). Deal them out and play in the normal way with the following addition. Each time a player lays down a domino they have to make a connection between the two words.

Blockbusters

If you draw a hexagonal grid on a piece of acetate (OHT) the task of setting up this game becomes straightforward. The question setter inserts a letter into each hexagon and teams compete to make lines across the 'board', as in the popular television programme. All the clues should come from the syllabus.

Balloon debate

Several students are each given the name of a different development in archaeology. They have to prepare in advance to answer questions on it, including providing examples. On the day of the debate the chosen students have to argue 'X has been the most important contribution to archaeology in the last 100 years.' The rest of the class have to each ask a question and will then vote for the winner. Over the course, similar debates could be used to ensure that all students have a go. The game builds up skills in argument too.

Rizla!

Papers are dealt out with methods written on them. Without looking at it, one student sticks their paper to their forehead. They then have ten questions to guess what they are. The other students can only answer yes or no.

TACKLING EXAM PAPERS

Ideally you should have become thoroughly familiar with the format and type of questions used in the exam during your course. Examiners do not try to catch students out and are highly unlikely to change their types of question without warning. The specific questions and any sources used are likely to be new to you but their format and what you are asked to do will be largely familiar. You need to work out what each paper or section wants you to do. To do this you need to look at the command words and the type of mark scheme used (▶ p. 398).

Looking at mark schemes and doing practice assignments are obviously essential and you will do this as part of your course. One way of helping yourself is to play the role of examiner. Try setting questions in the style of the exam. Produce a markscheme, write responses and then mark your work. An alternative is to swap questions with a friend. Either way, by putting yourself into this role you will gain insights into what you need to do.

In the exam

Most of you will have taken many exams already. As always the same golden rules apply. In addition, don't forget your ruler and magnifying glass!

Take a watch in and use it. Divide the number of marks into the time available. Allocate time per question and try to stick to it.

Use your time effectively. Read the question paper before you start. Where you have a choice, make sure that you have understood all the questions before you make your choice. Often the longest questions, particularly those with

Essay mark schemes

This shows in table form the hierarchy of levels for A Level and the undergraduate essays of two major university departments. Keywords and phrases have been extracted from the whole documents. Where statements sound similar they are shown at the same level.

Max mark 25	A Level	Degree Level	Max mark /16
		Critical thought and flair. Sound and relevant factual knowledge. Evidence of extensive reading, properly referenced. Logical, balanced and well supported arguments. Written without significant grammatical errors	15 or 73–9% Sound 1st
Level 5 21–25	Consistently analytical. Consistent corroboration with relevant detail from a range of contexts. Clear and consistent attempts to reach judgements. Strong communication skills. Strong conceptual understanding. Some evidence of independent thinking	Sound, competent, methodical and comprehensive. Lacking critical flair. Evidence of some reading beyond obvious texts which are referenced. Examples cited where relevant. Well written, without major grammatical errors	12 or 63–65% Solid 2:1
Level 4 16–20	Sustained analysis. Range of accurate and relevant supporting material. Covers main issues but may be unbalanced. Attempts to reach a judgement. Little narrative. Effective communication skills		
		Unoriginal and occasionally flawed. Where they are original they lack supporting evidence. Reading has been shallow. May be brief. Argument may be biased and not all may be relevant. May have significant grammatical or structural flaws. If several flaws are present it should be in a lower band	9 or 53–55% sound 2:2
Level 3 11–15	Understanding of relevant issues. Generally analytical with some narrative. Focused on the question but unbalanced treatment of it. Argued, but not consistently. Some relevant supporting material. Effective use of language	Not really satisfactory but shows just enough grasp of the subject. May be muddled and poorly argued. Weak and limited evidence with no sign of reading. Sections may be irrelevant. Arguments may be biased or simplistic. May be poorly written and structured	7 or 48–49% Solid 3rd
		Barely acceptable. Weak and shallow arguments. Lack of critical thought. Limited evidence. No reading. Poor English. Often confused or irrelevant although basic facts should be correct	5 or 45–47% Basic 3rd
Level 2 6–10	Some understanding of relevant issues. Lacking weight or balance. Relevant descriptions. Some irrelevance or inaccuracy. Some effective use of language		
Level 1 1–5	Largely narrative. Outline description. Very generalised. Lacking direction or links to the question. Limited communication skills	Unacceptably brief or muddled and flawed. Often irrelevant, difficult to understand and lacking basic understanding	3 or 30–39% Clear fail

Figure 12.16 *A level and undergraduate mark schemes*

quotations, look harder than they actually are. Try to avoid doing a question just because it contains a keyword you know about, you need to address the whole question.

On essay papers rough out a number of plans at once and add points later in case you forget them. They can save you time but don't spend too long doing this at the expense of the actual essay. If you finish early there is bound to be something you can improve on. Examiners are looking for:

- *Breadth*: have you considered all the ideas which might be appropriate to the question?
- *Relevance*: have you linked all your points to the command words in the question?
- *Support*: have you produced enough detailed specific evidence to illustrate the points you have made?

Writing under pressure is hard. If you find yourself struggling make sure you do the basics. This should ensure at least a pass.

1. Address the question. In your first sentence use the word 'because' in a clear 1–2 line answer to it. In your second sentence list the main points or evidence you will consider.
2. Write one paragraph on each of the points you have listed. Introduce the point, add some supporting detail and say how it helps answer the question. The last sentence in each paragraph should link to the next paragraph.
3. In your conclusion restate your argument highlighting the way your paragraphs have supported it.

And finally . . .

Your battery of fluffy toys might bring you luck in the exam but sound preparation is a surer way to success. If you have absorbed the lessons in this book you should be able to cope with whatever you are asked. Don't forget that all examination essays will have flaws. No examiner expects perfection and if you have worked throughout your course you should succeed.

Chapter 13

Doing an Archaeological Project

YOUR GOALS

You need to understand

- how to choose an appropriate topic
- where to obtain help and evidence
- how to plan and manage your time
- how to record sites and materials
- what to include and how to present your study.

Most courses, including A Level, require students to undertake a piece of personal research and submit their findings for assessment. This may be called coursework, a personal study or simply an archaeological investigation. Whatever its title it will have a set of written instructions as to the precise nature of your task. This will include guidance on what you must eventually produce and in which format. This chapter covers issues which are common to most students' experiences and needs. You should keep your specific research brief to hand as you read through this section. The examples provided here are from good A Level projects. They could equally be good investigations undertaken out of general interest.

HOW TO CHOOSE A TOPIC

Study the assignment brief issued to you. It may include constraints such as the word 'local' or

you may need to undertake some 'first-hand' observation. It is essential that you choose a subject that fits the requirements of your course, is based on evidence which is accessible to you and, most importantly, is something on which you will enjoy working.

It must be archaeological

Archaeology embraces many other academic disciplines and sources in attempting to understand past cultures. These range from biology through geology to architecture. It is common to find overlap emerging in a project. Graveyard surveys, for example, link strongly to social and economic history while studies of hedgerows will require some botanical knowledge. While links to other disciplines are clearly valid you must consider balance. Archaeological content should dominate the final work. For example, analysis of the structural evidence for different phases of building within a medieval castle is archaeological whereas exploring events and personalities linked to its use are usually of a historical nature. A general rule of thumb is that archaeology deals directly with the physical remains of the past whilst history is more concerned with analysing events using documentary sources.

You must be able to access your sources

Being able to visit your chosen sites, monuments, museum or archaeological unit should be high on your agenda. Research benefits from a first-hand approach and it is more than likely that you will need to make more than a single visit to your source(s) of evidence. A first visit – following initial research in the library or on the internet – will familiarise you with the object of your study. You need to get a feel for the extent of the site(s) or the range of artefacts available. Follow-up visits will be required for more detailed research. This might include surveying earthworks or sorting and drawing artefacts. Often students find that there are points they missed on previous visits which can be checked on later ones. If you have chosen sites at too great a distance such opportunities to revisit may be impractical. This is particularly true when students are tempted to select sites overseas. Your holiday visit to Pompeii may have fired your archaeological imagination but is unlikely to have resulted in meaningful research. The cost of a later visit to check measurements makes this a rather expensive option. Sites within range of home, school or college are your best bet.

Access does not just mean closeness. There are other people such as landowners involved. Public rights of way can be found on OS maps while better known sites are listed in gazetteers, often with directions for access. But in many cases there is no easy or direct footpath. Despite 'right to roam' legislation, if the site is on somebody's land you will need their permission to survey it. In 1999 a gamekeeper chased a student away from a stone circle in Derbyshire. His project was delayed for months while he then tried to get written permission from the landowner. It would have been better to have done this first. It is sometimes difficult to discover who owns particular fields, so build in time to find out and consider fallback projects in case permission is refused or you don't receive a reply. If you hope to use an artefact collection, you need to check with the keeper that this is possible and determine when you can have access to it. To give yourself the best opportunity in all cases, write early in your research programme, explain briefly your reasons for wanting access to the land or collection and offer a range of suitable times when you could visit. A stamped self-addressed envelope may add a degree of success to the response rate. Permission should be obtained from the site manager if you are studying an excavation and want to record more than a few cursory notes or photographs.

It is easy to get caught out with access issues. A common excuse for poor studies is that sites or museums were closed at the time the student visited. Check it out in advance. A more difficult situation is where the site is accessible but it is overgrown with vegetation. Summer grass or bracken growth can easily mask relatively minor features such as hut circles or medieval village remains. Winter is often the best time to visit earthworks. Even then you can still be frustrated. One keen fieldworker had to wait several weeks for snow to melt on Bodmin Moor before his barrow survey could be undertaken.

Supporting literature will vary in quantity according to the topic selected. Key texts to establish a context for your research are usually essential. Most studies benefit from an understanding of the relevant background. If you find too many books on your subject it will run the risk of lacking originality and it might be better to reconsider your focus. On the other hand, it is possible, as the case studies show, to identify

Figure 13.1 *A lovely day, but not the best one to survey Dun an Sticer Broch, Harris*

Summer vegetation totally obscures the interior and the entrances. The midges were bad too!

an aspect of our material past where there is little direct written material on which to draw. There are many untapped areas of archaeological potential. It is easier to say something new about the pattern of round barrows or pillboxes near your home than it would be to say something original about Hadrian's Wall. You should seek advice from your tutor on background reading and sources whatever your topic. Access to this material is also easier if it is a local site or collection. If your school or college does not have much, local museums and libraries probably will.

You also need to find the correct balance of available evidence to study. Too much and you run the risk of superficiality, too little and the problem will be achieving a meaningful outcome. The curator of your local museum might welcome an apparently sensible and enthusiastic student who offers to catalogue their Romano-British pottery collection; a concentration on just the samian ware might in reality be more feasible and appropriate for your study. If you do work with a third party such as a local archaeologist be sure to seek their professional advice but always refer back to your tutor who will better understand the requirements of your study.

So the first stage in your research is to ensure adequate and appropriate sources and access to them. Often at this stage some change may be needed to the original title in the light of your findings.

BASIC RESEARCH OPPORTUNITIES

There is a vast range of subjects to choose from. Before you select one, look again at exactly what your course requires.

A Level students

- At A2 level each student selects an individual choice of topic and question. Access to HE assignments are likely to be similar.

- Students must develop an investigation of a question, issue or problem in an archaeological context. It has to be based on named sites, monuments or museums and must consider how archaeologists might approach such an investigation. A level students are expected to explain the reasoning behind their choice of topic, to reflect on their proposed methods of enquiry, to place their work in its appropriate archaeological context by referring to previous related studies, to account for the methods they employ both for desktop research and field study, to gather relevant evidence and present it using appropriate media, to analyse and interpret their findings and finally to evaluate their efforts and answer the question they posed in their original title

- Pass level responses must go beyond a straightforward factual account of evidence they have identified. Evaluation and analysis feature strongly in high level responses. Full details from AQA.

- http://www.aqa.org.uk/qual/gce/ archaeology_new.php

Undergraduate students

- No standard practice. Some courses require research diaries on summer excavation work, others set investigations similar to those at A level in year 1 or 2.

- Students may undertake research for their extended essay or dissertation. Requirements vary from one university to another but the focus of such work tends to be sharper the higher one proceeds up the academic ladder. Requirements on other programmes such as OCR Vocational History and BTEC Nationals in Tourism or Countryside Management need to be checked carefully against specifications.

Sites and monuments

All sites can be studied in terms of spatial distribution and layout and their chronological development. Most can also be examined for typological development. Investigations can centre on any one, two or all of these factors to facilitate the depth of research needed. Whatever your choice of sites or monuments you should never go alone when doing fieldwork. Apart from the personal safety aspect, which cannot be overstressed, a companion can hold tapes or discuss your observations with you.

The extent of the task should have a strong bearing on the selection of sites. Single sites may not always be sufficient. While an Iron Age hill fort allows for both desktop research and field survey, a single pillbox would be too restrictive. A collection of coastal defences would be a sounder proposition. Studying a local group allows comparison and contrast to be developed which enables you to reveal your true archaeological investigative skills. Neolithic tombs provide such an opportunity. These monuments are widely distributed. For many students in the British Isles they are accessible and can be adapted to suit almost any purpose in terms of projects. A popular approach is to look at their distribution in terms of the Neolithic landscape, to establish original groupings or clusters, or to compare orientation. Other approaches include comparing inter-visibility or to report on the condition and current threats to the monuments.

Of course visible monuments, which include those you can find on OS maps, are rather like the tip of an iceberg. By far the greater proportion of evidence of past activity is hidden below ground. Those studies that only reflect on visible evidence may well fail to deal with the larger picture. Reference to aerial photographs and SMR documentation is useful in establishing evidence that cannot be recorded or accessed in other ways.

You may also be able to consult the results – usually published – of previous excavations on the sites. You need to decide how much of your

EXAMPLE 1

To what extent can archaeological methods be used to reassess the interpretation of Studford Ring as a Bronze Age cattle enclosure?

Keith decided to investigate a scheduled earthwork using non-invasive methods. The site had been interpreted as a Bronze Age cattle enclosure and he wished to examine the evidence on which this interpretation was based.

Sources

Bibliography included local antiquarian sources, regional (Yorkshire) studies and a comparative site reported in the *Yorkshire Archaeological Journal.*
Sites and Monuments Record – reference the main site and others in the vicinity
NMR via AHDS – air photographs
Ordnance Survey maps

Context

The landscape context of the site with reference to other known past human activity in the area

Studford Ring

0   10   20   30m

Letters refer to cross sections measured through ditch and bank systems

Cross sections of detch and bank from Studford Ring

2 m

2 m

Offset from North (0 degrees)

A – 165 degrees
B – 285 degrees
C – 10 degrees
D – 84 degrees

Figure 13.2 Keith's own survey plan of Studford Ring showing its banks and ditches with the use of hachures

EXAMPLE 1 *cont.*

To what extent can archaeological methods be used to reassess the interpretation of Studford Ring as a Bronze Age cattle enclosure?

and potential parallels was essential to the investigation. Hence the research at SMR with particular reference to Bronze Age and Iron Age enclosures/settlements and a basic understanding of land use from Cunliffe's Iron Age Britain (1995) underpinned the more focused local research.

Methodology

Keith blended desk-top research and fieldwork in his reassessment of Studford Ring. The desk-top element was comprehensive and results from a range of sources were clearly expressed and well-referenced establishing the physical nature of the site over the past two centuries and varying interpretations placed on the earthworks. The fieldwork enabled both a physical assessment to be made and reported with photographs (10) used appropriately to support the descriptive text. A basic survey was conducted resulting in a site plan of the earthworks and four cross-sections of the bank and ditch.

Discussion/analysis

Keith's research acknowledged the presence of evidence of occupation in the area of Studford Ring in the Bronze Age but pointed out that there is no direct evidence of contemporary use of the site. Similar sites in the north-east of England are dated to the Iron Age and while no direct evidence is present to support occupation at this period the possibility clearly exists.

Four possible functions are considered: defence, ritual, stock enclosure, settlement site. The first two are reviewed but considered unlikely explanations. Either of the last two possibilities could be argued on the evidence – Keith concludes that non-invasive methods cannot differentiate.

His site survey provides a sound example of using hachures.

evidence will be derived from such sources and how much from your study of unexcavated sites. Few personal studies achieve high grades by simply paraphrasing the work of others. Excavation reports are also a particularly difficult medium to summarise effectively. However, if sites have been excavated then you have no option but to investigate via the site report or archive.

Including a well-known site in a group study of several sites such as Chedworth and other Cotswold villas can lead to a loss of balance.

The data on one site far outweighs that easily obtainable on the others. This imbalance can be countered by a title which lays the stress on the better known site or which focuses on conservation and preservation issues. Sites with guidebooks should carry a health warning for students. They can seem a bonus when you are hard-pressed for time but the availability of such material can tempt you into producing a study which owes too much to others' work. At worst this can turn into an archaeological version of I-Spy.

EXAMPLE 2

A survey of ground and polished stone and flint axes from East Kent

'Hamid' set out to examine finds from a small area in some detail and to catalogue quantity, type and distribution. He hoped this might shed some light on Neolithic settlement in the region.

Sources

- Kent SMR
- Canterbury Archaeological Trust
- Kent Archaeological Review
- Archaeologia Cantiana
- Museums: British Museum, Canterbury, Dartford, Dover, Folkestone, Herne Bay, Maidstone, Powell-Cotton
- Wide bibliography including general prehistory texts and articles in archaeological journals

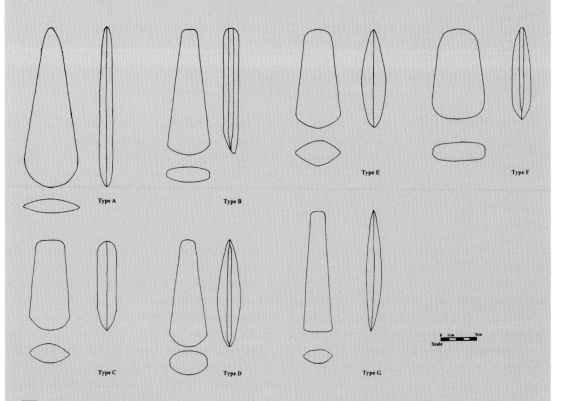

Figure 13.3 A type series of stone axes: the seven profiles against which the axes were matched for typological analysis

EXAMPLE 2 *cont.*

Methodology

Much previous research has been related to the petrological analysis (via thin sectioning) of axes to establish their source and the distribution patterns of products. Records on 125 axes were compiled from published data and museum records. Hamid used a self-devised sheet to list museum accession number; find spot; stone type; dimensions; completeness; condition; presence of cortex; other comments. The most complete were sketched in outline for shape comparison. Using typology and analysis of size and weight Hamid established a seven-type classification with description and illustration of one axe in each type. Charts were produced to show number of axes per group.

Having produced his catalogue, Hamid evaluated it and discussed its implications for understanding the archaeology of Neolithic Kent.

Content/discussion

Hamid acknowledged the difficulty in establishing an accurate number of axes. He observed that some are held outside Kent while others in Kentish museums were unprovenanced. More were likely to be in private collections and unpublished. Most were chance finds but others could be linked to archaeological sites or other Neolithic material. The section on raw materials acknowledged the work of others. Most axes were made from local flint but petrological analysis linked others to axe factories. He was able to construct distribution maps with links to known Neolithic sites and natural features. Further discussion centred on possible implications of the findings for exchange and identifying settlement and the function of the axes themselves.

Accompanying illustrations included location maps, six tables of data and typological drawings. No photographs were used; the project was acceptable without them. The project listed acknowledgements and had a comprehensive bibliography. The axe record sheets were placed in an appendix.

Artefacts

The potential for studying artefacts is vast. These range from Palaeolithic stone tools to relatively recent objects like clay pipes or horseshoes. However, artefacts are less frequently used as source material for projects than sites and monuments. This may reflect the pull of the outdoors and landscape archaeology but probably also stems from the greater barriers that exist between the researcher and the guardians of material culture. Artefacts are most likely to be in museums or with archaeological units. Individual excavators or collectors are less easy to identify as resources for students.

Most museum material is in storage. Some of it will be fully catalogued. Curators tend to display their better items so these objects are often unusual rather than representative. To fully explore a museum's holding of any particular aspect of material culture will require museum staff to locate and get out appropriate evidence. Many will do this but will want sufficient notice and a clear idea of what it is you wish to study. Arrangements will have to be made for frequent visits to work on the material as cataloguing and drawing are time-consuming activities. These can only be done during opening times which may mean Saturday or holiday appointments.

Archaeological units hold most recently excavated material and their time is even more limited than that of museum staff. Their role is not curatorial and it will need a personal introduction to access their store of artefacts. Some students obtain work experience placements with units and may be able to develop links through such activity. Other sources include local societies who may do some excavation or, more rarely, local excavators. Some metal detectorists might allow a study of their findings – such a recording and analysis of them could well prove fruitful.

Fieldwalking

Some students use their links with museums, units, universities or landowners to identify sites under the plough and arrange their own fieldwalking exercise. If it is well researched and planned this can lead to excellent, original studies. Farmers need to be approached sensitively for permission and in good time. Their schedule of activity needs to be known so that you can organise the fieldwalk at a convenient time both to them and yourself. You also need an initial visit to check that archaeological material is visible in the topsoil. Try not to be overambitious and do get some help. It takes longer to set up and walk an area of a field systematically and gather the evidence than you might think. Two students fieldwalking a 200 metre square could walk up to 10 kilometres each. On ploughed land that represents a considerable expenditure of energy! Washing, identifying and analysing the finds will also take much time.

Archaeology from the modern period

Most archaeological texts focus on later prehistory to the medieval period. However, this should not limit you and particularly if you live in a built-up area, you may find it easier to focus on standing buildings or more recent structures. Students have studied buildings ranging from docks to petrol stations. The remains of the industrial age and also of the Second World War are particularly rich sources for studies.

Industrial archaeology including agricultural evidence

Early transport systems such as canals and railways often leave linear traces, now often fading, of their routes. A keen eye for landscape and interpretation backed by older Ordnance Survey maps can be just what a student researcher needs. Both wind and water mills survive in a range of conditions and often have constructional sequences that can be ascribed to different phases of development. Where they have been converted into homes you may find the owners rather proud to show off original elements of the building. Mines are often landscaped after their closure and the danger of hidden shafts should discourage their use as a source for study. However, harbours, their associated buildings and tramways may survive in sufficient state to warrant investigation. Despite urban regeneration it is quite possible to identify buildings whose original purpose has now given way to new uses. Breweries, maltings, cinemas and mills all fall in this category. They lend themselves to questions asking, 'To what extent can an archaeological survey aid understanding of the development and function of the remains at X?

In his book ' Wall-to-Wall History' (Duckworth 1991) Richard Hodges presents a fascinating study of the typology of field walls and associated features such as gates and stiles on a Peak District farm at Roystone Grange. How many kilometres of our heritage of dry stone walls are still unstudied and unrecorded?

There is a vast range of vernacular farm buildings in the countryside. Even on modern farms you may not have to look far to find some older features. Records of this diminishing

Figure 13.4 *Fieldwalk finds presented with a scale*

archaeological resource are needed and your study could add to them. One rural structure which makes an ideal vehicle for manageable research to identify, record, illustrate, compare and produce distribution maps of is the dovecote. While there are some classic examples of free-standing structures (how many visitors to Avebury have noticed the circular dovecote opposite the entrance to the museum?), many are located in the end of barns or stables. Another disappearing feature are churn stands. Milk used to be collected from farms in churns placed at the roadside by farmers. They were put on stands so they could be easily lifted across to the lorries. Many stands still exist, though now redundant, and can be found, often rather overgrown, in hedgerows near to a farm's access onto a road. Styles vary (typology) and different materials were used. Very few are recorded.

The Defence of Britain

Research into modern military archaeology was boosted by the Defence of Britain project. It recorded some of the monuments slowly eroding away in the coastal and inland landscape. About 450 airfields were built during the Second World War particularly in the east. Coastal defences survive in many places simply because no one has bothered to remove them, for example the concrete blocks designed to slow a seaborne invasion (or were they for practice?) at Fairbourne, Gwynedd. Running in lines across the countryside are numerous pillboxes designed to hold up an invading army. These could be studied for typology or distribution. In towns, metal was collected during the war to 'help the war effort'. Careful examination of the tops of garden walls reveals the extent of such activity and provides fresh and original

EXAMPLE 3

Industrial archaeology: the Dudley (No. 2) Canal from Selly Oak to Halesowen, Birmingham

'Tom' attempted to evaluate the archaeological significance of the surviving surface evidence for 8 km of a canal abandoned nearly fifty years ago. The line of the canal passed through a park and housing and industrial estates. A significant feature was the Lappal tunnel which collapsed in 1917. At nearly 4 km it was one of the longest canal tunnels ever built.

Sources

■ Background texts and pamphlets on canals and industrial archaeology

■ Maps: Birmingham Canal Navigations; 1:25,000 OS for modern information; 1:10,000 OS (1967) for canal route shortly after closure; 1:2500 OS (25″ to mile 1881–2) showing sites of spoil heaps from the tunnel

■ Contacts: college library, Birmingham Central library archives, Country Park Ranger, local inhabitants with local knowledge/memories

Figure 13.5 *Students using tapes, ranging rods and clinometers to measure Painswick Beacon Hill Fort in order to construct profiles of the earthworks*

Methodology

Tom began with maps to establish the line of canal and accessibility. He planned to walk the length of the earthwork, observing and recording key features by note-taking, drawings (including profiles) and photography. He paid particular attention to bridges, wharves, overflows and tunnel spoil heaps, which had the appearance and the same fieldwork requirements as barrows.

Content/discussion

The first part of the line from the Worcester and Birmingham canal was easily identified in Selly Oak Park but the junction was obliterated in 1953 so Tom used local oral evidence and a dismantled towpath bridge to establish its position. Landscape interpretation revealed where the line of the old canal survived infilled between house gardens, which had been laid out when it was still a landscape feature.

Photographic evidence showed tunnel portals at the end of cuttings but like much of the canal these cuttings had been infilled. Locating boggy ground in the current landscape helped to reveal their original locations.

EXAMPLE 3 *cont.*

Industrial archaeology: the Dudley (No. 2) Canal from Selly Oak to Halesowen, Birmingham

The tunnel had been constructed by digging several shafts down to the proposed level of the canal and then cutting a bore on either side. The resulting spoil – red clay in this case – was brought to the surface. Once the tunnel had been cut and lined with brick the shafts were back-filled, but the bulk of the excavated material remained in heaps on the surface. Tom attempted to identify these 200-year-old spoil heaps from remains in a housing estate and adjacent Country Park by using an 1881 map. Erosion enabled him to determine the constituent material of the mounds and even retrieve reject bricks from the tunnel lining.

Towards Halesowen the canal ran on a huge earthwork embankment which was larger than the bank and ditch system at Maiden Castle. Tom was able to record profiles and compare them with eighteenth-century illustrations.

Tom's project included acknowledgements and a bibliography reflecting the Birmingham Canal Navigations and industrial archaeology. He produced plans, photographs and profiles of features, and map extracts were placed in an appendix.

archaeological evidence literally on the doorstep.

• http://www.britarch.ac.uk/projects/dob/index.html

Experimental archaeology

Planning, conducting and evaluating an archaeological experiment or reconstruction can seem an attractive option. It can make a worthwhile study but there are pitfalls to avoid. In many cases it is an advantage if you have some familiarity with the craft involved in the experiment. Prehistoric flint knappers or Romano-British potters had practice and experience on their side when they were making the artefacts we recover from excavations. Therefore if you don't have skills in knapping or wheel-made ceramics, you might be advised to avoid this type of project. Home-made hand-built pots, which do not resemble any archaeological material, 'fired' in a bonfire in the back garden do little

to explain or extend understanding of ceramics, their manufacture or firing techniques.

However, a student adept at woodworking might reconstruct and fire a bow, testing draw strength and range with different arrows and arrowheads. The groove and splinter technique of bone working for slender items such as pins can be reproduced with animal bone from the butcher and some sharp flint flakes. If you are able to visit experimental centres such as the Peat Moors Centre near Glastonbury you may be able to get advice on opportunities for developing these skills.

WHERE TO GET HELP AND ADVICE

During the topic selection process you will have identified an accessible range of resources. Where this involves the services of others, for example museum staff or SMR personnel, any request needs to be as clear and succinct as possible. The best practice is to make it clear that you have

EXAMPLE 4

To what extent can archaeological experimentation aid understanding of the efficacy of spindle whorls made of different materials?

Rebecca aimed to test the effectiveness of a range of different spindle whorls based on examples excavated on archaeological sites. She recognised a number of variables: material, design, dimensions, weight.

Sources

- Bibliography related to the craft of spinning and archaeological textiles
- Websites relating to the craft of spinning, sources of wool, archaeological sites and museum collections
- Examples drawn from Denmark, Meare West Village, Isle of Man, Gower, Merseyside
- Staff at museums in Lancashire and Cheshire

Context

Rebecca examined the nature and range of spindle whorls from varied sources. She contextualised the whorl within the hand-spinning process with some ethnographic parallels of the use of spindles and whorls. The nature of wool fibres was also discussed as a relevant aspect of an experiment into the efficacy of the process.

Methodology

A 'fair test' method was employed to eliminate variables as much as possible. Four whorls were made (wood, bone, modern tile, clay) and spindles (drumsticks) whittled to fit approx 14mm holes. Shetland wool was used throughout. Tests for efficacy were made on 50cm of yarn produced by each experiment relating to 'slubs' (lumps/irregularities of gathered fibres) and a strength test linked to the breaking point of each length.

Content/discussion/analysis

While noting her inexperience might influence the results, Rebecca made a sound attempt to produce and explain the outcomes of the experiment. In general terms the heavier the whorl the better the quality of the yarn and the greater its strength. Each of the four materials used was reviewed with a consideration for ease/difficulty of manufacture in past times (Rebecca used modern tools to create her artefacts).

Thought was given to development of the experiment to a higher level e.g. making several

Figure 13.6 *The four experimental spindles with whorls made from (l-r): clay, modern tile, wood, animal bone*

EXAMPLE 4 *cont.*

To what extent can archaeological experimentation aid understanding of the efficacy of spindle whorls made of different materials?

whorls of the same material but of different weights or developing/recording the turn-rate of the spindle.

An honest evaluation assessed the experiment as limited and the results as not necessarily 'presenting a real representation'. However the process – planning, researching, constructing the artefacts, running the experiment, recording and analysis – was distinctly educational and rewarding.

Figure 13.7 *Spinning with the modern tile in use as whorl*

already done some background research and focused on several questions to which you feel your contact might be able to offer answers. Don't pick a topic and send it to various possible sources of help expecting a completed project by return! Timing is also crucial. While you need to do exploratory work before making contact with requests for assistance or publications, you cannot afford to delay your approach for too long as agencies have their priorities and ordering material from them will involve a built-in time delay.

National resources

Whatever project you select there will inevitably be something of use on the Web. If nothing else, it can make access to sources of information faster. Start with one of the archaeological gateway sites (▶ p. 427). Of particular use for projects in England is the National Monuments Record (NMR) site. It is comprehensive and self-explanatory. It offers a search service, which is free 'subject to limitations', and free information packs. Topics available include 'Archaeology of England' and 'Aerial photographs of England'. A valuable link from NMR is to an alphabetical list of SMR addresses. These are your local sources of detail on known sites.

Museums

Museums often list 'supporting research', as part of their mission and many will have education officers who may be able to help. However, they are usually busy and their main focus is primary

Entry to cowhouse

Level of hay loft floor

Dutch barn with adjustable roof

Cowhouse

10   20 m (approx.)

Figure 13.8 *Diagram of types of barn*

The range and typology of such structures offer opportunities for fieldwork in most parts of the UK. Identification of examples, establishment of distribution patterns and recording techniques are all valid exercises, which might form the basis of local studies (after Lake 1989)

education so you need to book visits and be clear in advance about the help you want.

Units

Archaeological units are less easy to discover as they are professional organisations in the business of offering archaeological services to those who need, and will pay for, them. Although their focus is not curation or education their staff may assist if approached sensibly. Units can be found on the CBA website or via your SMR.

Figure 13.9 *Archaeological Data Service*

ADS is an unrivalled resource for archaeological researchers in the UK. The Archaeology Data Service provides free information on over 1 million sites. The online search engine provides short descriptive records. These can be used to access rich and detailed digital archives. Text resources include theses, monographs, journals and unpublished articles. There are also databases, images, CAD plans, survey plots, animations and virtual realities (◀ p. 371).

Libraries

Libraries vary hugely in the archaeology stock they hold. Local libraries may hold local collections including an archaeological journal but are most used for background texts or the (rather slow) inter-library loan service. University libraries (where archaeology is studied) or national organisations such as the NMR are the best option and will hold excavation reports and journals. However, you will need special permission to enter some university libraries and they do not usually let you borrow. It is worth persevering particularly with excavation reports, which are as near as you may get to the

evidence for some sites. Some older reports may be difficult to find. One last resort is to look for them at second-hand archaeological booksellers (▶ p. 427).

PLANNING AND MANAGING TIME AND WORD LIMITS

Every May, A Level projects are handed in with letters enclosed as appendices revealing that key information was still being sought only a few weeks earlier. There are many sources of information on time management and their advice is equally applicable to archaeological coursework. Once you have a plan, get started.

EXAMPLE 5

To what extent can field survey techniques help to understand the remains of the World War 2 army camp on Brayton Barff?

Paul examined a variety of resources related to this fairly recent site before undertaking a detailed field survey and recording of extant evidence. His aim was to consider the contribution that archaeological methods could make to an holistic study.

Sources

- Bibliography references several general works on twentieth century military sites published by English Heritage and the Council for British Archaeology.
- NMR – air photograph library
- HER – York
- Birmingham University Field Archaeology Unit
- Arts and Humanities Data Service (AHDS) and Archaeology Data Service (ADS)
- English Heritage Defence of Britain database
- Ordnance Survey maps 1845 – 2007
- Photographs – local library and local newspaper
- Local metal detectorist via ex-soldiers internet forum

Context

The army camp fell into disuse at least 40 years ago and has since been largely neglected. The Selby bypass destroyed a corridor across the site (approximately 30 per cent of the total area was lost though survey was undertaken by BUFAU – see above). A further 40 per cent is covered by a golf-course leaving 30 per cent of the original area containing brick structures standing to a few courses in height, many of which were difficult to access due to undergrowth and spoil-heaps.

Methodology

Paul attempted a summer survey but this was abandoned in favour of a December–February one when the undergrowth had died back. With an assistant holding tapes measurements and recording followed traditional methods. A GPS was used to plot fences around the site and

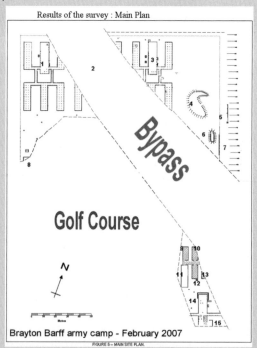

Results of the survey : Main Plan

Brayton Barff army camp - February 2007

FIGURE 5 – MAIN SITE PLAN.

Figure 13.10 *Plan of Brayton Barff Army Camp with individual buildings numbered for reference*

EXAMPLE 5 *cont.*

To what extent can field survey techniques help to understand the remains of the World War 2 army camp on Brayton Barff?

features in the woodland areas. Measurements were transferred into CAD software and plotted at 1:100.

All individual features and buildings were planned and described in detail. Illustrative photographs supported the text.

An aerial photograph taken in 1954 was rotated and rectified using computer software to fit a scan of the 1:2500 OS map and the overall site plan then resized to overlay the map.

Discussion/analysis

The plan overlay onto the aerial photograph provided evidence of very good agreement with buildings lining up properly within the boundaries of the camp.

The evaluation reflected on which questions about the camp the survey had answered and those which it had not and those which were capable of an answer without an archaeological survey. The main contribution of archaeological fieldwork was in terms of construction techniques which no other form of evidence could provide.

Figure 13.11 Photograph of Firing Range from the north-west showing state of site preservation

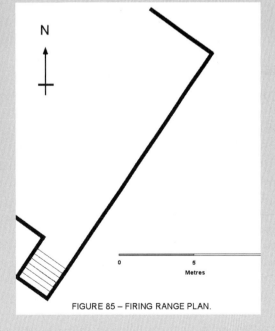

FIGURE 85 – FIRING RANGE PLAN.

Figure 13.12 Plan of Firing Range

Archaeology differs from many other subjects in the mix of indoor and outdoor activity. You need to get the sequence right so that you don't have to make repeated visits because you didn't ask the right questions on earlier visits. After an initial visit to get a feel for their site(s), most students carry out desktop research before returning to do detailed recording. That way they have more idea what they are looking for. You need to plan for delays. Letters from the SMR or landowner will not come back by return post. It may rain on the day you planned to do a fieldwalk. You need to start early, be patient and have other things to follow up while you wait.

PCs have made preparing studies much easier. You can collate information and notes as you go along, integrate visual images and perfect drafts more effectively. Try to ensure that you also record all sources used so that your references and bibliography are complete. Incidentally, nobody will believe that your hard disk crashed (and you forgot to make a back-up) the night you were printing the final copy. That excuse sounds like 'my dog ate it' to this generation of lecturers and examiners.

RECORDING EVIDENCE

How much of any site or range of artefacts you record will depend on the nature of the investigation and to what extent the site in question is central or more peripheral to the discussion. Wass (1999) is an excellent basic guide while Drewett (1999) provides a greater range of techniques.

Your record is likely to comprise four major types: drawn, written, photographic and diagrammatic. Drawings include location maps, plans of features or buildings, profiles of earthworks and elevations of structures. You may be able to illustrate relationships or phases through the medium of such illustrations. You will certainly need to make notes so that you can describe key features in your report. Photographs are useful in illustrating things you have identified and showing developments in the case of excavations. Tables and diagrams should be created where you have large amounts of data such as with fieldwork projects. They are also valuable for making comparisons and showing processes. A quick library search of archaeological texts will provide a wealth of examples.

Recording sites or features

Planning sites

You will probably wish to produce field drawings of earthwork sites. While drawing skills and surveying equipment obviously help, much can be achieved with simple gear: 20 or 30 metre tapes, ranging poles, a compass and marker arrows (try tent pegs with coloured ribbon) form a handy 'starter kit'. The simplest plans are likely to be made up from measuring or pacing the main features and roughly drawing hachures to indicate slopes.

For more accurate diagrams you will need to lay down a grid over the features to be recorded. A base line should be established and then a second main grid line should be fixed at right angles to the first. Parallel lines joined to each of these then form a grid. It is advisable to fix reference points so that you can return to the same grid, but you will need to do this sensitively and with permission from a landowner. You cannot leave obtrusive markers on public land or where grazing animals might damage themselves. Ideally this grid should be linked to reference points on OS maps. Once a grid is established you can plot it onto graph paper and by taking measurements from two fixed points to the feature, plot it by the process of triangulation.

When recording slopes, place marker arrows (one colour) along the upper edge and others (a different colour) at the lower extent of the slope. This enables the lines of the feature to be plotted and the arrows can be reused. Conventional hachures, where the head of the hachure represents the top of the slope and it gets thinner as

Figure 13.13 *A student drawing of the profile of earthworks at Crickley Hill including an example of the use of hachures*

the slope goes down, should be used. They indicate the direction and length of the slope. Steepness is indicated by heavier infill of the hachure, head shape or the closeness of the hachures.

Profiling features

If you want to draw a scale profile of an earthwork you may need more equipment. However, there are some simple methods which are effective. A horizontal line fixed across the earthwork at 90 degrees to its main alignment and kept level provides a baseline. Measurements are taken from it to the ground at fixed intervals that will establish the profile of your site. A series of shorter lengths may make maintenance of a level easier and can offer a solution for longer slopes as long as adjustments are calculated accurately. Ensure you record this. It is essential that you employ the same scale for both horizontal and vertical scales or your drawings will suffer from distortion. If you have access to more equipment, such as a level and measuring staff, your task will be quicker. Alternatively, your geography department may have clinometers or gradiometers which you could borrow and use to construct profiles in a series of angles and lengths.

If you follow the basic rules of setting out, measuring, plotting to scale and drawing up your field results it is possible for enthusiastic archaeology students to produce a decent original plan.

Recording excavations

Recording part of a current excavation site is similar to what the real excavation team will be doing. You need to consider how much detail you require in terms of plans, sections and photographs. You may need to ask about evidence relating to the various phases of occupation and to see particular finds, but it is unlikely that the specialist reports will be ready in time for you to see. A tape recorder might be a useful aid for when you have the chance to make enquiries.

Recording buildings

Photography and sketches of the lower levels and key external features are needed to illustrate building materials and phases. If you have internal access then room plans and details of construction and decoration can be added. You are unlikely to be able to get precise measurements for elevation drawings but using tapes, clinometers and some basic trigonometry can help produce a reasonable approximation.

Recording artefacts

There are archaeological conventions for the illustration of many finds and these can be studied in archaeological reports. Producing quality drawings is neither quick nor easy. You should consider the extent of your artistic skills and try them out against the recognised formulae for archaeological illustration so that you can judge your aptitude for this exercise. A reasonable alternative for those objects you may have collected yourself in fieldwalking is to scan them and trace the printout.

Often when there is a quantity of pottery to review attention is paid to what are called 'diagnostic' sherds for example rims and decorated pieces. The less significant sherds can then be grouped and described as collections. Such sherds may be counted and weighed and the information about them given in tabular form rather than by illustration.

Figure 13.14 *A scan of an artefact recovered by fieldwork*

Smaller objects like bronze brooches or flint tools require careful treatment by the illustrator and will always need to be drawn from at least two perspectives – front-on and side-on – to give a clear indication of their design. Sometimes in the case of objects, for example flint axes, it is the profile shape that is relevant in the report rather than a detailed drawing showing the flaking process. Each artefact should be drawn to a scale, shown in the drawing. Some description needs to be written to make clear to the reader matters relating to the object that the drawing does not necessarily convey, for example colour or texture.

A range of details should be used when cataloguing objects. These will include provenance, dimensions and description of key features.

	Quantity	Weight	Average Weight
Black Burnished Ware	77	676 gms	8.8 gms
Grey Ware	70	457 gms	6.5 gms
White Ware	2	50 gms	25.0 gms
Severn Valley Ware	18	117 gms	6.5 gms
Samian Ware	5	19 gms	3.8 gms
Other	13	126 gms	9.7 gms
Totals	185	1445 gms	7.8 gms

Figure 13.16 *Presentation of fieldwork results*

Figure 13.15 *A tracing made from the scan in Figure 13.14 with key features highlighted. This technique provides a good example of how those of us without good drawing skills can present illustrations*

WRITING UP

There are two considerations here: what does the reader of your study really need to know about your research? How can you best present the evidence? Assume that your reader has a sound archaeological understanding, but not necessarily knowledge of your particular topic, and address your work to them on that basis.

Refer again to the assignment brief. There may be specific advice on structure and presentation. This may include instructions, title pages, abstracts and appendices. It will probably mention plagiarism and referencing.

It is essential that you plan to produce a project which meets the criteria set out by your tutor or the syllabus. In the case of A level this means about 4000 words. This is not long so it is important that you aim for depth of argument rather than the superficial treatment of a large number of sites or artefacts.

Plagiarism

This means using other people's work unchanged or without acknowledgement. Avoid it at all costs. It is particularly easy to slip into accidentally where you are heavily reliant on one guidebook or report, or where you download material as notes from the internet. Be on your guard and if necessary adjust your question to avoid repeating somebody else's enquiry.

Presentation

Your original plan, probably somewhat adapted in the light of research, will form the basis for the work you submit. You will have sifted and sorted a range of materials and evidence and need a clear idea of the layout and balance of your work before you start writing. A flow diagram is useful.

Your illustrations should add to and explain points raised in your commentary. Avoid the temptation to put your photographs in just because you took them! Illustrations are probably best within or close to the text that refers to them. The ability to use a scanner is useful here. Always ensure that there is some annotation of any illustration. Transparent overlays are useful for illustrating distribution and your interpretation of phases. Maps can be traced as the base for these. Finally, if you are confident with IT think about a virtual walkabout (◀ p. 371).

KEY SKILL

Referencing

Referencing is an important part of a quality study and is insisted on at degree level. Get into the habit not only of listing your sources, both books and journals, but also of putting the page references into your draft notes as you select interesting comments or information. There are several referencing systems but the Harvard (author–date) version is becoming standard. Wherever you write something which is based on another's work you should reference that original work in a bracket immediately after your statement, giving the author's surname and the date of publication. In the bibliography you should list all your sources alphabetically by author. You also include date of publication, title, publisher and place of publication as shown below.

An example from case study:

> 'The discovery of eight flint axes from Creteway Down at Folkestone can be associated with finds of Neolithic date from the same area. (Clarke 1982)'.

The study's bibliography contained the following entry:

> Clarke, A. F. (1982) *The Neolithic of Kent — A Review. Archaeology in Kent to* AD *1500,* CBA Research Report No 48, pp. 25–30.

There are some variations on the Harvard system in use in different universities, so check with your supervisors exactly which format they want. At A level, the version above is acceptable.

Websites must also be referenced. No standard has yet emerged. You should list full web addresses and what they are in the bibliography. You could number them and use (web1) etc. in the body of the text although some universities may want the full address in the text.

Chapter 14

Additional Resources

STUDYING ARCHAEOLOGY IN THE UK

There are plenty of opportunities to study archaeology although the range of qualifications is relatively small. To get further information on any of them either contact your local institution or the Council for British Archaeology (CBA) Education service.

• http://www.britarch.ac.uk/educate/ed1.html

Introductory courses

Short courses are offered by Colleges of Further Education (FE) and the Workers Educational Association (WEA). Typically these will be 2 hours a week for ten weeks and are generally aimed at adults. Increasingly, colleges will offer an Open College Network (OCN) certificate for these courses. Sadly, major cuts in funding for adult education by the current government mean that these courses are rapidly disappearing. There are a few Access to Higher Education courses which cover some archaeology and there are also a number of archaeology Foundation Degrees including those linking forensic disciplines together.

• http://develop.ucas.com/FDCourseSearch/
  Gateway.html

Day schools or conferences are offered by university departments, FE colleges, local and national archaeological organisations and museums. Many of these involve lectures at university level although some are practically based. The two key sources on these are *Current Archaeology* (*CA*) and *British Archaeology* (*BA*) magazines.

Field schools, or training digs, are offered by universities and some local organisations in the summer. Details are advertised in *CA* and *BA* magazines. GCSE Archaeology was withdrawn a few years ago. However the new vocational GCSE in History contains significant archaeology options (up to 50 per cent) and offers the chance to undertake a basic fieldwork study and to compare historical and archaeological evidence in a study of 'Dark Age Britain'. Some of the BTEC Nationals including Travel and Tourism and Countryside Management include units where archaeology can be used for case studies.

AS and A Level Archaeology

These are offered by AQA. The AS can be taken separately or as the first stage of an A Level. Each award is broken down into two modules. Three of these modules are examinations which each last between 75 and 120 minutes.

AS Level (first half of A Level)

Unit 1: The Archaeology of Religion and Ritual

One from:
Prehistoric Europe – 30,000 BC to AD 43
Ancient Egypt – 3,000 BC to 50 BC
Roman Europe – 753 BC to AD 410

Unit 2: Archaeological Skills and Methods

Unit 2 requires you to analyse sources from a real archaeological site and answer a mini-essay on methods chosen from a short list. Unit 1 focuses on definitions and case studies and includes a longer piece of writing.

A2 (second half of A Level)

Unit 3: World Archaeology

A thematic approach covering settlement, economy, society and current issues in archaeology. It is assessed using essays.

Unit 4: Archaeological Investigation

A personal piece of fieldwork.

AS and A Level are offered in some FE colleges and schools. To find your nearest centre, contact the AQA or CBA. There are also some archaeology options in the Classical Civilisation A Level offered by OCR.

DEGREE LEVEL STUDY

Degrees usually involve study at university, although some courses have also been franchised to FE colleges. These may have a more practical or vocational focus than courses in universities.

At degree level there is considerable variety. You can study archaeology as a BA or a BSc, or in Scotland for four years for an MA. Detailed information can be obtained from the CBA or UCAS. Archaeology can be studied on its own, in combination or as part of other subjects. The information here largely applies to where it can be studied as a single subject. All courses will include elements on the development of archaeology, its methods and techniques, as well as the theory used to make sense of archaeological evidence. Beyond that they will vary considerably in their choice of topics.

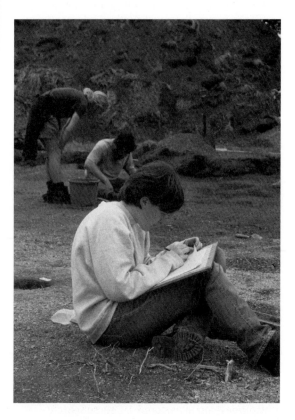

Figure 14.1 *Although it is sometimes difficult to arrange, you should try to get some practical experience of archaeology prior to applying or going to university*

In considering university courses you may want to give thought to the following:

- Is the course thematic or period based?
- Which periods can I study?
- Does the assessment pattern suit me? Is it continuous assessment or final exam based?
- What is the department strong in (e.g. science at Bradford, prehistory at Sheffield)?
- Does it have a practical or heritage element (for example Bournemouth)?
- What kinds of placements and excavation opportunities are on offer?
- How is it rated?
- Will I get the qualifications to get in?
- Do I need previous experience?

Market forces

Some courses have more applicants than others. They normally deal with this by asking higher grades from prospective students. If you are a standard A level student you simply have to get the grades. If you have a different educational background you should contact the department directly for advice before applying. Many are particularly keen on mature students, even if you haven't got A levels.

League tables

Universities are ranked on research and teaching. A good research record may tell you that the university has published good research or that it has a lot of researchers. You may not actually be taught by the key researchers. There also appears to be a bias towards larger departments in the way the tables are calculated. Bournemouth University in particular seems to have suffered in this respect despite producing important national research such as the MARS report. Teaching tables may reflect the quality of lecturing. One has to be a little careful interpreting these. Unlike A Level there is no systematic comparison of the quality of degrees from different universities. A 2:1 from one institution may or may not be as good as a 2:1 from another.

The website includes recent information on A Level points asked for. It also lists some of the specialisms on offer. With over 100 different possibilities for joint or part honours courses in archaeology, there are many other opportunities to study archaeology in other university departments. Examples include Maritime Studies at St Andrews or Wetland Archaeology at Hull.

STEPPING UP TO DEGREE LEVEL

If you have studied A Level Archaeology, you may find that there is not much of an initial step up. You may even find that you have less to do at first. As with most subjects there is considerable overlap between A Levels and many first year undergraduate programmes. In considering your choice of programme it may be a good idea to select different topics or periods from those you did at A Level to broaden your knowledge and maintain your interest. If your chosen course has a practical scientific or statistical element you may find this new. You will generally get some support at the university, but it might be worth refreshing your memory before you go.

University lecturers and undergraduates have identified the following areas as different from A Level or where students sometimes struggle:

- Working more independently or in groups
- Making interesting oral presentations
- Coping with theoretical concepts
- Adjusting to the idea that knowledge is always the product of interpretation
- Coping with maths and science elements
- Coping with wide chronological and geographical ranges
- Adjusting to the precision required in excavation
- Using academic libraries, journals and texts
- Writing essays in an academic style
- Using academic referencing from books, journals and web pages (◀ p. 422)

FINDING THE BEST INFORMATION

There are so many excellent sites, museums and written and electronic resources available to archaeology students that we can only list a fraction of those available. A much more detailed list linked to the topics in this book is available on the companion website. Since selection is subjective we have included those resources that we have found most useful and which our students have made most use of. Although we have tried to provide a good range, our choice is clearly biased towards our own interests. Another person's list would undoubtedly look very different. Other sources, which provide additional depth on topics contained in the text, are listed in the bibliography.

TWENTY VERY USEFUL BOOKS

The focus is largely on Britain and Europe and full details of each text are in the bibliography. Make sure your school or college buys a copy of these books.

General texts

- Ashmore, W. and Sharer, R. (1999) *Discovering our Past*. A good text for the visual reader, with diagrams well used to illustrate methods and thinking.
- Fagan, B. (2000a) *In the Beginning*. A detailed introduction to archaeology from an American perspective.
- Greene, K. (2002) *Archaeology: An introduction*. This has good coverage of reconnaissance, excavation and post-excavation techniques.
- Orme, B. (1981) *Anthropology for Archaeologists*. A great little text for getting you to think beyond European norms.
- Renfrew, C. and Bahn, P. (2004) *Archaeology: Theories, methods and practice*. This has become *the* encyclopedia of cases studies for a generation of archaeology students.

Archaeological sources and methods

- Coles, J. and Lawson, A. (eds) (1987) *European Wetlands in Prehistory*. An excellent insight into differential preservation and the value of wet sites.
- Drewett, P. (1999) *Field Archaeology*. For detailed coverage and clear explanations of methods.
- Muir, R. (1981) *Reading the Landscape*. A book to open your eyes to evidence of past activity embedded in the countryside.
- Schick, K. and Toth, N. (1993) *Making Silent Stones Speak*. Good on the use of experimental archaeology in investigating early hominid activity in Africa.
- Wass, S. (1999) *The Amateur Archaeologist*. A good aid for project work.
- Wilkinson, K. and Stevens, C. (2001) *Environmental Archaeology*. At last, a clear introduction to the archaeology of economics and ecosystems.

Period studies

- Cunliffe, B. (ed.) (1994) *The Oxford Illustrated Prehistory of Europe*. Well illustrated and authoritative.
- Hunter, J. and Ralston, I. (eds) (1999) *The Archaeology of Britain*. An excellent introduction to each period of British archaeology since the Upper Palaeolithic.
- Parker-Pearson, M. (1993) *Bronze Age Britain*. A very accessible and well-illustrated introduction to the Neolithic and Bronze Age.
- Wenke, R. (1999) *Patterns in Prehistory*. An overview of the majority of human history from a world perspective.

Archaeological themes

- Binford, L. (1983) *In Pursuit of the Past*. The introduction to understanding the formation of the archaeological record.
- Bradley, R. (1984) *The Social Foundations of Prehistoric Britain*. A ground-breaking book

which looks at how patterns in the archaeological record can be used to reveal the social and ritual nature of past societies.

■ Fagan, B. (1995) *Time Detectives*. A very readable series of case studies including several mentioned in this text.

■ Parker-Pearson, M. (1999) *The Archaeology of Death and Burial*. Wide-ranging and drawing on ethnography to examine past beliefs and practices.

■ Sherratt, A. (1997) *Economy and Society in Prehistoric Europe*. A stimulating series of essays on topics from horses to alcohol.

ARCHAEOLOGY BOOKSELLERS

There are often only limited ranges of archaeological texts in general bookshops. If you know what you want but can't get it, try these two specialist companies:

■ Castle Books: http://dspace.dial.pipex.com/ town/square/fe63/

■ Oxbow Books: http://www.oxbowbooks. com/

JOURNALS

In most subjects you would be unlikely to look at journals before university level. However, in archaeology it should be different. The first in this list are all very accessible and are often beautifully illustrated. The remainder are useful sources of case studies. Many good case studies only appear in journals.

British Archaeology (BA) http://www.britarch. ac.uk
Current Archaeology (CA) http://www. archaeology.co.uk/
Scientific American: http://www.amsci.org/ amsci/amsci.html
Antiquity: http://antiquity/ac.uk
Assemblage: http://www.shef.ac.uk/~assem/
The Prehistoric Society:
http://www.ucl.ac.uk/prehistoric/

GATEWAY WEBSITES

We have listed websites throughout the book where they provide more information on methods and case studies. To find other information you should head for one of the many archaeology gateway sites. Each of these will provide you with a huge number of links. You should be able to find something on almost everything you are looking for. We usually do.

These are a selection of the very best:

World Archaeology:
http://archaeology.about.com/
http://archnet.asu.edu/
http://odur.let.rug.nl/arge/
http://www.discoveringarchaeology.com/
http://www.bbc.co.uk/history/ archaeology/

Archaeology of the British Isles
http://www.britarch.ac.uk/info/uklinks. html
http://www.discoveryprogramme.ie/
http://www.cadw.wales.gov.uk/
http://www.english-heritage.org.uk/
http://www.historic-scotland.gov.uk/
http://www.spoilheap.co.uk/

Our current favourite is the anthropology site of Mesa Community College, Arizona which has great world archaeology case studies including short ethnographic and archaeological film clips.

http://www.mc.maricopa.edu/dept/d10/ asb/

If you want more, why not go online to the Archaeology Coursebook site www.routledge. com/textbooks/9780415462860. Unlike many of the sites listed, its focus will be on good case studies at the right level for seminars and essays.

PLACES TO VISIT

We have tried to ensure some regional coverage with our suggestions although there is inevitably a bias towards those which we have used and found useful.

Twenty museums to visit

There are two good websites which list many of Britain's museums:

- http://www.mda.org.uk/vlmp/
- http://www.museums.co.uk/

1 Ashmolean Museum, Oxford
2 British Museum, London
3 Devizes Museum (Neolithic-Bronze Age)
4 Ipswich Museum (Anglo-Saxon)
5 Keiller Museum, Avebury (Neolithic-Bronze Age)
6 Museum of the Iron Age (Danebury), Andover
7 Museum of Archaeology and Anthropology, Cambridge
8 Museum of London
9 Museum of Wales, Cardiff
10 National Museum of Scotland, Edinburgh
11 Newcastle University Museum (Roman)
12 Petrie Museum, London (Egypt)
13 Pitt Rivers Museum, Oxford (anthropology)
14 Salisbury Museum (Neolithic-Bronze Age)
15 Jewry Wall, Leicester
16 Lincoln Museum
17 Corinium, Cirencester (Romans and Saxon)
18 St Albans (Roman)
19 Manchester (Egyptian)
20 Tullie House, Carlisle (Roman)

Recreations and experimental sites

- Butser Ancient Farm, nr Petersfield
- Peat Moors Visitor Centre, nr Glastonbury
- West Stow Anglo-Saxon village, nr Bury St Edmunds
- Flag Fen, Peterborough
- Jorvik Centre, York
- St Fagins, Newport
- Bede's World, Jarrow
- Ironbridge Gorge, Telford

Visits to archaeological monuments

Where possible, several are grouped together to make a useful day out.

- Avebury–Keiller Museum–West Kennet–Windmill Hill
- Stonehenge–Durrington–Winterbourne Stoke
- Arbor Low–Stanton Moor–Creswell Crags
- Grimes Graves – West Stow–Thetford Castle
- Hadrian's Wall–Vindolanda–Housesteads
- Chedworth–Corinium Museum–Great Witcombe
- Fishbourne Palace–Butser–Mary Rose
- Maes Howe–Ring of Brodgar–Stones of Stenness
- Maiden Castle–Dorchester Museum–Cerne Abbas Giant
- Wharram Percy–Fountains Abbey–Rievaulx

Answers and Mark Schemes

Key task: test your understanding of geophysics (p. 18)

Resistivity area survey best for 2, 3, 4, 6, 8; also useful for 5, 9, 10.

Magnetometry area survey best for 1, 9, 5, 6, 10; also useful for 3, 4, 8.

Neither useful for 7.

Key task: test your grasp of dating methods (p. 108)

Spear (C14), shells (ESR, AAR, C14), seeds (C14), burnt flint (TL), mudbricks (archaeomagnetism, TL), Saxon bones (C14), kiln (archaeomagnetism), cave bones (uranium series or ESR for the calcite deposits), figurine (typology, TL, archaeomagnetism), boat timber (dendro, C14).

Glossary of Terms and Abbreviations

This list does not pretend to be precise in an academic sense. It is intended to give you a simple definition of words that may be new to you so that you can comprehend the sources you come into contact with. For greater sophistication you should use an archaeological dictionary. Every subject has a lexicon of acronyms and abbreviations. Archaeology (arx) is no different. The glossary contains those which you are most likely to come across and with which you should familiarise yourself.

Absolute dating: Giving the age of something according to a calendar or historic scale, e.g. BC, AD, BP. Also called as chronometric dating

Accelerator mass spectrometry (AMS): An advanced radiocarbon dating method which can work for tiny samples

Achieved status: Position or prestige in society earned through one's own efforts or qualities

Aerial survey: Locating and defining archaeological sites from the air. Photographing cropmarks and parchmarks during drought conditions usually produces the best results

Aggregation: Upper Palaeolithic sites where several groups have come together to cooperate in particular activities, for social reasons or to enable specialisation, e.g. Dolni Vestonici.

Anaerobic conditions: Where there is insufficient oxygen for the bacteria, which normally break down organic materials to thrive, for example waterlogged sites

Analogy: Interpreting something with reference to something else. For example, 'it is similar to X'

Animism: Belief in spirits

Anthropology: The study of humans. It has many subdivisions including Archaeology and Ethnography

Arable: Growing crops

Archaeological record: What survives in the ground before excavation or the records produced by archaeologists after the whole excavation and analysis process

Archaeology: The study of physical remains to help understand the behaviour of people in the past

Archaeometry: The application of scientific analysis to archaeological materials.

Artefacts: Can refer to anything made or modified by humans. Tends to be used most frequently for tools.

Ascribed status: Position or prestige in society due to inheritance

Assemblage: Artefacts from a particular period which typically appear together. Also used to describe a collection of materials, for example animal bones from a particular site

Atomic absorption spectrometry (AMS): Measuring light energy emitted by different elements. Different combinations provide different spectra

Attribute: A quality of an artefact which allows it to be grouped with others, for example colour, texture

Attritional bone profile: A table plotting the age and sex of animal bones which suggests that younger and old members of herds were killed. It suggests scavenging or selective hunting by humans or other predators

Augering: Using a drill to take a core through deposits in the ground

Band: A hunting and gathering based society with groups of under 100 people

Bayesian statistical analysis: This involves other observations and common-sense knowledge being used to modify probability statements.

Bigman: A non-hereditary position of status in some small-scale parties gained through the ability to amass and distribute resources – often through feasts.

BP: Before present (actually 1950). Absolute dating used for periods in the past where historical dates (BC and AD) are irrelevant, for example the Palaeolithic.

Cache: A store of food or artefacts

Caesium magnetometer: Cart-mounted magnetometers that use Caesium vapour to detect magnetic anomalies. More sensitive than conventional flux-gate machines they record straight line transects rather than using grids.

Calibration: Using one method to correct inaccuracies in another, for example using calendar dates from tree ring sequeces to calibrate raw radiocarbon dates

Canopic jars: Egyptian vessels in which organs from mummified bodies were stored.

Catastrophic profile: A table plotting the age and sex of animal bones which shows the natural distribution of animals in a herd. It suggests a natural disaster or unselective slaughter

Central place theory: A geographic model developed by Christaller, which predicts that central places would develop at regular spaced in an ideal landscape

Characterisation: Identifying the origins of materials from their physical characteristics

Chiefdom: A ranked society with the inherited or elected role of chief at the top. Likely to have some specialisation in crafts and types of building

Clan: A system of social organisation based on blood and marriage ties

Context: The position of an artefact, the layer of soil it was found in and other artefacts found with it

Coppicing: Repeatedly cutting trees back to a stump in order to encourage them to grow long straight poles which can then be harvested

Coprolites: Preserved faeces

Core: A prepared lump of stone from which tools can be made

Coring: Driving a hollow tube into the ground to get a stratigraphic sample of the subsoil

Cropmarks: Variations in the tone or colour of crops due to underlying archaeological features

Curation: Deliberately preserving artefacts, for example jewellery or weapons. This can result in artefacts from an early period being discovered 'out of sequence' on a later site

Cursus: Linear monuments, sometimes several kilometres long, constructed in the Neolithic period

Debitage: Waste from the manufacture of stone tools

Dendrochronology: Tree ring dating

Depositional processes: The various means by which archaeological material becomes buried

Desktop study: An office based search of historical and existing archaeological records about a site

Demic Diffusion: This is where one population expands faster than another and ultimately disperses till it occupies most of the available land

DHA: Direct historical approach. Using oral evidence and studies of a modern population to form hypotheses about an earlier culture in the same region

Diachronic change: Gradual change over a period of time

Disarticulated: Bones that are mixed up, no longer in the right places

Distribution patterns: Plots of archaeological finds either on a site or across a region which are analysed to determine the behaviour that caused them

DNA: Deoxyribonucleic acid. The material that makes up genes and determines the nature of living things

Doggerland: The ancient landscape now under the North Sea which once joined Britain to Europe.

Earthworks: Literally a series of 'humps and bumps' on the surface that indicate the buried remains of buildings, boundaries and field systems

Ecofacts: Natural material that is of archaeological interest. It could include human remains, food waste or environmental material such as pollen or snails. Not artefacts

Entoptic: Internally produced. For example, entoptic images are generated by the brain itself rather than reflecting what has been seen

Ethnicity: Identity of different groups based on their distinctive cultures

Ethnoarchaeology: Studying modern groups of people to understand the behaviour that leads to particular patterns of deposition

Ethnography: Observation based study of modern social groups

Excarnation: Defleshing a corpse in some way as part of mortuary ritual

Exchange: Not just trade, but any interaction where something passes between people. It could include information, gifts or money

Fall-off analysis: measuring the rate at which the number of particular artefacts decline as the distance from their source increases. It is used to diagnose particular modes of exchange

Faunal dating: Relative dating based on the evolutionary sequence in which mammals have developed

Feature: Non-portable archaeological remain such as aspects of a site for example posthole, hearth

Fieldwalking: Systematically searching ploughed fields for the remains of artefacts and buildings to detect likely settlement areas

Foragers: Groups subsisting on wild foods. Plant foods are usually the most important

Formation processes: How archaeological material came to be created, buried and transformed to create the archaeological record

Funerary rites: Events to mark the final rite of passage of a person. Overlaps with, but is not the same as, *mortuary practice*

Glyphs: Reliefs of figures or signs carved on stone. Usually Mesoamerican

Geochemical survey: Using techniques derived from chemistry to detect traces of past activity from soil samples. See phosphate analysis

Geophysical survey: Using techniques derived from physics to detect remains under the ground. See resistivity and magnetometry.

GIS: Geographical Information Systems: linked maps and databases

GPS: Global Positioning System. A handheld device for locating your position using satellites

Harris Lines: Horizontal lines in teeth enamel where growth was reduced during a period of stress.

Haplogroups: Particular sets of genetic variations. Think of them as branches of the homo sapiens family tree. Y DNA haplogroups are traced back to the first individual with that particular genetic mutation and are passed on by males, mtDNA can be traced back to the first female with that mutation and are passed down by females.

Hoards: Deliberately buried artefacts. May have been placed in earth or water for security, as offerings etc.

Hominans: Modern and extinct humans

Hominids: The great Apes. Includes Gorillas as well as human and many extinct species.

Hominins: sub-category of Hominids including humans and chimpanzees

Horticulture: Encouraging particular plants to grow, for example by weeding round them. Used to identify a stage in food production before agriculture

Horticulturalist: Groups subsisting largely on plant foods, some of which they may plant. May be mobile and not using permanent fields

Human: either just modern humans (us) or the Homo genus generally. Australopithecines Extinct African hominids living from 5 mya to around 1 mya. The gracile (slender) variants were the ancestors of the Homo genus.

Hunter-gatherers: Groups subsisting on a mixture of wild animal and plant foods. May be mobile

Iconography: Art that may have a religious meaning

Inclusions: Material added to clay to provide strength and improve the firing process. Also known as temper

Inhumation: Burial

In Situ: In its original place.

Intensification: Increasing production. Usually applied to food production but can apply to extraction or manufacture

Isotopes: Variations in the molecules of particular elements which have different numbers of neutrons.

Isotopic analysis: Identifying different ratios of isotopes in materials in order to pinpoint their source

Kin: Relatives through blood and marriage

LIDAR (Light Detection and Ranging): Similar to RADAR but transmitting and measuring the return of a short pulse of light (a laser) rather than radio waves. In aerial reconnaissance it measures the distance from the plane to the ground and is linked to a GPS system to provide a detailed contour survey.

Liminal: Something on the edge of normal society. May be a boundary or a group of people. May be seen as dangerous and likely to require ritual to deal with it

Lineage: A group sharing the same ancestor

Linearbandkeramik (LBK): The first farmers in central Europe, named after their pottery which was decorated with bands running around the vessels.

Lipids: fats

Lithics: Stone tools

Magnetometry: Detecting buried remains through magnetic variations between them and the surrounding soil

Market exchange: A system of exchange where producers compete in terms of prices. It is often associated with money or bartering and particular exchange sites, for example shops or markets

Mastaba: rectangular mudbrick structures that housed the entrance to underground tombs. These tombs were forerunners of the Pyramids.

Material culture: The total physical remains of a former society including artefacts, buildings, etc.

Matrix: The type of soil or other material in which an artefact is found

Mesolithic: A label given to the period from the end of the last Ice Age until the development of farming. Sometimes used to refer to groups living by hunting and gathering. In Britain dates range from around 8000 BC

Metallography: Studying the composition and structure of metals

Micro-contour survey: A detailed survey using accurate sensitive equipment to reveal subtle variations in the ground surface to reveal the plan of buried sites

Microliths: Tiny stone or flint blades. Associated with the Mesolithic period

Middens: A rubbish tip. In some periods may have had other functions including a source of fertiliser and a ritual site

MNI: Minimum number of individuals. The smallest number of animals that could have produced the bones in an assemblage

Moiety: Organisation of society based on the idea of two different subgroups

Monotheistic: Belief in one god

Mortuary practice: Ritual activity and preparation involving the disposal of a corpse

Native American Graves Protection and Repatriation Act (NAGPRA): A 1990 US law protecting human and cultural remains and repatriating materials from existing collections.

Natufian: The final Mesolithic culture of the Near East. Sedentary and with a range of tools for processing wild grains.

Neolithic: This label used to describe the period of the first farmers, before the use of metal tools. Increasingly it is used to describe the process of domestication including changing ideas about the world. British dates range from around 4500 BC

Neolithic package: The assemblage associated with the spread of agriculture across Europe including querns and polished stone axes, cattle bones and plant remains from emmer and einkorn wheat and barley.

Neutron activation analysis (NAA): Highly sensitive analysis of trace elements undertaken within a reactor

NISP: Number of identified specimens. A count of all the bones of each species in an assemblage.

NMR: National Monuments Record

Numen: the spirit of a place. It could also reside in objects or be linked to particular deities.

Obsidian: Volcanic glass that can be worked to produce hard, sharp edges

Optically Stimulated Luminescence (OSL) Dating: Similar to TL. It calculates the length of time since sediments such as quartz were last exposed to light.

Organic residue analysis: Using chemicals to extract and identify traces of plant and animal materials from pottery

Ossuary: A place in which the bones of the dead are stored, for example a charnel house

Palaeolithic: The first archaeological period. Before 8000 BC but subdivided into Lower, Middle and Upper on the basis of stone technology

Palimpsest: A collection of archaeological artefacts, ecofacts and material that may not be related. For example, they are together through accident or natural forces rather than human activity. Also used for a site with a mass of inter-cut features of different periods

Palynology: Studying pollen for dating and environmental reconstruction

Pastoralists: People who subsist largely from the animals they herd. May be mobile

Petrology: Studying the minerals in archaeological material to identify their source of origin

Phosphate analysis: Analysing soil samples to detect high phosphate which can indicate human or animal habitation

Planum method: An approach to excavating deposits where stratigraphy is very hard to detect and the fill seems to be homogeneous such as graves. It is also used on large open sites with few if any features. It involves trowelling successive articicial layers. More widely used abroad than in the UK.

Pollen dating: Using local pollen sequences to provide a relative date for a site

Polytheistic: Belief in many gods

Prestige goods chain: Where valuable items are exchanged between high status individuals, often over a considerable area

Primary products: The material gained by killing an animal, for example meat, skin

Probing: Using metal rods to detect walls and other buried features close to the surface

Propitiation: Offerings to gods, for example offerings in pits or deposited in water

Radiocarbon dating (RC): Absolute dating technique based on the known rate of decay of Carbon 14

Reciprocity: Exchange between social equals. Balanced reciprocity implies things of equal value are exchanged

Redistribution: A form of exchange where goods are collected by a central authority and then given to other people or places

Regression: Using clues from the earliest known maps and documents from an area and projecting them back in time to produce a picture of an earlier period

Relative dating: Determining where a site or artefact sits in a sequence in relation to other sites or artefacts

Remote sensing: Detecting archaeological remains from above the surface of the earth, usually from a satellite

Resistivity: Detecting buried remains through differences between them and the surrounding soil in their ability to carry an electrical current

Rites of intensification: Ritual to mark times of change or danger

Rites of passage: Ritual to mark events in the lives of individuals

Sampling: The careful selection of areas to investigate or materials to analyse. Usually based on mathematical probability to ensure that what is selected is representative of wider evidence

Secondary products: Materials gained from animals without killing them, for example milk, wool

Sedentary: Where a group is settled, that is staying in one place. Semi-sedentary groups stay for considerable periods, perhaps moving between sites on a seasonal basis

Segmentary society: Small, relatively self-contained social groups who may sometimes combine with similar groups to form wider alliances

SEM: Scanning electron microscope

Shadow sites: Sites that survive as low earth-works and are seen from the air in conditions of low sunlight

Shaman: Individual who can communicate with, and often interact with, spirits

Shovel pit testing: An alternative to field-walking for woods, pasture and gardens. Samples of soil from carefully selected test pits are sieved for artefacts

Sidescan sonar: A series of sonar pulses are emitted from a ship or towed device in a wide beam and the returning signal is recorded. The results provide an image of the seabed in the direction travelled.

Signature: Traces in the archaeological record that can be linked to particular patterns of activity

Site: A place where human activity has taken place

Site catchment analysis: Reconstructing the available natural resources within easy reach of an archaeological site to help construct a model of its economy and the diet of its people

SMR: Sites and Monuments Record

Social storage: When an individual gives something of value to another individual, creating an obligation on the part of the second person to return something at a later date. What is exchanged can vary enormously from an exotic gift to a meal, from military service to a bride.

Soil marks: Variations in the tone or colour of ploughed soil due to the destruction of buried features

Sonar: Form of underwater detection based on sound waves

Specialisation: This term can be used in several ways. Economic specialisation can be used to describe a group who rely on one primary means of supporting themselves, for example pastoralists. It can also mean a division of labour where different individuals perform particular tasks rather than working in similar ways, for example miners, iron smelters and smiths in the production of iron tools

State: Society with a territory, central authority and permanent institutions

Stelae: Carved stone pillars or statues

Stratification: A series of layers, strata or deposits laid down over time. Stratigraphy is the analysis of stratification or its use in relative dating

Structured deposition: Material entering the archaeological record through specific (possibly ritual) activities or behaviour patterns (not random). For example, particular animal bones being placed in ditches

Subsistence: The way in which a group acquires the food it needs e.g. fishing or herding. A subsistence economy is one which just produces enought to live on.

Superposition: The principle that in undisturbed stratification, the oldest layer in the sequence is at the bottom

Surface collection: American version of fieldwalking. It can usefully be applied to the systematic recovery of artefacts from places other than fields

Surface survey: Examining the landscape for evidence of underlying archaeological remains

Surveying: Precisely measuring the dimensions, position and orientation of archaeological sites and features

Syncretism: fusion of different systems of belief.

Taphonomy: 'The law of burial'. The processes which transform organic archaeological material in the ground

TAQ: Terminus ante quem. The latest possible date for a site or layer

Tell: A large mound created by successive settlement layers on a site over thousands of years

Temper: Material added to clay to give it strength and prevent it cracking during firing

Thiessen polygons: Shapes created by joining the mid-point between economic centres to provide models for exploring territories

Thin sections: Samples of rock taken for petrological analysis

TL: Thermoluminescence dating

Totemism: A natural object is adopted by a group as their emblem and as an object of worship

TPQ: Terminus post quem. The earliest possible date for a site or layer

Trace elements: Tiny amounts of rare elements within stone and metal. The balance of trace elements varies according to the geological source of the material

Transect: Walking or taking a sample across a landscape

Trend surface analysis: A way of illustrating the distribution of artefacts by using mathematical formulae to create a contour map

Tribe: A society that is larger than a band but still linked together by kinship ties. May number between several hundred and a few thousand people. Likely to be farmers or pastoralists. Unlikely to have wide variations in wealth and status

Typology: Organising artefacts into types based on similar attributes

Unit: An archaeological trust or commercial company that bids to do survey and excavation work

Use wear analysis: Using high-powered microscopes to study marks on tools and bones in order to identify the activity that caused them

Valletta Convention (1992): A Council of Europe agreement to document and preserve archaeological heritage. It has been ratified by the Parliament.

Votives: Artefacts deposited as offerings to gods or spirits

X-ray fluorescence (XRF): A non-destructive method of analysing the mineral composition of the surface of artefacts

Ziggurat: A Mesopotamian mudbrick temple. Stepped and shaped like a pyramid.

Bibliography

Ammerman, A & Cavalli-Sforza, LL (1984) The Neolithic transition and the genetics of populations in Europe. Princeton, Princeton U.P.

Anderson, S. (1985) 'Tybrind Vig' Journal of Danish Archaeology 4 Odense: Odense University Press

Armit, I (2003) Towers in the north, Stroud, Tempus

Ashmore, W. and Sharer, R. (1999) Discovering our Past, Mountain View, Calif.: Mayfield

Aston, M. (1985) Interpreting the Landscape, London: Routledge

Bahn, P. and Vertut, J. (1988) Images of the Ice Age, Leicester: Windward

Balter, M (2004) The Goddess and the bull: Çatalhöyük. *New york, free Press*

Balter, M (2006) First Jewellery? Old Shell Beads Suggest Early Use of Symbols. *Science* **312** (23 June 2006) p 1731.

Barclay, Gordon J. & Russell-White, Christopher J. (1993) Excavations in the ceremonial complex of the fourth to second millennium BC at Balfarg/Balbirnie, Glenrothes, Fife in Proceedings of the Society of Antiquaries of Scotland 123, 43–211

Barnett, J. (1998) 'Monuments in the landscape: thoughts from the Peak', Lecture at conference on Prehistoric Ritual, Oxford

Barrett, J. (1994) Fragments from Antiquity, Oxford: Blackwell

Barrett, J. and Bradley, R. (eds) (1980) Settlement and Society in the British Later Bronze Age, Oxford: BAR 83

Barton, N (1997) Stone Age Britain London, Batsford.

Bayliss-Smith, T. (1996) 'People–plant interaction in the New Guinea highlands' in D. Harris, (ed.) The Origins and Spread of Agriculture and Pastoralism in Eurasia, London: UCL

Bednarik, R. G. (1995). Towards a better understanding of the origins of body decoration. *Anthropologie* 33, 201–212.

Bednarik R.G. (2000) Beads and the orgins of symbolism. www.semioticon.com/frontline/bednarik.htm

Binford, L. (1978) Nunamiut Ethnoarchaeology, Orlando: Academic Press

Binford, L. (1983) In Pursuit of the Past, New York: Thames and Hudson

Binford, L. (1989) Debating Archaeology, San Diego: Academic Press

Bradley, R. (1984) The Social Foundations of Prehistoric Britain, London: Longman

Bradley, R. (1997) Rock Art and the Prehistory of Atlantic Europe: Signing the Land London: Routledge

Bradley, R. (1998) The Significance of Monuments, London: Routledge

Bradley, R. (2000a) The Good Stones, Edinburgh: The Society of Antiquaries of Scotland

Bradley, R. (2000b) An Archaeology of Natural Places. London: Routledge

Bradley, R. (2007) The prehistory of Britain and Ireland, Cambridge, Cambridge Univ. Press

Branigan,K (Ed) (2001) Urbanism in the Aegean Bronze Age. Seffiled, Sheffield Univ Press.

Brück, J. (1995) 'A place for the dead: the role of human remains in late Bronze Age Britain, Oxford Journal of Archaeology 61: 245–77

Bunson, M (1995) A dictionary of Ancient Egypt. Oxford, OUP.

Buckland, P. (1976) 'The use of insect remains in the interpretation of archaeological environments', in D. Davidson and M. Shackley (eds) Geoarchaeology, London: Duckworth

Burenhult, G (ed), (2003), People of the past, San Francisco, Fog City Press

Burger, J et al (2005) Ancient DNA from the First European Farmers in 7500-year-old Neolithic sites. Science 310 pp 1016–1018

Canaanite Amphorae Project www.amarnaproject.com/pages/recent_projects/material_culture/canaanite.shtm

Cann, R, Stoneking, M & Wilson, A (1987) Mitochondrial DNA and human evolution. Nature vol 325, pp 31–36

Caspari, R & Lee, S (2004) Older age becomes common late in human evolution. Online, Proceedings of the National Academy of Sciences. www.pnas.org/

Çatalhöyük project www.catalhoyuk.com/

Champion, T. and Collis, J. (eds) (1996) The Iron Age in Britain and Ireland: Recent trends, Sheffield: Sheffield Academic Press

Chapman, R., Kinnes, I. and Randsborg, K. (eds) (1981) The Archaeology of Death, Cambridge: Cambridge University Press

Clarke, D. (ed.) (1972) Models in Archaeology, London: Methuen

Clark, R. (2000) Mesolithic Hunters of the Trentino. Oxford: BAR 832

Coles, B. and Coles, J. (1976) Sweet Track to Glastonbury, London: Thames and Hudson

Coles, J. (1979) Experimental Archaeology, London: Academic Press

Coles, J. and Lawson, A. (eds) (1987) European Wetlands in Prehistory, Oxford: Clarendon Press

Collis, J. (1984) The European Iron Age, London: Batsford

Collis, J. (1996) 'Hillforts, enclosures and boundaries' in T. Champion and J. Collis (eds) The Iron Age in Britain and Ireland: Recent trends, Sheffield: Sheffield Academic Press

Cooper, N. (2000) The Archaeology of Rutland Water: Excavations at Empingham 1967–73 and 1990, Leicester: Leicester University Press

Cornwell, B. (1999) Stonehenge, London: HarperCollins

Cooney, G & Grogan, E. (1999) Irish Prehistory: a social perspective, Dublin, Wordwell

Council for British Archaeology discussion group on British Archaeology www.britarch.ac.uk/

Crossley, D. (1994) Post Medieval Archaeology in Britain, Leicester: Leicester University Press

Crow, J (2004) Housesteads. London, Batsford.

Crumlin-Pedersen, O (ed) (2003) Hjortspring. Roskilde, The Viking Ship Museum.

Cunliffe, B. (1992) 'Pits, preconceptions and propitiation in the British Iron Age', Oxford Journal of Archaeology 11: 69–83

Cunliffe, B. (1993) Danebury, London: English Heritage

Cunliffe, B. (ed.) (1994) The Oxford Illustrated Prehistory of Europe, Oxford: Oxford University Press

Cunliffe, B. (1995) Iron Age Britain, London: Batsford

Dark, K & Dark, P (1997) The Landscape of Roman Britain. Stroud. Sutton Publishing.

Darvill, T. and Fulton, A. (1998) MARS: The monuments at risk survey of England, Bournemouth and London: Bournemouth University and English Heritage

Darvill, T. and Thomas, J. (eds) (1996) Neolithic Houses in North-west Europe and Beyond, Oxford: Oxbow

Davidson, D. and Shackley, M. (eds) (1976) Geoarchaeology, London: Duckworth

De la Bédoyère, G (1998) Hadrian's Wall: History and Guide. Stroud, Tempus

Drewett, P. (1982) 'Later Bronze Age downland economy at Black Patch, East Sussex', Proceedings of the Prehistoric Society 48: 321–409

Drewett, P. (1999) Field Archaeology, London: UCL Press

Driessen, J History and Hierarchy. Preliminary Observations on the Settlement Pattern in Minoan Crete. In Branigan (2001)

Ellison, A. (1980) 'Settlements and regional exchange: a case study' in J. Barrett and R. Bradley (eds) Settlement and Society in the British Later Bronze Age, Oxford: BAR 83

English Heritage on-line press release 12/3/07. Precise dating gives Prehistoric past a human face. www.gnn.gov.uk/

Evershed, R.P. et al Processing of milk products in pottery vessels through British prehistory (2005) Antiquity 79, pp 895–908

Fagan, B. (2000) In the Beginning, New York: Prentice-Hall

Fagan, B. (1995) Time Detectives, New York: Simon and Schuster

Fash, W.L. (1991) Scribes, Warriors and Kings, New York: Thames and Hudson

Fischer, A (ed) (1995) Man and sea in the Mesolithic. Oxford, Oxbow Books.

Fleming, A. (1988) The Dartmoor Reaves, London: Batsford

Fleming, A. (1998) Swaledale, Valley of the Wild River, Edinburgh: Edinburgh University Press

Fried, M. (1978) 'The State, the chicken and the egg' in Cohen, N. and Service, E. Origins of the State, ISHI, Philadelphia

Gaffney, V & Stanic, Z GIS approaches to regional analysis: A case study of the Island of Hvar. www.arch-ant.bham.ac.uk/research/vince/index.htm

Gaffney, V Thomson, K, Fitch, S (2007) Mapping Doggerland: The Mesolithic Landscapes of the Southern North Sea. Oxford, Archaeopress.

Gamble, C. (1986) The Palaeolithic Settlement of Europe, Cambridge: Cambridge University Press

Gamble, C. (1999) Palaeolithic Societies of Europe, Cambridge: Cambridge University Press

Gamble, C. (2000) Archaeology: The basics. London: Routledge

Giddens, A. (1989) Sociology. London: Polity

Gilchrist, R. (1995) Contemplation and Action: The other monasticism, London: Leicester University Press

Gimbutas, M. (1991) The Civilization of the Goddess, New York: Harper Collins

Graslund, B. (1994) 'Prehistoric soul beliefs in Northern Europe', Proceedings of the Prehistoric Society 60: 15–26

Green, M. (2000) A Landscape Revealed, Stroud: Tempus

Greene, K. (2002) Archaeology: An introduction, London: Routledge

Grogan, E. (1999) 'Hilltop Settlement in South West Ireland', Lecture at conference on Late Bronze Age Landscapes, Oxford

Härke, H. (1990) 'Warrior graves? The background of the Anglo-Saxon burial rite', Past and Present 126: 22–43

Harris, D. (ed.) (1996) The Origins and Spread of Agriculture and Pastoralism in Eurasia. London: UCL

Haviland, W. (2000) Anthropology, New York: Harcourt Brace

Hawkes, C. (1954) 'Archaeological theory and method: some suggestions for the Old World', American Anthropologist 56: 155–68

Hedges, J (2000). Tomb of the Eagles. John and Erica Hedges.

Highfield, R (2006) The birth of bling. Daily Telegraph Online 24/6/06 .

Hill, J. D. (1996) 'Hillforts and the Iron Age of Wessex' in T. Champion and J. Collis (eds) The Iron Age in Britain and Ireland: Recent trends, Sheffield, Sheffield Academic Press

Hunter, J et al (1995) Studies in Crime: An introduction to forensic archaeology. London, Batsford.

Hunter, J. and Ralston, I. (eds) (1999) The Archaeology of Britain, London: Routledge

Ilkjaer, J (2002) Illerup Ådal- archaeology as a magic mirror. Aarhus, Aarhus University Press

Jackson, P. (1995) 'Footloose in archaeology', Current Archaeology 144: 466–70

Kemp, B. J (1993) Ancient Egypt, New York: Routledge

Kent, S. (1989) Farmers as Hunters, Cambridge: Cambridge University Press

Knecht, L. (1994) 'Late Ice Age hunting technology', Scientific American July: 82–7

Lake, M. (1989) Historic Farm Buildings, London: Blandford Press

Leroi-Gourhan, A. and Brézillion, M. (1966) 'L'habitation Magdalénienne No. 1 de Pincevent pres Monereau', Gallia Préhistoire 9(2): 263–385

Lewis-Williams, J. D. and Dowson, T. A. (1988) 'The signs of all times: entoptic phenomena in Upper Palaeolithic Cave Art', Current Anthropology 29 201–45

Loveday, R. (1998) 'Mother Dunche's Buttocks: a focus for Neolithic interest', Lecture to Neolithics Studies Group, London

Marcus, J. and Flannery, K. (1994) Zapotec Civilization, London: Thames and Hudson

Mays, S. (1998) The Archaeology of Human Bones. London: Routledge

Medieval Origins of Commercial Sea Fishing Project www.mcdonald.cam.ac.uk/projects/Medieval_Fishing/

Mellars, P & Stringer, C (Eds) (1989) The Human Revolution: behavioural and Biological Perspectives on the Origins of Modern Humans. Edinburgh, Edinburgh Free Press

Mellars, P (Ed) (1990) The Emergence of Modern Humans. Edinburgh, Edinburgh University Press.

Millett, M (1995) Roman Britain . London, English Heritage,

Milner, N (2007) Star Carr: Past, present and future. Oxford, Lecture.

Mithen, S. (1990) Thoughtful Foragers: A study of prehistoric decision making, Cambridge: Cambridge University Press

Moore, A., Hillman, G. and Legge, A. (2000) Village on the Euphrates, Oxford: Oxford University Press

Muir, R. (1981) Reading the Landscape, London: Michael Joseph

Orme, B. (1981) Anthropology for Archaeologists, London: Duckworth

Orton, C. et al. (1993) Pottery in Archaeology, Cambridge: Cambridge University Press

O'Shea, J. (1981) 'Social configurations and the archaeological study of mortuary practices: a case study' in R. Chapman, I. Kinnes and K. Randsborg (eds) The Archaeology of Death, Cambridge: Cambridge University Press

Parker-Pearson, M. (1993) Bronze Age Britain, London: Batsford

Parker-Pearson, M. (1999) The Archaeology of Death and Burial, Stroud: Sutton

Pedersen, L et al (eds) (1998) The Danish Storebælt since the Ice Age. Copenhagen Storebaelt

Pitts, M. and Roberts, M. (1997) Fairweather Eden, London: Century

Politiko Phorades project. www.scsp.arts.gla.ac.uk/Phorades/

Price, N. (2001) The Archaeology of Shamanism, London: Routledge

Prior, F. (1991) Flag Fen, London: Batsford

Rackham, O. (1986) The History of the Countryside, London: Phoenix

Reece, R. (1998) research in progress on the potential of hedges for locating early medieval settlement

Renfrew, C. (1973) Before Civilization, London: Jonathan Cape

Renfrew, C. (1984) Approaches to Social Archaeology, Edinburgh: Edinburgh University Press

Renfrew, C. and Bahn, P. (2000) Archaeology: Theories, methods and practice, London: Thames and Hudson

Reynolds, P. J. (1979) Iron Age Farm: The Butser Experiment. London: British Museum Publications

Richards, J (1997) Stonehenge:the story so far. London: English Heritage

Rue, D. (1989) 'Archaic Middle American agriculture and settlement: recent pollen dating from Honduras', Journal of Field Archaeology 10: 177–84

Schele, L. and Matthews, P. (1983) The Code of Kings, New York: Thames and Hudson

Schele, L. and Miller, M. (1986), The Blood of Kings, Austin: University of Texas Press

Schick, K. and Toth, N. (1993) Making Silent Stones Speak, London: Weidenfeld and Nicolson

Service, E. (1971) Primitive Social Organisation: An evolutionary perspective, New York: Random House

Sharples, N. (1991) Maiden Castle, London: Batsford

Shennan, S. (1975) 'The social organisation at Branc', Antiquity 49: 279–88

Sherratt, A. (1997) Economy and Society in Prehistoric Europe, Edinburgh: Edinburgh University Press

Schulting, R (2007) What the bones say: a bioarchaeological approach to Mesolithic burial remains. Oxford, Lecture.

Stringer, C & Mckie, (1997) R African Exodus: the origins of modern humanity London, Pimlico

Stringer, C (2005). The complete world of human evolution. London, Thames and Hudson

Stone, E & Zimansky, P (2004). The anatomy of a Mesopotamian City. Winona Lake, Eisenbrauns.

Stone Pages news bulletins on world archaeology http://www.stonepages.com/news/

Strudwick, N. and Strudwick, H. (1989) Thebes in Egypt, London: BM Press

Taylor, T. (1997) The Prehistory of Sex, London: Fourth Estate

Thomas, J. (1991) Understanding the Neolithic, London: Routledge

Tilley, C. (1994) A Phenomenology of Landscape, Oxford: Berg

Tilley, C. (1996) An Ethnography of the Neolithic, Cambridge: Cambridge University Press

Trigger, B. (1989) A History of Archaeological Thought, Cambridge: Cambridge University Press

Van Gennep, A. (1909) Les rites de passage, Paris: E. Nourry

Vanhaeren, M et al (2006). Middle Palaeolithic Shell beads in Israel and Algeria. Sciences 312 p1785

Waddell, J (2000). The prehistoric Archaeology of Ireland. Dublin, Wordwell.

Waddington, C. (1998) 'Cup and Rings in Context', Cambridge Archaeological Journal 8(1): 29–54

Wass, S. (1999) The Amateur Archaeologist, second edn, London: Batsford

Watson, A. (1997) 'Hearing again the sound of the Neolithic' British Archaeology 23 (April)

Welch, M. (1992), Anglo-Saxon England, London: Batsford

Wenke, R. (1999) Patterns in Prehistory, Oxford: Oxford University Press

Whitelaw, T (2001) From sites to communities: Defining the Human Dimensions of Minoan Urbanism in Branigan, K (2001)

Whittle, A. (1996) Europe in the Neolithic, Cambridge: Cambridge University Press

Whittle, A. (1998) Sacred Mound, Holy Rings. Oxford: Oxbow

Wilkinson, K. and Stevens, C. (2001) Environmental Archaeology Stroud: Tempus

Wilkinson, R. (2000) The Temples of Ancient Egypt, London: Thames and Hudson

Young, R (Eds) (2000) Mesolithic Lifeways. Leicester, Univ of Leicester

Zvelebil, M et al (Eds) (1998) Harvesting the sea, farming the forest. Sheffield, Sheffield Academic Press.

Figure Bib.1 *King Redwald from Sutton Hoo?*

From the evidence we have, this is what King Redwald from Sutton Hoo might have looked like if he had done Archaeology A Level.

Index

If monks had had to revise . . .